LETTERS FAMILIAR
AND FORMAL

The Other Voice in Early Modern Europe:
The Toronto Series, 20

The Other Voice in
Early Modern Europe:
The Toronto Series

SERIES EDITORS Margaret L. King *and* Albert Rabil, Jr.
SERIES EDITOR, ENGLISH TEXTS Elizabeth H. Hageman

Previous Publications in the Series

MADRE MARÍA ROSA
Journey of Five Capuchin Nuns
Edited and translated by Sarah E.
Owens
2009

GIOVAN BATTISTA ANDREINI
Love in the Mirror: A Bilingual Edition
Edited and translated by Jon R. Snyder
2009

RAYMOND DE SABANAC AND SIMONE
ZANACCHI
Two Women of the Great Schism: The
Revelations *of Constance de Rabastens
by Raymond de Sabanac and* Life of
the Blessed Ursulina of Parma *by
Simone Zanacchi*
Edited and translated by Renate
Blumenfeld-Kosinski and Bruce L.
Venarde
2010

OLIVA SABUCO DE NANTES BARRERA
The True Medicine
Edited and translated by Gianna
Pomata
2010

LOUISE-GENEVIÈVE GILLOT DE
SAINCTONGE
Dramatizing Dido, Circe, and Griselda
Edited and translated by Janet Levarie
Smarr
2010

PERNETTE DU GUILLET
Complete Poems: A Bilingual Edition
Edited by Karen Simroth James
Translated by Marta Rijn Finch
2010

ANTONIA PULCI
*Saints' Lives and Bible Stories for the
Stage: A Bilingual Edition*
Edited by Elissa B. Weaver
Translated by James Wyatt Cook
2010

VALERIA MIANI
*Celinda, A Tragedy: A Bilingual
Edition*
Edited by Valeria Finucci
Translated by Julia Kisacky
Annotated by Valeria Finucci and
Julia Kisacky
2010

*Enchanted Eloquence: Fairy Tales by
Seventeenth-Century French Women
Writers*
Edited and translated by Lewis C.
Seifert and Domna C. Stanton
2010

*Leibniz and the Two Sophies: The
Philosophical Correspondence*
Edited and translated by Lloyd
Strickland
2011

The Other Voice in Early Modern Europe: The Toronto Series

SERIES EDITORS Margaret L. King *and* Albert Rabil, Jr.
SERIES EDITOR, ENGLISH TEXTS Elizabeth H. Hageman

Previous Publications in the Series

In Dialogue with the Other Voice in Sixteenth-Century Italy: Literary and Social Contexts for Women's Writing
Edited by Julie D. Campbell and Maria Galli Stampino
2011

SISTER GIUSTINA NICCOLINI
The Chronicle of Le Murate
Edited and translated by Saundra Weddle
2011

LIUBOV KRICHEVSKAYA
No Good without Reward: Selected Writings: A Bilingual Edition
Edited and translated by Brian James Baer
2011

ELIZABETH COOKE HOBY RUSSELL
The Writings of an English Sappho
Edited by Patricia Phillippy
With translations by Jaime Goodrich
2011

LUCREZIA MARINELLA
Exhortations to Women and to Others if They Please
Edited and translated by Laura Benedetti
2012

MARGHERITA DATINI
Letters to Francesco Datini
Translated by Carolyn James and Antonio Pagliaro
2012

DELARIVIER MANLEY AND MARY PIX
English Women Staging Islam, 1696–1707
Edited and translated by Bernadette Andrea
2012

CECILIA DEL NACIMIENTO
Journeys of a Mystic Soul in Poetry and Prose
Introduction and prose translations by Kevin Donnelly
Poetry translations by Sandra Sider
2012

LADY MARGARET DOUGLAS AND OTHERS
The Devonshire Manuscript: A Women's Book of Courtly Poetry
Edited and introduced by Elizabeth Heale
2012

Letters Familiar and Formal

ARCANGELA TARABOTTI

❧

Edited and translated by

MEREDITH K. RAY

AND

LYNN LARA WESTWATER

ITER

Iter Inc.
Centre for Reformation and Renaissance Studies
Toronto
2012

Iter: Gateway to the Middle Ages and Renaissance
Tel: 416/978–7074   Email: iter@utoronto.ca
Fax: 416/978–1668   Web: www.itergateway.org

Centre for Reformation and Renaissance Studies
Victoria University in the University of Toronto
Tel: 416/585–4465   Email: crrs.publications@utoronto.ca
Fax: 416/585–4430   Web: www.crrs.ca

Iter and the Centre for Reformation and Renaissance Studies gratefully acknowledge the
generous support of James E. Rabil, in memory of Scottie W. Rabil, toward the publication
of this book.

Library and Archives Canada Cataloguing in Publication

Tarabotti, Arcangela
Letters familiar and formal / Arcangela Tarabotti ; edited and translated by Meredith K.
Ray and Lynn Lara Westwater.

(The other voice in early modern Europe : The Toronto series ; 20)
Includes bibliographical references and index.
Also issued in electronic format.
ISBN 978-0-7727-2132-7

1. Tarabotti, Arcangela—Correspondence. 2. Benedictine nuns—Italy—Correspondence.
I. Ray, Meredith K., 1969– II. Westwater, Lynn Lara, 1969– III. Victoria University
(Toronto, Ont.). Centre for Reformationand Renaissance Studies IV. Iter Inc V. Title. VI.
Series: Other voice in early modern Europe. Toronto series ; 20

BX4705.T277A4 2012
271'.97   C2012-906928-0

Cover illustration:
Portrait of Maria Salviati, 1543 (oil on canvas), Pontomo, Jacopo (1494–1557) / Galleria
degli Uffizi, Florence, Italy / The Bridgeman Art Library BEN 160888.

Cover design:
Maureen Morin, Information Technology Services, University of Toronto Libraries.

Typesetting and production:
Iter Inc.

Contents

Acknowledgments **xi**

Introduction
Arcangela Tarabotti: A Life of Letters **1**

A Note on the Translation **41**

Abbreviations **44**

Map of Seventeenth-Century Venice including the
Convent of Sant'Anna **45**

Letters Familiar and Formal Presented by Arcangela Tarabotti
to Her Most Illustrious and Esteemed Patron
Giovan Francesco Loredano **47**

The Tears of Arcangela Tarabotti upon the Death of the
Most Illustrious Signora Regina Donati **285**

Bibliography **297**

Index **309**

Acknowledgments

We could not have completed this project without the generous help of numerous colleagues. We are especially grateful to Mario Infelise, Ed Muir, Daria Perocco and Anne Jacobson Schutte for offering their expertise with regard to the religious, political and cultural context of seventeenth-century Venice. Paolo Cherchi helped us to track down some of the more obscure citations in the *Letters*. Diana Robin offered unfailing enthusiasm for this project as well as important insight from her own experience translating Italian women's letter collections. Albert Rabil Jr. shepherded this translation with remarkable care and never lost sight of the project's meaning, or our deadlines. We are thankful to Letizia Panizza, who read our manuscript with extreme care and helped us resolve some of the thorny linguistic issues we encountered in translating Tarabotti's unique and challenging literary style. Our appreciation also goes to Marianna Griffini for her editorial support and to Maura High for her thoughtful preparation of the manuscript. Our deepest thanks go to Elissa Weaver, who shared endlessly of her time and expertise as we brought this project from its first to its final stages. Finally, we thank our families for their belief in this project and in us. We dedicate this book to Owen, Sofia, Julia, and Anna.

Introduction

ARCANGELA TARABOTTI: A LIFE OF LETTERS

A Voice of Protest in Early Modern Venice

The life of the Venetian writer Arcangela Tarabotti, born Elena Cassandra (1604–52), was shaped by her early and unwilling entry into the convent of Sant'Anna in Castello, where she professed her vows in 1623 and spent the rest of her life.[1] Confined in this modest convent, which stood at the far end of the city, Tarabotti developed an acute awareness not only of her own marginalized condition but of that of the thousands of other involuntary nuns who populated Venice in the seventeenth century. With an insight all the more astounding for the narrowness of the confines in which she lived, Tarabotti grasped and then exposed through her works (seven of which we still possess) the political, social, and economic forces that stood behind the practice of coerced monachization, the enclosure of women with no religious vocation (see below). Beyond issues concerning the cloister, Tarabotti lay bare the hypocrisies that surrounded women's subaltern condition: how men deprived women of an education and then judged them to

---

1. Tarabotti herself wrote that she entered the convent when she was eleven, or in 1615 (see letter 99); the research of Emilio Zanette suggests instead that she entered the convent two years later (*Suor Arcangela monaca del Seicento veneziano* [Rome: Istituto per la Collaborazione Culturale, 1960], 27). Zanette's biography of Tarabotti, while sometimes paternalistic in its approach, provides essential information for the study of her life. Other important sources include Giuseppe Portigliotti, *Penombre claustrali* (Milan: Fratelli Treves, 1930), and Ginevra Conti Odorisio, *Donna e società nel Seicento* (Rome: Bulzoni, 1979). Since the 1990s scholarly interest in Tarabotti has intensified, leading to a number of modern editions of Tarabotti's works, in English and Italian. See (in order of publication): *L'"Inferno monacale" di Arcangela Tarabotti*, ed. Francesca Medioli (Turin: Rosenberg & Sellier), 1990; *Che le donne siano della spezie degli uomini: Difesa della donna* (1651), ed. Letizia Panizza (London: Institute of Romance Studies, 1994); *Satira e Antisatira*, ed. Elissa Weaver (Rome: Salerno, 1998); *"Women Are Not Human": An Anonymous Treatise and Its Responses*, ed. Theresa Kenney (New York: Crossroad, 1998); *Paternal Tyranny*, ed. and trans. Letizia Panizza (Chicago: University of Chicago Press, 2004); *Lettere familiari e di complimento*, ed. Meredith Ray and Lynn Westwater (Turin: Rosenberg & Sellier, 2005); and *La semplicità ingannata*, ed. Simona Bortot (Padua: Il Poligrafo, 2007).

1

be ignorant, for instance, or expected women (and not themselves) to be chaste and temperate. From her corner of Venice, Tarabotti took up the mantle of all women in their inevitable struggle against the injustices, big and small, of a patriarchal system. Tarabotti proposed (not entirely in jest) that only in the afterlife would the hierarchy be overturned and women finally favored.

Tarabotti's mission of advocating for women and exposing men's perfidy informs all of her works. In most of them Tarabotti offers an impressively synthetic—and necessarily abstract—analysis of gender dynamics. In her *Letters*, by contrast, such analysis gives way to practical application as she seeks to help real women resolve real problems and chastises real men for their reckless ways and their lack of consideration for women. As her theories are applied, they acquire subtlety (not all women are praised, nor are all men villains) and persuasiveness (some men's perfidy really is limitless). The wrongs of coerced monachization take on concrete shape in the person of Tarabotti, who repeatedly refers to herself as a prisoner and complains incessantly of her "constriction of the chest," a condition that is also metaphor for her suffocating confinement.

Also concrete in the *Letters* is Tarabotti's literary life. Whereas in her other works she voices frustration at women's exclusion from education, such protest crystallizes here in the writer's own figure as she responds to detractors who accuse her of ignorance and plagiary. These charges seem to have led Tarabotti to publish her letters in the first place, taking advantage of the pedigreed genre of the letterbook not only to prove her intellectual honesty but to affirm her literary worth. With her *Letters*, Tarabotti offers a flesh-and-blood example of the trials of the female intellectual and, through this very publication, her vindication as an accomplished woman of letters.

Women, Convents, and Society in Seventeenth-Century Venice

Tarabotti's Venice was home to some thirty-nine convents (with many more on the nearby islands) that housed a steadily increasing number of girls and women in the period following the Council of Trent. By the mid-seventeenth century, there were over 2,500 cloistered nuns in

Venice.[2] As recent scholarship has shown, the reasons for this grow-
ing convent population were complex and had little to do with religious vocation. Rather, as the interests of Venice's patrician families
intertwined with those of the state, convents provided a convenient
solution to a variety of problems. Faced with rising marital dowries,
middle- and upper-class families turned to the convent as a harbor for
their daughters, one that would protect their honor and the families'
reputation while easing their financial burdens. Although convents—
like bridegrooms—required a dowry, the fee was generally far lower
than that necessary to marry.[3] Patrician families may also have preferred their daughters to enter a convent rather than marry "down"
in the face of a diminishing pool of suitable bridegrooms, as Jutta
Sperling has argued.[4] In the case of Tarabotti—one of six sisters—it
is likely that her family simply did not have the means to supply each
daughter with a dowry adequate for marriage; it is also likely that because Tarabotti (as she tells us herself in the *Letters*) had inherited
her father's limp, her family considered her less likely than her sisters to find a suitable husband.[5] The divergent destinies of Venice's

2. At mid-century, there were about 2,500 women in Venetian convents (see Francesca Medioli, "Monache e monacazioni nel Seicento," one of three essays in Gabriella Zarri, Francesca Medioli, and Paola Vismara Chiappa, "De monialibus [secoli XVI–XVIII]," *Rivista di
storia e letteratura religiosa* 33, n. 3 [1997], 676–78). Jutta Sperling estimates the number of
nuns in Venice at 2,905 in 1642, with about 69 percent of these coming from patrician families, families of a higher social status than Tarabotti's; according to Sperling, in 1642 more
than 80 percent of patrician girls were nuns; *Convents and the Body Politic in Late Renaissance Venice* (Chicago: University of Chicago Press, 1999), 28, table 2.

3. By this period, convents required a dowry of about 1,000 ducats, a fixed sum established
by the Venetian senate. The average dowry for marriage, by contrast, ranged from eight to
forty times more, depending on the bride's social class (Medioli, "Monache e monacazioni,"
688).

4. In *Convents and the Body Politic*, Sperling posits a complementary rather than causal relationship between inflated dowries and high rates of coerced monachizations, arguing that
the increasing number of nuns was more closely linked to the patriciate's reluctance to surrender its exclusivity through downwardly mobile marriages for its daughters. On the issue
of aristocratic matrimony, see also Stanley Chojnacki, *Women and Men in Renaissance Venice: Twelve Essays on Patrician Society* (Baltimore: Johns Hopkins University Press, 2000).

5. Of Tarabotti's five sisters, two married and three remained at home (see Zanette, *Suor
Arcangela*, 4). Tarabotti's *Letters* feature two missives to her sisters that reveal great tension
in their relationship (see letters 106 and 188).

daughters, set on the path toward marriage or monachization without regard for their own desires, was a source of deep bitterness and anger for Tarabotti, who often returns to this theme in her works. In *Convent Hell*, for example, Tarabotti describes the starkly different conditions of nuns from their more fortunate sisters, the former condemned to a lifetime passed in a rough habit, the latter bedecked in pearls, ribbons, and lace.[6] Tarabotti's *Paternal Tyranny* launches a forceful attack at fathers for consigning their daughters with no religious vocation to a suffocating life in the cloister.

The economic rationale of the family was mirrored in the political rationale of the Venetian State, which encouraged the place-ment of girls and women in convents as a means to control the growth of the patriciate.[7] Tarabotti herself draws this connection in several of her works: in *Convent Hell*, for example, she calls upon families to recognize the economic and political factors driving the enclosure of women who did not have a religious vocation.[8] Although not all nuns were situated in convents against their will, even influential church figures recognized that convents were becoming less a haven for fe-male spiritual devotion than a repository for the city's unmarriageable daughters. The statement of the Venetian patriarch, Giovanni Tiepolo, that nuns made "a gift of their own liberty … not just to God, but to their native land, to the world, and to their closest relatives" stressed

---

6. *L'"Inferno monacale" di Arcangela Tarabotti*, ed. Medioli, 46.

7. For a discussion of the "civic ideology" that underlay the practice of coerced monachiza-tion, see Gabriella Zarri, "Monasteri femminili e città (secoli XV–XVIII)," in *Storia d'Italia*, Annali 9, *La chiesa e il potere politico*, ed. Giorgio Chittolini and Giovanni Miccoli (Turin: Einaudi, 1986), 359–429.

8. On coerced monachization, see Francesca Medioli, "The Dimensions of the Cloister: En-closure, Constraint, and Protection in Seventeenth Century Italy," in *Time, Space, and Wom-en's Lives in Early Modern Italy*, ed. Anne Jacobson Schutte, Thomas Kuehn, and Silvana Seidel Menchi, 165–80 (Kirksville, MO: Truman State University Press, 2001), and Medioli, "Monacazioni forzate: Donne ribelle al proprio destino," *Clio: Trimestrale di studi storici* 30 (1994): 431–54; Mary Laven, "Cast Out and Shut In: The Experience of Nuns in Counter-Reformation Venice," in *At the Margins: Minority Groups in Premodern Italy*, ed. Stephen J. Milner, 72–93 (Minneapolis: University of Minnesota Press, 2005); Giovanna Paolin, *Lo spazio del silenzio: Monacazioni forzate, clausura e proposte di vita religiosa femminile nell'età moderna* (Pordenone: Biblioteca dell'Immagine, 1996); Sperling, *Convents and the Body Politic*; Zarri, "Monasteri femminili e città."

the familial and civic—not religious—obligation that underlay the entrance of many girls into Venice's convents.[9] More generally, Cardinal Giovan Battista de Luca acknowledged the grim effects of the practice of coerced monachization on its victims, describing forced enclosure as a penance of "everlasting imprisonment, which is perhaps the second greatest after capital punishment."[10] Whereas a century earlier nuns were still permitted to leave the convent to visit with their families or to minister to the poor and sick, the reforms introduced by the Council of Trent included the institution of strict *clausura*, or enclosure, denying nuns even brief exits from the convent after the profession of vows.[11] As the reforms took hold, nuns' lives were increasingly circumscribed and their contacts with the outside world progressively more limited. This shift was reflected in convent architecture, as windows and doors were reduced in size or even bricked in and nuns required to communicate with visitors (who, at least in theory, were to be relatives or others with special permission) across grates and under supervision.[12]

Officially, the church prohibited coerced monachization. Chapter 17 of the Decree on Regulars and Nuns, which dated to 1563, required that applicants, before taking the veil, be examined in order to determine that they took this step of their own will and not

9. Qtd. in Letizia Panizza, "Volume Editor's Introduction," in Arcangela Tarabotti, *Paternal Tyranny*, ed. Letizia Panizza (Chicago, University of Chicago Press, 2004), 4, n. 6.

10. Qtd. in Medioli, "The Dimensions of the Cloister," 169.

11. On enclosure and its effects see, for example, Raimondo Creytens, "La giurisprudenza della Sacra Congregazione del Concilio nella questione della clausura delle monache (1564–1576)," in *La Sacra Congregazione del Concilio, quarto centenario dalla fondazione (1564–1964): Studi e ricerche* (Vatican City: 1964), 563–97; and Creytens, "La riforma dei monasteri femminili dopo i Decreti Tridentini," in *Il Concilio di Trento e la riforma tridentina: Atti del convegno storico internazionale* (Rome: Herder, 1965), 45–84; Francesca Medioli, "La clausura delle monache nell'amministrazione della congregazione romana sopra i regolari," in *Il monachesimo femminile in Italia dall'alto Medioevo al secolo XVII a confronto con l'oggi: Atti del VI convegno del Centro Studi Farfensi, Santa Vittoria in Matenano, 21–24 settembre, 1995*, ed. Gabriella Zarri (Nagrine [Verona]: Il Segno dei Gabrielli Editori, 1997), 249–82; Medioli, "Monache e monacazione nel Seicento," and Zarri, *Monasteri femminili*.

12. On convent structure and regulations see, for example, Anne Jacobson Schutte, "The Permeable Cloister?," in *Arcangela Tarabotti: A Literary Nun in Baroque Venice*, ed. Elissa Weaver (Ravenna: Longo, 2006), 19–36; Zarri, *Monasteri femminili*; and Medioli, "La clausura delle monache."

by force or undue persuasion.[13] Yet this provision was impossible to enforce, and the degrees and types of duress to which girls were subjected by their families difficult to detect and regulate.[14] In *Convent Hell*, Tarabotti included professed nuns themselves in her blame for the persistence of coerced monachization, arguing that, like fathers, they knowingly deceived girls into accepting convent life.

Tarabotti's Venice

As unbearable as Tarabotti found the convent, it did afford her the time to dedicate herself to intellectual pursuits. Recent scholarship has shown that convents offered women a space in which to develop their own creative identities, for example through lacework, music, or, as in the case of Tarabotti, writing. Although the conditions of enclosure grew increasingly restrictive after the Council of Trent, nuns continued to contribute to the artistic, intellectual, and economic life of their cities. In Venice, convents also played an important role in the city's rich civic mythology. Central to this were the legend of Saint Mark's visit to the island, where he received a prophesy that his body would remain there, and the story of the ninth-century *translatio* of the saint's body to the city; the presence of the saint's relics in the church of the city's rulers affirmed Venice's exceptionality and also its independence from Rome.[15] As Gabriella Zarri has pointed out, convents also possessed important holy relics from the Orient—including the bodies of Saint Zacharias, father of John the Baptist; Saint Anastasius, patron of Alexandria; and Saint Paul, patron of Constantinople; and important relics from female saints and Christian martyrs—which rendered the convents "direct participants in the symbolic construc-

13. Cf. *Conciliarum Oecumenicorum Decreta*, ed. G. Alberigo et al. (Bologna: Edizioni Dehoniane, 1973, rpt. 1991), 781.

14. As Schutte notes, girls were in most cases unlikely and even unable to go against the expressed wishes of their families or to question a destiny that may have been laid out for them from birth ("The Permeable Cloister?," 21).

15. Edward Muir notes that "as possessors of the Evangelist's body, the Venetian *duces* modeled their relationship to Mark on that of the popes' to Saint Peter. Just as the popes had inherited the authority of Peter, so had the Venetians inherited that of Mark. The popes were autonomous; therefore so should be the Venetian state" (*Civic Ritual in Renaissance Venice* [Princeton, NJ: Princeton University Press, 1981], 84).

tion of the city as a new Constantinople and Jerusalem."[16] That certain convents also hosted important Venetian civic rituals—the doge and Senate attended vespers on Easter, for instance, at the convent of San Zaccaria—suggested, as Zarri notes, a link between the prince's power and the civic role of the convents.[17] Because of the important role of the convents, the city chafed at the stricter rules imposed on nuns by the Council of Trent and after. The church's regulations were, however, eventually enacted because Venice's power in ecclesiastical matters was waning throughout the sixteenth and early seventeenth centuries.[18]

Venice had a long history of tension with Rome. In 1509, the Venetians suffered at Agnadello a humiliating defeat, orchestrated by Pope Julius II, that undermined Venetians' certainty of their glorious destiny even as it fueled mistrust of the Holy See. For much of the sixteenth century, however, Venice pursued an official policy of neutrality and accord with the church and chose to accept the decisions of the Council of Trent in 1564, the year of their issuance. The church for its part, in order to obtain Venetian support as it faced internal and external tensions, made some concessions to Venice, allowing, for instance, that bishoprics on the Terraferma be assigned to Venetian patrician families, while the Venetian state insisted on a symbolic power over religious matters, even if its real power was largely diminished. The church and state maintained a precarious balance in power in the late sixteenth century, a balance that was ruptured early in the seventeenth with the historic interdict confrontation between the church and the Venetian state. Tensions came to a head at the ascension to the papacy in 1605 of Paul V, who pushed for greater papal powers as Venice sought to curtail them with two laws that asserted the Republic's power over ecclesiastical property and one that asserted its power

---

16. Gabriella Zarri, "Venetian Convents and Civic Ritual," in Weaver, *Arcangela Tarabotti*, 41–42.

17. Ibid., 43.

18. On the issue, see, for example, Gaetano Cozzi, "I rapporti tra stato e chiesa," in *La chiesa veneta tra Riforma protestante e cattolica*, ed. Giuseppe Gullino (Venice: Edizioni Studium, 1990), 11–36; and Paolo Prodi, "Chiesa e società," in *Dal Rinascimento al Barocco*, ed. Gaetano Cozzi and Paolo Prodi, *Storia di Venezia*, vol. 6 (Rome: Istituto della Enciclopedia Italiana "Giovanni Treccani," 1994), 305–39.

to punish ecclesiastics. Early in 1606, the papal nuncio demanded that Venice yield unconditionally; the city—guided by the views of Paolo Sarpi, who counseled against surrender—did not, and by April the pope had excommunicated the Venetians and put their territories under interdict.[19] As the confrontation escalated, each side published propaganda, aimed at a broad European audience, to support their case; Sarpi's arguments against the church earned him excommunication, but also broad support in Europe and in Venice itself.[20] A year later a compromise, brokered by France, was reached and the interdict was lifted, but neither the pope nor the city emerged completely victorious.

The interdict struggle contributed to Venice's reputation for liberty, which, however exaggerated, nevertheless was to some degree accurate in describing the unusual freedom of the presses in the city. Indeed, one issue of continuing struggle between Rome and Venice regarded press censorship. In a 1596 agreement, Venice accepted Clement VIII's Index of Forbidden Books while also tightening state censorship and trying to limit inquisitorial interference, but Rome and Venice remained in disagreement in this area over the first half of the seventeenth century.[21] In the 1630s and 1640s, writers and printers were able, with striking impunity, to issue clandestine works in strident polemic with the Roman Curia and with the Barberini family. The Accademia degli Incogniti, many of whose members had libertine and antipapal leanings and were associated with such inflammatory works, thrived in this climate of freedom. Despite unorthodox attitudes, the group was not one of misfits and rebels. Indeed, the Accademia was the dominant cultural institution in mid-seventeenth-century Venice and represented the literary voice of the ruling class.

19. Some of the classic studies of the Interdict include Federico Chabod, *La politica di Paolo Sarpi* (Venice: Istituto per la Collaborazione Culturale, 1962); William J. Bouwsma, *Venice and the Defense of Republican Liberty* (Berkeley: University of California Press, 1968); and Gaetano Cozzi, *Paolo Sarpi tra Venezia e l'Europa* (Turin: Einaudi, 1979).

20. Gaetano Cozzi and Luisa Cozzi, "Paolo Sarpi," in *Storia della cultura veneta: Il Seicento*, vol. 4.2, ed. Girolamo Arnaldi and Manlio Pastore Stocchi (Vicenza: Neri Pozza, 1983), 19.

21. See Mario Infelise, "Books and Politics in Arcangela Tarabotti's Venice," in Weaver, *Arcangela Tarabotti*, 59. On seventeenth-century censorship in Venice, see also Paolo Ulvioni, "Stampa e censura a Venezia nel Seicento," *Archivio veneto* 104, no. 139 (1975): 45–93.

The success of Arcangela Tarabotti, who was closely linked to Incogniti circles and found within them influential if inconstant support, was indubitably fueled by the open publishing climate in these years, years when she came to prominence as a free-thinking writer whose works challenged church and state alike. But the period of freedom was only temporary. Whereas throughout the 1630s and early 1640s the Republic was able to reject Roman attempts to rein in Venetian publishing—and even expelled in 1643 the Roman nuncio who crusaded against the antipapal works of Ferrante Pallavicino—a changing international landscape eventually diminished Venice's independence. Indeed, the Republic, in the face of the 1645 attack on Candia, had to appeal for aid and seek rapprochement with the Holy See.[22] In this atmosphere of diminished Venetian autonomy, the tribunal of the Holy Office in 1648 brought to trial a printer linked to Incogniti circles, a proceeding that, as Mario Infelise notes, represented a successful effort by the Holy Office to restore control over Venetian printing.[23] If this change weakened the position of the Accademia and many of its members, its effect on Tarabotti is more difficult to discern. It was not this more restrictive atmosphere that inhibited Tarabotti's ability to publish her most controversial works—her *Convent Hell* and *Paternal Tyranny*, never published in her lifetime; these were, even without Roman interference, unpublishable in her city because of their polemic against the Venetian state. The increasingly strict publishing atmosphere that was taking hold in these years does instead seem to mark Tarabotti's final published work in 1651, a response to a treatise that denied women had souls. In this response, Tarabotti walks an uncomfortable line between orthodoxy and rebellion. But the 1650 *Letters*, which openly tout Tarabotti's reading and circulation of prohibited works, her attempts to publish—even by officially forbidden means— her controversial ones, and her disobedience of rules that governed nuns' lives, do not bear the marks of repression. The *Letters* are in this respect a testament to an era of publishing freedom that was coming to a close.

22. Infelise, "Books and Politics," 66.

23. On the trial, see ibid., 67–71.

Tarabotti's Life and Works

Despite Tarabotti's 1623 profession of religious vows, hers was a literary not religious vocation, and she used her pen to protest her own involuntary religious confinement and that of others, a protest she coupled with a more general defense of women. Tarabotti never resigned herself to the cloister. In her *Letters*, published two years before her death, she repeatedly depicts her life in the convent as an incarceration and "a hell where no hope of exiting can enter" (letter 163). Only her writing allowed her to escape Sant'Anna's confines and to survive within its walls, where the controversial writer with a "frank and impassioned way of speaking" (letter 59) found few friends. Tarabotti had little formal education and her writings protest women's broad exclusion from study as part of the same patriarchal system that allowed the practice of coerced monachization.[24] She describes herself as "a woman who lacks the illumination of art and study necessary to whoever professes letters" (letter 2) and defends herself from those who would criticize her by asking "what sweetness can lie in [the] sayings, what style, what explanations, what figures can be present in the compositions of a woman upon whom grammar or other learning has shed no imaginable light, and who in her spelling has only the dictionary as her guide?" (letter 44). Tarabotti used her lack of formal learning to counter her critics and to excuse errors in her works (particularly with regard to her citations of Latin sources),[25] but it was not an impediment to her writing: in her lifetime she published five prose

---

24. In the *Antisatire*, Tarabotti writes that men "have usurped a great advantage over [women], who rarely can dedicate themselves to the noble task of writing because they are by men's tyranny kept even from learning to read, let alone from the illumination of knowledge and letters" (*Satira e Antisatira*, 73; our translation).

25. Tarabotti was taken to task for errors in the Latin citations in her works. Critics charged that Tarabotti used only the Latin that she heard in the daily recitation of Scripture, a charge she accepts in part in her *Antisatire*: "Let them say … that I don't write with the proper style and organization (for I confess this myself), and that I use Latin sayings not because I know that language but because I have memorized a great number of these through the daily recitation of the Divine Office" (*Satira e Antisatira*, 75). Yet she also proudly advertised her particular style of writing: "I care little for all this, since I write only according to the rules that my fancy dictates" (76; our translations).

works in addition to her *Letters*, most of them quite controversial,[26] and composed at least six others, four of which have been lost.[27] Tarabotti probably also wrote verse, an aspect of her writing that has remained unexplored. She seems to claim credit in the *Letters* for certain poems written to mark felicitous events even as she expresses distaste for this sort of "occasional poetry." Much of the unattributed verse in the *Letters* may be hers and may lack attribution precisely because Tarabotti believed her authorship of it to be obvious. It is often consonant with Tarabotti's ornate and elaborate style (see below), and there is some later evidence to suggest that Tarabotti was known as a poet.[28]

At the center of Tarabotti's works are her assertion of women's superiority and her denunciation of men's injustice against them. In her earliest compositions, Tarabotti targets the practice of coerced monachization within the context of women's more general oppression. In *Paternal Tyranny*—published posthumously under the pseudonym Galerana Baratotti and with the less provocative title *Inno-*

---

26. The works Tarabotti published in her lifetime were *Convent Paradise* (*Paradiso monacale*), *Antisatire* (*Antisatira*), *That Women Are No Less Human Than Men* (*Che le donne siano della spetie degli uomini*), the *Letters*, and a short memorial work she appended to the *Letters*, entitled the *Tears upon the Death of the Most Illustrious Signora Regina Donati* (*Le lagrime … per la morte dell'Illustrissima Signora Regina Donati*). On the *Tears*, see below.

27. The two works that survived were Tarabotti's *Paternal Tyranny* (*Tirannia paterna*), printed shortly after her death as *Innocence Deceived* (*Semplicità ingannata*), and *Convent Hell* (*Inferno monacale*); see below. Beyond these, the *Letters* mention several seemingly devotional works that have not been found: *Contemplations of the Loving Soul* (*Contemplazioni dell'anima amante*), the *Paved Road to Heaven* (*Via lastricata per andare al cielo*), and *Convent Light* (*Luce monacale*); see letter 26. She is credited also with a *Purgatory for Unhappily Married Women* (*Purgatorio delle malmaritate*), mentioned in the presentation to the *Letters*, in letter 73, and in the preface to the *Antisatire*, but which also has been lost.

28. A nineteenth-century anthology attributes a poem to Tarabotti; see *Piccola galleria poetica di donne veneziane*, ed. D. Legrenzi (Mestre: Strennetta per l'anno nuovo, 1852), 17–18. There is certainly evidence of nuns writing poetry; Tarabotti's own correspondent Guid'Ascania Orsi of Bologna, for example, composed verse (a madrigal of hers is reproduced in Elisabetta Graziosi, "Arcipelago sommerso: Le rime delle monache tra obbedienza e trasgressione," in *I monasteri femminili come centri di cultura fra Rinascimento e Barocco: Atti del convegno storico internazionale, Bologna, 8–10 dicembre 2000*, ed. Elisabetta Zarri and Gianna Pomata [Rome: Edizioni di Storia e Letteratura, 2005], 171, n. 69). The writing that Tarabotti and Orsi traded likely included their verse, since poetry was in this era an important commodity of intellectual exchange.

cence Deceived[29]—Tarabotti blames fathers and the Venetian state for their betrayal of innocent daughters. Her indictment of the Venetian state—which has led some modern critics to view her as an early political theorist[30]—rendered the book unpublishable in that city. Though based on personal experience, the work eschews autobiography and concentrates instead on the overarching causes and effects of coerced monachization. Tarabotti warns that the practice results not only in the condemnation and future damnation of the unhappy victims who cannot abide convent life, but also in the eternal punishment of those who forced the girls into the convent against their will.[31] Tarabotti also protests against coerced monachization in *Convent Hell*, in which she recounts with bitterness how young girls are persuaded by their families and by nuns themselves that convents are heaven on earth, and realize too late that they are instead a hell in which body and mind are forever trapped. Again, Tarabotti predicts eternal punishment for this wrong: God does not look kindly upon the sacrifice of innocents, Tarabotti writes, since "the sacrifice that they make to Him of daughters and other relatives, forcefully imprisoned in an abyss, is too unjust and offends God with its stench."[32] With her assumption of divine support for her ideas despite their clash with state and church

29. Tarabotti, *La semplicità ingannata* (Leiden: G. Sambix [but Elsevier], 1654). The publishing information is false. Zanette suggests that the work was printed before 1654, perhaps as early as 1651, and thus before Tarabotti's 1652 death (*Suor Arcangela*, 439–45). This hypothesis is not followed by other scholars. Letter 58, addressed to Louis Matharel, suggests that Tarabotti herself renamed the work. On the change of title, see Simona Bortot, introduction to *La semplicità ingannata*, ed. Simona Bortot (Padua: Il Poligrafo, 2007), 79–80. *Innocence Deceived* was placed on the Index in 1661; see *Index librorum prohibitorum Alexandri XII pontificis maximi* (Rome: Ex typographia Reverendae Camerae Apostiolicae, 1664), 145, and Natalia Costa-Zalessow, "Tarabotti's 'La semplicità ingannata' and Its Twentieth-Century Interpreters, with Unpublished Documents Regarding Its Condemnation to the Index," *Italica* 78 (2001): 314–25.

30. See, for example, Stephanie Jed, "Arcangela Tarabotti and Gabriel Naudé: Libraries, Taxonomies and *Ragion di Stato*," in Weaver, *Arcangela Tarabotti*, 139.

31. On the publication saga of *Paternal Tyranny*, see Lynn Lara Westwater, "A Cloistered Nun Abroad: Arcangela Tarabotti's International Literary Career," in *Women Writing Back/ Writing Women Back: Transnational Perspectives from the Late Middle Ages to the Dawn of the Modern Era*, ed. Anke Gilleir, Alicia C. Montoya, and Suzan Van Dijk (Leiden: Brill, 2010), 283–308.

32. *Inferno monacale*, 92; our translation.

practice, Tarabotti called for a religiosity free from the hypocrisy of a hierarchy that abused its power.

The first work that Tarabotti succeeded in publishing, however, if not the first she wrote, was not a condemnation of coerced monachization but a work with a quite different tone: *Convent Paradise.*[33] This celebration of convent life for those with religious vocation was introduced by a *Soliloquy to God* in which Tarabotti declares herself converted to the religious life.[34] On the surface, the work seemed to be a retraction of *Convent Hell*, although, as modern critics have noted, Tarabotti never made a general condemnation of the cloister in any of her works, railing only against the abuse of it. Nevertheless, the fact that the title and some of the content were conciliatory rather than inflammatory, in contrast to those of her earlier works, made the *Paradise* easier to publish. The work gained the admiration of the literary establishment, in Venice and beyond, as the numerous encomiastic compositions that accompanied the volume attest. But the praise did not last long: it transformed into polemic when the writer published a second work the next year, her *Antisatire.*[35] A stark contrast to *Convent Paradise*, the *Antisatire*, which Tarabotti claimed she wrote at the behest of noblewomen (letter 207), was a witty response to Francesco Buoninsegni's *A Menippean Satire against Female Vanity*,[36] which criticized women's fashion excesses. Tarabotti cleverly parried the charges of the Sienese writer while also inserting other issues into the debate, including that of women's education. Despite its light tone, the *Antisatire*, with its emphasis on men's vanity and hypocrisy, was greeted with hostility by some literati. This negative reaction led to attacks on Tarabotti for some errors in *Convent Para-*

---

33. *Paradiso monacale* (Venice: Oddoni, 1643). A modern edition of the *Paradise* is planned by the editors of this volume, Meredith K. Ray and Lynn Lara Westwater.

34. A translation of the *Soliloquy to God* can be found in the appendix to Panizza, *Paternal Tyranny*, 155–57.

35. *Antisatira* (Venice: Valvasense 1644); modern edition by Weaver (see note 1).

36. *Contro 'l lusso donnesco satira menippea* (Venice: Sarzina, 1638). Buoninsegni's *Satire* was republished at least three times, twice together with Tarabotti's *Antisatire*. These two editions, although distinct, carry the same bibliographic information: Venice: Valvasense, 1644; on the issue, see the textual note in *Satira e Antisatira*, ed. Weaver, 109–12.

dise[37] and to accusations that she was not the true author of her works: *Convent Paradise* and the *Antisatire* were too different, her critics asserted, to have been issued by the same pen. A furious Tarabotti defended herself against such calumny. She wrote to her brother-in-law Giacomo Pighetti: "Certainly these fellows must have little experience with writing, since they marvel that the style of the *Paradise* should be different from that of the *Antisatire*, whereby they show that they do not know that style must be varied according to the topic" (letter 113). Refusing to be intimidated by her critics, Tarabotti persevered in her own defense and in that of all women, constantly positioning herself at the center of the literary and cultural wars over women's roles that unfolded in seventeenth-century Venice.[38] She continued this fight to the end of her life. Her last work answered a misogynous treatise originally published in Latin, the *Disputatio nova contra mulieres, qua probatur eas homines non esse*, or *New Disputation against Women in Which It Is Proved That They Are Not Human*, translated into Italian in 1647,[39] which argued that women had no soul. Tarabotti refutes the

---

37. Letter 99 details some of these criticisms.

38. The *querelle* on the merits of women had already been raging for centuries, but it took on new life in Venice at the beginning of the seventeenth century. At the end of the sixteenth century, Giuseppe Passi had published *The Defects of Women* (*I donneschi diffetti* [Venice: Iacobo Antonio Somasco, 1599]), a vitriolic attack on women. The next year two works in defense of women were published in the city: Moderata Fonte's *The Worth of Women* (*Il merito delle donne* [Venice: presso Domenico Imberti, 1600]) and Lucrezia Marinella's *The Nobility and Excellence of Women* (*Le nobiltà et eccellenze delle donne* [Venice: Giovan Battista Ciotti Senese, 1600]); modern editions and translations of both works are published in The Other Voice in Early Modern Europe series (Fonte, *The Worth of Women: Wherein Is Clearly Revealed Their Nobility and Their Superiority to Men*, ed. and trans. Virginia Cox [Chicago: University of Chicago Press, 1997]; Marinella, *The Nobility and Excellence of Women, and the Defects and Vices of Men*, ed. and trans. Anne Dunhill [Chicago: University of Chicago Press, 1999]). Marinella's treatise was composed specifically to respond to Passi's attack. The debates lasted until mid-century and conditioned the literary environment in which Tarabotti worked. On the issue, see Lynn Lara Westwater, "The Disquieting Voice: Women's Writing and Antifeminism in Seventeenth-Century Venice," Ph.D. dissertation, University of Chicago, 2003.

39. *Che le donne non siano della spezie degli uomini: Discorso piacevole, tradotto da Orazio Plato romano* [*That Women Are Not of the Same Species as Men: An Entertaining Discussion*] (Lyon: Gasparo Ventura, 1647). The name of the translator is false.

treatise's arguments one by one in *That Women Are of the Same Species as Men*,[40] published in 1651.

In 1650, however, Tarabotti had published another sort of book, the *Letters*,[41] which still mounted a general defense of women but, more important, aimed to solidify Tarabotti's own literary reputation. Published together with the *Tears*—a memorial work composed in memory of Tarabotti's dear friend Regina Donati in which Tarabotti justifies her bold publication of an epistolary collection—the *Letters* open a window onto her relationships with other writers as well as with a range of diplomats, political figures, friends, and family members. The *Letters* are an invaluable testament not only to Tarabotti's development as an author and to her life in the convent but, most important, to her efforts to construct her public image and to respond to her detractors.

TARABOTTI'S LETTERS

Tarabotti and the Epistolary Tradition

With the publication of her *Letters*, Tarabotti positioned herself within an extensive tradition of epistolary writing that stretched back to antiquity. The discovery of Cicero's letters in the fourteenth century had heralded the beginning of a new era for letter writing, quickly adopted by humanists as a tool to communicate ideas and showcase cultural and intellectual status.[42] Later, in the sixteenth century, Pietro Aretino

---

40. *Che le donne siano della spezie degli uomini* (Nuremberg: I. Cherchenbercher, 1651), available also in a modern edition by Panizza and in translation by Kenney; see note 1.

41. Tarabotti, *Lettere familiari e di complimento* (Venice: Guerigli, 1650).

42. Petrarch—himself an epistolarian who became an important model for letter writing in the early modern period—discovered Cicero's *Letters to Atticus, Quintus and Brutus* in 1345; in 1392 Coluccio Salutati came upon the *Epistolae ad familiares* (translated into vernacular Italian in 1544). As Paul Oskar Kristeller noted, epistolography was "perhaps the most extensive branch of Humanist literature" (qtd. in Giles Constable, *Letters and Letter-collections* [Belgium: Éditions Brepols, 1976], 39). The literature on humanist letterbooks is extensive: see, for example, Cecil H. Clough, "The Cult of Antiquity: Letters and Letter Collections," in *Cultural Aspects of the Italian Renaissance: Essays in Honor of Paul Oskar Kristeller*, ed. Cecil H. Clough (Manchester: Manchester University Press, 1976); M. Fumaroli, "Genèse

would make a splash with his pioneering first volume of letters, written in Italian rather than Latin, which revitalized and reinvented the genre.[43] Well before Aretino's lively, detailed missives earned him fame as Venice's "secretary of the world" (a self-designation that evoked the shift from the letter writer as a secretary in the service of a prince to one who served himself and his public) and inspired a revival of interest in the *lettera familiare*, women writers such as Isotta Nogarola, Cassandra Fedele, and Laura Cereta had composed and circulated letter collections, using them—as Tarabotti would—to establish their own literary status, advance their views, and respond to their critics. First circulated in manuscript during the fifteenth century, their letters presented compelling epistolary self-representations that contributed in no small part to the enduring reputation of all three women, and although their letters differ in many fundamental ways from those of Tarabotti (who must have known of them, whether or not she was able to read them in the Latin), aspects of their epistolary self-fashioning seem to presage her own.[44] Cereta also highlighted

---

de l'épistolographie classique: Rhetorique humaniste de la lettre, de Petrarche à Juste Lipse," *Revue d'histoire litterarire de la France* 78 (1978): 886–905; Judith Rice Henderson, "On Reading the Rhetoric of the Renaissance Letter," in *Renaissance Rhetoric*, ed. Heinrich F. Plett (Berlin: Walter de Gruyter, 1993), 143–62; and Diana Robin, *Filelfo in Milan: Writings 1451–1477* (Princeton, NJ: Princeton University Press, 1991).

43. On the vernacular epistolary vogue that developed in the wake of Aretino's first volume of *Letters* in 1538, see Amedeo Quondam, *Le carte messaggere: Retorica e modelli di comunicazione epistolare. Per un indice di libri di lettere del Cinquecento* (Rome: Bulzoni, 1981). See also Francesco Erspamer's edition of the first book of Aretino's *Lettere* (Parma: Ugo Guanda, 1995).

44. Although the letters of all three women circulated in manuscript form, those of Fedele and Cereta did not appear in print until the seventeenth century and those of Nogarola only in 1886. See *Clarissimae Feminae Cassandrae Fidelis venetae: Epistolae et orationes*, ed. Jacopo Filippo Tomasini (Padua: Franciscus Bolzetta, 1636); *Laura Ceretae Brixiensis Feminae Clarissimae Epistolae iam primum e MS in lucem productae*, ed. Jacopo Filippo Tomasini (Padua: Sebastiano Sardi, 1640); and *Isotae Nogarolae Veronensis opera quae supersunt omnia; accedunt Angelae et Zeneverae Nogarolae epistolae et carmina*, ed. Eugenius Abel, 2 vols. (Vienna: Gerold et socios; Budapest: Fridericum Kilian, 1886). All three letterbooks have been edited and translated in the series The Other Voice in Early Modern Europe published by the University of Chicago Press: see Isotta Nogarola, *Complete Writings: Letterbook, Dialogue on Adam and Eve, Orations*, ed. and trans. Margaret King and Diana Robin (Chicago: University of Chicago Press, 2004); *Cassandra Fedele: Letters and Orations*, ed. and trans.

in her letters the sacrifice and perseverance required of the woman artist and writer, demonstrating a kind of social consciousness that Tarabotti would echo.

Nonetheless, Tarabotti's *Letters* are perhaps best compared to those of Aretino, the "scourge of princes," who used his letters to establish his own literary persona, to reward friends and to punish enemies. Although Tarabotti professed distaste for Aretino's sharp quill, like Aretino she fully grasped the potential of the epistolary medium as a vehicle for self-promotion, self-positioning, and self-defense—this last being of particular significance to her given the continual criticism she faced. And if by the seventeenth century many letter writers were following the example put forth by Francesco Sansovino in his popular letter-writing manual, *Del secretario* (1564)—composing abstract letters that could be adopted as models—Tarabotti instead, like Aretino, placed herself squarely at the center of her epistolary narrative. Hers are not universal letters to be adapted and imitated so much as many self-referential epistolary narratives pieced together to craft a public image and to document a literary life, striking back at her critics.[45] Tarabotti's collection is composed not only of letters to friends and relatives, as suggested by the appellation "familiar," but also addresses important figures in the arenas of literature, politics, and the church: that is, highly placed or influential figures to whom she wished to demonstrate a connection. If the humanists employed letterbooks to establish their ties to a range of carefully selected correspondents, thereby bolstering their own standing, and used the space

---

Diana Robin (Chicago: University of Chicago Press, 2000); and *Laura Cereta: Collected Letters of a Renaissance Feminist*, ed. and trans. Diana Robin (Chicago: University of Chicago Press, 1997). On the women humanists, see for example, Margaret King and Albert Rabil, *Her Immaculate Hand: Selected Works by and about the Women Humanists of Quattrocento Italy* (Binghamton, NY: Medieval and Renaissance Texts and Studies, 1983; 2nd rev. paperback ed., 1991). On the development of women's vernacular epistolary writing in the sixteenth and seventeenth centuries in Italy, see Meredith K. Ray, *Writing Gender in Women's Letter Collections of the Italian Renaissance* (Toronto: University of Toronto Press, 2009). For a rich overview of women's literary presence in this period, see Virginia Cox, *Women's Writing in Italy, 1400–1650* (Baltimore: Johns Hopkins University Press, 2008).

45. On Tarabotti's *Letters* as a defense of her works and of her integrity as a writer, see Meredith K. Ray, "Letters from the Cloister: Defending the Literary Self in Arcangela Tarabotti's *Lettere familiari e di complimento*," *Italica* 81, no. 1 (2004): 24–43.

of the letterbook to position themselves within current debates over literature and culture, this is certainly Tarabotti's intention as well. As it had for the humanists, the published letterbook functioned for Tarabotti (as well as for her contemporararies such as Giovan Francesco Loredano, author of a volume of letters in 1653), as a reflection of the writer's credentials, accomplishments, and literary skill, while also highlighting relationships with scholars and patrons.[46]

The early modern letterbook was, no doubt, the product of careful consideration and planning, an important tool in establishing one's public reputation in the world of letters. Therefore, despite the desirability of a natural and spontaneous style, cited by many early modern epistolary manuals, published letterbooks like that of Tarabotti were hardly an unguarded reflection of the writer's personal feelings, experiences, and relationships—as some literary critics were, for a time, prone to see them. Rather, they were the product of careful consideration and editing, generally revised to varying degrees or, indeed, composed expressly for publication. Despite the requisite claims to the contrary frequently put forth in dedicatory letters, most epistolary collections were assembled with the authors' tacit permission, if not at their direct instigation. As evidenced in letter collections such as Paolo Manuzio's *Vernacular Letters of Various Noble Men* (1542)[47]—an important early entry in the epistolary arena—writers had come to expect and accept that their missives might be collected and published, and they often expressed the desire to polish them before they appeared in print. Although some of the letters in Tarabotti's collection were probably composed for publication rather than originating in real correspondence, others were certainly based on her actual epistolary exchanges. In fact, we are fortunate to have twelve

---

46. Many critics have likened the humanist letterbook to the modern-day scholarly dossier. See, for example, Vito Giustiniani, "La communication érudite: Les lettres humanistes et l'article moderne de revue," in *La correspondance d'Erasme et l'épistolographie humaniste* (Brussels: Editions de l'Université de Bruxelles, 1985), 109–33; Henderson, "Defining the Genre of the Letter," 94; and Robin, *Cassandra Fedele*, 35; see also Diana Robin, "Cassandra Fedele's *Epistolae* (1488–1521): Biography as Ef-facement," in *The Rhetorics of Life-Writing in Early Modern Europe: Forms of Biography from Cassandra Fedele to Louis XIV*, ed. Thomas F. Mayer and D. R. Woolf (Ann Arbor: University of Michigan Press, 1995), 187–98.

47. *Lettere volgari di diversi nobilissimi huomini, et eccellentissimi ingegni, scritte in diverse materie* (Venice: Paolo Manuzio, 1542).

of Tarabotti's mansucript letters, real missives that she actually sent, to compare with her published letters (and likely many more remain to be discovered in the archives).[48] We can see that many of her published letters bear resemblance to her real correspondence, albeit with some careful changes in wording or context (see, for example, letters 44 and 253 here). Although the existence of these documents cannot tell us whether all the letters in Tarabotti's collection had their basis in an actual epistolary exchange, they do suggest that the nun was in contact with many of the people who figure in her collection, from the friar Angelico Aprosio—a friend, then a bitter foe—to Vittoria della Rovere of Tuscany, whose patronage and protection Tarabotti sought for her *Antisatire* and (unsuccessfully) her *Paternal Tyranny*. In most cases, and where manuscript copies of published letters are lacking, other evidence confirms Tarabotti's relationships with the array of friends, patrons, and competitors who populate her letters.

Nuns and Letter Writing in Early Modern Venice

Tarabotti's letters speak compellingly to the deep importance that epistolary communication held for her as a cloistered nun. Enclosed in the convent of Sant'Anna from a young age and subjected to the increasingly rigorous environment of the post-Tridentine period, Tarabotti had limited opportunities to interact with the outside world. Although she frequented the convent parlor, receiving visits from members of the French diplomatic community in Venice, from her sometimes-patron Loredano, and from family and friends, she was as a professed nun not permitted to leave the confines of the convent. Letter writing, therefore, constituted an essential means for her to communicate with those who lived outside Venice or who were not

48. Seven autograph letters addressed to the friar Angelico Aprosio are housed in Genoa's Biblioteca Universitaria (BUG), E VI 22 and published in F. Medioli and F. De Rubeis, "La scrittura forzata: Le lettere autografe di Arcangela Tarabotti," *Rivista di Storia e Letteratura Religiosa* 32 (1996): 146–55; see also Medioli, "Alcune lettere autografe di Arcangela Tarabotti: Autocensura e immagine di se," ibid., 133–42. Five letters to Vittoria della Rovere of Tuscany are located in Florence's Archivio di Stato (Mediceo del Principato, 6152); these are transcribed in Francesca Medioli, "Arcangela Tarabotti's Reliability about Herself: Publication and Self-Representation (Together with a Small Collection of Previously Unpublished Letters"), *The Italianist* 23 (2003): 54–101.

permitted or able to visit her at the grille. Indeed, Tarabotti's *Letters* reveal the extent of her epistolary network and the variety of her addressees, who range from her sisters and brother-in-law, to the powerful Cardinal Jules Mazarin of France, to libertine writers such as the apostate friar Girolamo Brusoni. Most important, Tarabotti's *Letters* reveal her determination to establish herself as a serious literary presence by publishing an epistolary collection—something that had become almost *de riguer* among Italian writers by the seventeenth century—despite the many prohibitions against her, a nun, doing so. In fact, a variety of decrees issued in the later sixteenth and early seventeenth centuries repeatedly tried to regulate and even prevent nuns from writing letters (not to mention publishing them), fearing that epistolary communication offered too much interaction with the secular world, that it might expose nuns to influences from which they ought to be protected, and that it could prove difficult to monitor and control. Orders by the Patriarch of Venice Lorenzo Priuli in 1591 and Bishop Antonio Grimani in 1592, for example, had established strict regulations governing letter writing and insisted that any letters written or received by the nuns were subject to review by the abbess to ensure that both content and correspondent were acceptable.[49] A 1636 decree issued to Venice's female convents reiterated that letter writing was to be strictly regulated and limited to immediate family and others with express permission: ignoring such restrictions could result in confinement to one's cell, restriction of parlor privileges, exclusion from convent business, and suspension of eligibility for any kind of office within the convent.[50] Similarly, a 1644 order (issued in the same period in which Tarabotti was engaged in some of the very correspondence later published in her *Letters*) exhorted nuns not to write

---

49. See Bishop Antonio Grimani's *Constitutioni, et decreti approvati nella sinoda diocesana, sopra la retta disciplina monacale sotto L'illustrissimo, & Reverendissimo Monsignor Antonio Grimani Vescovo di Torcello. L'anno della Natività del Nostro Signore. 1592. Il giorno 7, 8 & 9 d'aprile*, chap. 46, "Delle Lettere, & Polize" (Venice, 1592), and Patriarch Lorenzo Priuli, *Ordini, & avvertimenti, che si devono osservare ne' Monasteri di Monache di Venetia: Sopra le visite, & clausura* (Venice, 1591), 10r.

50. Archivio Patriarcale, Venezia, Sezione Antica, Monalium 7, Order of Cardinal Cornelius Patriarch.

letters at all, even to their most immediate family.[51] Restrictions on letter writing by nuns in post-Tridentine Italy, intended to strengthen the separation of convent communities from the secular world, render Tarabotti's publication of a book composed entirely of personal correspondence all the more striking. Although there were a few precedents for epistolary publication by women religious, including works by Catherine of Siena, the Dominican tertiary Osanna da Mantova, and the Genovese nun Battistina Vernazza, such texts were—in addition to being published posthumously (and not originally intended for print)—distinctly spiritual in nature, distinguishing them from Tarabotti's manifestly secular letters.[52] Tarabotti's secular writings, in fact, made her something of an "anomaly" at a time when nuns who chose to write usually produced spiritual works or devotional poetry.[53]

If Tarabotti's epistolary activity allowed her to establish and maintain relationships with correspondents outside the convent and outside the city, the publication of her correspondence constituted her only effective weapon for confronting and refuting her critics. Tarabotti's literary career, as we have seen, was fraught with obstacles, turmoil, and controversy. With her published letters, Tarabotti was able to furnish public evidence of her talent as a writer and regain control over the story of her works' composition and publication, despite accusations that she had not written the works herself. In a passionate

51. Zanette cites Patriarch Giovan Francesco Morosini's order that nuns refrain from exchanging letters even with their closest relatives (*Suor Arcangela*, 366).

52. Generally considered to be the first book of vernacular letters written by a woman in Italy, Catherine of Siena's spiritual letters—which she dictated to a scribe—were first printed in 1500 by Manuzio. The letters of Osanna da Mantova were published with an account of her life written by her confessor: *Libretto della vita et transito de la beata Osanna da Mantova nuovamente corretto et con una nova aggiunta* (Bologna, 1524); on Osanna da Mantova, see Zarri, *Sante Vive: Profezie di corte e devozione femminile tra '400 e '500* (Turin: Rosenberg & Sellier, 1990). Battistina Vernazza was the author of various devotional works; her spiritual letters were published posthumously by Scotto in 1602 (see Daniela Soffaroli Camillocci, "La monaca esemplare: Lettere spirituali di madre Battistina Vernazza [1497–1587], in *Per lettera: La scrittura epistolare femminile tra archivio e tipografia secoli XV–XVII*, ed. G. Zarri [Rome: Viella, 1999], 235–61).

53. On Tarabotti's secular writing as an "anomaly," see Mario Rosa, "La religiosa," in *L'uomo barocco*, ed. Rosario Villari (Rome and Bari: Editori Laterza, 1991), 219–67.

letter to Nicolas Bretel de Grémonville, Tarabotti offers what may be seen as the raison d'être of her letterbook. She writes:

> Nonetheless let them say what they will; we will let them chatter, since the whole world will see, in a volume of letters that will soon see the light of day, whether that nonsense is true, that my writings need their polish to achieve glory. Your Excellency and other personages of merit will always be able to attest whether my letters reached your glorious hands in the same form in which they will appear in print. (Letter 99)

Tarabotti means to deflate her critics by offering firm evidence of her literary capacities and her integrity in the form of her *Letters*, which, collectively, document the composition of all her works. Tarabotti's *Letters*, therefore, are much more than a collection of personal missives; they are the defense and the reclamation of her own status as a literary figure in Seicento Venice.

Tarabotti's Epistolary Network

Despite all efforts by the church to limit or regulate nuns' epistolary activities, Tarabotti's network of correspondents is impressive. Included among her 256 published letters are many addressed to highly placed figures: three to Doge Francesco Erizzo and one to Doge Francesco Molino; a total of ten to the future doges Bertucci Valier and his son Silvestro; one to the duke of Parma, Odoardo Farnese; one to the future pope Alessando VIII; and one to the powerful cardinal Jules Mazarin in France. Five letters to Francesco Zati, the Tuscan resident at Venice, reveal that he was influential in placing her in contact with another important figure, Vittoria della Rovere, Grand Duchess of Tuscany, to whom she directs three letters and whose patronage she sought on more than one occasion.[54] Through letters to persons such as these, Tarabotti demonstrates the powerful connections she was able to establish despite her confinement to the convent.

---

54. Biographical information on these and other more occasionally addressed figures is provided in notes to the letters within the body of the collection.

More numerous still are Tarabotti's letters to literary figures, which include some seventy letters to named and unnamed correspondents. Foremost among these are her letters to members of Venice's Accademia degli Incogniti, the most powerful literary institution of the day.[55] The relationships Tarabotti established with members of this group played an important role in her literary success, increasing her fame and facilitating the publication of her works. The academy, which included nearly three hundred members from throughout the peninsula and beyond in its ranks, was a key arbiter of cultural taste in mid-seventeenth-century Italy. Influential academy members promoted vernacular literature of all genres and participated in shaping the nascent opera industry. The academy was also well known for its political and social stances. Some famous members of the academy inclined toward libertinism, though such a tendency was not universal. In general the academy tended to favor the independence of cultural and political life from religious control. Debates and controversies animated the academy, which thrived on questioning—sincerely or not—accepted political, social, and religious ideas. The many members of the academy with whom Tarabotti interacted and corresponded were likely compelled by her iconoclasm. Always in search of innovation, new names, and new conceits, they were also most certainly attracted by the singularity and forcefulness of this outspoken writer. Yet the hostility that Tarabotti faced over the course of her literary career had its origins within this same academy, where antiwoman sentiment ran rife. Tarabotti's letters document that many of her literary correspondents within the academy proved not to be faithful friends or support-

---

55. There are a number of studies dealing with the Accademia degli Incogniti. See, for example, Giorgio Spini, *Ricerca dei libertini: La teoria dell'impostura delle religioni nel Seicento veneziano* (Florence: La Nuova Italia, 1983); Paolo Ulvioni, "Accademie e cultura in Italia dalla Controriforma all'Arcadia: Il caso veneziano," *Libri e documenti* 5 (1970): 21–75. More recent studies include Monica Miato, *L'Accademia degli Incogniti di Giovan Francesco Loredan, Venezia (1630–1661)* (Florence: Olschki, 1998), which is marred by errors with regard to Tarabotti; and Nina Cannizzaro, "Studies on Guido Casoni, 1561–1642, and Venetian Academies," Ph.D. dissertation, Harvard University, 2001. For brief portraits of the members of the Incogniti, see *Le glorie degli Incogniti* (Venice: Francesco Valvasense, 1647); see also Michele Maylender's *Storia delle accademie d'Italia*, vol. 5 (Bologna: Licinio Cappelli, 1930), ad vocem.

ers; they tricked and taunted her and even went so far as to publish misogynistic works to provoke her.

At the center of the academy stood the nobleman Giovan Francesco Loredano, Tarabotti's patron and the dedicatee of her epistolary collection.[56] Loredano's support was instrumental in Tarabotti's efforts to publish several of her works—including her letter collection—and his backing lent authority to her literary ambitions. Tarabotti recognizes Loredano's important role in her literary life with the twelve letters she addresses to him within her published collection. Yet Loredano was not a wholly dependable ally; he repeatedly disappointed Tarabotti with his actions, as her published letters also attest. (Some of Loredano's own works reveal a persistent thread of misogyny; and he was behind the Italian translation of the treatise arguing that women did not have souls, mentioned above, to which Tarabotti responded.) Tarabotti's letters to Loredano indeed reflect a certain diffidence, alternating between respect, gratitude, and disenchantment.

Tarabotti had more stable relationships with other members of the academy. She addresses thirteen letters to Giovanni Dandolo, who wrote the letter of presentation for her letter collection and whom she encouraged to write his own work in praise of women.[57] Eleven letters are directed to Pietro Paolo Bissari, who praised Tarabotti effusively

56. Giovan Francesco Loredano (1606–61) was the most powerful figure in the mid-seventeenth-century Venetian publishing world. He was the author of numerous secular and religious works, as well as a volume of letters; for a full accounting of his publications, see Tiziana Menegatti, *Ex ignoto notus: Bibliografia delle opere a stampa del Principe degli Incogniti: Giovan Francesco Loredano* (Padua: Il Poligrafo, 2000). He also held a number of positions in the Venetian government, including as a member of the Council of Ten and as state inquisitor. On Loredano and the Venetian press see Mario Infelise, "Ex ignotus notus? Note sul tipografo Sarzina e l'Accademia degli Incogniti," in *Libri tipografi biblioteche: Ricerche storiche offerte a Luigi Balsamo* (Florence: Olschki, 1997), 207–23; and "La crise de la librairie vénitienne: 1620–1650," in *Le livre et l'historien: Etudes offertes à Henri-Jean Martin*, ed. Frédéric Barbier et al. (Geneva: Droz, 1997), 343–52.

57. The Venetian aristocrat Giovanni Dandolo (1613–61) was, like Loredano, a member of the Accademia degli Incogniti. In contrast to many other academy members with whom the nun associated, Dandolo remained a faithful ally of Tarabotti, who only expresses disappointment with him when he does not publish a promised work in praise of women (see letter 8).

in his own work;[58] and eight to Enrico Cornaro, who may or may not have been an academy member but who served as an intermediary between Tarabotti and other Incogniti.[59] The *Letters* include seven letters to Giacomo Pighetti, the husband of Tarabotti's sister Lorenzina and likely an early facilitator of her interactions with Venice's literary world as well as with the community of French diplomats with whom she corresponded.[60] Among her other correspondents from the academy are the writers Francesco Pona (five letters)[61] and Nicolò Crasso (three letters).[62]

Beyond the dozens of missives addressed to named academy members, Tarabotti directs many letters to two other academy members, Angelico Aprosio and Girolamo Brusoni, who had so infuriated Tarabotti that she expunged their names from the published collection. Aprosio, an itinerant friar and author, befriended Tarabotti but then betrayed her trust by condemning her works and literary abilities

58. Pietro Paolo Bissari (1595–1663), with whom Tarabotti exchanged a number of letters, was the founder in 1649 of the Accademia dei Rifioriti in Vicenza. Bissari was the author of *Bradamante*, a theatrical work to which Tarabotti refers in letter 219.

59. This lettered friend of Tarabotti's might be identified as Enrico Cornaro son of Paolo (c. 1600–63), a lawyer in Venice (ASV, sezione notarile, testamenti, 83.35). Cornaro's name does not appear in such academy membership rolls as the *Glorie degli Incogniti*, but he was clearly connected to the Incogniti's milieu; in letters 104 and 112, for example, Tarabotti thanks him for procuring a poem by the Incognito Giovan Francesco Busenello (1598–1659) for her *Tears*.

60. Giacomo Pighetti (d. 1647) was Tarabotti's brother-in-law, married to her younger sister Lorenzina. Bergamascan by birth, Pighetti practiced law in Venice, where he was also a writer of local acclaim. He contributed a Latin panegyric to Tarabotti's *Convent Paradise*. The *Letters* show that Pighetti, despite his family link to Tarabotti, at times antagonized her.

61. Francesco Pona (1594–1660), was a Veronese writer and doctor. In 1625 he published, under the pseudonym Eureta Misoscolo, *The Lantern* (*La lucerna*), which was placed on the Index of Forbidden Books, probably at least in part for its mention of reincarnation. He published an *Antilucerna* in 1648 (Verona, Rossi).

62. Nicolò Crasso (1586–c. 1655) was a widely published author and a prominent figure in the academy who also corresponded with Loredano (see Loredano, *Lettere, prima parte* [Venice: Guerigli, 1665], 8). Crasso had close ties to Cesare Cremonini, the controversial Paduan philosopher, who encountered trouble for his heterodox views regarding the immortality of the soul.

and seeking to publish against her.[63] Brusoni, another former friend, also dismayed Tarabotti when he chose to write on a topic she considered her own, that of coerced monachization.[64] The letters to Aprosio and Brusoni fall among the many in the collection directed at anonymous correspondents, named only with appellations such as "Signor N." or "Father N." (the initial derives from the Latin *nemo*, or nobody). Like those to Aprosio and Brusoni, these letters frequently turn on literary matters and reveal strained relations with the recipient, whose names, repressed as insult or precaution, can nonetheless frequently be deduced. In the case of Aprosio and Brusoni, Tarabotti includes a wealth of incriminating details to ensure their identification and thus humiliation. At least ten of the collection's anonymous letters were certainly meant for Aprosio; another ten were directed at Brusoni.

Tarabotti's epistolary relationships with women, by contrast, were rather less volatile, and also, judging from her letterbook, less voluminous—perhaps because women had better access to the convent parlor than men, and thus less need to resort to letters, or perhaps simply because she was in greater need of the kind of practical literary support her male contacts could best offer. Nonetheless, in four letters

---

63. Angelico Aprosio (1607–81), an Eremitani friar of the Augustinian order. Born in Ventimiglia (and also known as "Father Ventimiglia"), Aprosio traveled throughout Italy, spending periods of time in Genoa, Siena, Pisa, and Venice; it was in Venice that, as a member of the academy, he came into contact with Tarabotti. The friar initially encouraged Tarabotti, praising her *Convent Paradise*, but after the publication of the *Antisatire* their relationship soured, due largely to Aprosio's composition of the *Mask Lifted* (*La maschera scoperta*), which attacked Tarabotti and threatened to reveal her as the true author of the quasi-anonymous *Antisatire*; Tarabotti was able to block the publication of Aprosio's work; see E. Biga, *Una polemica antifemminista del '600: La "Maschera scoperta" di Angelico Aprosio* (Ventimiglia: Civica Biblioteca Aprosiana, 1989).

64. Girolamo Brusoni (c. 1614–c. 1686), a writer and apostate friar. He entered the monastery at sixteen, like Tarabotti without vocation, and fled it three times. Among his works are *La fuggitiva* (1639), *Orestilla* (1642?), *La gondola a tre remi* (1657), *I sogni di Parnaso* (c. 1660), and *Gli amori tragici* (no date). Tarabotti appears in at least two of his works: in the *Orestilla*, she is mirrored in the figure of the writer and forced nun Laura; and in the *Sogni di Parnaso*, after her death, Brusoni discusses his epistolary exchange with the nun, which he says compromises her literary reputation (see Zanette, *Suor Arcangela*, 130, 285, 371). Brusoni met Tarabotti, Zanette speculates, around 1640, and the two corresponded amicably before their friendship dissolved in a literary dispute.

to Aquila Barbara of Venice[65] and nine to Guid'Ascania Orsi, a nun and writer in Bologna,[66] for example, Tarabotti praises their works and responds to their kind words for her own, thus creating a small but nurturing community of lettered women. Tarabotti seems to feel at greater ease with these correspondents, freely sharing with them her frustrations at the obstacles that face women writers, as when she remarks to Orsi, "It takes great stubbornness to publish, being that everyone wants to say his part, especially against us women, because men obstinately do not want to admit that women know how to write without their help" (letter 24). Tarabotti also maintained a warm relationship with Betta Polani, a former inhabitant in Sant'Anna whose friendship remained an important source of support for Tarabotti even after Betta left the convent without taking the veil.[67] Tarabotti includes thirteen letters to Betta, including one (letter 26) in which the writer, ill and fearing death may be imminent, entrusts her friend with her literary works. Other female correspondents range from Tarabot-

65. We have little information on this correspondent, a noblewoman and writer, with whom Tarabotti seems to feel at ease despite their difference in social position. Tarabotti praises Barbara's writing but twice warns her of its danger. It is likely that Aquila was the wife of Almorò Barbaro, son of Pier Alvise, who lived from 1592 to 1660 according to Cappellari, or from 1598 to 1687 according to Barbaro, and who wed Aquila di Nicolò Boldù in 1632. She seems to have died before 1651, the year of the second marriage of Almorò (see Cappellari, *Campidoglio*, 1:105v.; Barbaro, *Arbori*, 1:203).

66. Guid'Ascania Orsi of Bologna was, like Tarabotti, a nun and a writer, evidently of both poetry and prose (see Graziosi, "Arcipelago sommerso," 146–81). In her correspondence, Tarabotti addresses Orsi with great familiarity; she repeatedly thanks her for her generosity and pledges her devotion. Tarabotti's letters show an interesting literary exchange between the two women: Tarabotti praises Orsi's letters, asks her for literary advice, and commiserates with Orsi about the difficulties women encounter in trying to publish their works.

67. Betta Polani (d. after 1654) was the niece of a convent sister of Tarabotti, Claudia Polani, and of Giovanni Polani, with whom Tarabotti corresponded with regard to her *Convent Paradise*. A novice at Sant'Anna for many years and a dear friend of Tarabotti's, Betta was compelled by her uncle Giovanni to leave the convent at the beginning of 1648 (see Zanette, *Suor Arcangela*, 113, 450). The two friends continued to keep in touch through Betta's visits to the convent and by letter. In Tarabotti's letter collection those to Betta stand out for their affectionate tone and for their frequency. Other documents on the Polani family can be found in ASV, Manimorte, Sant'Anna, Busta 15, fasc. 4.

ti's sisters to Isabetta Piccolomini Scarpi,[68] Tarabotti's partner in the brokerage of the fine lace for which Venice's convents were famous, to an unnamed "Mother N.," who sends Tarabotti a devotional work (letter 203).

Also prominent in Tarabotti's *Letters* are a number of missives addressed to members of the French diplomatic community in Venice. Limited by law in their contact with the Venetian patriciate, these transient residents in the Serenissima found a welcome interlocutor in the brilliant writer of Sant'Anna. Tarabotti, for her part, was flattered by the attention and friendship of her French contacts and hoped for their support in pursuing the publication of her works, particularly *Paternal Tyranny*, which she felt might receive a warmer reception in Paris, a city she described as a "paradise for women" (letter 136). Tarabotti includes several letters to the family of the French ambassador Jean des Hameaux;[69] she had an even warmer relationship with his successor, Ambassador Nicolas Bretel de Grémonville, who boarded his daughters in Sant'Anna under Tarabotti's care.[70] Tarabotti addresses seven letters to him, often addressing her literary tribulations in some detail; she also directs three letters to his wife, Anne-Françoise de Loménie, and, upon the family's return to France, two to their daughters. Through these connections, Tarabotti was also introduced to the marchioness Renée de Clermont-Galerande, to whom she addresses a

---

68. Tarabotti writes frequently to this correspondent regarding the lace Sant'Anna nuns create. Scarpi seems to have functioned as an intermediary between Tarabotti and her noblewomen clients in the contracting of this sought-after lace work.

69. Ambassador des Hameaux's tenure in Venice ran from 1642 to 1645. Tarabotti was in cordial contact both with his wife Anne des Hameaux (to whom Tarabotti refers with the Italianized last name of D'Amò) and her niece Marguerite de Fiubet (in letter 250 "de Giubet").

70. Nicolas Bretel de Grémonville (1608–48) was the French ambassador to Venice for a stormy period from July 1645 to October 1647. After less than two years, Bretel de Grémonville requested and obtained his departure from Venice, returning to Paris with his family, where he died on 26 November 1648; see *Dictionnaire de biographie française*, ed. M. Prevost and R. d'Amat (Paris: Librairie Letouzey et Ané, 1956), vol. 7. During his tenure at Venice, Bretel de Grémonville forged a close friendship with Tarabotti, visiting her in the convent parlor, writing to her, and even entrusting his daughters to the care of the nuns of Sant'Anna, as seen in letter 35. For information on his family members, see notes to letters 34 and 35.

total of four letters.[71] Tarabotti's relationship with the marchioness became progressively more tense due to two failed enterprises for which Tarabotti blamed the marchioness. First, she found the marchioness a difficult customer unwilling to respect an agreement regarding a lace collar Tarabotti had produced for her. Second, and more painful, was the loss of the manuscript of *Paternal Tyranny* that Tarabotti had been convinced to entrust to the marchioness's secretary, a certain Colisson. Although Tarabotti repeatedly asks the marchioness for news of both the man and the work, she received no satisfaction, and feared the *Tyranny* had been published in France under another's name.

The missives included in Tarabotti's *Letters* were composed over a period of about a decade, beginning around 1642 (when she composed the first work she would publish, *Convent Paradise*) and continuing up until the publication of the collection in 1650. None of the letters is dated and they are not arranged in any comprehensive chronological or thematic order, although the position of some seems to serve strategic purposes—for example, the letter to Doge Francesco Erizzo at the opening of the work advertises immediately Tarabotti's powerful connections, and the letter to Betta Polani at the end offers a humanizing conclusion to the collection and, as a tribute to a dear friend, serves as a bridge to the *Tears*, composed in honor of another cherished friend, which follows immediately after. Occasionally, brief groupings of two and three letters on a common theme occur, but more often missives dealing with the same topic are interspersed at long intervals throughout the volume, requiring the reader to reconstruct the narrative thread only after reading the entire collection, piecing together the many stories that are slowly portioned out, from Tarabotti's efforts to recover her lost manuscript of *Paternal Tyranny* to the deterioration of her friendships with Aprosio and Brusoni. The lack of an overarching organizational principle does not mean that Tarabotti was uninvolved with the assembly of her volume: indeed, we read at several points in the *Letters* themselves that she projected and planned its publication for many years and that, as we have seen,

---

71. The marchioness was part of Bretel de Grémonville's entourage in Venice. When the marchioness returned to France, she promised to help Tarabotti publish her *Paternal Tyranny*, an offer Tarabotti embraced. The venture ran aground, and Tarabotti's late letters to the marchioness express her deep disappointment.

she hoped her letters would function as proof of her literary authority and integrity. Perhaps she herself chose to arrange the letters in an apparently random fashion in order to attenuate and obfuscate certain episodes, for example, her involvement in the circulation of prohibited books or her efforts to publish controversial works such as *Paternal Tyranny*. In this manner she may have hoped to avoid the censure of religious and civil authorities and also to deflect the criticism of her detractors, for only an attentive external reader would be able to piece together the full text of the episodes she narrates. It is of course also possible, despite her declarations of involvement with the publication of the work, that it was the printer or an intermediary and not Tarabotti who determined the order of the letters.

While clouding certain storylines, the discontinuities in the letters' arrangement cannot obscure Tarabotti's close attention to evoking and describing her literary life. Many of the compositions, including those addressed to figures outside the world of letters, deal with matters relating directly to Tarabotti's activity as a writer: her works, the public reaction to them, her efforts to publish and promote them. Tarabotti seeks to defend herself throughout her *Letters* from the accusations launched against her and to establish, maintain, or expose the true nature of her relationship with writers such as Aprosio, Loredano, and Brusoni. Virtually absent, by contrast, is any sort of religious or spiritual thematics; firmly secular in nature, the letters highlight Tarabotti's status as a cloistered Benedictine nun mostly in condemnation of the practice of forced monachization, as when she reprimands even her good friend Bretel de Grémonville for choosing to place his daughters in a convent (letter 88). Tarabotti's customary passion for the defense of women and the condemnation of the unjust practices of patriarchal society and institutions, on the other hand, evident in each of her previous works from *Convent Hell* to *Paternal Tyranny, Antisatire*, and even the far less controversial *Convent Paradise*, is on clear display in the *Letters*. Here, too, Tarabotti is quick to praise the superiority of the female sex over the male, urging correspondents such as Giovanni Dandolo to write works in favor of women. She attacks the perfidy of men, as when she scornfully notes—playing on her status as a woman when it suits her—that Aprosio and others advance against her in a band to attack her writings, leaving her, a lone and vulnerable woman, to defend herself (letter 17). Yet although this theme, the defense of women and the biting critique of men, may be said to be the central element of most of Tarabotti's works, in the *Letters*, it is secondary to the major goal of the collection: to paint an epistolary portrait of Tarabotti as a writer of great talent and a woman of deep integrity.

Beyond Convent Walls: Cultural and Economic Exchange in the Letters

The *Letters* furnish rich details regarding the daily rhythms of life in a seventeenth-century Venetian convent and the difficulties often faced by nuns, from interacting with friends and family through the barrier of the parlor grille to navigating the tensions that inevitably arose among persons constrained to live, confined, in community. Often, Tarabotti complains of her poor health, the "continual constriction of the chest, which consumes me, I might say, to my very bones and nearly takes my breath away" (letter 17), or alludes to difficulties with the other nuns (letter 231, for instance). Tarabotti's *Letters* also shed valuable light on the many ways in which cloistered nuns were able to engage with and serve the broader community despite their enclosed state. The *Letters* reveal, for example, that the nuns of Sant'Anna, as in many female convents, took in young girls as boarders, educating them until their marriages, a practice known as *serbanza*. Often, the bonds engendered by this practice were intense, leading to long-term relationships between the nuns and the families involved.[72] In Tarabotti's case, the decision by the French ambassador and his wife to board their daughters in Sant'Anna led to a deeper relationship for the whole family with Tarabotti—a warm bond we see reflected in Tarabotti's words of congratulations for the birth of their son Marco—and, as we have seen, Tarabotti includes two letters to the girls following their return to France (letters 161 and 171). Nuns were often involved in helping to negotiate the marriages of their charges and others; several letters in Tarabotti's collection reveal her dedicated efforts—always in sympathy with the bride-to-be—to find an appropriate and appeal-

---

72. See, for example, Sharon Strocchia, "Taken into Custody: Girls and Convent Guardianship in Renaissance Florence," *Renaissance Studies* 17 (2003): 177–200.

ing spouse. In several cases, Tarabotti uses her connections to highly placed figures to faciliate the wishes of others, recommending and introducing people to others who can help them. Tarabotti's letters also provide insight into another area in which many female convents were involved: the contracting and production of the fine lace for which Venice, and its nuns in particular, had become famous by the seventeenth century.[73] The sale of the expensive lace collar for the Marchioness Clermont-Galerande that we find Tarabotti mediating in the *Letters* was a complex and delicate negotiation that necessitated her dealing with lacemakers within and outside of Sant'Anna.

Not only was Tarabotti a point of contact for the contracting of lacework; she was, interestingly, often the person to whom those outside the convent turned to locate controversial and indeed contraband literature. For a cloistered nun, Tarabotti was extraordinarily well informed regarding new developments on the Venetian literary scene. Francesco Maria Zati, the Tuscan resident at Venice, turned to her for a copy of a nonexistent work, presumed to be controversial, the *Soul of Zeno* (letter 214), supposedly inspired by the inflammatory *Soul of Pallavicino*, a clandestinely published work that presents the notorious Pallavicino as a martyr and that Tarabotti in the *Letters* openly claims to have possessed (letter 64). She also displays a good grasp of the current political situation, remarking several times in the *Letters* on the war in Candia, once even to Doge Erizzo (letter 19). As the *Letters* reflect, Tarabotti was, in fact, a kind of cultural broker, dealing in arenas as varied as literature and lace, marriage alliances and recommendations.The connections she established to important families and figures in Venetian society through the convent and, most important, through her activity as a writer, allowed her to mediate and direct a range of business from within the confines of Sant'Anna. In this, she was not alone—recent scholarship on nuns and convents has, increasingly, highlighted the many arenas in which they

---

73. On Tarabotti's involvement with lacemaking as well as her activities in the areas of *serbanza* and marriage brokering, see Meredith K. Ray, "Letters and Lace: Arcangela Tarabotti and Convent Culture in Seicento Venice," in *Early Modern Women and Transnational Communities of Letters*, ed. J. Campbell and A. Larsen (Aldershot, England: Ashgate, 2009), 45–73.

were active[74]—but in her unique voice, in her unrelenting dedication to promoting the cause of women and, especially, her own cause as a writer, Tarabotti was certainly unique. It is her individuality and the force of her own experience that emerge most indelibly from the *Letters*, indubitably Tarabotti's most personal work. At the same time, the *Letters* also constitute her most public work, in that they position her at the center of their narrative, as few letter collections, and no work by a nun had before.

Style and Rhetoric in the Letters

Tarabotti's writing exhibits a complexity and extravagance typical of much writing from the period. Like many of her contemporaries, Tarabotti displays a great fondness for metaphor and hyperbole, and much of her writing is built around elaborate conceits. Tarabotti's writing indeed assumes much of its force through her recourse to such rhetorical devices. In a typical passage Tarabotti writes:

> Figures of great esteem, most Serene Lord, do not come out with disdainful improprieties against women. Witness the many great literary men who flourish in the present centuries and the many modern swans whose song steals the glory of the Homers, the Virgils, and the Horaces. Among their number are many ravens with baleful quills flapping boldly about who, supposing themselves to be phoenixes in expressing themselves to the rays of the sun of glory, rather than

74. Zarri, "Venetian Convents and Civic Ritual," in Weaver, *Arcangela Tarabotti*, 37–56; Zarri and Pomata, *I monasteri femminili come centri di cultura fra Rinascimento e Barocco*; Elissa Weaver, *Convent Theater in Early Modern Italy: Spiritual Fun and Learning for Women* (Cambridge: Cambridge University Press, 2002); Craig Monson, *Disembodied Voices: Music and Culture in an Early Modern Italian Convent* (Berkeley: University of California Press, 1995); Robert Kendrick, *Celestial Sirens: Nuns and Their Music in Early Modern Milan* (Oxford: Clarendon Press, 1996); Kate Lowe, *Nuns' Chronicles and Convent Culture in Renaissance and Counter-Reformation Italy* (Cambridge, Cambridge University Press, 2003); and Elisabetta Graziosi, "Scrivere in convento: Devozione, encomio, persuasione nelle rime delle monache fra Cinque e Seicento," in *Donne, disciplina, creanza cristiana dal XV al XVII secolo*, ed. Gabriella Zarri, 303–31 (Rome: Edizioni di storia della letteratura, 1996).

immortalized find themselves with the feathers of their vanity singed and with the wings of impudence reduced to ashes forever. (Letter 17)

Transforming the literary world she inhabits into an aviary of swans, ravens, and would-be phoenixes, Tarabotti dramatizes her conflict with her adversaries by removing it from temporal and spatial specificity and projecting it into the atemporal space of myth. Her heavy reliance on analogy indeed frequently transforms her struggles into mythical (or biblical) battles and those involved in them into gods, goddesses, and other mythical creatures. The plays that Tarabotti frequently makes on the titles of her works, associating her *Convent Paradise* or *Convent Hell* with the otherworldly dimension, for instance, place her and her literary creations at the center of this metaphorical cosmography. Tarabotti simultaneously underlines the relevance of these titles and these works to her own unhappy biography, never letting the reader forget that in her writing metaphor is always anchored to fact and that her literary fancy demands real change. It is in this jarring encounter between conceit and reality that Tarabotti's writing distinguishes itself from that of her contemporaries.

Nevertheless, the *Letters'* rapid shifts between the metaphoric and the literal often create the marvel so keenly sought by seventeenth-century writers. The complex structure of the above passage, for instance, transforms it from a metaphorical into a real and awe-inspiring linguistic trap for her adversaries. In other passages, Tarabotti creates ambiguity as to whether she speaks literally or metaphorically. She writes, for instance, to a female author she greatly esteems:

I have just received the package from the heavens of your kindness. Since it is full of marvels, it renders me as astounded by the beauty of the flowers as I am embarrassed by the exceptionality of the favor and the nobility of your generous heart. Your garden indeed produces flowers that exceed natural ones in quality, and it is quite fertile with fruit and every other worthy quality. (Letter 192)

By blurring the distinction between conceit and reality, Tarabotti not only teases her readers but warns them of the potential for misreading metaphor.

Tarabotti also frequently elicits a comic effect by revealing the mechanisms of metaphors.[75] In letter 69, for instance, she writes:

> I suffer greatly from the constriction in my chest.... I was taught that, for a remedy, I should place a wolf's skin over the area that pains me, but never having been able to find one, I recall that in the Gospel our Lord calls wicked men wolves. Therefore I beg Your Illustrious Ladyship to intercede on my behalf with the excellent *avogadore* so that, should the occasion arise to condemn someone, he might skin him and send me the hide. If it improves my health I will forever pray for your success ....

Tarabotti insists on an intentionally ludicrous literal reading of a biblical metaphor, a reading that, in addition to provoking laughter, also fosters awareness of the importance of metaphor—and its proper interpretation—within her text. With frequent recourse to such metaphorical play, Tarabotti's *Letters* provide instances of the greatest humor in her oeuvre. This humor, far from a distraction, is instead a conduit that firmly connects metaphor to the reality, in Tarabotti's writing, of women's mistreatment at men's hand, a reality that no conceits could obscure.

The Afterlife of Tarabotti's Letters

One of the most striking aspects of Tarabotti's *Letters* is the silence that surrounds the volume's publication. Unlike Tarabotti's earlier works, all of which occasioned admiration or, more often, controversy, the *Letters* seem to have ruffled few feathers—despite the often unflattering portraits they offer of men such as Aprosio, Brusoni, and even Loredano. Tarabotti's 1643 *Convent Paradise* already featured within its leaves extensive praise of the work from important literary figures;

---

75. On the humor in Tarabotti's letters, see Lynn Westwater, "The Trenchant Pen: Humor in the *Lettere* of Arcangela Tarabotti," in Weaver, *Arcangela Tarabotti*, 158–72.

it also earned the writer new admirers, including powerful members of the Accademia degli Incogniti. When she published the *Antisatire* in 1644 to respond to Buoninsegni's *Satire* of female vanity, some of these same admirers quickly became vocal critics. Irritated by Tarabotti's quick-witted defense of women, they expressed their displeasure in responses such as Aprosio's *The Mask Lifted*, an attack on Tarabotti that also threatened to reveal her identity as the author of the *Antisatire*, which she had published only under her initials. *Convent Hell* and *Paternal Tyranny* were not printed in Tarabotti's lifetime, but they circulated in manuscript and Tarabotti spoke and wrote of them often. These works, too, engendered a range of responses: some admired her forceful voice, while others decried her prowoman stance and her criticism of the policies of the Venetian state and the church. Most damning, *Paternal Tyranny*, published posthumously as *Innocence Deceived*, was condemned by the church and placed on the Index in 1661.[76] Yet despite what might be described as the transgressive nature of the *Letters*—a strikingly public epistolary work by an enclosed nun at a time of increased restriction of nuns' epistolary activity—there is no evidence of the *Letters* giving scandal, nor of their arousing particular admiration. They do not appear to have caused any trouble for Tarabotti with church officials, and they were published with the necessary permissions—perhaps, after all, thanks to the inclusion of the *Tears upon the Death of Regina Donati* with the volume. Indeed, the *Letters* seem to have been accepted by the writer's contemporaries with equanimity, perhaps because the very structure of the work, as an epistolary collection, made it difficult for readers to piece together the stories Tarabotti was telling and thus some of her most provocative ar-

---

76. The church began to move against the book in 1654, when a report to the Congregation of the Index recommended the book's condemnation because it makes many statements against holy institutions; another report deplores the book's attitudes toward the church and church doctrine, and explains: "The book seems to smell of heresy and all of it is condemnable." The official censure of the book to the Congregation of the Index was issued in 1659, and contends that the author misreads Scripture, reflects Luther's opinions on women's roles, and even denies the human nature of Christ. It labels the work blasphemous and scandalous and warns that it could cause girls to reject convent life. This censure was so convincing that the Congregation decided to ban the book with no discussion in 1660; a degree to this effect was signed on July 4, 1661. On this condemnation, see Costa-Zalessow, "Tarabotti's *La semplicità ingannata*," 320–22.

guments remained veiled by the incomplete nature of each individual missive. Or perhaps the enduring popularity of letter collections, from which readers had come to expect self-promotion and animated cultural debates, made the publication of Tarabotti's collection less controversial. It is also possible that Tarabotti's death two years after the work was published suppressed the sort of petty literary squabbling that this book, like the *Antisatire*, might otherwise have occasioned. The lack of response to the last work Tarabotti published in her lifetime, *That Women Are of the Same Species as Men* (1651), might bolster this hypothesis.

Whatever the reasons for such a lack of interest, praise, or distaste for the *Letters* on the part of Tarabotti's contemporaries, it is surprising to a modern reader that a work so rich in detail, filled with insight into the literary life and tribulations of a woman writer and nun in Counter-Reformation Venice and dotted with polemics against the forced monachization in which church and state colluded, should have passed unnoticed for centuries. Tarabotti herself, despite her prolific and controversial writing, was largely forgotten until the early twentieth century, when Giuseppe Portigliotti turned his attention to her in his *Penombre claustrali* (1930). Portigliotti's study was followed by Emilio Zanette's *Suor Arcangela, monaca del Seicento veneziano* (1960), which furnished important archival information about Tarabotti and offered useful insights into the *Letters* themselves, which can baffle even readers familiar with the cultural and literary context of Seicento Venice. Ginevra Conti Odorisio returned Tarabotti to the spotlight in her *Donna e società nel Seicento* (1979); while Francesca Medioli located and published Tarabotti's manuscript *Convent Hell* in 1990, sparking a new wave of interest in the writer. Modern editions of Tarabotti's works followed (only *Convent Paradise* is not yet available in a modern edition; the *Tears* are excerpted in the present volume) and a volume of essays devoted to Tarabotti, which examined literary, political and religious dimensions of her works and contextualized her life culturally and politically, appeared in 2006.[77] Today, Tarabotti continues to inspire deep interest and admiration among those who read and study her works.

77. Weaver, *Arcangela Tarabotti*.

Tarabotti's *Letters* were not reprinted after their initial appearance in 1650 until their first modern edition in 2005. They did not circulate in epistolary anthologies and were not translated into other languages before now. The present volume, with its critical commentary and extensive explanatory notes, aims to extend the reach of Tarabotti's very forceful voice, which can be heard with the most clarity and immediacy in the *Letters*, to a broader audience of students and scholars alike. Published in translation here for the first time, Tarabotti's *Letters* are an invaluable resource for understanding Tarabotti's literary history as well as the intellectual, social, economic and political culture of Counter-Reformation Venice.

The Tears upon the Death of Regina Donati

Also included in the appendix to this volume is a brief excerpt from Tarabotti's least-known surviving work, *The Tears of Arcangela Tarabotti upon the Death of the Most Illustrious Signora Regina Donati*. Although published together with the *Letters* in 1650, the *Tears* are rarely considered by scholars and have never before been republished or translated. Yet the work is an interesting component of Tarabotti's oeuvre and one worth examining in greater detail as a literary text in its own right and for its role in the *Letters'* publication. Indeed, the *Tears* are closely linked to the *Letters*. One of the recurrent storylines threaded through Tarabotti's *Letters* is that of the death of Tarabotti's dear friend and fellow nun, Regina Donà (or Donati), and Tarabotti's subsequent decision to write the *Tears* as a memorial work in praise of her. Donà, who was clothed as a nun along with Tarabotti in 1620, died in 1645 at the age of thirty-six.[78] Her passing devastated Tarabotti: the loss of her friend, coupled with the departure of Betta Polani from Sant'Anna, left the writer (who often notes that she was not well-liked by her sister nuns) bereft and alone. At various points in the *Letters*, Tarabotti recounts her deep grief at Donà's death, writing of the "unbearable … suffering that torments me more each day" (letter 124). She claims that to console herself and to serve Donà's family she composed, on the night of her friend's death, a work that she describes as driven by emotion and lacking in grammatical and

---

78. Cf. Zanette, *Suor Arcangela*, 20, 30.

rhetorical order—a claim that is hardly borne out by a reading of the work. Although Tarabotti insists in this letter that she never intended to publish the work and that she did so only to please her friend's sister Andriana Malipiero (letter 124), it is clear from letter 148 that not only did Tarabotti plan—or eventually decide—to publish it, but that she hoped it would help pave the way for the publication of the *Letters*. In letter 148 to an anonymous correspondent, one who is clearly influential in the editorial world, Tarabotti uses the work and its irreproachable subject matter as leverage in seeking publishing permissions for the *Letters* themselves.[79]

> The darkest ink of my pen presents itself before the splendor of Your Excellency to beg illumination, that it too might legitimately appear on the world's stage. It requests licenses from secretary Quirini[80] and from the reverend father inquisitor, and I do not believe Your Excellency will refuse a happy outcome to such a request when he sees delineated at the end of the work the praises of my most beloved friend.

In fact, as we have seen, when the *Letters* were published in 1650, they were accompanied by the *Tears*. Yet the *Tears'* distinct frontispiece, its dedicatory letter, and its proemial verses in praise of Donà penned by Nicolò Crasso and an unnamed poet clearly mark the work as distinct from the *Letters*.

While Tarabotti's *Letters* show us how Tarabotti used the *Tears* to justify the publication of her letters, the *Tears* themselves show how such a justification took shape. Like no other surviving work of Tarabotti's, the *Tears* lack the polemical dimension that stood at the core of her other works and characterized even her partially conciliatory *Convent Paradise*.[81] In their unadulterated celebration of the reli-

---

79. On Tarabotti's *Tears* in relation to the publication of her *Letters*, see Ray, "Making the Private Public: Arcangela Tarabotti's *Lettere familiari*," in Weaver, *Arcangela Tarabotti*, 173–89.

80. Alvise Querini, secretary of the Riformatori dello Studio di Padova (cf. Aprosio, *Biblioteca aprosiana*, 169).

81. The polemic element of the *Paradise* is far from buried. Tarabotti begins the first book by writing, "God loves all creatures, but particularly Woman, and then man, even though

gious life (of which Donà, a voluntary nun, becomes the perfect representative), the *Tears* are perhaps similar to the apparently devotional works that are attributed to Tarabotti but have been lost: the *Contemplations of the Loving Soul*, the *Paved Road to Heaven*, and *Convent Light*.[82] If the lack of polemics and the devotional tone of the *Tears* set it apart from Tarabotti's other surviving works, the work is firmly connected to them by its insistent focus on the female experience, which she here elevates to sanctity. The work offers Tarabotti's vision of female and Christian perfection, a perfection which, centered on such traits as patience and silence, stands in marked contrast to Tarabotti's own qualities—her intolerance of the cloister for instance, or her compulsion to speak out, qualities on full display in the *Letters*. The Regina Donà of the *Tears* indeed functions implicitly as the antithesis of the author of the *Letters*, providing a vision of what the religious life could be when chosen; or perhaps it is better to say that Donà's figure serves as a complement to Tarabotti's, since Donà's experiences, as recounted by Tarabotti, alongside those Tarabotti recounts for herself, mark out the spectrum of experiences possible within the cloister walls. The *Letters* and the *Tears* are, therefore, most interestingly read together, providing not only a sense for the variety of women's convent lives but also for the range of Tarabotti's writing—a range which, in the absence of critical consideration of the *Tears*, has not been fully appreciated.

he doesn't deserve it" (41).

82. Giovanni Dandolo in his letter of presentation for Tarabotti's *Letters* attributes the *Paved Road to Heaven* to Tarabotti; Tarabotti claims this work and the two others in letter 26. Not only the titles but also the manner in which Tarabotti presents the works suggests that they were indeed devotional.

A Note on the Translation

Arcangela Tarabotti's *Lettere familiari e di complimento* brim with impassioned rhetoric and with the intricate structures, imagery, and metaphors typical of the writing of the Baroque period. In our translation of the *Letters*, we strive to maintain the distinctive tone and style of Tarabotti's writing while also making it readable for a modern English-speaking audience. Extensive notes accompany the letters to clarify references that were probably clear to Tarabotti's original addressees and to her contemporary audience but are now obscure. The most detailed notes appear at first mention of people, works, and important episodes in Tarabotti's life. We include no note where it is impossible to understand a reference or to identify a person referred to only by initials. The following points may also facilitate a reading of the translation:

Tarabotti's *Letters* were not arranged in a chronological or thematic order, although sometimes several letters on a similar topic appear in proximity. It is not known who determined the apparently chaotic order of Tarabotti's collection, but since this order may have been deliberate—to make some of the controversial elements of the collection less easily decipherable—and the order was in any case a fundamental part of the volume's presentation, we maintain it in our translation. While we preserve the original organization, our notes clarify the chronological and thematic ties between missives in order to make the *Letters* accessible to all readers.

We reproduce the *Letters* in their entirety. In order to facilitate their reading, we have modernized paragraph breaks and occasionally sentence structure. The *Letters* usually conclude with a complete salutation, but sometimes end abruptly, a usage we have maintained.

Frequently informal in style, Tarabotti's *Letters* at times display grammatical irregularities. In some cases, we have maintained these in our English translation, since they may reflect uncertainties in the linguistic and cultural preparation of Tarabotti, who had little formal education. They also seem to be characteristic of Tarabotti's impassioned style of reasoning. In the original, Tarabotti makes frequent use of superlatives to address her correspondents, referring to them repeatedly as, for instance, "Vostra Signoria Illustrissima." We have maintained these superlatives, where present, in each letter's opening address where they offer perspective on the relative status of Tarabotti's various correspondents and her relationship with them. We have, however, eliminated them within the body of the individual letters (preferring "Your Illustrious Lordship," for instance, to "Your Most Illustrious Lordship") to avoid weighing down the text.

Tarabotti Italianizes many of the names of her foreign correspondents and of their cities of origin. To maintain this interesting linguistic feature of her *Letters*, we have preserved Tarabotti's spelling of proper nouns within the body of the *Letters* while providing the standard spelling in our notes (for example, D'Amò/des Hameaux). Similarly, we have maintained Tarabotti's original spellings of Italian and Venetian proper names, even where these may vary from letter to letter (Loredano/Loredan).

Tarabotti frequently plays on the titles of her works and those of her associates. Since the meaning of certain passages often hinges on such wordplay, we have chosen to translate titles in as literal a manner as possible: the *Inferno monacale*, for instance, becomes *Convent Hell*. In some cases, these titles may be at variance with those under which existing English translations of these works have been published.

Tarabotti includes frequent citations from biblical, philosophical, and literary sources. We provide the original sources for these citations when available, even though it is probable that Tarabotti used one or many general repertories and, for her biblical citations, that she relied on her memory of liturgy and of the breviary. For biblical citations, we refer to the *Biblia Sacra juxta Vulgatam Clementiam: Editio Electronica* (http://vulsearch.sourceforge.net/html/index.html), ed. Michael Tweedale et al. (London, 2005). For English translations, we rely on the Douay-Rheims Bible, referenced at http://www.latin-vulgate.com.

We retain in the original the Latin citations that Tarabotti includes in the *Letters*, providing their translation in the notes. We make no alterations to them, even if they are erroneous, since Tarabotti speaks frequently in the *Letters* themselves about the criticisms she receives for the errors in her Latin citations (see for example letter 89).

While much of the period poetry included in the *Letters* cannot be attributed with certainty, it is likely that Tarabotti penned at least some of it (on the issue, see also our introduction).

We have largely maintained Tarabotti's often obscure use of abbreviations within the letters, spelling out only those of which we can be certain (e.g., *V.S.* = *Vostra Signoria* = Your Lordship) or reasonably certain (e.g., *m.* = *marito* = husband [in letter 68]). Except for standard abbreviations, such as *V.S.*, we note the abbreviations that we spell out.

Tarabotti frequently refers to her correspondents or to third parties anonymously, using a title and an initial or an initial alone to refer to them (generally, an *N.*). We maintain this usage (Signor N.). Sometimes she uses the same designation within a single letter to speak of different people.

Some of Tarabotti's published letters also exist in manuscript form. After referring the reader to the appropriate sources for a detailed presentation and discussion of the manuscript letters, we subsequently make mention only of those cases in which the comparison between the manuscript and the printed letter is of particular interest.

When citing passages from Tarabotti's other works or those of her contemporaries we have used, where available, published English translations. In all other cases, translations are our own unless otherwise noted.

Abbreviations

APV: Archivio Patriarcale di Venezia

ASF: Archivio di Stato di Firenze

ASV: Archivio di Stato di Venezia

BMV: Biblioteca Marciana di Venezia

BUG: Biblioteca Universitaria di Genova

Boerio: Giuseppe Boerio, *Dizionario del dialetto veneziano*. Venice: Giovanni Cecchini, 1856.

DBI: *Dizionario Biografico degli Italiani*. Rome: Istituto della Enciclopedia Italiana, 1960.

PL: *Patrologia Latina*, ed. J.-P. Migne. Paris: Migne, 1844–55.

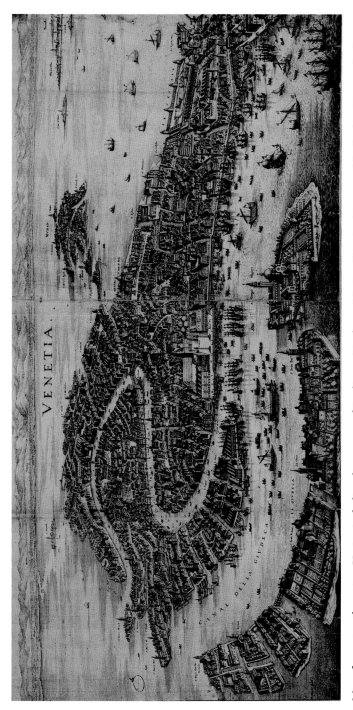

Map of seventeenth-century Venice, including the convent of Sant'Anna. Matthaeus Merian. *Venetia.* Courtesy of the Sterling Memorial Library Map Department, Yale University.

LETTERS FAMILIAR AND FORMAL

PRESENTED BY ARCANGELA TARABOTTI
TO HER MOST ILLUSTRIOUS AND ESTEEMED PATRON
GIOVAN FRANCESCO LOREDANO

GUERIGLI
VENICE
1650

MOST ILLUSTRIOUS AND EXCELLENT PATRON[1]

With the expressions of respect my frailty has permitted, I have honored many gentlemen and persons of the world who are great in virtue, birth, and position. Since I know that all the qualities I have admired in others are combined in Your Excellency, I resolve to collect all my letters in a single volume and honor your person with it, thereby imitating the ancients, who dedicated a day to every deity and consecrated the whole year to Jove supreme. I know the world will condemn me for my temerity in so exalting these weak and imperfect writings, but I hope also for compassion, at least from those courteous enough to recognize that the lightest pages naturally fly to the highest heights. For me it will suffice if Your Excellency enjoys them, as your most singular virtues will ensure. I am also reminded that in the Gospels the Lord accepted with more affection the small offering of a poor woman than ever the rich treasures of great men.[2] In closing, I humbly dedicate myself to Your Illustrious Excellency as your most humble and obliged servant,

   Arcangela Tarabotti

---

1. Tarabotti dedicates her *Letters* to the Venetian nobleman Giovan Francesco Loredano (1606–61), who controlled in large part the Venetian publishing industry and was the central animator of the Accademia degli Incogniti.

2. Cf. Luke 21:1–4.

SIGNOR GIOVANNI DANDOLO'S LETTER TO THE SIGNORS GUERIGLI[3]

You asked me, Signors Guerigli, if Arcangela Tarabotti's letters are worthy of publication, and I ask you in turn if publishers are worthy of such a fine work. I say this because the only press I would deem worthy of these letters is one that printed characters of gold. To offer you my opinion, I have read all her letters and compared them with those that have achieved fame and renown; it seems to me now that hers are gold while theirs are but brass, since theirs have made a clamor but hers have weight and worth. I admire the style: when it is heroic it is without equal and even the most familiar moments are sublime. In this it resembles a royal palace in which every room, even the lowliest reserved for servants, never ceases to be regal. Her conceits are striking, fitting, erudite, and vivacious, and, most important, they are not distorted by artifice nor are they beholden to other literary lights. They are instead quick, natural, and so well ordered that, together with the excellence of her style, this new Arachne[4] masterfully weaves of them a cloth in which the loveliness of the background draws attention to the flowers, and the beauty of the flowers adds splendor to the background. The fact that she is an Archangel makes it clear that her pen is from Paradise. Regarding the title, you can put whatever you like as long as the name of she who wrote the book is present, since we know (as that great thinker said) that Caesar was followed by Augustus. In any case, it seems to me that we can in good conscience call this a collection of miracles rather than a compilation of letters, since certainly every letter is a miracle of art and nature. The intellect of this great woman can without hyperbole be called divine, because she has already constructed in three volumes Paradise, Inferno, and Purgatory; *nor did she disregard the earth, which she ennobled with another volume,* The Paved Road to Heaven.[5] *And like Jove who struck*

---

3. The Venetian aristocrat Giovanni Dandolo (1613–61) was a writer and member of the Accademia degli Incogniti.

4. The story of Arachne, the great weaver who challenged the goddess Athena and was transformed into a spider for her temerity, is recounted in Ovid, *Metamorphoses*, bk. 6.

5. The "Dantesque" trilogy of works referred to here includes Tarabotti's first published work, *Convent Paradise* (*Paradiso monacale*) (Venice: Oddoni, 1643); her *Convent Hell* (*Inferno monacale*), which circulated in manuscript form; and, evidently, a *Purgatory of Unhap-*

down the giants with bolts of lightening, she with her Antisatire *struck down Buoninsegni and other outsized intellects who dared to rise up against the female sex.*[6] *She has written many other small works that adorn her virtuous person like stars, but she has published few of them, since the rays of her modesty conceal and suppress them, whence many people of letters yearn to see them but cannot.*[7] *These virtues, however great, are but the least measure of her glory. Her saintly manners, her innocence, her prudence, her charity, and her exemplary works separate her from the earth and lift her to Heaven. I remind you of this since, if you have a perfect description of her manners and her life, I am sure you will publish this work in glorious fashion, to the honor of your press. In closing, I thank you for esteeming my judgment. As I bid you farewell, I pray that you will give me the same chance to serve you as you give me to love you.*

---

pily Married Women (*Purgatorio delle malmaritate*), mentioned in letter 73 and in the preface to Tarabotti's *Antisatire*, but which, if completed, has been lost; this is also the case for *The Paved Road to Heaven* (*La via lastricata per andar al Cielo*), referred to again in letter 26.

6. The reference to the giants who sought to scale Mount Olympus only to be struck down by Jove's lightning bolts is applied here to the controversy surrounding the publication of Tarabotti's *Antisatire* (*Antisatira* [Venice: Valvasense, 1644]) in response to Francesco Buoninsegni's satire of feminine vanity, *A Menippean Satire against Female Vanity* (*Contro 'l lusso donnesco satira menippea* [Venice: Sarzina, 1638]).

7. The reference includes perhaps two other lost religious works mentioned by Tarabotti, along with *The Paved Road to Heaven*, in letter 26: the *Contemplations of the Loving Soul* (*Contemplazioni dell'anima amante*) and *Convent Light* (*Luce monacale*).

1

TO THE MOST SERENE PRINCE OF VENICE
FRANCESCO ERIZZO[8]

Since my lucky stars have happily enriched the labors of my poor intellect by placing them before Your Serenity's eyes, I am moved by devoted respect and reverent desire to record this enormously fortunate day with white chalk, as the ancients would have done.[9] To reciprocate in some measure the honor that Your Serenity bestowed upon me by deigning to glorify my writing with your gaze, I present to you my *Paradise*. I pray that it be to your liking, if for no other reason than that it is prelude to what awaits you in Heaven after the great accomplishments of a glorious life.

I nevertheless admit that bewilderment and ambivalence accompany my boldness as I present to Your Serenity these compositions which lack every attribute of good writing; but your serene heart, a treasury of all that is great, will receive them with such grace that my fears will become ambition. In publishing my work, I would with great respect have had it fly to seek protection at your feet, but with self-reflection I came to understand that my humble compositions were an offering commensurate to the majesty of a hero like Your Serenity. You who vie with the great Alexander[10] in magnanimity and valor could not receive gifts ill-suited to your immense merit and your generous nature, if the virtue of your heart and the strength of your arms had not granted you a wealth of experience.

---

8. Francesco Erizzo was doge of Venice from 1631 to 1646. Tarabotti turns to him as a friend and protector of women, offering him a copy of her *Convent Paradise* (thus dating this letter to 1643 or later). Erizzo's good relationship with Tarabotti or at least with the convent of Sant'Anna is suggested by the medal he had cast in honor of the convent during his tenure as doge (see E. Cicogna, *Storia dei dogi di Venezia* [Venice: Giuseppe Grimaldo, 1864], vol. 2).

9. The expression derives from the ancient Roman practice of noting auspicious dates by marking them on a calendar with white chalk.

10. Alexander the Great, king of Macedonia and conqueror of the Persian empire (356–23 BCE).

You deserve the most noble and opulent scepters and kingdoms and even vaster realms, and not dark ink, poorly formed letters, and flimsy pages. For this reason the most beautiful queen of the Adriatic circled your head with the doge's crown, and by honoring you with the glorious horn that surrounds your temples, Astrea was seen returning to earth from Heaven, and people now flock from the most remote parts of the world to learn how to dispense true and upright justice.[11] Your heart is also home to marvelous prudence, insuperable strength, and indisputable temperance; whence, since you are not only the son but the glory of the virgin Adriatic city, refuge of Justice and of all the other virtues that are represented with feminine figures and called with feminine names,[12] I hope that you will not scorn the most humble homage of a woman who can present nothing more fitting to you than a *Paradise*. I beseech you to welcome it, if only to avoid betraying your own nature and jeopardizing the kindness that runs in your most illustrious and serene blood. Your lineage enlightens the world, consoles our native city, and glorifies the Venetian empire, particularly with the successes achieved under your command. Whence, since you grace everyone so generously, you are loved by your subjects, feared by your enemies, and revered by the female sex, whose merit you recognize, not ungratefully, but kindly, just as the greatest and wisest kings in the Holy Scriptures did.

Heartened by your admirable qualities, I ask you to pardon the boldness with which I dare to appear before you with these words, and I pray you not be offended by those sentiments against men that you will see throughout my works. Kneeling before you to kiss your garments, I remain Your Serenity's.

11. Tarabotti describes the doge as the personification of Astrea, goddess of justice. In the civic mythology of Venice the city itself was held to be the incarnation of justice.

12. Venice's complex civic mythology was based upon the identification of the city with the "feminine" virtues. Like a chaste maiden, Venice was characterized as a politically inviolable and incorruptible power. Dating its foundation to the Feast of the Annunciation in 421, the city closely identified itself with the Virgin Mary.

2

TO THE MOST ILLUSTRIOUS SIGNOR COUNT COMMENDATOR PIETRO PAOLO BISSARI[13]

I return to Your most Illustrious Lordship that sonnet which, containing within itself all Platonic theology, displays on paper the divine nature of your spirit. Only you, who understand so much, are capable of appreciating how much I enjoyed your kind exposition. And because I would like to be able fully to show you my enjoyment of the honors I undeservingly derive from your kindness, I am sending you *Paternal Tyranny*.[14] If the clumsiness of its composition renders the reading of it tiresome, the reverent and respectful awe with which I send it to you will serve as a balance. Should the sting of some of the concepts cause you shock and dismay, let these be removed by my sincere, truthful assertions exempting Your Illustrious Lordship from those men of whom I speak.

As for the rest, I beg you not to show it to just anyone. Knowing the complete imperfection of the work, I must force myself, like a tyrant, to turn it over to Knowledge itself. Do not condemn it should you find it full of errors, for as such, it conforms to the nature of tyrannies. But a woman who lacks the illumination of art and study necessary to whoever professes letters can certainly hope for understanding from Your Most Illustrious Lordship who, being all perfection and kindness, will indulge my failings. Beseeching you thus, I pray you receive every happiness from the loftiest of Lords, and I reaffirm myself Your Most Illustrious Lordship's.

---

13. Pietro Paolo Bissari (1595–1663), a frequent correspondent and faithful ally of Tarabotti's. Here she sends him a copy of her *Paternal Tyranny* (*Tirannia paterna*; see n. 14 below) with the request that—given its provocative theme—he share it with others judiciously.

14. *La tirannia paterna*, a polemical work by Tarabotti that takes aim at the practice of forced monachization, of which she herself was victim. The work was published posthumously in 1654 as *Innocence Deceived* (*La semplicità ingannata*) under the pseudonym "Galerana Baratotti"; it was placed on the Index of Forbidden Books in 1661.

3

TO THE MOST ILLUSTRIOUS SIGNORA N. NEGRI[15]

That fame which, trumpeted by the cleverest and most distinguished man alive, introduced Your Illustrious Ladyship to me as the glory of and exemplar for the most worthy women of our age, obliges me to consecrate myself to you in pure devotion. I know that I should receive the punishment of Icarus, but if the illustrious count and commendator Bissari was the Dedalus who fashioned the wings of my boldness, I can and must hope for your indulgence and forgiveness.[16] The declarations of such a great gentleman have given me advance assurance; in fact his guarantees encouraged me to pledge my servitude at the feet of Your Illustrious Ladyship's kindness, thereby beatifying myself in this convent Paradise.

I beseech you not to disdain those offerings that, pouring forth from the depths of my heart, could not be refused even by deities. If I feared disdain as I trust in kindness, I would with humble appeals implore this honorable man to defend me, but I do not know which one of you would prevail, as an Apollo would be pitted against an Athena.[17] I must believe, then, that you, to whom Heaven with great generosity granted all the graces, do not lack mercy, since your quintessence is none other than perfect goodness. Therefore do I boldly, but even more reverently, reveal to the lofty heights of your merit the lowliness of my condition. This may seem excessive disparity, but it is in fact a worthy comparison, since masters are usually contrasted with their servants. So with true heart do I declare myself to Your Illustrious Ladyship, who, as the delight of beauty, the formula of wisdom, and the pride of modesty, makes it clear that her qualities are admirable but not imitable, just as immutable will always be my respect and

---

15. This *lettera di complimento*, a formal letter, is offered as a sign of Tarabotti's respect and devotion to her correspondent, of whom little is known. She may have been a relative of Vincenzo Negri, a member of the Accademia Olimpica along with Pietro Paolo Bissari, with whom Tarabotti corresponded regularly and whom she mentions here.

16. The mythological hero Dedalus constructed wings of wax in order to flee Minos's maze.

17. Tarabotti imagines a contest between Bissari/Apollo (god of music, poetry, and the sun) and Negri/Athena (goddess of wisdom and patroness of the arts).

reverence. With this, praying to Heaven for bounteous grace for you, I devote myself on bended knee to Your Illustriousness.

4
TO THE ILLUSTRIOUS COUNTESS N.

The felicitous results of the honorable endeavors of Your Illustrious Ladyship's illustrious consort must necessarily be shared with and transmitted to you by merit of the marital affection commanded by God himself. Brimming with emotion, I therefore rejoice with you. May you, who are kindness itself, please accept these heartfelt writings, which will serve to impress upon you the seal of my steady and eternal servitude, since the ancients equated black with steadfastness.[18] With this I most devotedly offer my respects.

5
TO THE MOST ILLUSTRIOUS SIGNOR COUNT
COMMENDATOR PIETRO PAOLO BISSARI[19]

So that Your Illustrious Lordship might understand that your authoritative commands are for me explicit law, I will to fulfill them set aside those considerations which should be dearest to me and, with feeble strokes of ink, humbly rush to pay my respects to that lady who, praised by Your Illustrious Lordship as a marvel of our century, can be nothing less than a miracle of our times.

I know that if I undertook this enterprise on my own, there would be no punishment commensurate to my audacity, but since I do it to serve one to whom I am indebted, I believe I deserve compassion and forgiveness. For both of these you must plead this time with your kindest intercession; it is (please pardon my saying) the rightful duty of a gentleman. I therefore boldly pray that you take it upon yourself to

---

18. Tarabotti here underlines the resoluteness of her words, drawn in the black ink of her pen, but she may also imply her own steadfastness, since Benedictines wore a black habit. On the equating of the color black to the quality of steadfastness, see, for example, Fulvio Pellegrino Morato, *Significato de' colori e de' mazzolli* (Pavia: Andrea Viani, 1593), c. A7r.

19. In this letter Tarabotti assures Bissari that she will use her pen to honor his mother, Giulia, as she does in the subsequent letter (letter 6).

present these signs of my servitude to that most illustrious lady—your mother—and to those other ladies, with due apology for my frailty. In the eternity of their merits, my servitude will be eternal. And in the meantime I beseech for you the fullness of all the graces, and I implore you not scorn that I should be Your Illustrious Lordship's.

6

TO THE MOST ILLUSTRIOUS COUNTESS GIULIA BISSARI[20]

Those most precious greetings that Your Illustrious Ladyship presented to me by way of your son, the most illustrious commendator, pleased and honored but also confused and embarrassed me. The praise that your kindness bestowed upon my most imperfect *Paradise*, although it cannot fully please me since I know I do not deserve it, nevertheless flatters me since it comes from such a great lady and mistress. For both the greetings and the praise I would like to offer your great person the most humble thanks that can emanate from a heart that is all gratitude and devotion.

But, Most Illustrious Ladyship, even if the Graces are usually bare, I am nevertheless ashamed to present before you my own signs of gratitude, which lack conceits, are stripped of merit, and have no other adornment than a most reverent respect. May you, who are kindness itself, enjoy the sincere eagerness of my resolve and forgive the poverty of my gifts, neither adorned by study nor embellished by art. Pardon also the excessive audacity of my pen, while I worship you for having, among your other accomplishments, enriched the world with the most eminent hero that Fame has ever extolled. But since the glorious praise of such an esteemed man deigns not to be recorded in inexperienced and coarse writing, and so that you will not believe me overly bold in trying to recount the indescribable glories of the pen and of the sword of so famous a gentleman, I will conclude by rendering thanks to God and to my good fortune, which with no merit on my part gave me the chance to pledge myself to you and your son as your servant and virtual slave.

---

20. Tarabotti thanks Giulia Bissari, mother of Pietro Paolo, for her kind greetings and praise for *Convent Paradise*.

I will add nothing more but to say that with deep and soulful respect I devote myself to the incomparable and perfect kindness of Your Illustrious Ladyship, and pledge to make it my duty in my prayers (however feeble they are) to beseech His Divine Majesty with incessant pleas for your and your family's unending prosperity. Bowing before you I pray you to accept respectfully my servitude, which I pledge will be steady and eternal so that I may always be Your Illustrious Ladyship's.

7

TO THE ILLUSTRIOUS SIGNOR GIOVANNI DANDOLO

Since the incomparable kindness of Your Illustrious Lordship undertakes the most worthy cause of publishing the singular privileges and glorious praise of my sex, I beseech you not to defer any longer, as I am certain that your rare genius will have no need to go begging for conceits where the material alone abounds in merit.[21] Your mind, which, almost like an oyster shell, contains within itself pearls of candid and pure sentiment, will rightly instruct the pen to flow with gems of lofty expression in praising the female deity.

It was surely fitting that Truth, the daughter of Time, should not have appeared on the world's stage to praise the greatest marvel created by God, except as introduced there by a member of the lying sex, to its even greater consternation. Just as the divinity of women is the ornament of all mankind, so it was apt that she should be described by one so distinguished with all the gifts of nature, grace, and fortune. At the sound of so sonorous a trumpet, men will blush at how they have slandered those who gave them life, and they will not dare oppose a new Minerva in men's clothing. They will hold their wicked tongues when they see that, from the treasury that contains the greatest mysteries of the world, the arrows of female virtue strike at their falseness, and in this guise Your Illustrious Lordship will come forward to declare that you are the only truthful man, just as you are the sole phoenix among the greatest intellects. It is no wonder that the shining heavens of women, studded with so many virtues, has permit-

---

21. Tarabotti refers to *On Women's Divinity*, which she discusses also in letter 8 to Giovanni Polani. The work, if ever written, has been lost.

ted that such a gentleman as yourself should know their purity. Nor is there anyone who does not know that only the blind cannot see the rays of the sun.

That sex which, more deserving of the title "most bestial" than "strongest," has been rendered as blind as a mole through its own pretension and temerity, does not understand and wickedly labors to degrade women, who were exalted by Wisdom itself above the choirs of angels.[22] But this is of little matter when, in the vanity of this world, there is no beauty that is not contaminated by the deformity of these monsters, nor sanctity that is not profaned by their audacity. You, however, sharper-eyed in your virtue than Argus,[23] know the truth and rightly reveal that women are the ladder to Paradise, desiring thus to affirm to all men that they will never be permitted to ascend above women, because God in His justice will not allow men to trod upon those who are not inferior, but in fact have superior graces that privilege and ennoble them.

Consider, I beseech you, how favored your illustrious family has been by women, and, if you think ingratitude befits a gentleman of your stature, then leave off praising them. I will not mention that you were born of a woman, for this is a blessing that men sadly abuse; but I must descend into more marvelous particulars. The most blessed Virgin created, among the most noble sons of the Queen of Adria (who is under her protection) the most worthy house of Your Illustrious Lordship. Whence, having received the honor from such great subjects, this city chose to be commanded by a certain Enrico Dandolo,[24] who, in the glorious and sublime conquest of Byzantium, had occasion to demonstrate how greatly he was favored by Juno and

---

22. In Ps. 44:10, Mary is at Jesus's right hand in Heaven, above the angels. The reference may also be to the Rose of the Blessed that is situated above the three choirs of angels in Dante's *Paradise* (cantos 31 and 32), in which the women of the New and Old Testament, and Mary most prominently, are placed.

23. In Greek mythology, the beast with one hundred eyes who is transformed into a peacock.

24. Enrico Dandolo (c. 1107–1205), ancestor of Giovanni, was in 1192 the first Dandolo to become doge. He commanded the Venetian fleet in the fourth crusade when, in 1205, the Christian troops conquered and sacked Constantinople, capital of the Byzantine Empire. For his central role in the conquest, Dandolo was offered the imperial crown, which he refused.

Bellona,[25] who made the sea sail with as many victories as ships. In sum, your most fortunate and admirable house gave signs from the beginning—through its family name that expresses a sympathetic connection between *Dandolo* and *donne*,[26] and through its symbol of a white cross[27]—that a gentleman would be born who would, with pious sincerity, express (without irony) the glories of feminine purity and make public the attributes granted to women by the heavens.

If, therefore, Your Illustrious Lordship will be that golden pen that enters into the most secret arcana of the greatness and merits of so sublime a sex, and will be rewarded with deserved applause, I beg you in that case to concede that women have obliged you with their favors. Meanwhile, the Muses glory that their crowns of laurel never elicited greater acclaim than when encircling the temples of Your Illustrious Lordship and your most illustrious brother,[28] who have furnished our age with our own Demosthenes and Cicero.[29] You are the two columns of Hercules who constitute the extreme limits of knowledge, to whom Almathea bequeathed her horn and whom the Graces themselves suckled.[30]

I do not call to mind for Your Illustrious Lordship these honors rightly conferred upon you by my sex as a reprimand, however; but I well remind you not to abuse the good graces of women while in the hands of the Fates lies the thread of your life, which I pray God may be long and happy to crown your great achievements. I am Your Illustrious Lordship's.

---

25. Juno, wife of Jove, queen of heaven and protector of marriage and of women, symbol of power; Bellona, goddess of war and wife of Mars.

26. *Donne*: in Italian, "women." With a Baroque sensibility, Tarabotti frequently plays on the phonic resonances between words in this way.

27. Giovanni's pseudonym was "Crocebianca," or "Whitecross" (see G. Melzi, *Dizionario di opere anonime e pseudonime di scrittori italiani* ... [Milan: Pirola, 1848], vol. 1, ad vocem).

28. Matteo Dandolo (b. 1611), elder brother of Giovanni and like him a writer, was the addressee of two letters in Tarabotti's collection.

29. That is two say, with two great orators.

30. The two Dandolo brothers are as exceptional as the Pillars of Hercules, which stand between the Mediterranean Sea and the Atlantic Ocean; as rich with talents as if Amalthea, Jove's nurse, had given them her cornucopia; and as if the Graces themselves—the three goddesses who incarnate beauty—had raised them.

8

TO THE ILLUSTRIOUS SIGNOR GIOVANNI POLANI[31]

Experience, always the teacher of truth, has already led me to know of Your Illustrious Lordship's most courteous disposition in favoring me, which gives me courage to impose upon you once again. Thus I beg you in your unparalleled kindness to pass the enclosed letter on to the most illustrious and excellent Loredano, together with the work that he was kind enough to imparadise with his most celebrated pen. I will not remind you of the excuses I wish to be made in my name to this most eminent personage, knowing well your prudence and how you are a devoted protector of my interests.

I beseech you not to allow the most illustrious Signor Giovanni Crocebianca[32] to see the book, for until he has fulfilled his debt by finishing his promised discourse *On Women's Divinity*,[33] I deem him unworthy of seeing the *Paradise*, which, having become the target of mens' malicious tongues, seeks shelter beneath the kindest shadow of Your Illustrious Lordship. Please do not hesitate to defend it from the blows of its detractors with your authority.[34] It is true that the marks left by sharp teeth are invisible wounds from which your valor may not be able to defend me completely; but come what may, I don't care about praise, because I know I do not deserve it, just as I would not

31. Giovanni Polani (d. before 1654) was a relative of Tarabotti's close friend Betta Polani, who likely introduced Tarabotti to him. He was an important literary go-between for Tarabotti, who here asks him to give a copy of her *Convent Paradise* to Loredano, along with a letter thanking Loredano for his contribution to the work. There is in fact an introductory letter to the *Paradise* in which Loredano, addressing Polani, writes, "With the sense of debt with which one receives favors from Heaven I received the book your illustrious Lordship, in his kindness, sent to me." Tarabotti's letter of thanks to Loredano follows below (letter 9).

32. Giovanni Dandolo; see n. 27.

33. See n. 21.

34. Tarabotti's *Convent Paradise*, initially praised by the Venetian literary community, became a target of criticism, especially after the publication of her controversial *Antisatire* in 1644. Perhaps irritated by the content of this latter work, critics started to denigrate the *Paradise*. Tarabotti was attacked for errors in the text (some were hers, but many were introduced in the printing) and plagiarism, by critics who maintained that the *Paradise* and the *Antisatire* were too different to have been composed by the same author. Tarabotti seizes the opportunity in the *Letters* to respond to these accusations (see for example letters 13 and 51).

wish my words to encounter in others those sinister conceits that my own just and righteous intentions do not merit.

I have perfect faith in your courtesy, since I see your favors rain down upon me, just as the heavens flooded graces upon Your Illustrious Lordship, from which inundation I feel myself immersed in a sea of obligation, which will keep me Your Illustrious Lordship's.

9

TO THE MOST ILLUSTRIOUS AND EXCELLENT SIGNOR GIOVAN FRANCESCO LOREDANO[35]

The admiration with which I read, and reread, Your Excellency's most accomplished, even divine, letter so stunned me that my mind, rather than thanks, can formulate only confusion. But these are not the first miraculous effects of your celebrated pen, which has managed to steal the glory from all the writers of the world. You are a miracle of nature and a prodigy of knowledge; whence it is no surprise if you should be able to form prodigies that are admirable, but not imitable. The words with which you deigned to honor my weak composition are so sweet that readers, like bees sucking the honey of your most divine style, deeming it the very quintessence of Paradise, will set aside the sterile banalities produced by a sterile female mind. My *Paradise* will consider itself the more glorious with such a champion than ever the Earthly Paradise with the Cherubim or the Empyrean with the Fisherman.[36] Let each of them give way, then, to the angelic Loredano, who, more valorous than they, with the shining shield of his letter forbids the malice of any Aretino[37] to enter my Paradise. All my glories are the fruit of your generosity, which knows how to enrich even holy poverty.

35. Tarabotti thanks Loredano for having composed a letter of presentation for *Convent Paradise* (see the preceeding letter to Giovanni Polani).

36. The Cherubs, the angelic order that, after the Seraphs, is closest to God, guard the earthly Paradise (Gen. 3:24). The Fisherman is Saint Peter, guardian of heavenly Paradise.

37. That is, of a sharp-tongued critic. Pietro Aretino (1492–1557), called the "scourge of princes," was known for his biting characterizations of his contemporaries and for his often misogynous writing.

Therefore, my *Paradise* comes to seek shelter under the wing of your capable patronage. May you, the embodiment of courtesy and the exemplar of kindness, not scorn the humility with which I thank you for the honor you have conferred on me, and may you be pleased with the humbleness of the gift, forgiving me my excessive audacity, while I reverently declare that I will pray to His Divine Majesty for the worthy exaltation of your person and your house, as I will do for all my life, pledging myself to you always.

10

TO THE ILLUSTRIOUS SIGNORA MARGHERITE DE FIUBET, NIECE OF MADAME D'AMÒ, WIFE OF THE AMBASSADOR OF FRANCE[38]

My heartfelt prayers present themselves before Your Illustrious Ladyship to entreat you, on bended knee, not to grant an audience to the Signors N., for reasons I will explain to your most courteous kindness later.

My mind, so dazzled by the marvels of your rare qualities, would nonetheless aspire to dictate to the pen conceits worthy of the enormity of your merits and the vastness of the favors that rain down on me from your heavenly kindness. But what does a person of no consequence know and what can she do in comparison to one so infinitely great? A lowly person compared with such a lofty personage? An earthly object compared to a heavenly one?

I mean to say, Illustrious Mistress, that my thanks, bare and lacking in every grace, do not dare appear before you, in whom the Graces abide, clothed and adorned in the richest ornaments and costumes that they have ever worn. And who could ever give thanks for a gift from Paradise, which is exactly what your conversation is: dear, spirited, and worthy in every respect. One admires in Your Illustrious Ladyship, even at your tender age, a beauty so rare it renders you

---

38. Marguerite de Fiubet (in letter 250 referred to as "de Giubet"; d. between 1645 and 1650), was the niece of Anne des Hameaux, wife of the French ambassador Jean des Hameaux, whose tenure in Venice lasted from 1642 to 1645. Tarabotti refers to the des Hameaux with the Italianized last name of d'Amò or di Amò, and was in cordial contact with both Marguerite and Anne.

a celestial Venus, since your majestic aspect is heavenly, just as the gown you were wearing when I was lucky enough to see you in person was the color of the heavens. The prudence and refinement of your intellect reveal you as a Minerva, and your noble birth and decorous wealth show you to be a Juno. In your candid wisdom all the virtues have found a home, drawn by your inner purity no less than by the external fairness that shames the pearls you wear. Revel, too, as you may rightfully do, in having been born to be an ornament to our age, while the world may rejoice in having produced that precious pearl[39] compared by the wise man to the realm of the heavens, and upon whose discovery the good merchant *abiit et vendidit omnia quae habuit et emit eam*.[40] Meanwhile, I will rejoice in hearing my praises sung by an earthly angel.

That I might therefore reciprocate in some way as befits your merit and fulfills the obligations of my duty, I will perpetually beseech the Lord God to grant you incomparable honors and prosperity, declaring myself entirely prepared to carry out your commands, as well as those of her illustrious excellency,[41] the immense excess of whose regal kindness I admire. In going so far as to honor and favor me, who does not deserve it at all, this excessive kindness makes her most noble courtesy shine forth all the more. Deign, therefore, to present her with my servitude and devotion, together with the respects of Lady N., while both of us offer our entire selves to Your Illustrious Ladyship, and I beg you to receive me and keep me as Your Illustrious Ladyship's.

11

TO THE ILLUSTRIOUS SIGNOR GIOVANNI DANDOLO[42]

I, who am ignorance itself, give birth to a new marvel upon experiencing the excessive kindness of Your Illustrious Lordship, since it is neither custom nor obligation for those of your status to respond to

---

39. Tarabotti writes "Margherita preziosa," playing on her correspondent's Italianized name, Margherita, which is also a word for pearl.

40. Matt. 13:46: "went his way, and sold all that he had, and bought it."

41. Anne des Hameaux, Marguerite's aunt and wife of the ambassador of France.

42. Here Tarabotti thanks Dandolo for a letter in which he praised her, but she wishes that Dandolo would praise women in general and not her in particular (see also letter 7).

the tiresome chatter of their lowest servants, in order by their silence to show the poor fools their temerity.

You, however, who through the sympathetic similarity between your family name, *Dandolo*, and the name of women, *donne*, partake in their divinity beyond the limits of the human condition, are pleased with noble impartiality to favor everybody with your praise, including me, who is less worthy than anyone. I recognize myself to be undeserving of such exalted favor, so that I feel obligated to thank you with particular fervor for the honor I receive. Whence I can truthfully assure you that Fame will restrain herself in spreading news of the divine attributes of your pen when it reaches her ears that Your Illustrious Lordship uses it to praise the very model of ignorance and a cicada who screeches in the darkness of ignorance with no light of learning. May your kindness take pity and not so humiliate one who is not entirely lacking is self-knowledge. If you praise your negligence, I curse my excessive zeal if it prevents women from enjoying the sense of your elevated reasoning. My letter was not sent as a spur to your virtue; but rather it was a reverent reminder so that the splendid heavens of women might remain perfectly adorned with the luminous strokes of your precious pen, which, jealously guarding its nursemaids, the Graces, would prefer to deprive me of all graces by only giving me to myself.

I don't wish you to lack passion or feeling in praising women; on the contrary, I hope that with a brilliant and witty turn of phrase you succeed in winning the hearts and minds of them all. I do not concede to you, however, that men have no reason to fear those blows which, originating from the strongest arm of wisdom, will render their defenses useless. I beg you not to permit your divine intelligence to mention virtues that I do not possess, and which in you reign as if in their proper and absolute domain, unless you wish to remain beaten and knocked down by slanderers, to the perpetual shame of my sex. My shortcomings will be enough to bring down and impoverish even the nobility and richness of your admirable eloquence: desist, therefore, from risking so precious a treasure. Meanwhile, on bended knee, I beg you to make clear to those villains who say that women are their cross to bear, that Christ deigned to die embracing, or rather nailed to, the trunk of a cross, by which means most ungrateful man was redeemed and Paradise filled with the elect, just as women fill the world with people and with virtue.

To conclude, I will address that lofty comment with which you called me a phoenix. While, on the one hand, Your Illustrious Lordship is the phoenix of enlightened minds, I continue to be one for the ignorant, and most humbly I offer you my respects.

12

TO THE MOST ILLUSTRIOUS SIGNORA ISABETTA PICCOLOMINI SCARPI[43]

Here is that *punto in aria* lace that has driven me mad and emboldened me to make recourse to Your Illustrious Ladyship's sea of favors. I confess that in this business only the green color[44] of the gown that adorns your most gentle person fuels my heart's hopes of succeeding in supplying this work to the marchioness, to whom I am bound by my word, which I have always valued beyond my life itself. I find no other relief in the present uncertainties than to know that I have depended in this matter upon the most virtuous lady in the world, recognized as such by all. If you abandon me, I will have lost my map and I fear I will drown in the Syrtes of despair.[45]

---

43. This letter, like others to this addressee, makes mention of the famous *punto in aria* lace produced in Venetian convents. Isabetta was an intermediary between Tarabotti and the Marchioness di Galeranda, who requested, as we read elsewhere, a lace collar (see letters 149, 164, and 174). Venetian lace, which reached the height of its splendor in the seventeenth century, was famous in all of Europe for its delicacy and the complexity of its designs. In contrast to other Venetian art industries, lacework was produced in private spaces, houses and convents, and it was not well recompensed (see Pietro Molmenti, *La storia di Venezia nella vita privata dalle origini alla caduta della Repubblica*, 5 [Bergamo: Istituto italiano d'arti grafiche, 1910–12], 2:190–94; 3:61). On Tarabotti's activities in this regard see Meredith K. Ray, "Letters and Lace: Arcangela Tarabotti and Convent Culture in Seicento Venice," in *Early Modern Women and Transnational Communities of Letters*, ed. A. Larsen and J. Campbell [Farnham, U.K.: Ashgate, 2009], 45–73).

44. The color green commonly symbolized hope.

45. The Syrtes are two great embayments on the Mediterranean coast of northern Africa: Syrtis minor, in current-day Tunisia, and Syrtis major, in Libya, present numerous rocks and cliffs that make navigation perilous.

But what am I saying, my most courteous lady? I ought hope and await the illumination of your most prized favors amid the obscurity of my ignorance and of my prison. I already received a prelude of them when, surprised by your visit on the first of May, the day in which the greatest delights of spring flourish, I allowed myself to hope for your gracious favors, since I saw myself honored with a flower to which I attribute the effects of that reverent servitude that I profess to you eternally and which need remain hidden under the veils of silence no longer.

My heart presents itself, therefore, at this juncture of the most holy season of our Lord's birth, to wish you all the happiness of which you are worthy. Do not scorn this expression of debt, while, like the angels, I announce to you and to all your illustrious house the peace and joy of the Holy Spirit (may He grant you honors and prosperity), commending myself as always to Your Illustrious Ladyship.

13

TO FATHER N.[46]

A few days ago I received a letter from Signor N. by way of the nun on duty, who only now tells me that Your Lordship handed it to her and adds that—after having already spoken with you about my excessively imperfect compositions—she heard you express concepts which were as far from the truth as are the greater Indies from this city of ours. I was truly astonished, not because I am unaccustomed to hearing the vanities of the world—even though I remain outside of it—but because an immaculate conscience cannot without disgust hear things

---

46. Likely Angelico Aprosio (1607–81), an itinerate writer and member of the Accademia degli Incogniti. The friar initially encouraged Tarabotti, praising her *Convent Paradise*, but after the publication of the *Antisatire* their relationship soured, due largely to Aprosio's composition of the *Mask Lifted* (*Maschera scoperta*) that attacked Tarabotti and threatened to reveal her as the true author of the quasi-anonymous *Antisatire*; Tarabotti was able to block the publication of Aprosio's work (see E. Biga, *Una polemica antifemminista del '600: La 'Maschera scoperta" di Angelico Aprosio* [Ventimiglia: Civica Biblioteca Aprosiana, 1989]). Aprosio helped circulate the rumors that Tarabotti had not authored the works that appeared under her name, a charge she rejects in this letter.

that can stain it and damage its reputation. *E 'l mio nemico del mio mal si rida.*[47]

Your Lordship should know that, not to boast but in defense of the truth, I feel obliged to tell you that my offspring have no father but my rough intellect, nor other mother than my selfsame ignorance, and whoever believes otherwise is mistaken. If I wanted to deceive the world and to appear in the booksellers' shops dressed in clothes that were not my own, it would be akin to wanting to drive the sun's chariot with the certainty of falling, and I would well merit in that case the mockery and derision of lettered men.[48]

If Your Lordship would deign to hear from my own lips my honest defense of my innocence, I would consider it a most singular favor, and I assure you that I would show you the truth as clearly as the sun shines at high noon.

If I bore you, I ask Your Lordship to excuse me with your excessive kindness, well recognized by all, while I along with these others admire you and kiss your hands. I am Your Lordship's, etc.

14

TO THE MOST ILLUSTRIOUS SIGNOR COUNT COMMENDATOR PIETRO PAOLO BISSARI

The redoubled favors that I receive from Your Illustrious Lordship would require another intellect and other eloquence than mine in order to render proper thanks. I should invent new ways to express gratitude, but your benevolence, which has no equal, seeing my capabilities unable to match my mind's desire, will appreciate the silent devotion of my heart.

47. "And my enemy mocks my pain": cf. the final composition in Petrarch's *Canzoniere*, the *Canzone alla Vergine: Ma pur in te l'anima mia si fida, / peccatrice, i' no 'l nego, / Vergine; ma ti prego / che il tuo nemico del mio mal non rida* (RVF 366.72–75 ["But even so in you my soul confides, / A sinner, I admit, / but Virgin—I implore / Let not your enemy deride my plight," trans. James Wyatt Cook, *Petrarch's Songbook* (New York: Medieval and Renaissance Texts & Studies, 1995); cf. also Ps. 24:3 and 40:12.

48. That is, if Tarabotti sought to circulate the work of others under her own name, she would fail with grave consequences, similar to Phaeton, child of the Sun, who sought to possess what did not belong to him: driving his father's chariot through the sky, he capsized, transforming Libya into a desert and bringing destruction to all of Africa.

I presented your odes to the illustrious and excellent Signor Ambassador,[49] who in leafing through them said that he received them like a gift from God, since they were presented by an angel, and in fact he seemed to admire that which no one else can imitate. They were also enjoyed by these gentlewomen, as are the most courteous manners of Your Illustrious Lordship, by which they confess that they are singularly honored, just as I see my most reverent servitude decorated with excessive favors. All together we humbly bow to Your Illustrious Lordship, etc.

15

TO THE MOST ILLUSTRIOUS AND EXCELLENT SIGNOR GIOVAN FRANCESCO LOREDANO[50]

Since Your Illustrious Lordship drank from the river Lethe[51] in order to remove my guilt for having written to you, I feel obliged to refresh your memory that exactly twenty-four days ago today, with the pretense of a book rather than your heart's devotion, you honored me with a personal visit in which I felt myself blessed by your favors.[52]

Two days later an angel—I know not whether of light or of darkness[53]—brought, in Your Illustrious Lordship's name, a copy of the *Soul of Pallavicino* into the Purgatory of Sant'Anna.[54] I would have left it there to be purged, but since I know that soul to to be a slanderer,

---

49. Most likely Nicolas Bretel de Grémonville (see n. 115), the French ambassador to Venice from 1645 to 1647, with whom both Tarabotti and Bissari had close relations.

50. This letter centers on two books concerning Ferrante Pallavicino (1616–44), the iconoclast and member of the Accademia degli Incogniti. One of the books to which Tarabotti refers here is the controversial *Soul of Ferrante Pallavicino* (*L'anima di Ferrante Pallavicino*), published after Pallavicino's death. The second book to which she refers is Pallavicino's *Joseph* (*Giuseppe*, 1637), which Loredano pretended to seek in Sant'Anna some days earlier; Tarabotti reprimands him for having visited her only for this purpose.

51. Lethe, the mythological river of oblivion in Hades, from which the souls of the dead drank and so erased the memory of their past lives on earth.

52. On this visit from Loredano, see also letter 111.

53. Tarabotti may make a veiled reference to Angelico Aprosio.

54. *L'anima di Ferrante Pallavicino* (Lyon, n.d.). The work has been linked to Loredano (on this work see also letter 64).

I feared a satire against nuns.[55] Nevertheless, out of respect for the person who sent it, I brought it into our convent Paradise, but I heard its erroneous opinions. *Summopere cavendum est, omne mendacium, omne quoque genus mandatij magnopere fuge*[56]—even though I know that all of these souls are well supplied with crowns, rosaries, crosses, and medals in order to fly to Heaven by means of indulgences. I feared a schism and decided that the best course of action was to send it back to Your Illustrious Lordship,[57] who, being an always benevolent Jove, will not condemn (I believe) the goal of my good intentions.

It was you yourself who asked me insistently for Pallavicino's *Joseph*,[58] and I say that this great patriarch is a Jew we can deal with since he never engaged in usury and it would not have been difficult or inappropriate, as you write, to find him among one hundred virgin brides of Christ, even if he fled from one gentile woman who had been tainted by a man.[59]

As for the rest, I do not steal souls because I am not the devil; in fact, since I am an Archangel, I assure their health. In short, men

55. The reference is probably to Pallavicino's criticism of nuns in the *Postman Robbed of His Mailbags*, which contains a number of antifeminist arguments (*Corriero svaligiato* [Nuremberg [Venice]: Stoer, n.d. (but 1641), published under the pseudonym Ginifacio Spironcini; modern edition by A. Marchi, ed. [Parma: Università di Parma, 1984]). Tarabotti responded to these polemics in her *Semplicità ingannata* (*Innocence Betrayed*). See the modern edition by Bortot and the English translation and edition by Panizza, which includes a translation of another of Pallavicino's antifeminist diatribes (158–62), to which Tarabotti also responded.

56. "Above all, lying must be avoided; also shun as far as possible every kind of duplicity." Cf. for example unknown author, *Sententiae*: "Summopere est cavendum omne mendacium, quamvis nonnunquam sit aliquod mendacii genus culpae levioris, si quisquam praestando mentiatur" (*PL* 83:1177C).

57. That is, she realized the danger in keeping a forbidden book in the convent.

58. Tarabotti scolds Loredano for teasing her: the previous day he had asked her for Pallavicino's *Joseph*, and now denies having done so. On this episode see letter 111 and Zanette, *Suor Arcangela*, 350–54.

59. The practice of usury was associated with the Jews. In a series of allusions, Tarabotti compares, with irony, her own efforts to locate Pallavicino's book *Giuseppe* to Joseph's actions in Egypt (Gen. 39:1–20). Loredano had played on Joseph's refusal of Potiphar's wife, described in the book. He denies asking Tarabotti for the book because he would not have sought among Sant'Anna's one hundred women the story of a man who could not tolerate even one (cf. Loredano, *Lettere* [Venice: Guerigli, 1655], 333). Tarabotti refutes this assertion.

always want to insult under the guise of praising. To you, however, who by semidivine actions remove yourself from their number, I consecrate with heartfelt devotion all that I am and all that I am worth, and I beg God that, just as His name will be eternal, so will you have never-ending life that the world may always be blessed by your celestial pen. And on bended knee, I thank you for the praise that you bestowed upon me, and I remain Your Excellency's, etc.

16

TO THE MOST ILLUSTRIOUS AND REVEREND SIGNOR
FRANCESCO MARIA ZATI, RESIDENT OF TUSCANY AT
THE MOST SERENE REPUBLIC OF VENICE[60]

When I sent Your Illustrious Lordship a letter for delivery to her highness,[61] my pen was in mourning for the baleful calamity of the death of my brother-in-law[62] and could not express wishes for happiness. Nevertheless my heart, although wrapped in sadness and troubles for so great a loss, did not fail to pray to Heaven during the recent holy Christmas holidays that you be filled with prosperity and contentment, just as now I predict that you will achieve the holy Church's greatest honors in the new year, to the glory of God and the splendor of the Vatican.

May it please you to receive these wishes that my reverent devotion pronounces, while I most humbly pray you regard my works with a benevolent eye, since I admit that I lack the light of letters. This admission would make me guilty of temerity, rather than defending my innocence, since I dared to send them to you. If I had known, however, that Your Illustrious Lordship was a member of the most no-

---

60. Francesco Maria Zati, resident of Tuscany at Venice from 1642 to 1652 (L. Bittner and L. Gross, *Repertorium der diplomatischen Vertreter aller Länder seit dem Westfälischen Frieden* [Oldenburg: G. Stalling, 1936–65], 1:537). Zati, who represented the interests of Ferdinando II de' Medici, the Grand Duke of Tuscany, at Venice, functioned as an intermediary for the correspondence between Tarabotti and Ferdinando's wife, Vittoria della Rovere. This letter is datable to the end of 1647, shortly after Christmas.

61. Vittoria della Rovere (perhaps in reference to letter 84).

62. Giacomo Pighetti, husband of Tarabotti's sister Lorenzina, died 10 October 1647 (Zanette, *Suor Arcangela*, 408).

ble and virtuous Accademia della Crusca,[63] I would never have dared to do this. If to properly judge a verse of that musical swan Marino those fine intellects took as many days as it took to make the world,[64] what will it take to criticize the writing of a monkey among writers and a cicada who shrieks, bothering anyone who hears her? It is true that those works which are not read do not suffer criticism, and that the criticism of lettered men is like the shadows in painting, which make the merit of the work stand out all the more. This befalls the best writers, but I can expect nothing but the derision of men, whom Your Illustrious Lordship exceeds in sublimity as much as cypresses exceed other plants in height, and I honor you most humbly.

17

TO THE MOST SERENE DUKE OF PARMA
FERDINANDO FARNESE[65]

Because I am unable to respond worthily to the courteous letter of Your Serenity while restraining my affections within the boundaries of reverence, I know not what to do but once again devotedly consecrate my heart to you.

With regard to my infirmity, were God willing, I wish I could vow to follow your prudent advice that I revere; and I would gladly do so since, among all the infirm, I profess to be one who more than any other feels antipathy for doctors and medicine. But a good regimen alone, and the adherence to moderate living, are not enough to secure my life, let alone my health. A continual constriction of the chest, which consumes me, I might say, to my very bones and nearly takes my breath away, comes over me in the autumn and spring with such vehemence that often it reduces me to a state in which I might

---

63. The Accademia della Crusca was founded in Florence in 1582 with the goal of establishing norms for the correct use of Florentine Italian. It does not appear, however, that Zati was a member of this group (see S. Parodi, *IV Centenario dell'Accademia della Crusca: Catalogo degli accademici dalla fondazione* [Florence: Accademia della Crusca, 1983]).

64. The reference is to the famous poet Giovan Battista Marino (1569–1625).

65. The duke to whom Tarabotti writes was actually Odoardo Farnese (1612–46), who became the Duke of Parma in 1622. He married Margherita, daughter of Cosimo II de' Medici and Maria Maddelena, Archduchess of Austria, in 1628.

suddenly render my soul to my Creator. So be it; it pleases the Father of all things.

But, leaving aside these melancholy subjects, I will go on, with the confidence granted me by Your Serenity, to discuss more fully than in my previous letter the ridiculous enterprise of those who have taken it upon themselves to attack my *Antisatire*.[66] Know, therefore, that even if many people told me that others were employing their pens against me, I was reluctant to believe it, feeling certain that I was more than safe from their malicious blows so long as I live under the protective shield of Her Most Serene Highness, the grand duchess of Tuscany, whose name alone, Vittoria, promises me a triumph in every circumstance.[67] I persuaded myself that, since the duchess is a Pallas worthy of every lettered person's adulation, there would not be a writer bold enough to contradict those labors I sent to shelter under her patronage. Do not believe, however, that I harbor ill will toward these men; rather, I consider myself obliged that they demonstrate so high an opinion of me as to believe me more robust than a Hercules, advancing against me in such number.

It is true that, these being men who perhaps feign chivalry, like knights errant they appear incognito under deceptive garments and so enter the society of those of whom the Gospel says, *Veniunt ad vos in vestimentis ovium intrinsecus autem sunt lupi rapaces*.[68] And who could deny that they are wolves if, upon seeing an innocent little lamb, they advance against her to take her life by swallowing up what little applause she receives from the ingenuousness of others. Your Seren-

---

66. The publication of the *Antisatire* led some of Tarabotti's critics to write responses. Girolamo Brusoni, a writer with whom she exchanged several letters, threatened to compose an *Antisatira satirizzata* (*Antisatire Satirized*; see letter 99) which does appear to have ever been published; the publication of Aprosio's *Mask Lifted* was blocked (see n. 46). Luigi Sesta's *Censura dell'Antisatira* (*The Antisatire Censured*) appeared in 1656, after Tarabotti's death. On the polemics surrounding the *Antisatire*, see Biga, *Una polemica antifemminista*, and Weaver's introduction to *Satira e Antisatira*.

67. Vittoria della Rovere (1622–94), known for her patronage of artists and for her relationships with Florence's convents. Tarabotti dedicated the *Antisatire* to her; in another missive (letter 94), she asks the grand duchess's help in publishing *Paternal Tyranny*.

68. Cf. Matt. 7:15, "Beware of false prophets, who come to you in the clothing of sheep, but inwardly they are ravenous wolves." Tarabotti, by using the word "incognito," would seem to be linking these attacks to the Accademia degli Incogniti.

ity, who has read my book,[69] knows full well that when I speak against men I make a solemn declaration to exclude those who are good; whence these, by attempting to avenge themselves against me, show they are insulted, and therefore guilty and members of the worst company of men. That it is true that they alone set themselves apart from good men is proved by a dedicatory letter addressed by one of them to women, all of whom the writer declares to love, demonstrating the vain inconstancy of his soul by showing him to have in his breast a monstrous heart capable of many and varied affections.[70] I do not understand them. But another fashions himself a preacher of wine's splendors, confessor of liars and patron of drunkards, not knowing how to argue against me with other, better terms at the very beginning of his *Mask Lifted* than by exalting Bacchus' liquor, in which alone, he concludes, truth lies as if at its center.[71] It is clear, Most Serene Lord, that this man is one of those who never offer the truth except when, their minds blurred by wine vapors, they speak in a manner contrary to their nature and inclination. Let them howl, then, as they will, like dogs at the moon, against the purest rays of my truthful words, whose splendor nothing will jeopardize, and I will hold those men in little esteem.

Did I not fear to bore you with overlengthiness, I would recount to Your Serenity my dealings with these great writers who, having once urged me with a thousand adulations to expose my *Convent Paradise* to public light, now, with a perfidy that could only occur in men's hearts, decry it and doubt that it could be the fruit of my labors.[72]

---

69. The *Antisatire*.

70. The reference is to the writer and apostate friar Girolamo Brusoni (on this letter see also Zanette, *Suor Arcangela*, 279). Once friends, Tarabotti and Brusoni fell out over a literary dispute (see especially letters 141 and 231).

71. Tarabotti is referring to the work by Aprosio.

72. Tarabotti was particularly incensed by the accusation that she was not the author of *Convent Paradise* (see also letter 99 to Nicolas Bretel de Grémonville), partly because, as she says here, her accusers are the same men (such as Aprosio and Pighetti) who encouraged her to publish it. Tarabotti makes reference to these accusations in the *Antisatire* as well, where she laments: "Many malicious or ignorant men assert that *Convent Paradise* could not have been dictated to me by my own mind … or else that, if it were, it must have received ornamentation, adornment, and rich strokes of philosophy and theology from lofty and intelligent minds" (*Satira e Antisatira*, 74).

But I intend to pass over these details in silence, since I take pride in the fact that these men say those compositions are not the product of my talents, which appear (more as a result of their envy than the merit of my pen) so perfect that one might doubt my sterile intellect produced them. Would to God they were so perfect and provoked these doubts caused by envy, which makes the things of others seem more perfect than they actually are. On a similar theme Ovid said:

> *Fertilior seges est alieno semper in agro.*
> *Vicinumque pecus grandius uber habet.*[73]

To the vice of envy, they add, in extraordinary measure, that of adulation, for one of them in his writings and published works extolled my name and praised it above the stars, and another urged me with exhortations and praise to publish my imperfect compositions.[74]

These manners of theirs I nevertheless deride, and I am reminded of Crates of Thebes,[75] who likened adulation to the fruit of the fig tree, which is eaten only by cuckoos and baby blackbirds. Whence I am most certain that the ignorant alone, not the lettered, will turn their eyes and minds to those concepts which, after various praises, these men offer against a woman. They cannot but sicken worthy gentlemen and fine minds. I am well convinced of this by the example of Signor Buoninsegni, who with noble and generous kindness left it to these troublemakers to dispute those interpretations which I consigned to print, never intending to offend him but only to jest.[76]

---

73. Ovid, *Ars amatoria*, book I, verses 349–50: "The crop is always better in our neighbour's field; his cows more rich in milk" (trans. Lewis May, *The Love Books of Ovid* [Whitefish, MT: Kessinger Publishing, 2005]).

74. Tarabotti likely refers here first to Brusoni and then to Aprosio.

75. Cynic philosopher (4th–3rd century BCE).

76. At several points in the *Letters*, Tarabotti notes that others, not Buoninsegni, criticized her *Antisatire*, and that their criticism was fueled not by affection for Buoninsegni but by scorn for women and for her in particular (see for example letter 113). Buoninsegni himself declared his admiration for Tarabotti in a letter to Aprosio: "I offer infinite thanks to that mother who wished to honor me, esteeming my little trifle, composed to entertain our serene patron for an hour in the academy, worthy of censure by her lofty intellect" (letter dated Siena, 15 September, 1644, BUG, E VI 6, Int. I, quoted in G. Portigliotti, *Penombre claustrali* [Milan: Treves, 1930], 285 and Weaver, ed., *Satira e Antisatira*, 25).

Figures of great esteem, most Serene Lord, do not come out with disdainful improprieties against women. Witness the many great literary men who flourish in the present centuries and the many modern swans whose song steals the glory of the Homers, the Virgils, and the Horaces. Among their number are many ravens with baleful quills flapping boldly about who, supposing themselves to be phoenixes in expressing themselves to the rays of the sun of glory, rather than immortalized find themselves with the feathers of their vanity singed and with the wings of impudence reduced to ashes forever.

But here let the pen rest and the heart be light in adoration of Your Serenity's merit, while I, who have at the center of my thoughts my wish to honor you, beg pardon for the lengthiness of this letter. If I have bored and offended you, the fault belongs to the great confidence that your kindness allows me to practice with you. And humbly I honor you.

18
TO THE MOST ILLUSTRIOUS AND EXCELLENT SIGNOR GIOVAN FRANCESCO LOREDANO[77]

If Your Excellency exhorted me to have my *Letters* printed, and with most kind gestures offered to be that favorable deity who would make them public, it now seems that your advice and promises have disappeared, or rather from that oracle that once proffered favorable responses without my asking I now see the desired result too long delayed. Deities, however, are not held to their word, and since their judgments are incomprehensible mortals should not complain of them. One ought rather ask their pardon for one's own faults in order to receive subsequent favors. Whence I, recognizing this debt, bowing before Your Excellency, admit my faults if I sinned out of ignorance, and I assure you that I welcome a negative response as much as the favor of one of your most courteous visits, and while I await you I most humbly kiss your garments and remain your servant.

---

77. This letter highlights Loredano's complex role in the publication of Tarabotti's *Letters*: here she obliquely criticizes him for his inconstant support of her work.

19
TO THE MOST SERENE PRINCE OF VENICE
FRANCESCO ERIZZO[78]

The affectionate greetings sent me on various occasions by Your Serenity and your majestic portrait, which I daily honor as I reflect on your great merit, have rendered my cell celestial and focused all my worldly glory on that ultimate goal that leaves nothing more for my ambition to desire, since I recognize that I have been (may I say) beatified by your favors in this convent Paradise.

It is true, Most Serene Sir, that it is natural for worthy princes to congratulate their subjects; but with what sort of thanks can I, in whom there is not even a shadow of merit, repay your generosity in having conferred upon me such honors, which flow from the regal magnanimity that distinguishes you as the most worthy, the most accomplished and virtuous prince whose glorious fame was ever hailed by public acclaim? Certainly I have no way to thank you, for one cannot give thanks in proportion to the immensity of those favors that derive from such a high place.

Nonetheless, I hope that the kindness of so great a gentleman will not scorn the admiration and the sincere compliments of a heart that is stunned and reverent in contemplating a majesty beyond human confines, of almost divine nature, because even God himself welcomes those thanks that derive from the purity of a devout soul.

Be certain, Your Serenity, that I have no movement, breath, or emotion that is not perpetually employed (as I can do nothing else) in begging, with ardent prayers, that His Divine Goodness grant you all the graces that derive from His omnipotent hand. Nothing less is demanded of the favors rained down upon me by your kindness, to the dismay of the derisive Momusses.[79] May your regal magnanimity welcome the disposition of my soul, which has no guide in its desire to serve you, and, prostrate at your feet, I beg you to forgive the humble temerity with which I send you the *Hieroglyphic Olive Branch* of peace

---

78. This letter, which offers generous praise of the doge and thanks him for his support, presents Tarabotti as a part of Erizzo's circle. She contrasts the doge's backing with accusations from her detractors.

79. Momus: in Greek mythology the god of satire, censure, and unfounded criticism.

with the Ottomans, which the whole world awaits through your most prudent command.[80]

I would also like to repay you in more fitting fashion, wherefore I am transported by a fervent wish to be more learned in order to be able in some way properly to describe the exalted qualities of so great a hero. I am even moved to envy the eloquence of Demosthenes and Cicero, to record for posterity the glorious memory of a prince whose heroic and lofty deeds are enough to bury in the sea of oblivion all those more famous actions and undertakings that fuel the arrogance of any crowned head. Only the commemoration of your deeds ought rightly remain in the coming centuries as a model and example for the world's greatest rulers.

Confident, therefore, in the foundations of your infinite merit and in your inimitable kindness, prostrate at your feet I beg your forgiveness for the lengthiness of this letter, and reverently I kiss your robes.

20

TO THE MOST ILLUSTRIOUS SIGNOR NICOLÒ FOSCOLO[81]

Here, at last, are carried out your commands, which for me will always be inviolable. I am mortified that my constant indisposition delayed my serving you. May you, who as much abound in kindness as I am

---

80. Tarabotti refers in all probability to a lost work of the same title by Guid'Ascania Orsi of Bologna (like Tarabotti, a nun and writer), the *Olivo geroglifico*, which likely traced the tensions in the Adriatic between Venice and the Ottomans that threatened to provoke an open war. Despite the hopes for peace that the book seemingly voiced, these tensions led to the war of Candia, which erupted shortly after Erizzo's death and which Venice lost after twenty-two years of fighting. Peace was reached in 1669. The Serenissima had to give up the island of Crete, strategically located at the center of the eastern Mediterranean, which Venice had controlled for 465 years.

81. There were several Nicolò Foscolos in Venice in this time period and it is difficult to determine with which one the nun corresponded. Tarabotti includes only this one letter to him. It is possible that this is the Nicolò (1596–1643) who was the brother-in-law of Elena Foscolo, another of Tarabotti's correspondents (cf. A. Cappellari, *Campidoglio veneto*, Marciana mss. Italiani, classe 7, nos. 15–18, 577). Tarabotti sends him a piece of writing he had requested and which Tarabotti says she produced unenthusiastically.

filled with imperfections, forgive that failing, which merits pardon since it is unintentional.

Your Illustrious Lordship will find much confusion within these pages. This is typical of my pen, guided as it is by an intellect unused to proper writing. The content itself is dull, and I did it most unwillingly and quite poorly.

May Your Illustrious Lordship receive these wishes of my heart, and be content with a trifle in place of the greatness I wish I could produce; while I continue to pray that the supreme Lord of lords grant you the return of your health, again declaring myself Your Illustrious Lordship's, etc.

21

TO SIGNOR N.[82]

Yesterday I sent two letters to Your Lordship asking you to notify me of their arrival. Now I send you two small notebooks to look over; although they may seem the same, your intelligence will see clearly that there are some differences. They are teeming with errors, but since these befit my intellect and the writings of a woman lacking in learning, they ought to be pitied by your kindness. The style is not concise, a natural failing of mine, and also because when composing a response one can be neither too charming nor too vivacious. The work is muddled, because I have no other rhetorical rules than those which my own poor judgment dictates. If the sentences are not balanced, or rather if they are missing some elements, this derives no less from my ignorance than from my illness, which for fifteen days now has incessantly oppressed me in such a manner that I am forbidden to write and read attentively anything of value.

---

82. The work to which Tarabotti refers in this letter to an insider in the publishing world might be the *Antisatire*, and in this case the recipient could be Loredano, Aprosio, or Pighetti, since each of them urged the nun to respond to Buoninsegni's *Satire*. More likely, Tarabotti refers to her treatise *That Women Are of the Same Species as Men* (*Che le donne siano della specie degli uomini* [Nuremburg: I. Cherchenbercher, 1651]), a work that responded to one denying women had souls (*That Women Are Not of the Same Species as Men: An Entertaining Discussion* [*Che le donne non siano della specie degli uomini: Discorso piacevole*] [Lyon: Gasparo Ventura, 1647]; see n. 191). In this case she would be discussing an earlier draft of the work that was printed in 1651, after the publication of her *Letters*.

May Your Lordship have pity on me, and know that tomorrow eight days will have passed since a gentleman lent me the little work you will find here, along with the command that I should respond to it.[83] I obeyed him willingly, being naturally inclined to such material by a certain disposition that invites me to take up the pen, since I cannot wield the sword, to defend my sex, and since there are no more gentlemen who defend women, but only insult them. Adieu.

22
TO THE MOST ILLUSTRIOUS SIGNOR N.[84]

In grave circumstances, redoubled petitions and renewed prayers must summon compassion among men, for they are so dear to God, who wants us to ask and plead so that He can then grant us favors. I mean to say that, if I imposed on Your Illustrious Lordship this morning with my letter, I am not unworthy of the pardon of your response to the present missive, since my ardent desire to serve Lady N. leads me again to take pen in hand to relay to you this news. It seems, from certain particulars gathered by people familiar with the workings of government, that M. rightly may not and ought not expect more than that assigned to him by his father. It is the opinion of many that a husband is needed to protect these ladies and to keep them at a safe distance from the blows of this man. Engage the excellent Signor Ferro[85] in a little public discussion of the truth of the matter as you did the other night, and you will certainly make him cede. Would that I could speak to him myself, for what I lack by defect of ignorance I would make up in ardor and love. Do not, I beg you, share in the opinion of

83. If Tarabotti is in fact discussing the *Antisatire*, her version of the treatise's genesis here differs from the one she gives elsewhere, when she says her response was solicited by noblewomen (letter 207).

84. This letter highlights Tarabotti's participation in matters that regard women beyond convent walls. It seems she is trying to help several women to protect their inheritance, which is threatened by a certain "M.," perhaps a relative of theirs. On this episode, see also letters 104 and 140.

85. Tarabotti mentions a Ferro in another letter regarding this matter (letter 140). He may perhaps be a relative of Suor Marcella, whose lay name was Elena Ferro and who entered Sant'Anna in 1643 (see Zanette, *Suor Arcangela*, 72).

adversaries, when from the tumult of this war one may expect some victory. I hold it as a point of pride.

May Your Illustrious Lordship not divulge anything to Signor N. about this, and I ask Your Illustrious Lordship to remember me, etc.

23
TO SIGNOR N.[86]

My obligations, together with a slight and unusual indisposition, kept my pen from fulfilling that duty of debt and thanks I owe you. Nonetheless, my heart responded in your favor, while, dazed at the consideration of your kindest offers, it offers you all that may come of my frailty.

I regret that you have undertaken to respond to my words in order to please your friends, and my enemies, for I would not want you to acquire the title of "malicious" which suits them so well. Truth will make all these things known to the world, while I insist that I did not intend to offend Signor Buoninsegni or others in my *Antisatire*, nor did I speak about those who don't deserve it, as can clearly be seen. May the liars be rebutted!

I will glory in testing myself against you, for even if I am vanquished, I will not lack praise for my courage in daring to write against your celebrated pen.

For the rest, your commands will always be dear to me, and I kiss Your Lordship's hands. And excuse the multiplicity of errors that results from the hurry of the messenger who awaits me, and keep me.

---

86. Zanette identifies this anonymous correspondent as the writer Girolamo Brusoni (c. 1614–c. 1686; see *Suor Arcangela*, 277), another member of the Accademia degli Incogniti. Here Tarabotti reprimands him for his decision to respond to her *Antisatire*; she refers most likely to his *Antisatire Satirized*, which seems never to have been published and which Tarabotti mentions elsewhere (see letter 99).

24
TO THE MOST ILLUSTRIOUS GUID'ASCANIA ORSI[87]

The most courteous expressions of Your Illustrious Ladyship, together with the humanity of your dear and adorable conceits, overcome the emotions of those who profess to serve you in such a way that you possess all the affection of your servants. Such has befallen me, Illustrious Lady, for, seeing myself excellently honored by the grace, the affection, and the honors of so great a lady, I feel my heart tormented by its inability to demonstrate with external signs the sincere proof of my internal respect and the ardent feeling I profess and share with you.

Let Your Illustrious Ladyship be assured, however, that all that I am and all that I am worth, I am and I am worth because of you, and you may treat me as your subject.

> *E ciò ch'a me di far non è permesso*
> *Prego da Dio le venga ognor concesso.*[88]

Give me occasion to employ my feeble talents, so that through experience you may know the purity of my devotion.

I would consider it an honor to be able to kneel before you, my dearest Lady, known as you are by all as the universal glory of our sex; and where you raise me up from this respectful act of servitude, I am all the more humbled. But may the effects of your courtesy give way to the affections of my obligation. I will await some word with regard to the favor, which will be as dear to me as health itself, which I so dearly crave.

Your Illustrious Ladyship will excuse me if I sometimes delay, albeit with great sorrow, in offering my respects to you, and attribute it to the fact that it is the season for taking the purge.

For the rest, I am caught up with the inexplicable malice of certain people who wish to defend Signor Buoninsegni, who is so very

---

87. Guid'Ascania Orsi of Bologna was, like Tarabotti, a nun and a writer, and Tarabotti's letters to her convey great warmth and deep respect. In this letter, after praising Orsi's writing style, Tarabotti bemoans the difficulties women writers face.

88. "And what is not permitted to me / I pray that God always grant to you." The verse may be Tarabotti's own.

kind.[89] Illustrious Lady, it takes great stubbornness to publish, being that everyone wants to say his part, especially against us women, because men obstinately do not want to admit that women know how to write without their help. I laugh at such chatter. Pardon my long-windedness, for I respectfully and affectionately kiss your hands, living each day ever more Your Illustrious Ladyship's, etc.

25

TO THE MOST ILLUSTRIOUS SIGNORA BETTA POLANI[90]

Never let it be the case that I should forget Your Illustrious Ladyship. In the greatest afflictions of the heart and in the gravest torments of these afflicted limbs, the memory of my dear lady Betta will flourish always; this I swear to you with all the sincerity of my soul, which, being poised to depart this earthly dwelling, relays first to my heart these affectionate conceits, then recorded by my pen, while I declare myself yours, and affectionately kiss you.

26

TO THE MOST ILLUSTRIOUS SIGNORA BETTA POLANI[91]

Because the pilgrimage of my life has reached the ends of this earth, to you who have been the complete mistress of the dearest part of myself, I send my works, the dearest things I have and what I most regret leaving behind. I would say they ought to be burned, but I have no one in here that I can trust. *The Contemplations of the Loving Soul*, the

---

89. The allusion is to the scandal provoked by the publication of Tarabotti's *Antisatire*, which she composed in response to Buoninsegni's *Satire*. Tarabotti insists that those who conspire against her are motivated not by love for Buoninsegni but by hatred toward women and toward her.

90. Betta Polani (d. after 1654), a novice at Sant'Anna for many years, was one of Tarabotti's closest friends in the convent before she was compelled to leave in 1648. The two remained in close contact through visits and letters, as Tarabotti's epistolary collection attests.

91. In this letter Tarabotti, sick and convinced her death is imminent, tries to arrange for the things that are most precious to her: her literary works. She implores her dear friend Betta to print some of them and to destroy the others.

Paved Road to Heaven,[92] and *Convent Light* may be printed, if you so wish.[93] The rest should be thrown into the sea of oblivion, I pray you *in visceribus Christi.*[94]

Pray for this soul, for I will certainly do the same for you from beyond. Love me even if I am dead, and adieu forever.

27

TO SIGNOR N.[95]

In the grim and cloudy day of my thoughts and in the dark and gloomy night of my ailments, the divine Petrarch could not have foretold the climate from the signs of the sun because *obscuratum est sol.*[96] Had he been as capable an astrologer as he was a perfect poet, he might well have predicted a flood of tears and threatening comets from those baleful events that my heart presages. So be it. O God, alas it is true that *Inquietum est cor nostrum donec requiescat in te.*[97] I am not content, sir, no, and there is no end of repugnance all around.

I found a benefice of twenty-four ducats annually for that priest; if you would like to oversee it, Your Lordship may tell me so in writing.

As for the discussion that took place with the gentleman your relative, it was sincere and in that style of speech employed by me in these matters, and which I esteem good for the soul, as it is certainly preferable to live in the world than to cover oneself with the religious

---

92. In the Italian, *La via lasciata dal Cielo,* most likely an error for *La via lastricata per andar al Cielo,* the work mentioned by Giovanni Dandolo in his letter of presentation for the *Letters.*

93. All these works have been lost. See Dandolo's letter of presentation.

94. Cf. Phil. 1:8: "For God is my witness how I long after you all in the bowels of Jesus Christ."

95. This letter touches on many topics: a vague prediction of ill fortune, negotiations for a priest looking for a benefice, and a bitter reference to cloistered life for those who have not chosen it.

96. Cf. Petrarch, *E ria fortuna po' ben venire meno / S'a i segni del mio sol l'aere conosco* (RVF CLIII.14); the Latin quotation comes from Luke 23:45 ("And the sun was darkened").

97. Cf. Augustine, *Confessions,* vol. 1, chap. 1, "Our heart is restless, until it repose in thee" (trans. Edward B. Pusey [New York: Modern Library, 1949], 3).

habit and, with one's heart out in the world, to drown in a glass of water.[98]

Lady N. sent me the anniversary gift,[99] and I send it to you, having had your promise to receive the same. I oblige you to do this, and I entrust myself to your prayers.

28

TO THE MOST ILLUSTRIOUS SIGNORA N.[100]

With my heart swimming in tears, I inform Your Illustrious Ladyship of my unlucky tribulations. My dear friend has died: she who, ever faithful over the course of twenty-five years, may be acclaimed by fame as the model of true friendship. I am without my soul and I have lost every blessing. Have compassion for me, for pity's sake, and be assured that there is nothing left to console me but having gained Your Illustrious Ladyship as my lady and mistress, to whom, in grief, I dedicate myself.

98. It seems Tarabotti tried to dissuade a relative of her correspondent from choosing the religious life, either for himself or, more likely, for one of his relatives.

99. Tarabotti may refer to a gift or payment made on the anniversary of the profession of vows.

100. Tarabotti communicates to an anonymous female correspondent the news of the death of Regina Donà who, along with Betta Polani, was one of the Tarabotti's few friends in the convent. Regina and Arcangela entered Sant'Anna together as novices and took the veil on 8 September 1620 (Zanette, *Suor Arcangela*, 83). The death of Regina on 31 March 1645 (ibid., 378) was a devastating loss for Tarabotti, worsened further by the departure of Betta from the convent. After Regina's death Tarabotti wrote in her honor the *Tears upon the Death of the Most Illustrious Signora Regina Donati* (*Lagrime ... per la morte dell'illustrissima signora Regina Donati*), a brief encomiastic work published along with the *Letters* and excerpted in the appendix to this volume.

29
TO THE MOST ILLUSTRIOUS COUNTESS S.[101]

I cannot, nor ought not, nor do I wish to set aside the expression of Your Illustrious Ladyship's sublime virtues, while the loftiness of your merit acts as an invincible obstacle to doing so. Let us forget this quarrel, I pray you, and let happen what may. I will be prouder to be honored by such a lady, and such distinguished gentlemen, than if I, like Saint Paul, had been snatched up to Heaven to hear the voices of the angels.[102] My Illustrious Lady, I am not one to critique a song, note its trills, observe its warbles, assess its transitions, or pass judgment on its languor, since I am most ignorant about it; I will merely try to harmonize, with the recitals of your song, the great dissonance between your great favor and my lowly merit. Truly my most imperfect *Paradise* had need of an angelic voice to make people consider it Paradise in fact.[103] Knowing this, Your Illustrious Ladyship, by virtue of your kindness, deigned to prove it to be so.

Furthermore, I understand that men always act with their own interests in mind. Your Illustrious Ladyship must excuse me if I speak the truth, though it be contrary even to your illustrious spouse. But let these gentlemen take care, lest they run into a Megaera rather than a Eurydice; whence they will need the aid of your voice to remain

101. Tarabotti repeats her plea, expressed in another letter to the countess, who was apparently a singer, that she come to Sant'Anna to perform a concert (see letter 90). Music was an important part of convent life (see for example C. Monson, *Disembodied Voices: Music and Culture in an Early Modern Italian Convent* [Berkeley: University of California Press, 1995]; and R. Kendrick, *Celestial Sirens: Nuns and Their Music in Early Modern Milan* [Oxford: Clarendon Press, 1996]). In the second part of the letter, the nun polemicizes against self-interested men (including the husband of her correspondent). She makes her usual exception for good men.

102. 2 Cor. 12:2–4.

103. It seems that Tarabotti here thanks her correspondent for contributing, along with other poets, an encomiastic poem for her *Convent Paradise*. Two female poets wrote dedicatory verse for the volume: Lucrezia Marinella and an "incerta," or unknown woman. Since Marinella was not a noblewoman, the recipient of this letter must be the other poet, who was perhaps hesitant to have her name appear in print.

unscathed.[104] It is true that these illustrious ones stand outside the human condition, so that, since they are not men, I am certain they will favor me.

These days of waiting will seem like centuries to me, and in the meantime I will pray for these gentlemen, on the merit of their good deeds, entry to that Paradise which Your Illustrious Ladyship so well deserves, being an angel in presence, voice, and habits and belonging to that sex which is destined for eternal glory. I am obligated to be your servant out of both debt and desire, and as such, I offer you my respects in the name of my friends and Lady R. in particular.

30

TO THE ILLUSTRIOUS SIGNOR GIOVANNI POLANI

Yesterday, despite my debt to you, I could not respond to Your Illustrious Lordship's kind letter because I had to be at the grille.[105] Please excuse this failure, which since it was involuntary is not unworthy of pardon. If I do not thank you for being the one who inspired the flight of Loredano's most glorious quill, it is for no other reason than that I deem myself to be as unworthy as I am desirous to do so. The honors that I receive are too grand for me to render proper and worthy thanks. Nevertheless, proclaiming my inability, I am in a certain way satisfying the demands of my devotion.[106]

Just one word, let alone such spirited and kind praise, contained in one of the excellent Loredano's letters in praise of any work, no matter how imperfect, would suffice to prove it worthy for all time. This letter, which issued from the trove of the most florid and secret treasures of knowledge, could imparadise Hell itself, let alone make

---

104. Tarabotti warns men that, in their voyage from Hell to oppose her, they might encounter not Orpheus's Eurydice but the enraged and dangerous Megaera, one of the three Furies.

105. In the Italian, *a finestra*: literally, at the window, located in the convent parlor. Here nuns could converse with visitors from behind a grille and under supervision. In Seicento Venice visitors were required to obtain permission to visit the convent from the Provveditori ai Monasteri, but in reality, many did not. The nuns' parlor often functioned as a kind of salon, a social space for friends, relatives, writers, musicians, and others to meet, and as an arena where business matters, often regarding family affairs like marriages, were discussed.

106. Tarabotti here discusses the letter of presentation composed by Loredano for Tarabotti's *Convent Paradise*, with which she was very pleased (see letter 8).

heavenly my *Convent Paradise*. Everything beautiful and delightful in my work will owe its life to the supreme courtesy of Your Illustrious Lordship, who, although I did not deserve it in the least, was kind enough to make a heavenly rivulet spring from the immense sea of Venetian knowledge to irrigate with fertile waters the sterility and aridity of my conceits. The writing contained in a letter so full of wit is able to draw out the heart from the reader's chest (almost as if by magic) and direct it to read my *Paradise*. I confess that my weakness had need of defense from the spite of malicious men, but I would never have dared hope for such high and noble protection. Such favors come from the kindness of Your Lordship, who knows not how to distribute them but with a most liberal hand. Many writers believe that the Evangelist whose name you carry lives also in the Earthly Paradise, placed there by God so that at the end of days he might come to fight against the Antichrist in defense of our true faith.[107] I too, also in imitation of His Divine Majesty, now deem you to be forever the defender of my *Convent Paradise*, so that you will work to defend the truth it contains against the malicious untruths and sophistic contrivances of the Antichrist's heralds.

But it is better that I hold my peace, since I deem the silence that always befits my religious profession perhaps more appropriate than mere thanks. I therefore pass to other matters to thank you for your efforts to retrieve that story[108] for me and to let you know that C. is not capable of this task, since it is more the job of a friar than anyone else.

I did not understand what you wanted to say about the illustrious Signor Francesco, since I knew nothing of the honor of the sonnets that he bestowed upon me; but His Reverence[109] revealed the code, so I feel I must complain to this gentleman, since he is capable

---

107. That is, Saint John the Baptist. According to the Byzantine tradition, Saint John waits with Enoch and Elijah to battle the Antichrist (see W. Bousset, *The Antichrist Legend*, trans. A. H. Keane [London: Hutchinson, 1896], 208).

108. The reference (*favola*) may be either to a work Tarabotti wished to obtain or to a piece of information.

109. S[ua] R[everenza]: likely Angelico Aprosio, whom Tarabotti often addresses as *vostra Signoria reverenda* ("Your Reverend Lordship").

of pretending, which until now I would perhaps have doubted.[110] May Your Illustrious Lordship be pleased to deliver the attached missive of thanks, since, if I did not repay this debt as far as I am able, I would add knots to the ties of obligation that make me, by my choice, his and Your Illustrious Lordship's, etc.

31
TO THE ILLUSTRIOUS SIGNORA N.[111]

The devotion that I profess toward the illustrious count, Your Illustrious Ladyship's brother, combined with the reports of your great merit from a knowledgeable person, assure me that, since you are the very idea of kindness, you will not disdain me for offering you, along with my reverent servitude, this small stillbirth of my most sterile intellect. I pray you forgive me if it does not seem perfectly appropriate for a religious person, since I fell into the error of composing it and having it printed not by my own inclination but to obey commands I cannot ignore. Please excuse its manifold defects and pardon my excessive boldness.

I am not without hope that your eminence and kindness will show me compassion and forgiveness, since I know it is the habit of those of your stature to appreciate the gifts of their servants; presenting myself as such to you, I kiss Your Illustrious Ladyship's hands.

32
TO THE ILLUSTRIOUS BETTA POLANI

Since communicating the troubles of the heart to true friends is a great relief to disconsolate souls, I feel obliged to transmit to Your Il-

---

110. The *Biblioteca aprosiana*, or *Aprosian Library* (by "Cornelio Aspasio Antivigilmi," that is, Angelico Aprosio [Ventimiglia], [Bologna: Manolessi, 1673], 173–75) contains four laudatory sonnets composed by "F.B." (perhaps Francesco Buoninsegni [see Weaver, *Satira e Antisatira*, 11, n. 9] or [Giovan] Francesco Busenello) in honor of Tarabotti. A note by Aprosio explains that Tarabotti sent the sonnets to him herself. The letter that accompanied the sonnets is included in Tarabotti's *Letters* (letter 154).

111. With the requisite expressions of modesty Tarabotti offers her anonymous correspondent one of her works, probably the *Antisatire* (which she states elsewhere, as here, was composed only at the request of others; see below, letter 33).

lustrious Ladyship the bitter news of the death of she who gave me life.[112] I have lost everything good with the loss of the one I affectionately called mother. It is true that we all must pay this tax to the earth, since *statutum est hominibus semel mori*.[113] But it is also true that our humanity cannot receive such blows without mourning. Please pray that God grant me some consolation, as I, amid my deep distress, revere you.

33

TO HER MOST SERENE HIGHNESS VITTORIA DELLA ROVERE, GRAND DUCHESS OF TUSCANY[114]

The reverent blush with which I appear before Your Serene Highness cannot be conveyed by the weakness of my pen, so tentative and imperfect. Please excuse (on bended knee I pray you) my boldness and cover it with the cloak of kindness that adorns you, so that you will see it as pure devotion and deem it worthy of pardon.

I do not know whether my religious state increases or diminishes my guilt, but I wish to suppose that such a state renders me, if not innocent, at least pardonable, since it is the privilege of people in religious orders to criticize freely things that are poorly done and to see their own sacrifices better appreciated by God than those of people in the world. I do not lack hope therefore that Your Highness, who is adorned with divine qualities, will appreciate the gift that with the dedication of this little work I give you with devout and religious hand

---

112. Tarabotti's mother, Maria Cadena dei Tolentini, died around age seventy-four in February 1648 (ASV, notarile, testamenti, b. 620, n. 233). Maria's will, drawn up in 1647, left ten ducats to her daughter in Sant'Anna.

113. Heb. 9:27: "it is appointed unto men once to die."

114. Tarabotti dedicated her *Antisatire* to Vittoria della Rovere of Florence. This letter illustrates Tarabotti's strategy with regard to publishing this work: while it is clear from other letters that she had every intention of publishing it, she often (as in this letter) claims the opposite, insisting that she wrote it at the request of a group of noblewomen and that they forced her to publish it. A virtually identical manuscript copy of this letter, dated 9 July 1644, is in the Archivio di Stato of Florence, Mediceo del Principato, 6152, cc. 29r–v (F. Medioli, "Arcangela Tarabotti's Reliability about Herself: Publication and Self-Representation [Together with a Small Collection of Previously Unpublished Letters]," *The Italianist* 23 [2003]: 54–101).

and heart. The work undertakes to denounce not Signor Buoninsegni but his wicked *Satire*, which attacks women's fashion. It was not my intent to defend women's vanities, nor to offend that gentleman, but rather to revere Your Serene Highness and to follow the commands of many noble ladies whom I am obliged to obey as a servant. I proceeded on the belief that this composition of mine would not be seen in public, since I deemed it worthy of no other light than that of fire. But since those powerful people, rather than showing me gratitude, mortified me by their betrayal, I have resolved that the printed work will seek protection beneath the wing of that same deity to whom I dedicated the manuscript.

May your kindness please pardon this error of excessive boldness, which, were it not spawned by great devotion, would merit severe castigation. I am nevertheless ready to undergo the punishment that your always upright and irreproachable justice will determine for me, and I fully admit my guilt in order to mitigate my crime before Your Serene Highness's regal mind. I continue to pray His Divine Majesty grant you boundless prosperity and success, and I most reverently bow to you.

34

TO THE MOST ILLUSTRIOUS AND EXCELLENT SIGNOR NICOLO BRETEL DI GREMONVILE, AMBASSADOR OF FRANCE TO THE MOST SERENE REPUBLIC OF VENICE[115]

These weak strokes of my pen transmit no less to Your Excellency than to the illustrious and excellent ambassadress[116] my soul's most devoted and reverent sentiments to rejoice in the felicitous birth of that son[117] who, drawing life from admirable parents, will by consequence be a glory to posterity and an exemplar of virtue. Please do not reject my

---

115. Nicolas Bretel de Grémonville (1608–48) was the French ambassador to Venice from July 1645 to October 1647 and a close confidant of Tarabotti's.

116. Anne-Françoise de Loménie, who married Nicolas Bretel de Grémonville in 1632.

117. Bretel de Grémonville's son was baptized on 12 June 1646 with the name Marco, in obvious homage to the city of his birth. At the baptism, attended by Doge Molino, to whom Tarabotti also wrote, Marco was carried by the Marquis di Galeranda, the husband of another of Tarabotti's correspondents (see ASV, Collegio/Cerimoniali III, 123r).

dutiful expression of debt and reverence, and receive these wishes proclaimed to you by my heart, which, always raised up to His Divine Majesty, will pray that your magnanimous hopes be fully realized.

In the meantime I most reverently communicate to you a thousand affectionate congratulations from these most illustrious girls,[118] and I kiss Your Excellency's no less than Madame's hands, saying to the child:

> *Perché mostrarti un vero sol pretendi,*
> *luminoso fanciul, nasci fra l'onde,*
> *e perché tua virtù già sparga incendi*
> *in seno del leon i rai diffonde;*
> *Come si trovin le dolcezze intendi*
> *in mezo a le salsedini profonde;*
> *anzi perché di sol tutto comprendi*
> *il fonte a te col mar non si confonde.*
> *Sí che un sole tu sei nato fra noi,*
> *e spargerai lasciando il mar fra poco*
> *sovra le cime alpine i raggi tuoi.*
> *Io dal gallico Giove un cenno invoco*
> *perché so che a quel cenno i lidi eoi*
> *avran da novo sol splendor e foco.*[119]

---

118. Bretel de Grémonville's young daughters, entrusted to the nuns of Sant'Anna for their education. The girls were boarded at Sant'Anna for a period as young lodgers or "putte a spese," as they were called in Venice, to be educated by the nuns.

119. "Since you mean to show yourself to be a true sun / luminous child, you are born amid the waves, / and so that your virtue may already spark fires / it spreads its rays in the heart of the lion; / you understand how sweetness can be found / amid the salty depths; / in fact, since you comprise all the sun / THE SOURCE does not confuse you with the sea. / Thus you are a sun born in our midst, / and soon leaving the sea / you will spread your rays over Alpine peaks. / I invoke a sign from the Gallic Jove / since I know that with such a sign the Aeolian shores / will have from this new sun splendor and fire." The authorship of these verses is uncertain, although it is not likely to have been Tarabotti herself, who elsewhere declares her distaste for this type of occasional verse (see letter 243, in which she asks Guid'Ascania Orsi to find someone to write a poem in honor of Marco's birth).

35

TO THE MOST ILLUSTRIOUS AND EXCELLENT SIGNOR NICOLÒ BRETEL DE GREMONVILLE, AMBASSADOR OF FRANCE TO THE MOST SERENE REPUBLIC OF VENICE

The circumstances under which Your Illustrious Excellency chose to share such a singular favor with me last night would merit comment from the most famous pens. That you wrote me with your own hand, at the fifth hour,[120] when your heart was rejoicing with overflowing happiness for the birth of a son, is an occurrence that transcends my understanding. My heart is insufficient, my pen incapable, my speech too humble to render graceful thanks for such graces. At the sight of Jove adorned, Semele was reduced to ashes,[121] and I in the courteous reading of Your Excellency's important letter was stunned in such a manner that I retained no senses that allowed me to thank you for having shared your happiness with me in this way.

The consolation I experienced in hearing of the birth of this most desired son hardly allowed me to skim these most courteous lines which, if tender, prick me nevertheless. The ease of the birth that did not belabor Madame must be attributed to the virtue of Your Excellency, since, given that the child must be a living portrait of you who tend to favor not offend women, he could not bring trouble to a woman who merits the reverence and respect of all men.

At your bidding I asked the mademoiselle of Rouen[122] how she will like the company of a brother, and I find that she is so jealous for Your Excellency's love that if she were a boy I would fear an outcome like that which befell the world's first brothers.[123] But women are not driven by such cruelty. She cries and grieves at her parents' happiness, but with such prudence that she astonishes anyone who is with her.

---

120. That is, after midnight (Zanette, *Suor Arcangela*, 306). On the calculation of the hour in Tarabotti's time, see Molmenti, *Storia di Venezia*, 3:166.

121. Having persuaded Jove, the god of thunder, to appear before her in all his splendor, Semel was burned to ashes at the sight.

122. One of Bretel de Grémonville's daughters; perhaps called thus after the city of Rouen in Normandy, the family's native land (see Zanette, *Suor Arcangela*, 309).

123. Cain and Abel. On the jealousy of Bretel de Grémonville's daughter at the birth of her brother, see also letter 129 to Madame de Grémonville.

Please pity her, and continue to love her; while rejoicing anew at the happiness of both of Your Excellencies, my heart continues to sing:

> *Non temete il furor di squadre infide*
> *o del veneto mar guerriere genti:*
> *sa rintuzzare i barbari ardimenti;*
> *è risorto fra voi gallico Alcide.*
> *Già la destra fatal, che i mostri ancide,*
> *sfida l'idra ottomana a pugne ardenti,*
> *per secondare i fortunati eventi.*
> *O come il cielo al nobil parto arride!*
> *Del superbo Ibraim l'empia fortuna*
> *già cede al nome e apresta i funerali*
> *a' maometani dèi la tracia luna.*
> *Ed a ragion paventano gran mali*
> *se chi dovea fra gigli aver la culla*
> *fra i leoni dell'Adria ebbe i natali.*[124]

36

TO FATHER N.[125]

Since the fifth element of which I am formed is sincerity, I resolve finally to make it clear to Your Reverence that I have always despised

---

124. "Do not fear the fury of infidel troops / or the peoples who would war on the Venetian sea: / he knows how to blunt barbaric audacity; / the Gallic Alcides has risen in your midst. / Already his deadly right hand, which slays monsters / threatens the Ottoman hydra with bold fists / to favor fortunate outcomes. / O how Heaven smiles upon this noble birth! / The impious luck of the arrogant Ibraim / is already ceding to his name, and the Thracian moon / prepares funeral rites for the gods of Mohammed's followers. / And with good reason do they fear great troubles / if the baby who should have been cradled among lilies / was born amid the lions of Adria." The author of these verses is not known; see n. 119. Tarabotti depicts Bretel de Grémonville's newborn son as an Alcides, that is, a newborn Hercules. Playing on common iconography, she says in the final lines that the Grémonville child will be an even more fearsome foe to the Muslim world since he was born not in France (among lilies) but in Venice (amid lions).

125. This letter, according to Zanette meant for Aprosio (*Suor Arcangela*, 266–67), reveals the deep animosity between Tarabotti and Aprosio that arose from her *Antisatire* and his response, the *Mask Lifted*.

friarly insolence and that I can only ridicule those dogs that howl at the moon.

You may cease writing me, because your letters will not in the future be read by me, and I will give them the reception they deserve, just as I will esteem your compositions, be they printed or manuscript, as much as all the lettered men of Italy have valued your published writings against Father N.[126] May God grant you what you deserve.

37

TO THE MOST ILLUSTRIOUS SIGNOR GIOVANNI DANDOLO

The most noble marriage of Your Illustrious Lordship, which promises through your children to provide to posterity the perfect ideals of most accomplished gentlemen and noble women, encourages me to fly with my pen to wish that those joys promised you by such gracious nuptials will be uninterrupted.[127] Please accept, I pray you, my dutiful offering of sincere and devoted congratulations, and receive the wishes of my heart, which implore that Heaven bestow upon you unequaled graces, devoting myself to be Your Illustrious Lordship's, etc.

38

TO THE MOST ILLUSTRIOUS MATTEO DANDOLO[128]

The servitude that I profess with regard to the most worthy status of Your Illustrious Lordship requires that, at the recent happy conclusion of the most worthy marriage contracted by the illustrious Signor Giovanni your brother, I be bold enough to join the universal acclamations of the entire Venetian Senate to rejoice with you, with all of your illustrious family, with our native city. Please do not disdain this page,

---

126. P[adre] *N.* Zanette explains that Tarabotti alluded to Aprosio's many publications against Tommaso Stigliani, to whom she refers with the generic *N.* (ibid., 267).

127. With this letter Tarabotti congratulated Giovanni Dandolo, who was married to Orsa Gabriel on 18 February 1644 *more veneto* (Venetian calendar [1645]) (ASV, Avogaria di Comun, Indice di matrimoni patrizi per nome di donna, 86, ter. 1 [reg. V., 87]).

128. Like letter 37, this letter also addresses the marriage of Giovanni Dandolo, brother to Matteo.

rather admire in its candor the purity of my most devoted respect, since I will never fail to be Your Illustrious Lordship's, etc.

39

TO THE MOST ILLUSTRIOUS SIGNOR GIOVANNI DANDOLO[129]

So regally has Your Illustrious Lordship favored me with your most divine pen, and so richly have you decorated my poor talents that, to tell you the truth, I would not trade places with queens. Your kindness has so gladdened my labors that I feel like a goddess, and I keep saying to myself, as that rash Niobe[130] did:

> *Who denies my fortunate condition?*
> *Who can doubt my future?*[131]

I do not fear that I will see, as she did, my children pierced through by the arrows of Phoebus, since a greater sun rendered them immortal for me.[132] Nor may anyone any longer believe that my off-spring are adulterous, since I, like an eagle, show them clearly to be legitimate, for I saw them resist not the splendors of the sun's sphere, but the rays of two blessed spheres, which are the most luminous ones that God created.[133]

---

129. The thanks that Tarabotti offers in this letter are for Dandolo's letter of presentation for the *Letters* themselves.

130. Niobe, the personification of maternal grief, paid for her pride when jealous Latona sent her son Apollo (Phoebus), god of the sun, to kill Niobe's twelve children with his ar-rows. Inconsolable, Niobe cried herself to death and was transformed into a weeping mar-ble statue (Ovid, *Metamorphoses*, book 6, 165–312, trans. Brookes More [Boston: Cornhill Publishing, 1922]).

131. Ibid., 193–94. Tarabotti quoted in Italian from Ovid's original: *Sum felix (quis enim neget hoc?) felixque manebo / (Hoc quoque quis dubitet?)*

132. Tarabotti refers to the works, written by her, that Dandolo mentioned by name in his letter of presentation.

133. Tarabotti makes reference to the notion, present in Pliny and in various bestiaries, that the eagle subjected its eaglets to a test in order to verify their legitimacy: it made them gaze directly into the sun. An illegitimate eaglet would blink and thus be forced from the nest. Tarabotti states that she and all the world can see that her works are legitimate, that is to say,

My tongue should quiet itself since it knows not how to utter anything of worth, and my heart should enjoy those qualities that, coming from such a sublime place, would make deities proud; while I humbly bend my knees to you.

40

TO THE MOST ILLUSTRIOUS AND EXCELLENT SIGNOR GIOVAN FRANCESCO LOREDANO

Your Excellency's favors have made prideful an archangel who prays, genuflected, that she will not be cast out of the most delightful paradise of your grace as a result of this fault. The courteous visit of your illustrious and excellent spouse was the reason for this sin, and it adorned my servitude with so much glory that there is nothing left for me to desire.

With my heart's voice I thank you for the favor, and with my pen I record the troubles of a certain Monte, who hopes (from nowhere else but Your Excellency's heroic compassion) for relief from the ruin that threatens him.[134] Upon a mount God redeemed the world, and upon this Monte you will redeem the house of a poor gentleman which is now lost in afflictions and tribulations.[135]

Your justice can be no less apparent to the world than your marvelous virtue. Being a perpetual admirer of this and honoring your merit, I kiss Your Excellency's robes.

---

the work of her own pen, because they are able to resist something even stronger than the rays of the sun: the light of two great minds, Loredano and Dandolo, who support her work.

134. The nun asks her powerful correspondent to help this person, probably the Vicentine Lauro Monte mentioned in letters 209 and 215, whose difficulties were likely of a legal nature.

135. Tarabotti makes a word play on the gentleman's name, Monte, the Italian for "mount."

41

TO THE MOST EMINENT AND EXCELLENT SIGNOR ENRICO CORNARO[136]

Lady N., aware that during the two most solemn days certain prisoners are usually granted their freedom by grace, and knowing that she was imprisoned although innocent, hoped, through the grace of Your Eminent Lordship at this holy Christmas holiday, to leave this hateful prison. But, seeing that the infant Christ, still in his mother's womb, does not hear her requests, she hopes to obtain her liberty at least by the Resurrection, when He, grown into a man and experienced in prisons and torment, will perhaps have mercy on her suffering.

In the meantime, she goes about this convent purgatory singing the *miseremini*, and with prayers awaits angels, among whom is Your Eminent Lordship. Since you are the one who ought to bring her the greatest relief, we beg you to honor her with a visit during these holy holidays; and while, as Christ is born, we pray that all happiness may be born with him, and as the year dies, that her misfortunes die with it, we both remain Your Eminent and Excellent Lordship's, etc.

42

TO THE MOST ILLUSTRIOUS AND EXCELLENT SIGNOR NICOLÒ BRETEL DE GREMONVILLE, AMBASSADOR OF FRANCE TO THE MOST SERENE REPUBLIC OF VENICE

Your Illustrious Excellency's precious greetings, accompanied by festive wishes for these holy holidays, invites us reverently to thank you for such honors and to proclaim in return your redoubled happiness and graces.

Her ladyship's miscarriage pierced our souls, and the news of her gradual recovery restored consolation to our hearts. May the blessed Lord allow her to achieve the complete restoration of her health, as we, with the most insistent of prayers, unceasingly pray to

---

136. It is probable that this correspondent is Enrico Cornaro son of Paolo (c. 1600–1663), a lawyer in Venice (ASV, sezione notarile, testamenti, 83.35). The letter shows how Tarabotti tried to help other women who were put in convents against their will.

Heaven, which we will forever beg to watch over the illustrious house of Gremonville, to which I am, etc.

43

TO SIGNOR N.[137]

Your Lordship's onions and shoots produced such wonderful flowers that you ought to admire them, since they were gathered in Paradise by the hand of that N.[138] so beloved by your heart and celebrated by your pen in the person of Arcangela.

If in the past days you sent me pomegranates, the king of fruit, and I send you a rose, the queen of flowers, and if in the dead of winter the angel of the Lord presented Saint Dorothy with roses amid her atrocious martyrdom, I too, who am an Archangel,[139] a bride of Christ in the martyrdom of religion, present to Your Lordship the same roses in this coldest of seasons.

I harbor a doubt, however, that there might be some trick hidden beneath those sweetest of pomegranates, for, if the serpent tempted Eve with fruit in earthly Paradise, Your Lordship, too, came to tempt me with pomegranates in convent Paradise.[140] Therefore no one should marvel if I fall into the sin of complaining, since the first man, no less than the first woman, succumbed to the sin of gluttony.

I resolved to return the favor of the flowers and the fruit; as for the accusations and lies, I bite my tongue, and suspend my pen by offering you my respects. Adieu.

---

137. The recipient of this letter may be Aprosio or Brusoni, who at times lauded and at times denounced the nun's writings. Tarabotti gives a vivid image of such instability in the letter's final lines, where she contrasts the lovely gifts of fruit (perhaps metaphorical) from her correspondent and his "accusations and lies" against her.

138. Tarabotti indicates herself.

139. In the Italian, *Arcangela*.

140. According to some interpretations, the fruit of the Tree of Life was the pomegranate.

44
TO THE MOST EMINENT SIGNOR N.[141]

Your Eminent Lordship looked upon the miscarriage of a sterile mind, not the happy birth of a lofty intellect. I understand your meaning, and I offer you the greatest possible thanks for the kindness you demonstrate toward me in praising what ought merit reprehension. My pen does not drip diamonds, but the despair of poor prisoners.

I agree that a stillbirth of the mind, conceived and delivered in the obscurity of the purest ignorance, should not see the light of day. I wish Your Eminent Lordship to remove, with religious authority, the most obvious errors in these pages, which my own affection cannot hide; in fact I know that, in order for a good critic to correct them entirely, he would have to throw them into the fire.[142] Let your supreme intelligence consider what sweetness can lie in its sayings, what style, what explanations, what figures can be present in the compositions of a woman upon whom grammar or other learning has shed no imaginable light, and who in her spelling has only the dictionary as her guide. In such a woman, unused to writing anything but the occasional letter, there cannot be sufficient ability to compose without errors.

As for the rest, I am sending you the end of the work, a reading appropriate for these times—appropriate, I mean, in terms of the subject matter. On the other hand, it is absurd to see a Paradise, which ought to be formed of meanings and concepts that transcend the confines of human understanding, fabricated out of air, with no foundation in learning, uneven in its sentences, poor in erudition, rich in errors, and adorned with the trifles of various poets. But sir, one who

141. Tarabotti penned this letter to Aprosio when their relationship was at its high point. She speaks with great dissatisfaction about her *Convent Paradise*, which she is still completing, even asking for editorial input from Aprosio, who had evidently already praised the work (on this issue, see also the manuscript letter she wrote to Aprosio, dated 25 September 1642, at the Biblioteca Universitaria di Genova [BUG], E VI 22, c. 129, published by F. Medioli [with the erroneous date of September 24] as an appendix to "La scrittura forzata: Le lettere autografe di Arcangela Tarabotti," *Rivista di Storia e Letteratura Religiosa* 32 [1996]: 149, n. 1).

142. Tarabotti addresses Aprosio with nearly identical words in a manuscript letter regarding *Paternal Tyranny*; cf. the letter dated 17 September 164? (BUG, E VI 22, c. 122 [Medioli appendix to "La scrittura forzata," 147]).

is not in love with God cannot speak of him. I was much better able to describe *Paternal Tyranny* and to erect the workings of *Inferno* than to describe the greatness of *Paradise*.

If Your Eminent Lordship is able to confess me at the next festival of the Blessed Virgin, please give me notice, for I will take it as a most singular favor. In the meantime, I offer you my respects, and to your holy prayers I commend myself most humbly.

45

TO SIGNOR N.[143]

I write to you in keeping with Your Lordship's note of yesterday evening, begging that you deign to treat with the greatest attention this matter that is so important to me.

Let Your Prudence's first consideration be whether the subject is worthy of the person you mentioned, in all ways and specifically in parentage. Be sure that there is not even a shadow of suspicion that the inquiry originates from here, because rather than aid the interests of this lady, it would ruin them.[144] You can say that the disagreement with Signor N. caused these rumors to fly about the city, or make up some other excuse, for Your Eminent Lordship, being of the virile sex, will not have to go searching for lies most kind in order to set this affair on the proper path. May your goodness not fail to attend to this, for your intelligence will not lack the ability to help me. Afterward, I will await word, but I do not wish for long delays.

In the meantime, since you intimated that you do not have the time to skim those lines that contain nothing worthwhile but their explanation of the truth so despised by men, please favor me with their return, for, since that work is my daughter and a virgin, I would not

143. With this letter Tarabotti attempts to arrange the marriage of a woman who evidently comes from an important family, perhaps the same woman to whom Tarabotti refers in another letter on a similar topic (letter 22). Alongside the marriage negotiations, Tarabotti here asks that her correspondent return to her a literary work.

144. Tarabotti attempts to hide her role in these negotiations, whose precise nature remains unclear. Perhaps the family of the bride-to-be is trying to reject one candidate in order to choose a more suitable one.

want her to encounter, while in your hands, the fate of other unfortunate women.[145] I offer you my respects.

46

TO THE MOST ILLUSTRIOUS AND EXCELLENT MADAME DI AMÒ, AMBASSADRESS OF FRANCE[146]

If serving Your Illustrious Excellency depended on me alone, I would always place your commands before my very life. But because I must depend on the will of others, I am also forced to settle for what I must, not for what I would wish and desire for your service.

Only now have I received an example from the women who make lace in the round.[147] I am sending it to Your Excellency to see if it might meet your approval, in order to make sure immediately that you receive everything you requested, insofar as I am able with my diligent but ineffectual efforts.

As for that design that is characteristic of us,[148] they demand sixty ducats per *braccio* as a final price. If you will deign to signal me your wishes, I will have them start immediately, and they will take upon themselves the obligation of making six *bracci*.[149] Those who do the finest work will work on the large pieces.

As for the rest, to you once again I dedicate myself and the living spirit of my soul, that I might employ them to my last breath as

145. Tarabotti probably refers here to her *Paternal Tyranny*, which she circulated as a manuscript. She asks that the work ("my daughter and a virgin") be returned to her for fear that her correspondent will mistreat it, as he evidently has other works (or women).

146. In this letter Tarabotti negotiates the price of a piece of lacework her convent sisters were making. Tarabotti seems to have acted as a broker rather than a maker of lace, and thus she expresses frustration at the fact that, since she depends on others' work, she cannot satisfy her recipient's request as soon as she had promised.

147. On the production of lace in seventeenth-century Venice, see n. 43.

148. In the sixteenth and seventeenth century, Venetian lacework was varied and there were frequent innovations in its design and production. Tarabotti makes reference here to a type of lace that the Sant'Anna nuns produced.

149. The *braccio* was the major measure of length in northern and central Italy, defined as "the length of the two arms extended when measured from the tips of the middle fingers" (Ronald E. Zupko, *Italian Weights and Measures from the Middle Ages to the Nineteenth Century* [Philadelphia: American Philosophical Society, 1981], 40).

your servant. I regret that the weakness of my abilities does not suffice to serve worthily a lady of such merits, to whom I most humbly bow; and the lady N. and I declare ourselves slaves of the illustrious lady Margherita,[150] ardently longing for her most desirable conversation, the honor of which we anxiously await. In the meantime I pray that Heaven grant Your Illustrious Excellency an abundance of graces.

47

TO THE MOST ILLUSTRIOUS SIGNORA GUID'ASCANIA ORSI[151]

One who is possessed of worthy qualities readily ascribes the same to others. So it is that Your Illustrious Ladyship quickly lent credence to those reports about me that, perhaps more affectionately biased than they were truthful, reached your ears. I would like to be such as you have persuaded yourself I am, in order more worthily to offer and grant that reverent observance that you have deigned to declare not unwelcome. Be assured, therefore, of a devoted reciprocity in feelings from me, with which I will forever glory in the good fortune of every opportunity to serve you and the illustrious Lady N., whose affectionately partial servant I will always be in equal measure.

With regard to the gift you sent me, I offer you the greatest thanks, regretting that you have behaved toward me in such a way that my servitude might seem more a result of your kindness than of your merit and my devoted election.

I must also inform you that not I, but my lady sister, was gravely ill; whence I delight that I was able to declare myself your servant in a period of good health, in order to be able to execute your commands, by which I will forever esteem myself highly favored and with which I commend myself to Your Illustrious Ladyship, etc.

150. The niece of the des Hamaux (Marguerite de Fiubet), who was also the recipient of some of the nun's letters.

151. Tarabotti here addresses Orsi, a frequent correspondent, to thank her for the compliments she gave to Tarabotti and for a gift, and to promise her eternal dedication. She also clears up a misunderstanding: it was not the nun but her sister who had been ill.

48

TO THE MOST ILLUSTRIOUS AND EXCELLENT
SIGNOR N.[152]

My illness has begun to recede and once again I can discuss the things that give me pleasure. Last night, therefore, I heard from one of our lay sisters[153] that the parish priest of Santa Margarita[154] is like a viper deaf to that truth proclaimed by the pages my pen marked. He asserts—I know not with what foundation of reason—that my compositions cannot be my own offspring. Then I recalled the conceits of Your Excellency, and I held them up to myself as gospel proof: that is, that I cannot listen to such impertinences except from such fools. I did indeed laugh, because the idea is absurd. These good people are accustomed to laughing and singing upon the death of their near and dear and praying for their immortality in the next life; and therefore we ought not marvel if they wish not to hear that someone lives immortally in this world. Your Excellency is certainly a prophet for me, and I wish to be your sibyl.

Believe me that in the persecutions of your adversaries, you seem as a sun surrounded by impertinent clouds, which eventually must disperse in tears of regret before the splendors of your merits. Be assured of this, and I bow to you.

49

TO MY MOST ILLUSTRIOUS SIGNORA BETTA POLANI[155]

I receive the admonishments of Your Illustrious Ladyship as expressions of your affection, but that I should leave off writing is quite im-

---

152. In this letter to an anonymous correspondent, Tarabotti derides her detractors who, jealous of her literary success, spread the rumor that she is not the true author of the works attributed to her.

153. The lay sisters (*converse*), as opposed to the choir nuns (*monache da coro*) entered into the convent with a smaller dowry and did not profess final vows. Inferior in convent heirarchy to the *monache da coro*, the *converse* performed much of the convent's menial labor.

154. The parish church that looked out on the Venetian campo of the same name.

155. This letter to Tarabotti's close friend expresses the nun's anguish at the death of Regina Donà, who was Tarabotti's convent sister and dear friend, and at Polani's departure from the convent.

possible. In this prison and in my illness nothing else will satisfy me. I have lost my friends, I am a shadow without you; whence if I had not this diversion, I would be dead by now. Physicians say that *contrariis contraria curantur*,[156] and to me it seems things are otherwise, because only a tempered pen can temper my suffering. It does not frighten me in the least to hear that my studies will cause my death, because I will not mind changing surroundings, varying my torments, conversing with other angels, and frequenting other demons. You know what Saint Paul said: *Cupio dissolvi, et esse cum Christo.*[157] And Petrarch also sang: *La morte è la fin d'una prigione oscura.*[158]

May the Blessed Lord do with me what he wishes; and you may avail yourself of my weakness, as I kiss you lovingly.

50

TO SIGNOR CAVALIER FRANCESCO PONA[159]

It is not difficult for me to believe that these gentleman academicians should be stunned at the appearance of my obscure hand before the light of Your Excellent Lordship. They presume that I believe myself to be a phoenix when they see me come before a sun to recover my strength, which would indeed be a rejuvenation, and so have reason to be astounded and amazed. But, Most Excellent Sir, these persons are quite mistaken, for I know and confess myself to be a bat unable to look into the shining rays of your splendors.

I am confident of receiving some degree of health from you who, absorbed in the study not just of letters, but of medicine, deign

---

156. This maxim, "Opposites are cured by opposites," can be attributed to Hippocrates but many authors cite it. Cf. H. Walther, *Lateinische Sprichwörter und Sentenzen des Mittelalters und der frühen Neuzeit in alphabetischer Anordnung* [Göttingen: Vandenhoeck & Ruprecht, 1982], 2:7, 424–25.

157. "I wish to be dissolved, and to be with Christ" (cf. Phil. 1:23, "But I am straitened between two: having a desire to be dissolved and to be with Christ, a thing by far the better.")

158. "Death is the end of dark imprisonment" (*The Triumphs of Petrarch*, trans. Ernest Hatch Wilkins [Chicago: University of Chicago Press, 1962], "Triumph of Death," 2:34, 61).

159. Francesco Pona (1594–1660), Veronese writer and doctor and a member of the Accademia degli Incogniti. Tarabotti in this and other letters turns to Pona for both literary and medical advice.

with the *lapis filosoforum*[160] of your kindness to touch my unhappy person in order to transform it from the base metal of its ailments to the prized gold of perfect health. It is impossible for me to render you proper thanks for such lofty favors, and so I hold my tongue.

Regarding the prescription you gave me, I conferred with these excellent gentlemen, who not only approved it as useful for my malady, but praised it highly. It remains for me to try it: and, if it is true that the patient's hope and faith in the doctor accomplish more than the doctor and the medicine themselves, I consider myself already cured. It is true that imagination has never sufficed for me, but this time your merit gives me great confidence.

For the rest, I say to Your Most Excellent Lordship that, being a nun, I wish to reprimand falsehoods, no matter how obliging and kind. Your intelligence should know, therefore, that Arcangela Tarabotti cannot be a wandering star, but rather a fixed star condemned to the heavenly cloister forever; and not finding here the holy and orderly hearts to which you refer, in consequence my errors come to be disorderly and worthy of reprehension and blame. May they be pitied by you, however, for that is enough for me, and I resign myself to Your Illustrious and Excellent Lordship.

51
TO FATHER N.[161]

It has come to my attention that Your Paternity has some doubt as to whether the *Convent Paradise* that has appeared in print can be the work of my own mind, as if you did not believe that a female, in amends for the first woman who destroyed a Paradise, could create a new one. Therefore, I am resolved to thank you for this opinion of yours that renders me ambitious, while your doubts seem to me extraordinary praise, since from so esteemed an intellect as yours I hear my compositions judged to be such that they could not be the daughters of so weak an intellect as my own.

---

160. The philosopher's stone, believed by alchemists to chage base metal into gold and silver.
161. In this letter, which is addressed most probably to Aprosio, Tarabotti refutes with brilliant sarcasm the accusation that she did not write the *Convent Paradise*.

From anyone else but Your Paternity, I would receive this lack of faith without comment, as befits one who aspires to no other glory but to follow the inspiration of her talent. And just as I know how to deride the arrogance of men who disdain the minds of women, so I know I can rest easy in this case in the purity of my conscience. But I cannot remain silent while a priest denies faith in Paradise. Perhaps you must do so in order to render my *Convent Paradise* akin to the heavenly one in which you do not believe.

Be that as it may, I profess myself obliged by your sentiments, begging you in my role as nun to retract your incredulity and declare yourself a convert to the true faith, if only to forbid me an even greater excuse to commit the sin of pride. I offer you my respects.

52

TO THE MOST ILLUSTRIOUS AND EXCELLENT PROCURATOR SILVESTRO VALIER[162]

Some days ago A., on behalf of Your Excellency's illustrious and excellent father,[163] informed me that, if I need favors, I must appeal to that purple[164] that no less enjoys being honored by your young person than it does being ruled by your wise heart. Now I have an occasion to carry out these orders, which hearten me such that, even if I am fearful, I am not hopeless, since such an eminent personage provided me a guarantee. Nevertheless I do not ask your pardon for my boldness, for that would seek out punishment, but I nevertheless expect it from the beauty and goodness that distinguish you as an angel given by God as a singular grace to our native city.

---

162. Silvestro Valier (1630–1700) was a powerful figure in the Venetian Republic. As a young man he was named *procuratore*, one of the republic's most prestigious posts. He also served for a time at the court of the Venetian pope Alessandro VIII (Pietro Ottoboni, also a correspondent of Tarabotti's). In 1694 he was elected doge. Here, Tarabotti asks him to help a young man connected to the family of her friend Betta Polani.

163. Bertucci Valier, also a correspondent of Tarabotti, elected doge in 1656.

164. Purple cloth symbolized high status. It was worn by cardinals and, in Venice, by the patrician class. See Pietro Molmenti, *La storia di Venezia nella vita privata dalle origini alla caduta della Repubblica* (Turin: Roux e Favale, 1885), 411.

Perfection already yearned for Your Excellency's most worthy qualities, but now that a most powerful sun at the dawn of its life is casting the light of high noon in your heart, you have been proven to be a heaven. Heaven protects the innocents and from Heaven come graces. Whence, from such a serene heaven, studded with so many merits, I am not without hope that I will receive your grace and protection for this young man who sinned out of ignorance. He will explain the urgency of his need and I implore such high protection since he is the representative of the Polani sisters, who are my dear friends and sole mistresses.[165]

I pray that Your Excellency's kindness, although I've done nothing to deserve it, deign to believe that an important cause moves me to bother you. I humbly kiss your excellent father's garments and pledge that I am Your Excellency's, etc.

53

TO THE MOST ILLUSTRIOUS SIGNOR N.[166]

The courteous promises Your Illustrious Lordship made to me on Saint Peter's day[167] nourished my heart with the hope to see you again soon, but because I see your return has been delayed, I fear that, with the example of that old saint who reneged on his promise to Christ, you too have decided it is acceptable not to keep your word to me. I know indeed how all men are tarred by the same brush, and thus it is no less a grave sin than madness to believe any of them. Nonetheless, I beseech Your Illustrious Lordship to come see me, and I promise that

---

165. From the *Letters* we discern that Tarabotti knew at least two women in the Polani family: her friend Betta and Betta's aunt, Claudia, also a nun in Sant'Anna.

166. This letter was probably intended for Girolamo Brusoni. Tarabotti and Brusoni were correspondents and, for a time, literary confidants, brought together by a shared outrage at the practice of forced monachization (Brusoni, like Tarabotti, was coerced into taking vows) and by common cultural interests. Their friendship deteriorated, however, into a literary rivalry. If Brusoni is the addressee, Tarabotti must have written this letter prior to the final dissolution of their relationship, for while she responds to insults by Brusoni, she also invites him to visit her in Sant'Anna.

167. Celebrated 29 June.

my conversation will not be combative or religious but literary since I have to discuss my literary reputation.[168]

It will nevertheless be trying and difficult to trust you since, with mockery and to my face, you derided that defect with which my father wanted perhaps to mark me as his daughter.[169] In any case I am proud of my limp because with it I will be sure to be among those who are invited to that great supper from which others of you, with straight bodies but limping souls and crippled deeds, have been excluded forever by our Father.[170] Adieu.

54

TO THE MOST ILLUSTRIOUS SIGNOR N.

In one of the coming days Your Illustrious Lordship may receive a letter directed to the illustrious Signor N., and I beseech you in your charity to deliver it to me by hand. If you deem letter carrying unworthy of your greatness, know that I will pay for this leaf of paper with many prayers to God for your happiness and success. You who so value your spirit will need be pleased at an offer that is so advantageous to you.

For the rest, those women who desire a husband should consecrate themselves to the god Giagantino or the goddess Prena[171] rather than listen to the chatter of Your Illustrious Lordship, who little cares for the prayers of virgins and has even less pity for the complaints of widows. I would have much to say on these matters, but words are wasted on vipers.

168. If Brusoni is the addressee, perhaps Tarabotti refers to the rumor (which he helped circulate), that she had not authored her own works, or else to her fear that Brusoni would write and publish on the theme of forced monachization, which she had already treated in unpublished works she shared with him. Brusoni did, in fact, publish a work on this subject, the *Tragic Loves* (*Amori tragici*; no publishing information; see Zanette, *Suor Arcangela*, 132).

169. That is to say, that Tarabotti had a limp like her father. Years later, in *Sogni di Parnaso* (1660), Brusoni repeated the insult, calling Tarabotti "crippled in body and mind" (*zoppa di corpo e di ingegno*).

170. The reference is to the parable of the marriage feast that Christ told his disciples (cf. Matt. 22:1–14).

171. Giagantino and Prena; gods of fertility seemingly invented by Tarabotti.

N. told me that the man who feigns himself deaf[172] would like money to give to the Ns. Your Illustrious Lordship must again put your tail in your ear at this request,[173] while I, all ambition and vainglory for the honors that I receive from your most kind visits, fan out my peacock feathers. It is true that while I strut about like a peacock, if I observe the lowness of my merit, I am quite mortified at myself, and shouting inside *Domine non sum digna*,[174] I dedicate myself to Your Illustrious Lordship, etc.

55

TO THE MOST SERENE PRINCE OF VENICE
FRANCESCO ERIZZO[175]

The generous proposition that Your Serenity made to your great Senate calls all voices and all tongues to acclaim you and bless you always. The fact that these most prudent senators showed their pleasure at the offer by accepting it showed the whole world that victories should be awaited from nowhere but your most invincible arm, which in other instances has rendered itself formidable to enemies. Your Serenity should glory in the fact that in the future the valor of the Alexanders and Caesars will cede place at the mention of your own, since they undertook their bold enterprises in the flower of youth, and you at the ripest age make yourself known and distinguished as leader no less of the military forces than of the city of Venice, not thirsting for empire but defending the Holy Faith.

I confess that these considerations make me envy the pens and the intellects of the great Loredano, the divine Dandolos, the glorious Valier, the renowned Businello, the most learned Crasso, and many

---

172. *'l capo di petra*, or stone-headed person; one who does not wish to hear.

173. *Si ponga … la coda nell'orecchio*. Medieval bestiaries attribute this action to serpents, who cover their "ears" with their tail. Tarabotti did not expect her correspondent, whom she describes as deaf to the pleas of women, to respond to this request either.

174. "Lord, I am unworthy." First verse of the Communion prayer (and cf. Matt. 8:8).

175. This encomiastic letter to the doge of Venice centers on the campaign against the Turks planned by Erizzo (who died before seeing it begin).

other erudite and worthy writers.[176] I envy, I say, their knowledge, which would enable me worthily to describe the glories of a prince who deserves the leadership of the world. But since my pen is too weak, I pray that Your Serenity, with merciful compassion, consider the devotion of my heart, as I, with varied words, bow to you and beseech that you please concede this act of great charity that will be explained to you by the person who brings you these letters. The request is honest, and I am not without hope that such a generous prince will grant it in these most holy holidays, when great heroes are wont to bestow graces.

In the meantime I will pray that Heaven lengthen your life's thread for a century, and that in the new year you may not only see the Ottoman Empire destroyed but that with new and fortunate victories you may bring it under the dominion of your most beloved republic, for which (no less than for Your Serenity) I pray armies of angels to help. I am and will always be your most humble servant and subject.

56
TO THE MOST ILLUSTRIOUS SIGNOR GIOVANNI DANDOLO

Bound by the prayers of a worthy personage whose commands I am obliged to obey, I must beg that Your Illustrious Lordship deign to present the attached recommendation to the excellent *avogador* Loredano,[177] whose kindness I would no sooner doubt than I would that the sun shines or that fire heats. I myself do not dare to fly to that great light; since I know that I am such a small moth, I fear that I would be reduced to ashes. I flee this chance to bring myself before one who, like God, has the power to hasten the life of mortals. I turn therefore to Your Illustrious Lordship in these holy days of confession, pardon, and grace.[178] I confess my temerity, plead for forgiveness, and am not without hope of grace, which is an act of great charity. If you

---

176. Giovan Francesco Loredano; Giovanni and Matteo Dandolo; Silvestro, Andrea, or perhaps Bertucci Valier; Giovan Francesco Busenello, and Nicolò Crasso; all acquaintances of Tarabotti.

177. A public prosecutor of the Venetian Republic.

178. Perhaps Lent, the period of penitence and reflection.

have need of prayers for your soul, embrace the occasion that is presenting itself to you, and I bow to you.

57
TO FATHER N.[179]

I don't know if Your Lordship has more greatly satisfied my senses or damned my soul by sending me your beautiful *Argiope* in these holy days. Well do I know that my mind, transported to the Parnassian paradise, left off its contemplation of the celestial one; and that my heart—held rapt as it read by those lines which were most perfect though drawn in black ink—was distracted from admiring the lines I should have read instead, traced with blood in the book of my Lord's humanity. I admired the noble intentions, the gentle words, the sweet turn of phrase, the marvelous verse, when I should have been contemplating the cruelest of intentions, the disgraceful words, the bitter gall, and the stunning way in which men rendered death unto Him who gave them life. I pitied the passions and the jealous blows of those earthly lovers instead of weeping for the suffering of Christ and considering the hammer blows that crucified our Savior. In short, I more greatly enjoyed this musical fable than the mournful tragedy of the Cross, and you are to blame. I confess myself before Your Illustrious Lordship, and while I await absolution, I heartily thank you for the honor and I hope that this Holy Week will be full of spiritual pleasure for you. To see Christ risen, I go with the Marys to the Holy Sepulcher, letting you go with the disciples to Emmaus;[180] and I offer you my respects.

179. Tarabotti addresses the Genovese friar Giovan Battista Fusconi, who had sent her a copy of his *Argiope* (Venice: Gio. Pietro Pinelli, 1649; the dedication is dated 29 December 1645), a musical drama that is the subject of this letter. Tarabotti praises the work, even as she reprimands the author for having distracted her from her religious responsibilities at Easter time. Fusconi was the secretary of the Accademia degli Incogniti according to Michele Maylender (Maylender, *Storia delle accademie d'Italia* [Bologna and Trieste: L. Cappelli, 1926–30]. See also C. G. Jöcher, *Allgemeines Gelehrten-Lexikon* (Leipzig: Johann Friedrich Gleditsch, 1750–51, ad vocem). Fusconi was closely linked to Loredano and edited a collection of *Love stories* (*Novelle amorose* [Venice: Guerigli, 1656]), to which numerous Incogniti members contributed.

180. Depicting herself as having been absolved of her "sin" (of reading secular literature) by Fusconi, Tarabotti affirms that she will rededicate herself to religious observance during this

58

TO THE MOST ILLUSTRIOUS SIGNOR LOUIS MATHAREL, RESIDENT OF FRANCE AT THE MOST SERENE REPUBLIC OF VENICE[181]

I am sending a small work of mine to Your Illustrious Lordship, in the hopes that you will help me by sending it to France, where—since freedom of belief is enjoyed there—it may perhaps not be looked at askance for having undergone a second baptism.[182] I beseech your kindness also to ask that person[183] that the book be printed in duodecimo and properly corrected, and that the typeface be bold but attractive.

I know that these reminders are unnecessary for Your Illustrious Lordship's intelligence, but I know that I will be no less pitied than helped by your kindness, which keeps me Your Illustrious Lordship's, etc.

59

TO THE MOST ILLUSTRIOUS AND EXCELLENT SIGNOR GIOVAN FRANCESCO LOREDANO[184]

I present myself before Your Illustrious Excellency with such bewilderment in my heart, caused by your most reverent homage, that my

---

holy period, just as her correspondent will do. Both of them, therefore, are about to make a (metaphorical) pilgrimage to the holy sites. Emmaus was the village near Jerusalem where the risen Christ appeared to two disciples (Luke 24:13–31).

181. Louis Matharel was the chargé d'affaires for France at Venice from February 1648 to November 1651 (Bittner and Gross, *Repertorium*, 1:244). His years in Venice were marked by tensions between France and the Serenissima (see Zanette, *Suor Arcangela*, 314–17). This letter concerns the second episode in the drawn-out history of Tarabotti's efforts to have her *Paternal Tyranny* printed in France.

182. It seems that Tarabotti planned to publish *Paternal Tyranny* in France under a new title, perhaps as *Innocence Deceived* (*La semplicità ingannata*), the title under which the work was in fact published, posthumously, in 1654.

183. Probably the same person mentioned in letter 132.

184. In this letter Tarabotti returns to Loredano a book he lent her and asks for another. Such exchanges attest to the important role played by Loredano as a mediator between Tarabotti and the intellectual world beyond the convent. She also mentions the condemnation of a misogynous work that Loredano probably translated into Italian and certainly helped to disseminate (see n. 191).

pen, aware as it is of its own imperfections, cannot express it. I believe I can truthfully say that even the pages I write upon blush on my behalf.

But since one cannot kneel before the confessor without giving back to others what belongs to them, in these holy days I send to Your Excellency your *Damsel*, which, having been married and then become a vagabond, indeed having shared herself with men, should no longer stay in this convent, nor does she any longer deserve the title of *Faithful Damsel*.[185] As I received it, of course, I return it to you, and I humbly renew my prayers for *The Soul of Zeno*,[186] which was without a doubt seen in octavo.[187]

Even Mistress N. is going around dressed like a pope,[188] perhaps to rekindle the memory of that Joan who, in accordance with Socrates's view, made clear to everyone that women are by nature able to command even the pontificate, even if many sorry souls howl the contrary.[189] But of them I believe scripture says, *Qui habitas in cælis-*

185. *Donzella … Donzella fedele*. Tarabotti plays on the title of a work she had borrowed from Loredano. It was authored by Antonio Santa Croce of the Olivetano order, a member of the Accademia degli Incogniti (on this episode, see Zanette, *Suor Arcangela*, 343).

186. *L'anima del Zeno*. Tarabotti requests this work not for herself but for Francesco Maria Zati, the Tuscan resident at Venice (see letter 214). It is at least the second time she asks Loredano for this book (see also letter 100), after having already asked Giovanni Dandolo (see letter 64). The book was greatly sought after and was supposedly based on the life of Renier Zeno (1575?–1647), the Venetian senator and great critic of the Roman Curia and of aspects of the Republic. It was purportedly modeled after the controversial *Soul of Ferrante Pallavicino* (*Anima di Ferrante Pallavicino*), which, in narrating the biography of Pallavicino, launched a fierce attack against the church. It is remarkable that others should have turned to Tarabotti, a nun, for such works, and demonstrates how closely connected she was to literary and even libertine circles. But, as Zanette notes (*Suor Arcangela*, 358–62), *The Soul of Zeno* did not actually exist: it was an invention (see letter 214), perhaps of Loredano himself, who alludes to it in the *Soul of Ferrante Pallavicino* ("Second Vigil," 73).

187. The rumors circulating in Venice about this nonexistent work even described its format, "in otto fogli."

188. Elegantly.

189. Tarabotti refers to the apocryphal but enduring legend, dating to the Middle Ages, of Pope Joan, a woman believed to have served as pontiff in the ninth century. By the sixteenth century the validity of the legend had begun to be called into question, a dismissal that Tarabotti links to other attacks on women. Socrates' discourse on women's equality is in Plato's *Republic* (bk. 5).

videbis eos.[190] I want to believe, however, that these wits will be more cautious in criticizing women now that the Holy Church has declared to the whole world that they are not only part of mankind, but that they also have divine qualities, and it strikes down those who deny that women have souls with the same punishments that it usually reserves for heretics who deny the existence of God.[191]

But to other matters. During his last visit Signor N. planted a suspicion that gives me no rest. He alleged that I have fallen from Your Excellency's grace, which I value more than any treasure. I cannot fathom the reason, nor do I want to believe that it is because, since you are not used to my frank and impassioned way of speaking, you misunderstood my words. I imagine instead that the frequency of my letters bothered you, and if this were the case I pledge never to write you again, but instead with the pen of my heart ceaselessly to mourn such a great loss, and I pledge myself to Your Excellency, etc.

60

TO THE MOST ILLUSTRIOUS SIGNORA BETTA POLANI

If a repentant sinner receives God's pardon, I am not without hope of the same from a goddess like Your Illustrious Ladyship. I repent not

---

190. "You who dwell in Heaven shall see them." Cf. Ps. 2:4, *Qui habitat in cælis irridebit eos* ("He that dwelleth in Heaven shall laugh at them"). It is unclear whether the text's variation on the Vulgate is intentional.

191. Tarabotti refers to the controversy over the publication of the treatise *That Women Are Not of the Same Species as Men* (*Che le donne non siano della specie degli uomini*), which denied that women had souls—an idea that was not only antifeminist in nature, but heretical. The treatise, written in Latin and published in Germany, was translated into Italian and published in Venice in 1647, where it was linked to the Incogniti; indeed it is likely that Loredano himself had a hand in it. See the edition by L. Panizza, with notes and an introduction in English, *Che le donne siano della spezie degli uomini: Women Are No Less Rational Than Men* (London: Institute of Romance Studies, 1994). The Inquisition reacted strongly to the treatise, placing the blame for it in 1649 on the printer Francesco Valvasense, who was already imprisoned, condemning him to an additional period of imprisonment at the discretion of the Sant'Uffizio, prohibiting him from continuing his work as a printer and forcing him to abjure (on Valvasense's trial, see M. Infelise, "Libri e politica nella Venezia di Arcangela Tarabotti," *Annali di Storia Moderna e Contemporanea* 8 [2002]: 40ff). This is likely the punishment to which Tarabotti alludes. The Inquisition did not attack more highly placed figures, such as Loredano.

having communicated my reverent respect in response to your most kind words. The reasons are understandable, however, since my illness always interferes with my ability to repay my debts. It suffices that my affection for you will be firmer than a rock in the wind or a cliff in the thundering sea. Please ask of me freely what you will, as I kiss you with all my heart and bow to you.

61

TO THE MOST SERENE PRINCE OF VENICE, FRANCESCO MOLINO[192]

That fame which, sung by Signor Pighetti, my dearest brother-in-law, has introduced you to me as the kindest prince to ever wield a scepter, stirs in me a most ardent desire to join the universal acclamation of the whole Senate and rejoice with Your Serenity that the Queen of Adria has wreathed your temples with the ducal diadem, to the consolation of our native city and the glory of the Venetian empire. Our blessed Lord placed you in the stormy skies of Italy as a rainbow of peace for its peoples, and He will ensure that the graces of your glorious horn will stretch further than the horn of plenty of fabled poets.[193] May His peoples rejoice, Thracians tremble, and the Ottoman hide,[194] as you see that Heaven has unexpectedly contributed to your success although you have no personal ambitions. The name alone of such a religious hero[195] will bolster your armies with courage and terrify foes. That man who in the past showed himself in bellicose matters to be a Caesar will now, with the prudence of peaceful decisions reveal him-

192. Francesco Molino succeeded Francesco Erizzo as doge of Venice (1646–55). In this encomiastic letter, Tarabotti offers him a copy of her *Convent Paradise*, just as she had to Erizzo.

193. Tarabotti refers to the *corno*, the cap worn by Venetian doges, so called for the horn-shaped protuberance at its back. The cap could by extension stand for the doge himself or for Venice.

194. As Molino was ascending to the office of doge, the war in Crete continued and the Turks prepared to invade Dalmatia. Tarabotti echoes the hopes of the Venetians that Molino might eliminate these threats against the Republic.

195. Tarabotti flatters her powerful correspondent by comparing him to a saint of the same name, but does not specify which of several saints by this name she intends.

self to be a Cato: *Ut utrunque tempus et bellorum et pacis recte possit gubernare.*[196]

In the meantime I will pray with ceaseless orations for armies of angels to help against the foes of the Holy Faith, and I send you a *Paradise* that you will appreciate at least because it is presented to you by the most passionate and faithful servant of your serene family. I mean by this Signor Giacomo,[197] who has never without tears mentioned the most august name of Your Serenity's brother, of dear memory.[198] Now I think his heart is too small a vessel to contain the overwhelming happiness he feels at this prudent Senate's election of your most worthy person, whose garments I reverently kiss.

62

TO THE MOST EXCELLENT SIGNOR GIACOMO PIGHETTI[199]

This morning, to satisfy Your Lordship, these words poured fourth from my pen, which, if they are not worthy of appearing in a prince's hand, are at least filled with the desire to fulfill your commands. Please receive them and correct them with the same sincere affection with which I send them to you. I know that the errors they contain in conceits, structure, and spelling are infinite, but I also know that your infinite kindness will pardon them. Please do not deprive me of these hopes and send these lines back corrected. Meanwhile, I will continue to pray for an abundance of happiness for you, and I affectionately kiss my lady sister.[200]

---

196. "That in times of war and peace he may govern properly." Cf. Justinian, *Institutiones*, bk. 1, "Proem."

197. Giacomo Pighetti, the brother-in-law who, according to Tarabotti at the beginning of the letter, praised the new doge (see also letter 62 to Pighetti).

198. Probably Domenico Molin, the writer and politician, who died in 1635.

199. This letter seems to address the composition of letter 61 above, written to congratulate the new doge Francesco Molin; Tarabotti was evidently encouraged in this undertaking by her brother-in-law Pighetti and now she asks him to look over her work.

200. Lorenzina, Tarabotti's sister and Pighetti's wife.

63

TO THE ILLUSTRIOUS MONSIGNOR OTTOBON, AUDITOR OF THE ROTA[201]

I see in the courteous reply of Your Illustrious Lordship the impossibility of the affair, and at the same time I realize my request was as inopportune as my boldness was worthy of chastisement. Nonetheless I am certain not only of kind understanding, but also of merciful pardon from the clemency of Your Illustrious Lordship, who is the exemplar of perfect goodness. *Tunc enim homo perfectus est quando amore et bonitate plenus.*[202] The appreciation with which you received my letters and honored me with your precious words assures me of this, as do your kind actions which, the less deserving I am of them, embarrass me all the more.

These, however, are the effects of your courtesy, celebrated by all as admirable, in virtue of which I dare to beseech you once again, if the opportunity presents itself, to assure this illustrious and excellent lady that, although my request was prompted by important personages, I willingly await in any case the punishment determined by her always infallible justice.

I would also like to say that I do not thank you for such honors because I confess myself incapable of thanking you, and I declare myself Your Illustrious Lordship's, etc.

201. Pietro Ottoboni (1610–91), auditor of the Sacred Roman Rota for fourteen years, was elected cardinal in 1652 and named bishop of Brescia in 1654. Upon the death of Pope Innocent XI in 1689, he was elected pontiff and took the name Alexander VIII. In this letter, Tarabotti asks for his help in an affair she does not specify. She mentions other correspondence the two exchanged, giving the impression that this letter does not represent an isolated case of contact, even though this is the only one in the collection explicitly directed to Ottobon.

202. "When man is full of love and goodness, then indeed is he perfect." The citation seems to be based on a saying that is found in various sources: *Tunc homo est perfectus, quando est charitate plenus* ("When man is full of charity, then is he perfect"; quoted in *De modo ben vivendi* [*PL* 184: 1208c], author uncertain, and also in Defensor Locociagensis, *Scintillae* [*PL* 88: 0599d]).

64

TO THE ILLUSTRIOUS SIGNOR GIOVANNI DANDOLO[203]

Although I may commit the sin of temerity in my frequent recourse to the kindness of Your Illustrious Lordship, I am not unworthy of pardon, while, recognizing my error, I kneel before you most devoutly to make my confession and await absolution through that penance imposed on me by your kind hand. It is certainly true that Your Illustrious Excellency, being accustomed openly to condemn the defects of others, is ill suited to the office of confessor, whose duty is to hide them. Nonetheless, knowing how great is the value of your prudence, I believe you know *Tempore congruo loqui et tempore congruo tacere.*[204]

I beg you, therefore, to favor me with the volume entitled the *Soul of Zeno.*[205] I am curious to speak with the souls of dead men, for, to tell the truth, one hears nothing but lies from the living. If Your Illustrious Lordship does not have power over their souls as you torment their bodies with the subtlest contradictions, please request it from that god who sent the *Soul of Pallavicino*[206] here to convent Hell.

Your Illustrious Lordship must in your kindness excuse me if I bore you too greatly, and I remain Your Illustrious Lordship's, etc.

65

TO THE MOST ILLUSTRIOUS SIGNOR COUNT PIETRO PAOLO BISSARI

As I continue to read with the greatest pleasure Your Illustrious Lordship's most erudite and charming books,[207] it feels as if my mind has

---

203. Tarabotti asks Dandolo for a coveted book that she cannot find.

204. "There is a time for speaking and a time for silence." A variation on Eccl. 3:1–7, "All things have their season, and in their times all things pass under Heaven.... A time to keep silence, and a time to speak."

205. See above n. 186.

206. That is, Loredano. *The Soul of Pallavicino* (*Anima del Pallavicino*) was a clandestinely published work in which the author, believed to be Loredano himself, enacts a fictional conversation with Ferrante Pallavicino, the apostate friar who was caught on his way to France and beheaded by religious authorities in Avignon (on the topic, see also letter 15).

207. On Bissari's works, see letter 2.

entered a delightful Paradise where I find not only the noblest flowers of verse but the most mature fruits of true learning.

> *Perché nel lume de' suoi bei concetti*
> *Tanta dolcezza scorge alma ben nata*
> *Che non ricerca in terra altri diletti.*[208]

I read and admire, and in admiring I adore the inventiveness, the beauty, and the variety of such varied and precious conceits. I would like to be a bee that I might suck the honey from one of the lovely flowers of your eloquence, but I realize that, all your words being charming and sweet, I cannot imbibe them without harming my own intellect, which is incapable of such goodness, remembering that *Amor non recipit de impossibilitate solatium, nec accipit de difficultate remedium.*[209] I find, however, even in these pleasures, things that, bringing a blush to my face, lift me out of myself, while I feel myself—of no stature in my own person and intellect—raised up by your celebrated pen and acclaimed as that which I am not.[210] But since I do not believe I am such, I accept the judgment of Your Illustrious Lordship, while Saint Jerome teaches us: *Non ideo te bonum aestimes, si bonus praediceris.*[211] On bended knee, therefore, I wish to thank you, but my hand slows the course of my pen, because my mind, confused by the marvels of Your Illustrious Lordship's own pen, can form nothing but confused expressions. I however retain so great an awareness of your infinite merit that I confess to being Your Illustrious Lordship's, etc.

---

208. "Because in the light of your beautiful conceits, / The well-born soul discovers such sweetness / That it seeks no other pleasure on this earth."

209. "Love does not take solace in the impossible, nor does it accept a cure for difficulties." This saying was transmitted in various sources; see for example Petrus Chrysologus, *Sermones* (*PL* 52: 595C).

210. Tarabotti perhaps refers to Bissari's praise of her and other women in the first volume of his *Scorse olimpiche*. Bissari writes: "Tarabotti shines like a new Archangel, and, divine in her habits, immortal in her compositions, she shows herself, under the heavens of a sacred cloister, not to lack the other qualities of an Archangel" (11).

211. "You do not therefore deem yourself to be good if you are predicted to be good." Saint Jerome is cited in the widely read patristic collection compiled in the ninth century; see Defensor Locociagensis, *Scintillae* (*PL* 88: 646C).

66

TO THE ILLUSTRIOUS SIGNOR MATTEO DANDOLO[212]

The prudence of Your Illustrious Lordship, which undertakes nothing by chance, demonstrated your maturity to me even in the matter of printing *Paternal Tyranny.* Not having denied me your efforts in response to my requests, perhaps so as to not leave me, alone, deprived of your kind manner, you let the outcome illustrate how inopportune were my demands and how bold my temerity. Furthermore, since you confer nothing save favors of great import, you chose to mortify my audacity by not granting that through you I might know where N. resides. It is as if pleas for favors so slight are an inconvenience for the greatness of people like you. My aim, however, was not blameworthy, for not excessive boldness but excessive confidence in the courteous qualities of Your Illustrious Lordship caused me to commit so grave an error, from which, because *abissus abissum invocat,*[213] a greater error was born, which was that of not availing myself of your courteous inclinations.

Here, then, is a third, which is that of bringing the imperfections of my pen before your high intellect, which, known by all men of letters as admirable, exceeds in sublimity that of other men as men exceed other animated beings.

If I sin too greatly in boldness, with reverent trepidation I ask your compassion, kissing Your Illustrious Lordship's hands.

67

TO THE MOST EMINENT AND EXCELLENT SIGNOR ENRICO CORNARO

I have immediately carried out the command of Your Eminent Lordship with such a sense of consolation that my pen is not sufficient to describe it. I mean that I fulfilled it with regard to my works, about which you recently inquired. I considered it my great fortune, however, that they did not wander before the eyes of the most sublime

---

212. Tarabotti asks her correspondent for a favor, although he has refused two other requests from her. She expresses polite annoyance at these refusals.

213. Cf. Ps. 41:8, "Deep calleth on deep."

intellect that exists today, and I confess that still I would prefer to conceal them from the divinity of your spirit; but your authoritative commands persuade them to present themselves with great humility for your most kind critique.

Your intelligence will see a chaos of errors and a most imperfect *Paradise*. Nor should the *Antisatire* be condemned by your courtesy. I am certain, however, that your noble soul knows only to be kind in judging and measured in condemning the writings of a woman who, unschooled in letters, can well hope for compassion from wise men, among whom Your Eminent Lordship is second to none.

I ask you to receive and enjoy from the illustrious Lady N. this infinitesimal sign of our immense obligation, and together we offer you our respects.

68
TO THE MOST ILLUSTRIOUS SIGNORA N.[214]

I immediately carried out the commands of Your Illustrious Ladyship by informing A. of the age, profession, and expectations of the bridegroom. I found her most willing to take him, as long as he does not ask too much and is content with a dowry appropriate to her status. One thousand ducats are difficult to put together at this time; she has many sisters and little fortune, times are hard, and needs are great. She smiled upon hearing that he is a young man; she asked if he had a shop, and if he does not, I believe that he will now have a good opportunity with the dowry for a good income, furnishings, and property. It seems to me he ought to be satisfied. And to know whether she is a good and upstanding woman, you must seek the sieve of the Vestals,[215]

---

214. This letter describes with great clarity how nuns, from within the convent, helped to arrange marriages. In the negotiations described in this letter, Tarabotti places herself solidly on the side of the bride, who was probably a boarder in the convent and of whom Tarabotti was evidently quite fond.

215. Valerius Maximus (*Factorum e dictorum memorabilium*, 18, 1.5) and Pliny the Elder (*Naturalis historiae*, 28.2) report that the vestal virgin Tuccia, unjustly accused, carried a sieve full of water from the Tiber to the temple to prove her innocence.

for I don't recommend that you trust these Thomases[216] who could taint her virtue with a single touch.

I am not pleased with the agreement of my lady with M.; nonetheless, I trust your intelligence and your reason. At least establish that the goods should return home upon the death of the one who now unjustly usurps them.[217] In any case the chariot of the moon led by a mule implies that, since the moon is cold and barren, and likewise the mule cannot reproduce, he should therefore not place his hope in posterity.[218] May Your Illustrious Ladyship excuse the bother I cause you, nor say anything to Lady N. with regard to this match.

I was about to seal this letter, and Lady N. came to me with more favors from Your Illustrious Ladyship, and so I respond.[219] The proposal for a husband[220] for A. is a bit low; I do not know if it is a joke or serious. Proposing an upstanding man is a thing of repugnance in these times, and his status as a widower also speaks against him, for when wives die young you can believe that it is as a result of their husbands' mistreatment. But let us leave aside these jests; in all seriousness I say to Your Illustrious Ladyship that I would like to marry off A., as long as she can be well placed. Her dowry should befit her station, and if women are crosses to be adored only when gilded, you may blame the wicked greed of men who sold God himself for a few coins.[221]

---

216. That is, the opinion of those skeptics who would doubt the girl's chastity only because it is their nature to distrust everything; their skepticism can create ruin. The allusion is to the Apostle Thomas who doubted Christ's resurrection and wanted to touch his body before believing (John 20:24–30).

217. Tarabotti expresses her disapproval of a certain financial agreement among unspecified parties.

218. Tarabotti warns that the greediness of M. can only be shortlived, since he will have no heirs. For the image of the carriage and the moon, see Vincenzo Cartari, *Immagini degli dei de gl'antichi* (Venice: Tomasini, 1647), 58.

219. Before sending this letter, Tarabotti receives another missive from her correspondent regarding the marriage negotiations for A., who is presumably the same bride mentioned above. Her correspondent seems to have proposed another match, a suitor of whom Tarabotti disapproves.

220. In the original text, Tarabotti employed the abbreviation "m." for *marito*, or husband, here.

221. That is, Judas.

Tomorrow, which is a day of devotion, I will await Your Illustrious Ladyship not only to discuss this marriage, but also to discuss the concerns of those female wards who, sheltered under the mantle of your protection, hope for relief from nowhere else. I ask you for the favor of this visit, on the condition previously established with Lady N., which is not to disturb her ever again.

In the meantime I leave it to you to admit whether you are defaulting on your promise to favor me, who is Your Illustrious Ladyship's, etc.

69

TO THE ILLUSTRIOUS SIGNORA N.[222]

I cannot help but complain of the scant charity of Your Illustrious Ladyship. I suffer greatly from the constriction in my chest. I have no priest, nor can I receive a courteous favor from you. I was taught that, for a remedy, I should place a wolf's skin over the area that pains me, but never having been able to find one, I recall that in the Gospel our Lord calls wicked men wolves.[223] Therefore I beg Your Illustrious Ladyship to intercede on my behalf with the excellent *avogadore* so that, should the occasion arise to condemn someone, he might skin him and send me the hide. If it improves my health I will forever pray for your success, and to Your Illustrious Ladyship, etc.

---

222. In this letter of light tone but serious intent, Tarabotti scolds her correspondent, who evidently had not fulfilled a promise that regarded her health. Here uses her health, which often provides a tragic strain in the *Letters*, to make a joke at men's expense.

223. This comparison appears several times in the Gospels: see, for example, Matt. 7:15 and 10:16 and Luke 10:3.

70

TO SIGNOR N.[224]

Your Eminent Lordship, who is full of grace, seeks to fulfill every measure of kindness, and thus congratulates me assuming that my book has been printed, for which I warmly thank you. You should know, however, that I believe this to be Grossi's invention,[225] as I shall explain more clearly in person. It is true that I received the marchioness's letter[226] delivered to the Lumaga brothers,[227] but I do not understand from it that the work has been printed, nor much less find news from Monsieur Martini.[228] I do not place faith in words; I need actions to appease me, otherwise I will do as I wrote previously in a letter to the same lady.[229] I offer you my respects.

224. In this letter to an anonymous addressee, Tarabotti again takes up the topic of her *Paternal Tyranny*, which she had entrusted to a Frenchman so that he would print it in his homeland. Her correspondent had told her that the book had indeed been printed; the nun does not believe the news because she distrusts her French agent.

225. No further information is available about Grossi, not mentioned elsewhere in Tarabotti's letters.

226. Marchioness Renée Clermont de Gallerande, a correspondent of Tarabotti's, had been an intermediary in Tarabotti's attempt to have her *Paternal Tyranny* printed in France. Tarabotti had entrusted it to her when the French delegation was preparing to return home. The letters to the marchioness in Tarabotti's collection reveal the frequent tensions that characterized her interactions with the noblewoman, born primarily of the marchioness's failed promises to help her publish her controversial work.

227. Upon departure from Venice, the French delegation had charged the Lumaga (or Lumago) brothers, perhaps bankers, to oversee their financial affairs, as we see in letter 149. In another instance, the ambassador Bretel de Grémonville, departing for France, writes to the doge on 14 October 1647, asking that the three thousand ducats necessary to pay his debts be given to the Lumago brothers (ASV, Esposizioni Principi, Collegio, Registro 56, 154r).

228. Martini, whose identity is uncertain, evidently remained in Venice after the French delegation had left.

229. Tarabotti seemingly refers to another missive (letter 149), in which she threatens "disgrace and blame before the whole world" if her *Paternal Tyranny* were to be printed under another's name.

71
TO THE ILLUSTRIOUS SIGNORA GUID'ASCANIA ORSI[230]

After having sent for the *Olive*[231] hundreds of times, at last a gentleman retrieved it from the messenger. Truly the work is wonderful, and worthy no less of the intellect of Your Illustrious Ladyship who formed it than of our most serene sir who will receive it. It would be a pity if it were lost; and from you, who are made of graces, nothing could come to me if not graces and supernatural favors. To be able to reciprocate for once the debt of so many obligations to you is the ultimate goal I seek. But, my illustrious Lady, I blush at presuming to return celestial graces with earthly favors. Your kindness must command me, therefore, that by my actions I may give you proof of my heart's devout and reverent observance, with which affectionately revering you I declare myself wholly ready for your commands and I dedicate myself eternally to Your Illustrious Ladyship, etc.

72
TO THE MOST ILLUSTRIOUS AND EXCELLENT SIGNOR ANDREA VALIERO[232]

A star most well disposed to my fortunes led Your Excellency to hear my imploring requests, which you granted with great kindness. I speak of the graces of that divine sonnet with which you deigned to ornament my present composition, for which I swear that I could nei-

---

230. This letter attests to the nun's literary ties, which were maintained through reciprocal favors. Orsi had sent a work to Tarabotti, which the nun had lost and then found and will now give to "our most serene sir," probably a reference to the doge Francesco Erizzo (see letter 19).

231. We can presume that the *Olive* was a literary work of Orsi's, a writer; it is probably the *Hieroglyphic Olive Branch* to which Tarabotti refers in letter 19. No trace has been found of Orsi's literary works (which perhaps were never printed), save a madrigal reproduced in Graziosi, "Arcipelago Sommerso," 171.

232. Tarabotti here thanks Andrea Valiero (1615–91) for the dedicatory sonnet to Vittoria della Rovere, which appeared anonymously in her *Antisatire*. Beyond his roles as senator and general, Valiero was a poet and historian; he wrote *La storia della guerra di Candia* (Venice, 1679) and some works that were never published. Cf. Weaver, *Satira e Antisatira*, 34; Cappellari, *Campidoglio*, 4:429–30.

ther hope for nor expect greater applause or glory. Your Excellency understood the lowness and crudeness of the construction; in order for it not be recognized as a poor, unsophisticated hovel, you honored me by placing a sumptuous and noble façade before it. This was composed of the noblest marbles of charming conceits made of such sparkling and precious jewels of eternity that it lent a certain splendor to the shadows of my ignorance while also blinding readers to the many errors of my *Antisatire*. I do not know how to express my obligation to you except to confess my pen's inability to do so. I will thank you, therefore, even if I am well aware I know not how to and cannot do so.

Your Illustrious Lordship's composition is nonetheless marred in one aspect, for since your glorious name does not appear there, nor does it appear incognito elsewhere than in my book, it will be adored by all people just like the Athenians adored an unknown God. I, idolizing your divine qualities and daring to bring my own imperfections before your eyes, most humbly bow to you.

73

TO THE MOST ILLUSTRIOUS AND EXCELLENT SIGNOR LORENZO PISANI[233]

I send an earthly *Paradise* to Your Illustrious Excellency so that your intelligence may recognize that the pen that knows how to tell the truth about men's tyranny also knows how to imitate God (without arrogance, however) while it builds Paradises and Infernos, not forgetting to make a Purgatory for unhappy women as well.[234] Therefore, if Your Excellency wishes to enjoy the delights of Paradise (and not to declare yourself a Calvinist by not believing in Purgatory), you should

---

233. It is not clear which Lorenzo Pisani is Tarabotti's addressee in this brief letter, the only one in the collection directed to him. Perhaps it is Lorenzo son of Marco (1585–1645), Head of the Council of Ten; alternatively, it could be Lorenzo son of Bortolo (1611–48), member of the Quaranta (the appeals court of Venice) (ASV, M. Barbaro, *Arbori de patritii veneti*, ad vocem). Tarabotti might have known him through a Prudenzia Pisani who was a nun at Sant'Anna according to some convent documents from 1644–50 (cf. APV, Collezione Antica, "Monalium," 1644, 1647, 1650). In this letter Tarabotti sends Lorenzo Pisani her *Convent Paradise* as proof of her literary talents.

234. The references are to Tarabotti's works: her *Convent Paradise*, *Convent Hell*, and her *Purgatory of Unhappily Married Women* (which has been lost).

use your authority in such a manner that everyone may understand that without Purgatory, one cannot enjoy the blessings of Heaven. All women will then be forced to applaud your great merit and admit you as a guardian angel of their sex, and I to declare myself always devoted to the sublime qualities of Your Excellency, etc.

74

TO THE MOST ILLUSTRIOUS
SIGNOR GIOVANNI DANDOLO[235]

Because I was in bed afflicted with a most powerful dizziness, only now have I heard how Your Illustrious Lordship's excellent father-in-law has passed on from this valley of tears to the blessed lands of Paradise, and more with the pain of my heart than with my actual pen I grieve with you. Your Illustrious Lordship must believe that I feel my soul eternally obliged to share in your difficulties and in those of your illustrious house. I wish it a happiness suited to its merits that I might also rejoice, as is the duty of your true and most devoted servants, among whom I am second to none. I devote myself to Your Illustrious Lordship, etc.

75

TO THE MOST EMINENT AND EXCELLENT
SIGNOR NICOLÒ CRASSO[236]

Eager to receive two exceptional favors from the kindness of Your Eminent Lordship, I have been trying from time to time for a number of days to take up pen to beseech you; but then recognizing that I have no merit with you other than my internal devotion, I fling it far away.

235. A condolence letter written upon the death of Dandolo's father-in-law, Zaccaria Gabriel.

236. One of four letters addressed to the writer Nicolò Crasso (1586–1655c.), friend to Tarabotti and member of the Accademia degli Incogniti; Crasso also corresponded with Loredano (see Loredano, *Lettere, prima parte* [Venice: Guerigli, 1665], 8). Crasso had ties to Cesare Cremonini, the controversial Paduan philosopher who encountered trouble for his heterodox views regarding the immortality of the soul. Here, Tarabotti asks for verses he had composed for Giovan Francesco Busenello (see n. 237) and alludes to a request described more fully in letter 76: that her correspondent compose the introduction to one of her works.

Finally the prompting of the person in need and my knowledge of the generosity of your noble heart give me courage to come reverently to beg you for that most kind response you gave to one of the compositions of the illustrious Busenello.[237] I hope also to immortalize a most beautiful and virtuous gentlewoman[238] with the lines of your esteemed pen, more miraculous than Apelles's brush.[239] If Your Eminent Lordship will deign to favor me, let me know and I will explain more thoroughly the requirements of this lady. Meanwhile I beg on bended knee for your kind pardon as I humbly make my request by reverently kissing your hands.

76
TO THE SAME[240]

If my face blushed at writing to Your Eminent Lordship, now my heart has taken comfort in the reading of your most kind letter. I certainly will not be able to send you the response you merit, but you who are all kindness will take pity on the imperfection of my intellect no less than of my pen, as my thankfulness in pure devotion comes to thank you to the best of its weak ability. I enjoyed the effect of those most graceful verses, I felt sorry for the effort you had to make to remember them, and I remain eternally obliged, but I recognize that I am a Tantalus amid the waters.[241]

---

237. Giovan Francesco Busenello (1598–1659) was a lawyer, librettist, poet, and member of the Accademia degli Incogniti; he composed poetry and plays that were set to music, some by Claudio Monteverdi. Tarabotti repeatedly expresses admiration for his work; from her *Letters* we learn that Busenello visited Tarabotti in the convent parlor.

238. Regina Donà, the dear friend and convent sister memorialized in Tarabotti's *Tears*, to which she refers here.

239. Famed early Hellenistic painter (fourth century BCE), known for his portraits of Alexander the Great.

240. In this letter, Tarabotti thanks Crasso for the composition he wrote for Busenello that she had requested in letter 75. She also explains in more detail the poems that she would like Crasso to compose for the *Tears* that memorialized Regina Donà. Two of his poems appear in the work.

241. That is, she cannot reciprocate as she would like. Tantalus, in Greek mythology the son of Zeus, who, having abused the hospitality of his hosts, was punished by being immersed

As for the composition that I desire and that Your Eminent Lordship courteously promises me, the subject will be an oration I am sending to you that I wrote some time ago.[242] This gentlewoman was of most noble, or rather serene, birth, tall, of notable beauty, and endowed with exceptional virtue; she was my sister in affection, and indeed her love grew always closer to the highest degrees of an uncorrupted and perfect friendship. She died at around thirty-six years of age and I feel compelled to reciprocate her love with whatever weak talents God has granted me. But since I know that my pen is unable to express even a small particle of this saintly soul's merit, I take recourse to the heavens of Your Eminent Lordship's knowledge to crown her with praise in this world just as I believe her to be crowned *Regina* in the other.[243] Such is the promise of the kindness of Your Eminent Lordship, who knows how to favor even those who don't deserve it, and I bow to you reverently.

77
TO THE ILLUSTRIOUS SIGNORA BETTA POLANI

Your Illustrious Ladyship's kindness continues to honor me with your most precious words, and I am not able to respond promptly, since I am tormented by a most stubborn pain that leaves me no comfort at all. Please have compassion, for pity's sake, on my state, rather than condemning me as it seems I deserve if one judges by appearances only, and I bow to you, kissing you with affection.

78
TO THE MOST EMINENT AND EXCELLENT SIGNOR
ENRICO CORNER

I bring wishes of happiness to Your Eminent Lordship in these holy festivities along with my bothersome requests for visits in these days of rest. In the former your kindness will see the continuation of my

---

up to his neck in water he could not drink, looking up at trees heavy with fruit he could not eat.

242. The *Tears* for Regina Donà.

243. Regina, the name of Tarabotti's friend and the Latin or Italian for "queen."

perpetual fidelity and will appreciate my heartfelt affection, and in the latter you will understand the urgency of my need, which is great. I will not continue with other formalities to excuse my temerity. Instead, remembering your kind acts, I will conclude by praying His Divine Majesty that, just as on the night of the most holy birth all the deserts of Libya blossomed,[244] so may all the flowers and fruits of contentment and glory blossom in Your Eminent Lordship, and may a continuous peace and tranquility accompany you for a century. I remain Your Eminent Lordship's, etc.

79

TO SIGNOR N.[245]

I have received a *Paradise* that seems to have been issued from Hell, so blackened by smoke is it. Kindly exchange it, I beg you, because I must send it to an important personage.

 Please greet Lady Paulina warmly in my name, and tell her that I await a visit from her along with your baby, who has truly remained impressed in my mind, since I saw how he exceeds others of his age in his size; and in his beauty I consider him a true angel destined to defend my *Paradise*, having been born a twin to it.[246]

 May God keep you and content you.

---

244. According to a prophesy in the Old Testament, the earth would burst into blossom upon the birth of Jesus Christ (see Isa. 35:1–2).

245. In this letter to an addressee identified only through the name of his wife, Paulina, Tarabotti complains of the condition in which she has received a copy of her *Convent Paradise* and asks her correspondent (perhaps a printer or bookseller) for another copy.

246. Tarabotti refers to her correspondent's son as "twin" to her book since he was born at the same time as her book was published.

80

TO THE MOST ILLUSTRIOUS SIGNOR GIOVANNI DANDOLO[247]

Since the authoritative voice of Your Illustrious Lordship calls Fortune—which is always obliged to obey the higher deities—"propitious," I can do nothing but expect a happy outcome in the wedding of Lady N. That she is with me in heart I cannot believe; but given (not conceded) that this could be, I would like to unite her heart with my own to make a twin star to place in the heavens of your favor, where there are stars so courteous that they shine light even on my imperfections. From your own reflection, Illustrious Signor, in the dark and jumbled sea of my ink, you see shine forth those marvels that, perhaps hyperbolically, you mention to me. The wise say that wonder is the daughter of ignorance, but to me it seems that it is the mother of wisdom, since it was wonder at what they observed that led the ancient philosophers to discover all of the sciences. I want to conclude that Your Illustrious Lordship, in your wonder at my unpolished writing, clearly shows the refinement of your intellect, while, penetrating perhaps too deeply in their deficiencies, you know not how to stay on the surface of my simplicity, and thus you marvel at my excessive boldness. That you offer yourself as my servant is too great an impropriety, since Heaven willed me to be born subject and therefore servant.

But to other matters. This morning I had to use that gift from the excellent *avogador* Loredano given to me the other day by Your Illustrious Lordship. I would like very much to have a letter in favor of our convent against those in the Vicentino[248] who took from us, despite the prohibitions against doing so, certain crop yields which by right belonged to the Signors Aviani.[249] I want it to be quite firm. If

247. This letter to Dandolo intertwines literary and practical matters. Tarabotti mentions Dandolo's praise of certain of her works (playing on the "marvelous," a common Baroque motif). She also speaks of the marriage of a certain Lady N.; and, finally, of the daily business of the convent, now involved in a legal dispute.

248. The land surrounding Vicenza, in this period under the control of Venice.

249. This reference remains rather oblique. Tarabotti seeks the intervention of Dandolo in spurring Loredano to defend the rights of Sant'Anna with regard to its lands in the Vicentino, which were perhaps being used illegally. The Aviani mentioned here may have had ties to the convent through a sister Lugrezia Aviana, who appears in a series of convent docu-

you manage to obtain it, Your Illustrious Lordship may in fulfillment of your desire receive what you sought from the illustrious Signor N., and I bow to you.

81

TO THE MOST ILLUSTRIOUS SIGNORA ANDRIANA MALIPIERO[250]

The bitterness of the pain that pierced my soul upon the passing of Your Illustrious Ladyship's sister and my cherished friend has not allowed me to fulfill with you those duties of condolence which befit such a terrible loss. But I need consolation myself, since such a dear and affectionate companionship, which I enjoyed for many years, has carried away my heart and has left me more half dead than alive. Neither can the illustrious lady your aunt find peace, and she says that if our most beloved Regina was Your Illustrious Ladyship's sister and my friend, to her she was a daughter, since she raised her from a most tender age.[251]

Let your prudence take consolation; in fact let us all console ourselves and resign ourselves to the will of the Lord, saying with Saint Job, *Dominus dedit, Dominus abstulit.*[252] She is certainly in Heaven and

> *A chi piange per lei, per lei sospira*
> *O lo sprezza o no 'l cura o non l'ascolta.*[253]

---

ments from 1652 regarding a dispute, which she eventually won, with her brother Francesco over the patrimony of their father Gerolamo (cf. ASV, Sant'Anna di Castello, b. 17; Lugrezia's name also appears in several rolls of nuns [APV, Collezione Antica, "Monalium," 1644, 1647, 1650]).

250. The recipient of this letter of condolence was a noblewoman who was the sister of Tarabotti's dear friend and convent sister Regina Donà, recently deceased. Andriana Donà married Giovanni Malipiero on 30 June 1621 (ASV, Avogaria di Comun, *Libro d'oro*, Reg. 4, c. 164v). Tarabotti dedicated the *Tears*, composed in Regina's honor, to Malipiero.

251. No other Donà appears among the chapter nuns in 1633, 1647, or 1650, but it is possible that the aunt to whom Tarabotti refers was a maternal aunt or a relative who lived outside the convent.

252. Job 1:21, "The Lord gave, and the Lord hath taken away."

253. "Whoever cries for her, sighs for her / Either disdains Him or cares for and heeds Him not."

And I commend myself to Your Illustrious Ladyship with the pen of my heart.

82
TO SIGNOR N.[254]

I could not respond to the graceful jests of Your Lordship because I was compelled to jest with the doctor, the confessor, or the surgeon. I have been in bed since the middle of this past January, always in mortal languor, and now at the appearance of spring my attacks have blossomed in such a way that, renewed so frequently, they would frighten even the most hearty constitution. I see my hopes, on the verge of birth, die. I mean, when I begin to recover, I languish again. So be it.

Lady N. will certainly come on Monday. I leave it up to Your Lordship to act as you wish, since I only intend to please you, to whom I belong, etc.

83
TO THE MOST ILLUSTRIOUS AND EXCELLENT SIGNOR FRANCESCO MARIA ZATI, RESIDENT OF TUSCANY AT THE MOST SERENE REPUBLIC OF VENICE[255]

Since Divine Bounty has allowed me yet to suffer amid the miseries of this life, I must not carelessly neglect the duty demanded by the debt of my fidelity to wish Your Illustrious Lordship in the impending most holy festivities such joys and contentments as filled the world at the birth of the infant Christ. In that blessed night, the holy shepherds saw the earth blossom and other marvels. I pray Heaven to see marvelous graces blossom for Your Illustrious Lordship in the new year, graces commensurate with the greatness of your merit, which I sincerely admire. Beseeching that the enclosed letter be delivered, I most reverently bow to you and remember Your Illustrious Lordship, etc.

---

254. Tarabotti discusses with her unnamed correspondent her poor health and also some business, described only obliquely, between herself, her addressee, and an unidentified lady.

255. In this letter, one of five addressed to Zati, Tarabotti offers Christmas wishes and asks that he give a letter to Vittoria della Rovere (letter 84).

84

TO HER MOST SERENE HIGHNESS VITTORIA MEDICI DALLA ROVERE, GRAND DUCHESS OF TUSCANY[256]

With the most humble pleas that can come from a respectful heart devoted to the greatness of Your Serene Highness, I pray you most humbly bowed not to disdain these words of mine which aim to pledge to you my most reverent servitude and to wish you holy festivities filled with all the felicities that Heaven can bestow. Please enjoy these regards, while I deem it superfluous to ask pardon for my boldness from your incomparable kindness. I predict also with the new year new prosperity for your glorious person and famous victories for your serene house, of which I am and will always be (no less than of Your Most Serene Highness) a most humble servant.

85

TO THE MOST ILLUSTRIOUS ANDREA VENDRAMINO[257]

Your Illustrious Lordship's cherished aunt and my beloved friend, in her passing from this valley of tears to Heaven's most delightful chambers, took my heart with her and I can therefore find no words of condolence commensurate to the inestimable loss. You, who are all prudence, console yourself with the bitterness of the pain, since I, having lost half of myself and that true friend which the wise man deemed a treasure,[258] will be able to take no comfort but that which will be supplied by the hope of seeing her again in Paradise.

---

256. This letter of good tidings for Christmas and the new year is that to which Tarabotti refers in the previous letter to Francesco Maria Zati (letter 83); it may be dated to 16 December, 1645 (see the manuscript copy in the ASF, Mediceo del Principato, 6152, c.32r [Medioli, "Reliability," 90]).

257. Andrea Vendramino was the nephew of Regina Donà, the "beloved friend" to whom she refers in this letter—probably Andrea son of Giovanni (1628–1686); his father married the sister of Regina and of Andriana Donà in Malipiero (another correspondent of Tarabotti).

258. Perhaps a reference to Sirach 6:14, "A faithful friend is a strong defence: and he that hath found him, hath found a treasure."

86
TO THE MOST EXCELLENT SIGNOR GIACOMO PIGHETTI[259]

If I carefully consider my interests, I find no reason valid enough to persuade me that my book deserves to come to any other light but that of fire. Please don't urge me to do anything else, most excellent Lordship, so that I won't have to count you too among the deceivers. My supreme ignorance does not permit that such nonsense, coming from a mind shut away without the light of letters, appear before the eyes of the world to be subjected to the malicious censure of men. The brief time in which I composed the volume manifests it as an intellectual miscarriage and a caprice built on air, provoked however by a most just cause. My religious status detests such profane writing, and my pen must not serve to trumpet a failure that obscures the beauty of humanity and, to put it better, would impoverish the heart of eloquence. Our century is prolific enough in its own troubles and won't want to be defamed with a style that is a stylus of its abuses. Men will certainly not reform their ways at the sight of their ugly habits; indeed they will say that I have had occasion to experience the multiplicity of their deceptions. They will certainly be lying, because, just from reading the words our first father said upon creation, I learned not to believe any of them.[260] Women are criticized enough in general by writers without my putting myself in danger of being the target of their slanderous tongues. I must not provoke such an indomitable creature since I lack the learning to undertake my defense.

I appeal to you, who quite prudently know these to be infallible truths, to give back to me all those most imperfect writings. I do not doubt your incomparable kindness. Meanwhile, I give you my word of honor that the false praises that could come to me from the

259. Here Tarabotti asks her brother-in-law Pighetti to return her manuscript of the *Antisatire*, claiming that she does not intend to publish it (although it is evident in other letters that she means to do just that). The cordial relationship evident here between the two would be interrupted when Pighetti showed the manuscript to Aprosio and encouraged him to write a response to it. In time, Tarabotti and her brother-in-law would make peace, and she lamented his death in a later missive (letter 16).

260. Tarabotti traces the root of male dishonesty to Adam, who, she says elsewhere (see letter 122), blamed Eve to excuse himself.

virile sex do not entice me at all, rather they persuade me to avoid them; and fondly I offer you my respects and send greetings to the good graces of the lady my sister,[261] whom I kiss dearly.

87

TO SIGNOR N.[262]

From that text from which, since it is entitled *Paradise*, I hoped for every consolation, I receive an inferno of pain. The errors are infinite and so conspicuous that they do not seem to be caused by the press but by the author. I feel myself dying of shame because in this way I can only attract the laughter of everyone, all the more so since as a woman it will appear to the masses as if I, like a monkey, wanted to imitate lettered men without having an idea of what I was saying.

I therefore pray Your Lordship to take pity upon me and, if you do not have the patience to oversee the printing with the diligence that is needed, to tell me so in the spirit of confidence that I deserve, and I will be satisfied by your sincerity. I do not distrust your kindness but at times one cannot do what one would like; for this reason I pray you not to deny me the fruits of your candor in this affair, while I attest that I am compelled to have these two folios reprinted at my own cost since they are so distorted in their conceits, as Your Lordship will see. From your niece[263] you can learn the truth and you can also gain assurance that important reasons motivate me to do this. If the expense were mine I swear to God that I would give everything to the devil; in any case a perpetual rage would trouble me more than the loss of a thousand scudi.

The lady your niece sends her greetings, and, praying you to pardon me, I offer you my respects.

---

261. Lorenzina, Tarabotti's younger sister and Pighetti's wife.

262. This letter—one of the oldest letters in the collection, composed in 1643 at the latest—regards errors in Tarabotti's first printed work, her *Convent Paradise*, and attests to her frustration at not being able personally to oversee the printing. The letter was certainly directed to Giovanni Polani who helped her to put the *Paradise* to press (see also letter 89).

263. Betta Polani, Tarabotti's friend who was long a novice at Sant'Anna but never took vows and left the convent after many years.

88

TO THE MOST ILLUSTRIOUS AND EXCELLENT SIGNOR NICOLO BRETEL DE GREMONVILLE, AMBASSADOR OF FRANCE TO THE MOST SERENE REPUBLIC OF VENICE[264]

Certainly no other pen than that of Your Illustrious Excellency could have composed the most gracious page that I receive from your most considerate courtesy. Such are the sparkles of its conceits, so illustrious its forms, so resplendent its favors, so conspicuous and sweet the graces it displays to me that even I, accustomed to your kind admiration, am now dazzled and confused. Illustrious and Excellent Lord, I would rush to your feet to beg pardon for my silence, were it not born of the most humble respect I owe to so important a personage. My quill dared not undertake so lofty a flight; it feared a precipitous fall and did not risk to delineate with black ink the candor of the most devoted servitude ever recorded in the annals of eternity.

Overwhelming me even further, you had your precious words precede mine, but know that your favors could not come before me without lowering themselves. You wish me to excuse you, and yet you know that the actions of a god cannot be censured by a woman. Content yourself with penitence although you were never guilty, unless perhaps of a kind theft. You say your patronage is useless to me, and yet it is what grants me glory before the world. You add that I need nothing, since, having taken a vow of religious poverty, I possess no other riches than to be Your Excellency's servant. You oblige me to keep you in my memory, and affect not to know that you will never be erased from it, not even at the end of my life. Kindly take care that your modesty does not diminish the rest of your qualities with such contradictions. Be that as it may, I would like to thank you for so many honors, but I cannot, because the graces conferred on me by you are

---

264. In this letter, probably written around the beginning of 1648, Tarabotti thanks Bretel de Grémonville for a letter in which he had evidently written of her with high praise. She congratulates him also on the birth of his second son after the family had returned to France. She criticizes, however, the ambassador's decisions for his daughters. She also sends news regarding a treatise recently translated into Italian and published in Venice that maintained that women had no soul.

celestial and immortal, and those that I offer you in return are earthly and mortal.

And who could doubt that your graces are celestial, when they bring me news of the birth of an angel,[265] who with his elder brother[266] will enrich our age with a Plato and an Aristotle. Much may be expected of them because of the lofty qualities of their parents, and we must believe that, having both been produced in the city of Venice, they will also have Venus for their friend.[267] In the meantime let them enjoy the Graces who serve as their nursemaids and let Your Excellencies take pride in the fact that your children wear the splendors of their parentage upon their visage and that they clearly demonstrate that, if their beauty is angelic (as the philosophers have it), it cannot be separated from a goodness that makes them shine marvelously. My astrology teaches me as much; please accept my celebration of this nativity as emerging from a heart that knows only to carry the happiest wishes to the illustrious house of Gremonville, while in the distance I see

> *Quest'Alcide novell'erger sul colle*
> *Ove premio al valor Gloria s'estolle.*
> *Già fatto si prevedo*
> *Scorrer la scena, ed essaltar Parigi,*
> *Se fia che 'l patrio brando aruoti in giro.*
> *Già l'ottomano e 'l Medo*
> *Incatenati al pie del gran Luigi*
> *Porger sudditi bacci al pied io miro.*
> *Il genitore ammiro*
> *Farsi maggior nel figlio e in cetre e in marmi,*
> *La Francia a lui sacrar le moli e i carmi.*[268]

---

265. As we learn in this letter, the second son of Bretel de Grémonville was conceived in Venice but born in France. Since the ambassador left Venice in October 1647, the boy must have been born no later than July 1648. Bretel de Grémonville died November 26 of the same year.

266. Marco, born in Venice.

267. Venice was linked to the Virgin Mary but connected with Venus, the goddess of love, too, on the basis of the same phonetic similarity.

268. "I see this new Alcides rise up on the hill / Where glory, the prize of valor, appears. / Once grown up, I foresee him / rush on to the stage and Paris exult / if he wields the sword

But on to the rest. It is difficult for me to believe that Your Excellency regrets your hurry in returning to France, although I well know that our desires are usually followed by remorse. Too dear is one's home, too sweet the sight of one's family, and very tender those domestic conversations, all things that were decidedly far away in this city; nor were you permitted any visits but to poor imprisoned women.[269] That you then should take leave of the charms of that court to delight in the parlor of Santa Anna seems (you must pardon me) impossible to me, and I receive such words as befitting a gentleman who in his kindness has no peer. I know I ought at least feign to believe, but my sincerity does not allow it.

I am the one who, during other conversations, turns her mind to those most courteous visits she enjoyed from both Your Excellencies, and thinks herself stolen away to the Third Heaven, although on coming back to my senses I weep for the loss; and now I will surely fall in your opinion, in confessing forthrightly that it is much better not to have enjoyed happiness than to lose it.

I rejoice in the good health of madame, just as I regret that your daughters must experience P[aternal] T[yranny].[270]

I carry out the commands of Your Excellency and, with regard to the news asked of me, I tell you that my heart is heavy over the death of my most beloved brother-in-law, Signor Pighetti,[271] and my body is beset by my constant indisposition.

---

of his country. / I see already the Ottoman and the Mede, / enchained at the foot of the great Louis, / offer kisses of the vanquished at his feet. / With pleasure I see his father / aggrandized in his son, and in cither and in marble / France dedicate to him monuments and song." Even though Tarabotti expresses distaste for this type of poetry (see letter 243), she seems here to take credit for these verses.

269. The Republic, to prevent representatives from other governments from receiving too much power or information, tried to limit their official contacts as much as they could (see Pietro Molmenti, *Curiosità di storia veneziana* [Bologna: Zanichelli, 1919], 48–49). For this reason, Tarabotti says, Bretel de Grémonville had no other option but to visit nuns, a type of contact that did not compromise state affairs.

270. With her allusion to her own work, Tarabotti seems to indicate that Bretel de Grémonville had chosen life in the convent for his daughters, who had been boarders at Sant'Anna.

271. On the death of Giacomo Pighetti, see also letter 16.

On the feast of Saint John, Lady N. was joined in matrimony to a young gentleman of high position who, in keeping with his nature, treats her as befits a French gentleman.

Lady N.[272] enjoys a most happy life in her own house, nor does she want to subject herself to the sex which is (truly) too arrogant.

Your Excellency may have seen the impertinence of a certain man, for a little work has been published that is peppered throughout with heretical ideas and concepts asserting that women are not of the same species as men, that God did not die for them, and that they cannot be saved.[273]

Your goodness must excuse me if I bore you with these trifles instead of responding concisely to your letter which, being full of such delightful thoughts, I consider a Paradise; and thus with adoration in my heart I bow, etc.

89

TO SIGNOR N.[274]

I do not know on what basis Your Lordship says that I have not kept my word to you. You have no reason to complain, for no one tried to prevent you from expressing your thoughts. That father V[enti] M[iglia][275] was not planning on clearly revealing my name in his work is a lie, for it circulates with my name as clearly shown as it is in the *Paradise*, and this is the infallible truth.

I, too, realize that there are many errors in the Latin phrases in the *Paradise*, but the fault lies more with the press than with me, as the illustrious Signor Giovanni Polani and others can attest, knowing

---

272. Tarabotti refers to a different "Lady N." than the one mentioned just above.

273. On this controversy, see letter 59.

274. This letter, almost certainly directed to Girolamo Brusoni, regards the controversy that surrounded Tarabotti's *Antisatire*. Both Brusoni and Aprosio had written responses to Tarabotti's work (see above n. 66). Tarabotti blocked the publication of Aprosio's work because it publicly revealed her name (see n. 46). In this letter, on the other hand, she denies that she tried to stop the publication of Brusoni's work, which nonetheless appears never to have been printed. She also responds to Brusoni's criticism of her *Paradise*.

275. That is, Aprosio, a native of Ventimiglia.

my pain at finding these unseemly mistakes.[276] Your Lordship should know, therefore, that I never deemed it without imperfection, as my writings attest, and if it was an error to publish it, the fault was my brother-in-law's.[277] I swear to you I know nothing of the letter sent to you in his name, and I believe that the devil puts his tail where he can't put his head![278] Nonetheless I wholeheartedly regret that my brother-in-law should have occasion, for the fault of others, to complain of me, for I sincerely love him as a brother and admire his merits, just as I pray to our Lord every desirable happiness for Your Lordship.

90

TO THE MOST ILLUSTRIOUS COUNTESS S.[279]

Those promises which, dictated by an excess of kindness, issue forth from the mouth of a lady of Your Illustrious Ladyship's stature and from gentlemen of such reputation as the illustrious Matteo and your husband, have no need of prodding or petitions to be spurred on to effect. Doubting nothing, but moved by a most vehement desire to have my ears graced by the sweetest song of Your Illustrious Ladyship, I beg you with reverent reminder to deign to see that actions follow words and also to ask on my behalf that these illustrious sirs also deign to agree. Since they are treasure troves of courtesy and the essence of kindness, I feel confident that they will not, with my humble prayers, deny this honor.

Music partakes of the glories of Paradise and I invite Your Illustrious Lordships and Ladyship not to deny my convent Paradise the glories of music unless you wish it to be an imperfect Paradise, and in return I assure these sirs that, for the period in which I am thus de-

---

276. See letter 87.

277. Giacomo Pighetti, who Tarabotti says had encouraged her to publish the work (see letter 196).

278. Brusoni had evidently accused Tarabotti of having sent him a letter pretending that it was from her brother-in-law.

279. Tarabotti invites her anonymous addressee, along with her husband and a certain Matteo, to the convent to entertain the nuns with their song. The correspondent seems to be the same one as in letter 29, which postdates this missive. The lay status of the musicians means that the concert would probably have taken place in the parlor.

lighted, they will remain untouched by the qualities I generally mete out to men; indeed I will count them among the angels. Although we are women, they ought not fear that, like the women of Thrace, we will greet the harmony of their voices with stones, for if those women were impious and pagan, we are Christians and religious, and if Orpheus was the enemy of women, their illustrious lordships[280] have nothing in common with him but the marvelous excellence of their playing and singing.

Therefore I will anxiously await news from the bearer of this letter as to whether my wishes will be granted by your favor next Monday. In the meantime, awaiting a concert of your voices, I too will compose a concert from your great merit and my respectful devotion which, bowing to these illustrious sirs, declares itself forever Your Illustrious Ladyship's, etc.

91

TO THE MOST ILLUSTRIOUS SIGNOR N.[281]

Since Your Illustrious Lordship, with the usual flattery of men, affects to appreciate my letters, I will feign to believe you and therefore I will continue to bother you, with your consent, without even blushing.

I inform you, therefore, that Lady Death, indignant (I believe) with Lady N.[282] because she did not wish to continue wearing those mourning clothes that mark us as dead even though we are alive, has set out to deprive her of those dearest to her. But not having had the fortune to pluck me from the number of the living, thanks to the favor bestowed on me by my Bridegroom, she now stands with scythe in hand, posed to snap off that last stem remaining in the lady's most desolate family.[283] I would deem this occurrence advantageous for her had they already settled with Signor N. But since everything is to the contrary, I fear that, given the uncle's testament, matters might go in

---

280. The addressee's husband and Signor Matteo.

281. Tarabotti tells her anonymous addressee of her recovery from a grave illness and updates him on the situation of a certain lady.

282. Perhaps Tarabotti's friend Betta Polani, who left the convent after many years.

283. If Tarabotti writes of Betta, the "stem" could be her uncle Giovanni, who would be the uncle mentioned shortly after.

the opposite direction: that is, the mule will remain loaded with gold and the ladies will be left with only a bit of fodder. Such is the way of the world: previously they were trying to broker a marriage for her, and now I understand that as a result of her brother's delays she is reduced to the state of one of those mummies that come from Egypt.

This is all an example for us, Illustrious Signor. Go ahead and plunder the sea of Love in order to take possession of what, once obtained, only bores you. Take care to have your feet bound by lovely hands just as your heart was injured by a pair of lovely eyes, for in any case it can be said: oh, foolish ones, how greatly you deceive yourselves! I speak of men in general, and, in particular regarding the aforementioned affair, I await Your Illustrious Lordship, to whom I most humbly bow, praying that you do not reprimand me if I send you too much to read, for it is customary to provide one's accusers with the trial proceedings.

92

TO THE MOST ILLUSTRIOUS SIGNOR
GIOVANNI DANDOLO[284]

Since the Fates still insist on holding together the threads of this unhappy life, I beg a visit of you, bowing reverently before Your Illustrious Lordship, and imploring your forgiveness if, in order to serve others, I overstep the limits I should obey. The sight of this moving skeleton will perhaps astonish you, and you may think me a shadow; nor should your prudence be surprised, while, with my usual sincerity, I explain to you what has befallen me in these past days.

Your Lordship should know that I was overtaken by a most fierce constriction in my chest, which deprived me at the same time of my breath, and, one could say, of my life. It seemed to me in those languors that my soul escaped from this prison and arrived at the river Acheron, where I saw a throng of souls waiting to be ferried to the

---

284. In this letter, Tarabotti recounts to Dandolo a vision she had of the afterlife when she was gravely ill. In her otherworldly vision, God, too, affirms the superiority of the female sex and condemns men's sinful treatment of women.

kingdom of death.[285] Accompanied there by sorrow, and by horror, I stopped to consider my surroundings. In those shadows, by divine will, I couldn't see the light of the two beautiful angels who were helping me to the shores, where I asked to be taken along with the others to the dark banks.

Then the old helmsman,[286] raising his shaggy brow and fixing his admiring eyes on me, said: "Oh, little fool, no woman ever entered this place: indeed, you should know that the countless souls you see here are all men, most of whom have been damned on account of the great disdain with which they treat women, and particularly their wives. Be aware that in this place the most fierce punishments of the Divine Hand are meted out against those who want always to dominate women, who by righteous consent will from hereon will triumph."

As soon as that horrendous voice had penetrated my ear, I was surrounded by the whitest of clouds, and I was presented to God by the angels; when he kindly received me, I rejoiced tremendously, thinking that I would remain there eternally with my Lord. But he said to me: "My most beloved, it is still not time for you to come enjoy what I have promised you, for it is necessary that you to return to the world to warn men of their damnation. I will give you, as I gave Moses, this tablet wherein these wicked men will be able to see that they have no part in the Kingdom of Heaven. In my name you must preach this truth liberally, nor should the knowledge that they abhor your preaching hold you back. You see that in Paradise women increase my incidental glory, and that through their hands the greatest graces of my omnipotence pour forth."

After he spoke, I woke up by his command and saw my friends, who, huddled around my bed, were inconsolably lamenting my death. At my first breaths they dried their tears, and I immediately asked if the illustrious Signor N. had attended my funeral, as he was obliged to do by his word.[287] They then exchanged glances, and they did not

---

285. Allusion to Dante (*Inferno*, canto 3, 70–129). Tarabotti transforms the Dantesque journey into a narrative that punishes the wrongs done to women and justifies her polemics against men.

286. Charon.

287. The identity of this Signor N. is not specified.

know how to answer me in order (I believe) not to disgust me. But finally they said: "You know well that for the most part all men are untruthful." Then I truly would have been shocked, if I hadn't been reassured that in Heaven, and in Hell, my long-held opinions are no caprice, but rather inalterable truths, which in the future I will emphasize more than ever.

But if I bore Your Illustrious Lordship with the long-windedness of my writing, no less than with the dull and melancholy content, no matter. Please deign to sample, among so many tastes, this small taste of mortification, and do not fail to visit very soon, because we must deal with a matter more secret than you believe; I bow down to you.

93

TO THE MOST ILLUSTRIOUS AND EXCELLENT SIGNOR BERTUCCI VALIER[288]

The most deferential spirits of my soul rush to congratulate Your Excellency for the glorious nomination to procurator of your illustrious and excellent son[289] who—a sun in the eastern sky with all the light of his splendors, which are not at all inferior to those of his father—illuminates the world with shining rays of virtue. He does not wish to be less than his parent, upon whose powerful shoulders he sees all Italy carried and supported. The purple robes, which confer honors, could

---

288. An important figure in the Republic, Bertucci Valier (1596–1658) held many important offices that culminated in his election as doge in 1656.

289. Silvestro Valier (1630–1700) was nominated procurator in 1649. The office of procurator was, after that of the doge himself, the most important one in the Republic, and it carried, as the doge's, a life-time appointment. Frequently a new doge was elected from the ranks of the procurators; this occurred to Silvestro himself who was elected after having held many other important offices, including a period as ambassador to the Venetian pope Alexander VIII (Pietro Ottoboni, another of Tarabotti's correspondents). Valier, like many other Venetian nobles in this period, received the position of procurator upon a payment of more than twenty thousand ducats, which the Republic needed to finance the war against the Turks (Francesco Sansovino, *Venetia città nobilissima et singolare* [Venice: Steffano Curti, 1663], 725; Cappellari, *Campidoglio*, 4:430). The nomination to procurator was always an occasion for a family's great jubilation, as we see with Tarabotti's congratulations to Silvestro's father (see Capellari, *Campidoglio*, 4:12).

hope for nothing more than a subject who so augments their dignity, for which Lady N. and I heartily rejoice once again. And since it is customary for great princes, in their greatest jubilation, not to scorn the respects of the lowest peasants and their humble gifts, I beg Your Excellency, with such a favor, not to scorn this small sign of my great respect. Upon the birth of God, the shepherds' offerings were as dear to him as those of the Magi. Therefore the illustrious and excellent procurator, now reborn in greatness, ought not despise this humble gift I offer his lovely bride, who indeed seems a celestial Venus.[290] At this I respectfully rejoice and kiss Your Excellency's robes, while wishing for your most serene house a male child who will bring glory to this Republic.

94

TO HER SERENE HIGHNESS VITTORIA MEDICI DELLA ROVERE, GRAND DUCHESS OF TUSCANY[291]

The most remarkable favor which I have received from Your Serene Highness's royal kindness surpasses the limits of my understanding. When have I ever before merited the great honor of receiving your most precious words from the very hands of the lord Resident?[292] I must certainly mark in white[293] the lucky day that was itself marked, to my good fortune, by such a favorable event. I would further like to offer you the most humble thanks that can issue from a heart filled with complete respect and devotion; but if the Graces, though daughters of Jove, go naked, neither do I, in my religious poverty, have the orna-

---

290. In 1648 Silvestro married Betta Querini (Biblioteca del Museo Correr, M. Barbaro, *Alberi dei Patrizi Veneziani*, ad vocem).

291. A version of this letter, dated 8 April 1645, can be found in the Archivio di Stato di Firenze (Mediceo del Principato, 6152, c.31r–v [Medioli, "Reliability," 88–89]). Tarabotti asks the grand duchess to help her publish *Paternal Tyranny* outside of Venice, placing her hope in della Rovere's authority as well as in the fact that her patron is located in Florence, where the attack on Venice's government and its noblemen might be more acceptable than it ever could be in the Serenissima. Della Rovere seems not to have responded directly to the request, and Tarabotti turned her publishing ambitions instead to France.

292. Francesco Zati, who appears elsewhere as an intermediary between Tarabotti and the grand duchess.

293. *segnar in bianco*. See n. 9.

ments to clothe my thanks in such a way that they might be worthy to appear before the eyes of the most glorious and worthy princess who lights up the world today.

Your Highness nourishes my ambition too generously for me to be able to offer the proper thanks, and I see your unparalleled kindness all too graciously open the path for my boldness, with which, prostrate at your feet, I dare beg you to lend me the support of your most authoritative patronage in order to obtain from Rome, or else from Florence, the publishing privileges[294] to have my *Paternal Tyranny* printed, which for certain reasons I do not seek in my own state. Indulge (I most humbly beg you) the audacity of my request, while I assure you on my word that the abovementioned work contains nothing that goes against the Holy Faith or against good manners.

I will await your favor, since I need fear neither good nor bad outcome to the boldness of my request, as it is for such persons as yourself to concede and intercede for important favors. And among other things, with the most ardent of prayers I will beseech God to award you the regal crown together with the greatest happiness you could desire, and a century of life, which you, the phoenix of princesses, well deserve. I also hope the upcoming feast of the Resurrection will be filled for Your Most Serene Highness with all those rewards that can come from the omnipotent hand, and I humbly bend my knees before you.

95
TO THE MOST ILLUSTRIOUS SIGNORA BETTA POLANI

The first breath that God has conceded me after I have long yearned to breathe I will blow into my quill to make it fly to Your Illustrious Ladyship, sending it as ambassador of my afflictions and bearer of my thanks for your kind visits. You must know, therefore, how my bed bloomed with torments to such an extent that I could truly say, *Non est dolor sicut dolor meus.*[295] My afflicted mind, my weak limbs, my half-dead heart made me believe that I had lost my life. I do not know

---

294. *Le licenze*: the official permission necessary in order to publish a book.

295. A variation on the biblical verse Lam. 1:12, *Attendite et videte si est dolor similis sicut dolor meus* ("Attend, and see if there be any sorrow like to my sorrow").

if these symptoms were due to my illness or to not seeing Your Illustrious Ladyship, who is the dearest object to my eyes, the nourishment of my heart, and the life of my soul, which having already pledged itself to your divinity cannot live away from it. Adieu.

96

TO THE MOST ILLUSTRIOUS SIGNOR MARIN POLANI[296]

The reports Your Illustrious Lordship gave me regarding the illustrious Lady Betta, your sister and my most beloved friend and only mistress, have created such strange effects in me that I myself cannot understand them. I am glad that she is pained to be separated from me; her distress sorrows and cheers me. Her sighs brighten my darkness and her tears make me shed through my eyes the essence of my heart. She is veritably the simulacrum of true friendship and of faith, and I reciprocate her affection to such an extent that I find no peace away from her. With her departure from me, I felt my soul leave my breast, whence I now am just a body full of wretchedness. I see myself separated from the most dear, kind, prudent, and gracious gentlewoman that God, Nature and the Graces have ever fashioned. Her incomparable modesty and skill in governing a household would enable her to lead a world. That head, which encloses a more-than-divine intellect, should honor crowns, and those industrious hands should wield scepters.

Your Illustrious Lordship has much to praise in her governance, to admire in her actions, to learn from her discussions, and occasion to marvel at her traits of perfect courtesy, kindness, grace, goodness, religiosity, and Christian piety. She suffices to create a Paradise, since where one finds her most fortunate person it can be said that there is *aggregatio omnium honorum*,[297] while in her alone is contained all the goodness and beauty that the world possesses. Ap-

---

296. Marin Polani was the brother of Betta Polani, the dear friend Tarabotti praises in this letter composed after Betta's departure from Sant'Anna. Tarabotti attempts to convince Marin of Betta's merits, perhaps because he had not yet found her a husband (see letter 91).

297. "The accumulation of all honors." Cf. Boethius, *De consolatione philosophiae*, PL 63.0724a, *Liquet igitur esse beatitudinem statum bonorum omnium congregatione perfectum* ("It is in fact the highest of all good things and it contains all the good things within itself,"

preciate, Your Illustrious Lordship, these glories of hers and value her as you would all treasures combined together. All the gold in Peru and all the pearls and jewels on earth are not worth a twig in comparison to the pure gold of her heart and the candor of her purity, which robs the splendor from oriental pearls. Let all jewels cede their place to the most precious gems that adorn the nobility of her heart. Please revere her, Your Illustrious Lordship, in my name, and console her by assuring her that in response to her laments and tears I am a grieving Echo[298] and that her love is superseded by an Anteros who has become a giant,[299] while I will say, as that great mind did:

> *Creda ognun a suo modo, io già non credo*
> *Che possa lontananza un caro oggetto*
> *Sveller da un cor, ch'a prova in me lo vedo.*[300]

Please forgive me, Your Illustrious Lordship, if I bore you and ask you to deliver these messages, a favor which does not deserve refusal from so kind a Mercury.[301] Fondly bidding adieu to the illustrious lady, I bow to you.

97

TO MY MOST ILLUSTRIOUS SIGNORA BETTA POLANI

You ask me with great urgency for details of my health. I must not and cannot deny these to you, even though they are unhappy, ominous, and baleful.

Since the first of December I have been in bed, oppressed with a shortness of breath that brings on a fever, robs me of my senses, and kills me a hundred times a day, if one can die so frequently. I have no more spirit; I have lost my strength because my nourishment con-

---

Consolation of Philosophy, trans. Joel C. Relihan [Indianapolis: Hackett Publishin, 2001], 51).

298. The nymph Echo, transformed to stone and condemned to repeat the words of others.

299. Anteros, brother of Eros and god of unrequited love.

300. "Let each believe what he will, but I do not believe / that distance may remove from the heart / what is dear, and in myself I see the proof." Citation not indentified.

301. Mercury, messenger of the gods.

sists of nothing but barley juice and milk with linseed. Such misery is compounded by my being in a dormitory that would better be called a mortuary since next to my cell is a nun *in extremis laborantem*,[302] whence instead of relief for my suffering, I frequently hear loudly thunder in my ear these fearful words: *Proficiscere anima christiana de hoc mundo*.[303] Death and Time are playing chess and we are a trio of invalids, nor do we know who will be taken by our common enemy. May His Divine Majesty do with me as He pleases, since in any case you can only ever delay but never avoid this passage. I am more troubled by the fluctuating waves of the bitter sea of this world than I am fearful of shipwreck in departing it.

I was used to a most exacting attention to my ills, thanks to your love and the charity of my regal Regina,[304] who forgot her own station to save me. Now I am attended with little affection and indifferently, as you know. Nonetheless I hold it to be indubitable that the lack of care cannot speed the time I am destined to die since *constituisti terminos eius, qui præteriri non poterunt*.[305]

I do not deny in the meantime that, in the face of the shrieks of the priest who banishes souls from this world, I feel my hair curl or my blood chill. My soul itself, rattling in my chest, knows not how to determine if those calls are for it. From such events you can deduce what my life is like. Please beseech the Lord for me with prayers for some shade of health, but I believe firmly that I will be forced, after long suffering, in the end to die. So be it. I would not in any case want to live eternally in such misery. Adieu.

---

302. Near death.

303. "Go forth from this world, Christian soul" (Catechism of the Catholic Church, art. 12, par. 1020).

304. Regina Donà, the fellow nun whose death in 1645 is lamented several times in Tarabotti's *Letters*.

305. That is, the moment of death is decided by God alone (cf. Job 14:5).

98

TO THE MOST REVEREND SIGNOR N.[306]

In the course of the reading I sent to Your Illustrious Lordship you will have found much more that is profane and mordant than eloquent or spiritual, since my pen is not able to speak of the erudite souls in the schools of Paradise, as you say, but instead of those enclosed by paternal tyranny in convent Hell. In merit of your kindness let not the fact that I talk universally of men cause you scandal, since the innocent and good ones, with their selfsame acts, subtract themselves from the masses of wicked ones. It is not with presumptuous heart that I share these vain words with you, but rather I speak obediently, and Your Reverend Lordship knows well that *melius est obedire quam sacrificare.*[307] I bow to you.

99

TO THE MOST ILLUSTRIOUS AND EXCELLENT SIGNOR NICOLO BRETEL, SIGNOR DI GREMONVILLE, AMBASSADOR OF FRANCE TO THE MOST SERENE REPUBLIC OF VENICE[308]

Your Excellency asks me with such urgency for the responses against my *Antisatire* that I am obliged to inquire after them, but more with the desire to serve you than because I care to see them. Thus far the *Antisatire Satirized,*[309] which is the best, has not been put to press. The *Mask Lifted*[310] has not been seen and quite likely they both could have been reduced to ashes in the *Funeral for Feminine Luxury* that came

---

306. Tarabotti likely refers in this letter to *Convent Paradise*, as she excuses herself for not having done a better job with the subject matter, accustomed as she is to writing against forced monachization, not about nuns with a vocation.

307. Cf. 1 Sam. 15:22, "For obedience is better than sacrifices."

308. Tarabotti reports here on the reactions provoked by her *Antisatire*—from the various works composed in response to it to the accusations that she had not authored her own works.

309. *Antisatira satirizzata*, by Girolamo Brusoni.

310. *La maschera scoperta*, by Angelico Aprosio.

from Bologna.[311] The *Hercules Slayer of Geryon*[312] will respond to the *Antisatire Satirized* with bolts of lightning, and since comedies are called masks, *Boldness: A Comedy* will be the response to the puppet-like father of the *Mask*.[313]

To Your Excellency, in whom I confide everything, I will soon send a little highlight which will give you a sense for the tenor of the comic work.[314] In the meantime, so that your refined intellect may gather its content, I will say that Truth—dressed up as Momus[315]—speaks the prologue and, to be frank, I hope that she will be well received because she is facetious, mordant, and contains within herself many truths that speak against the Zoiluses of our time,[316] and against the FRIARS of this world,[317] and she jokes a lot about nosy meddlers.[318] If these men take offense, it matters little to me; he who stings must be stung and he who damages another's reputation deserves to have his honor pierced. These captious intellects quibble too much with me, and they have no regard for the fact that I am a woman and that I profess no knowledge, since I came to live in these cloisters when I

---

311. *Funerali delle pompe feminili*: yet another response to the *Antisatire*, composed, according to Zanette, by Silvio Foccacci (*Suor Arcangela*, 278).

312. *Ercole geromicida*. Someone—probably Tarabotti herself—was planning a response to Brusoni's work that was perhaps never completed or at least never published (nor does Brusoni's work seem to have appeared in print). This is the only mention of the *Hercules* in the *Letters*. Hercules killed the monster Geryon as one of his labors.

313. That is, Aprosio, whose lack of originality Tarabotti mocks. The *Comedy* (*Ardire comedia*) seems to be another work Tarabotti was planning in response to her critics. Although there is also no mention of this work elsewhere in the *Lettere* nor trace of a manuscript or printed volume, the details she provides about it below suggest that it was partially completed.

314. That is, the *Comedy*.

315. Momus, the Greek god of criticism.

316. That is, against her critics. Zoilus (c. 400–c. 320 BCE), Greek rhetorician and philosopher, known for his sharp censure of Homer; his name became a synonym for malicious critics.

317. The word "friars" (*frati*) is fully capitalized in the original text, an unusual instance. Both Aprosio and Brusoni were friars, and Tarabotti criticizes them here and elsewhere in the *Letters*, along with other religious, for lacking in faith. "Of this world" (*di questo secolo*) has the dual implication of "contemporary" and "secular."

318. *Li dazieri degl'impacci*. The Venetian expression *tor dazi d'impacci*, according to Boerio, signifies to mix oneself up in the problems of others, perhaps for one's own benefit.

was eleven years old without ever having basked in the light of learning, as I testify in all of my writing.[319]

They criticize me because the style of the *Paradise* and of the *Antisatire* are different.[320] They say that calling Alexander the Great incontinent in the *Paradise* was a very grave error, but I disagree, since, even if he used great continence with Darius's wife and daughters,[321] an ear of wheat does not make it summer,[322] and in other instances he acted most incontinently, even going so far as to marry a maiden who was his subject.[323] They criticize me for calling Dante a vain poet and for putting Saint Anthony in the place of Saint Paul. It is true that I might have created such an anachronism, but these condemnations have no substance and are characterized more by malice than rigor.

Nonetheless let them say what they will; we will let them chatter, since the whole world will see, in a volume of letters that will soon see the light of day, whether such nonsense is true, that my writings need their polish to achieve glory.[324] Your Excellency and other personages of merit will always be able to attest whether my letters reached your glorious hands in the same form in which they will appear in print.

As for the rest, I will continue to serve you until my last breath, even if I have received some information that the affair threatens to end unhappily.[325] But come what may, dangers do not frighten me, and

319. Tarabotti says she has had no literary instruction because she entered the convent at age eleven. Zanette, however, convincingly dates her entry into Sant'Anna to 1617, at age thirteen (*Suor Arcangela*, 26–27). Perhaps Tarabotti mistakes the date, or perhaps she shifts it in order to strengthen her point.

320. Tarabotti mentions this criticism, which fueled suspicion that she had not authored her own works, at other points in the *Letters* (see, for example, letter 113).

321. During the victorious battle of Issus (333 BCE), Alexander, having captured the family of King Darius, treated the women with the greatest respect. For this reason Darius himself admired him. Alexander went on to marry Darius's daughter, Barsine.

322. An echo of the proverb "One swallow does not make a summer."

323. There are numerous episodes of unchastity attributed to Alexander the Great, who took many lovers, male and female.

324. This letter, which dates to before Bretel de Grémonville's departure from Venice in 1647, and, given the references to the controversy over the *Antisatire*, probably a few years earlier, attests that Tarabotti had planned the publication of her *Letters* for some time.

325. It is not clear what task Tarabotti undertook for the ambassador.

for you, *le alte non temo e l'umili non sdegno*.[326] Rest assured of this, Your Excellency, on the solid basis of your immense merit and of my affection, which pledges itself to you ever anew.

100
TO THE MOST ILLUSTRIOUS AND EXCELLENT SIGNOR GIOVAN FRANCESCO LOREDANO[327]

Since all souls fly to their center, which is God, to be rewarded or punished according to their merits or demerits, I write to you to see if the *The Soul of Zeno* has come to Your Excellency, who is a god of our century, immortalized by your own pen. If that *Soul* has flown to the tribunal of Your Excellency, I beseech you on bended knee (as one must before deities) to send it to convent Paradise, or rather to condemn it to the Hell of the living. I say in one or in the other since in this place such great contrasts are linked so unusually: Paradise, Hell, angels, and demons. I will not declare which group I belong to because it would insult your great wisdom.

Deliver it to the pleasures of Paradise or condemn it to the torments of Hell, since in any case I will be able to carry out the duties of an archangel and to perform those of a demon, too, remaining Your Excellency's, etc.

101
TO THE MOST ILLUSTRIOUS LADY AQUILA BARBARA

If Your Illustrious Ladyship's stature did not inhibit the freedom your affection and kindness offer, I would say, regarding those heretical thoughts you write me about, that I think you should step back over the threshold into the Church.

---

326. "I do not fear the lofty, and I do not disdain the humble." These verses are pronounced by Clorinda in Tasso's *Gerusalemme liberata*, canto, stanza 46, line 6 (*Jersualem Delivered*, trans. Ralph Nash [Detroit: Wayne State University Press, 1987]).

327. In this letter Tarabotti makes the first of two requests to Loredano to obtain *The Soul of Zeno* (*L'anima del Zeno*), a work that was much sought after in Venice but that did not actually exist (see also letter 59). Tarabotti also asked Giovanni Dandolo to locate the volume (see letter 64).

My illustrious and kind Lady, I swear to you on the altars of Truth that I have been little or not at all in Parnassus to consort with those Apollos and those Muses whom, I confess, I am unworthy of visiting, much less imitating. I am deprived of the light that you, with too much, indeed overflowing, affection see shine forth in my compositions, which are arid, sterile, and cold, in keeping with the season and with my age. I am beginning to lose all vitality, and in fact to have no living part except the memory of being servant to Your Illustrious Ladyship, etc.

102
TO SIGNOR N.

In two most courteous letters from Your Lordship, I find charming conceits yet inconsistent thoughts. You say in the first that you believed I had already flown amid angels, while you go on in the second to say that, if you asked me for news from the other world, you didn't intend Heaven. I truly cannot understand such equivocation, since, if you believed me amid angels, my reports therefore would necessarily come from Paradise. You cried for my death, and now you're disgusted to know I am revived. You made offerings for my soul yet you would like it to have suffered the torments of the damned. You thank me for having erased with my words your worry about my death, and you would like me dead forever, since you think only a fool would choose to leave the Empyrean merely to return to Hell.

Be aware, Your Lordship, that the contradictions expressed to me in these letters and your curious questions have split my mind in two. I will resolve everything, however, in my next dispatch. In the meantime I offer you my respects.

103

TO THE MOST ILLUSTRIOUS SIGNORA ISABETTA PICCOLOMINI SCARPI[328]

If Your Most Illustrious Ladyship were a mortal creature, I would begin to doubt the reliability of women, but because I know you are a goddess, I fear that you may be too lax with the women working on the *punto in aria* lace.[329] R. has not sent so much as a scrap of it, and I see that the more rapidly time passes, the more her hand delays the promised work, which will force me, too, to go back on my word.

Praise God, I am somewhat recovered from my illness, although my condition is worsened by a multitude of obligations contracted from my sickbed to repay the graciousness of Your Illustrious Ladyship, to whom I eternally pledge my humble devotion. Awaiting the prized fruits of your favor I kiss you dearly, and declare myself yours.

104

TO THE MOST EMINENT AND EXCELLENT SIGNOR ENRICO CORNARO[330]

Your Noble Lordship's servant presented me with the precious words of the illustrious B.,[331] when I, having long lamented the delay, had lost hope of ever receiving them. I did not immediately open the letter, thinking it to be the same document you sent me regarding the interests of the illustrious ladies P.[332] But as soon as he left and I realized I held in my hands the treasure I so desired, I knew myself to be obliged to extend to you immediately the highest expression of thanks my

---

328. Tarabotti writes frequently to this correspondent regarding the lace Sant'Anna nuns create.

329. See above n. 43.

330. Tarabotti expresses gratitude to Cornaro for having sent her some poetry, probably penned by Giovan Francesco Busenello (see letter 112), for the *Tears*, in honor of Regina Donà, which Tarabotti published with her *Letters*.

331. The reference is likely to the poet and member of the Incogniti Giovan Francesco Busenello. In letter 112 Tarabotti says she is "in love" with his verse.

332. This may be a reference to the noblewomen Tarabotti seeks to aid in letters 22 and 140.

poor mind has ever brought forth, using my pen, always the sincere ambassador of my heart's affection. I admire the graceful, if funereal, composition, and I worship the author, saying,

> *In sua bocca sì belle son le lode*
> *Che più dolce armonia qua giù non s'ode.*[333]

I am pleased to hear a swan sing the passing of my Regina, and I glory in knowing that at my request, an Apollo has made her immortal, pledging myself to Your Most Noble and Excellent Lordship, etc.

105
TO THE MOST REVEREND SIGNOR N.[334]

Some days have passed since I received out of Your Reverend Lordship's kindness a little book in which I saw that you, upon the most steadfast basis of scripture, have fabricated the *Victory of Women* in response to those sacrilegious pages that assert they are not of the same species as men, that Christ did not die for them, and that they will not be saved. Truly what was needed to refute the false opinions of a heretic was nothing less than a pen from Paradise, and, to really confuse and terrify him, a trumpet of the Holy Spirit. All women have had the luck to have as their champion a George who, as God's servant, not at all inferior in sanctity to that other George who was Christ's soldier,[335] has wielded the sword of truth and slain the dragon, fending off the blows of liars, whose tongues are called *gladius acutus* in the Holy Book.[336] Therefore I am obliged to pray that Heaven regenerate

---

333. "From him, so lovely is the praise / That no sweeter harmony is heard down here."

334. Tarabotti directs this letter to a man of the cloth named Giorgio, who had evidently written a work entitled *The Victory of Women* (*Vittoria delle donne*) in response to the treatise denying that women had a soul (see above n. 191). It seems that this work was written before Tarabotti herself responded to the treatise. No trace of this *Victory of Women* remains; a work entitled *Victory of Women* (*La vittoria delle donne*) by Lucrezio Bursati (Venice: Evangelista Deuchino, 1621) does not concern this polemic.

335. Saint George (third century CE), revered in Venice, was a defender of women who, according to the Golden Legend, killed a dragon to save a princess.

336. "A sharp sword." Cf. Ps. 56:5.

Your Most Reverend Lordship like the phoenix, so that for a century the Holy Church may enjoy such a defender and women a protector whose piety and Christian charity is beyond human measure.

Because of the most singular favor bestowed upon me out of your kindness, I feel myself obliged to thank you with the warmest sentiments of my soul and to pray to Heaven that, just as the blessed shepherds and the Magi witnessed the sprouting of shoots of green in the desert on holy Christmas night,[337] you, in the desert of this world, may feel the love of your God sprouting ever more strongly in your heart, so that it may produce marvels the faithful can admire. I most humbly ask your holy blessing.

106

TO THE S[IGNORE] A. C. T[ARABOTTI][338]

It is madness to write to those who do not deign to respond. Nevertheless, it is always proper that whoever is oldest should demonstrate more sense. It is not for me to imitate you if you do not live up to the debt of kinship and affection that, as sisters, we ought to all share with one another. Therefore, in keeping with my duty at this holiest of holidays, I wish you all the physical and spiritual comforts that I could want for myself. I pray that Blessed God may rain down upon you the most florid and gracious graces that are bestowed in Paradise.

I implore you to recognize my affection, which I remind you springs ever new. I kiss you both tenderly, sending—more with my heart than my pen—happy wishes by the thousands to you, Illustrious Mistresses, to whom I reverently bow.

---

337. See above n. 244.

338. Tarabotti directs this letter to two of her five younger sisters, possibly Camilla Angela, Lucia Caterina, or Angela; Zanette proposes the latter two (*Suor Arcangela*, 19–21), perhaps because Camilla Angela died in 1644 (ibid., 63). The letter reveals the tensions in Tarabotti's relationship with her family, in this instance because Tarabotti feels hurt by her sisters' lack of attention. The tensions are less palpable in the other letter in the collection directed to her sisters (188).

107
TO THE MOST ILLUSTRIOUS SIGNOR COUNT
COMMENDATOR PIETRO PAOLO BISSARI

May it never be the case that the requirements of admiration and awe cause me to ignore those of obligation and respect, nor may the common masses' impertinence dissuade me from devotedly performing those acts of adoration toward Your Most Illustrious Lordship that I promise will be eternal. Therefore, bowing humbly, I pray to God that, just as on the night of Holy Christmas Heaven and Earth were seen to rejoice with bountiful marvels, so too may portents of heavenly grace and marvels of earthly pleasures be seen in you, that every person might be invited to rejoice in them. I pray also that in the new year all the most glorious events that can honor a kind and most noble individual will grace Your Illustrious Lordship, to whom, dedicating my weak talents, I bow.

108
TO THE MOST ILLUSTRIOUS AND EXCELLENT SIGNOR
GIOVAN FRANCESCO LOREDANO[339]

God, who sees into our hearts without error, knows how much my intent did recoil, my mouth refuse, and my pen flee from begging Your Excellency that the case of Signors Marcantonio Muti and Gio[vanni] Maria Scotto[340] be introduced. Nevertheless, I have had to cede to the renewed requests of these personages and prostrate myself at your feet, calling upon your generous piety to obtain this favor. The parties involved assure me that this is an affair of the purest charity, which will miraculously produce peace between both these families, which otherwise threaten one another with destruction or death. Therefore I most humbly entreat Your Excellency to ignore my lack of merit, but to recall that God lends his ear to the voices of the weakest and his aid to those who invoke it with faith.

---

339. In this letter Tarabotti asks her powerful associate for help in resolving a conflict between two families.

340. The Muti and Scotto families were both well-known Venetian families.

Therefore I await, prostrate on the ground, a benign affirmation that you will intercede for these persons, but unsure of receiving it, I remain in the same state of fear experienced by those accused of capital offenses who await the sentence for or against them. While I beg favor for my desires, I wish perfect health for the excellent and noble lady Laura,[341] humbly kissing Your Excellency's robes.

109

TO THE MOST ILLUSTRIOUS SIGNOR COUNT
COMMENDATOR PIETRO PAOLO BISSARI[342]

The glorious pen of Your Illustrious Lordship, accustomed to executing marvels, would wish to deceive me by claiming that the quintessence of precious gold you distill is but base metal, that the Paradise of your compositions is akin to those confused and obscure Paradises that I am wont to create, and that I am so devoid of feeling that bitter absinthe should seem to me the sweetest nectar. I beg Your Illustrious Lordship's pardon, but you are greatly mistaken, for although I do not keep in my cell the *lapis philosophorum*,[343] impossible to produce, I do have the touchstone of other weighty ancient and modern authors, among whom I see shine the purest gold of your divine learning.

In short, in your acumen you present everything to me upside down, because in marking my imperfections you did not paint a great expanse on a modest canvas, as you say, but rather you delineated a giant in the nothingness of my merit, and from the insignificant earthly glimmer that is me, you make me appear a star.[344] Therefore may the stars always favor your illustrious house, and I pray that God grant you endless favors, declaring myself Your Illustrious Lordship's, etc.

341. Loredano's wife, Laura Valier (see *Vita di Gio. Francesco Loredano Senator Veneto, descritta da Antonio Lupis* [Venice: Valvasense, 1663], 22).

342. Tarabotti chastises her friend for the modesty with which he speaks of his own compositions and the excessive praise he lavishes on her even though she does not deserve it.

343. The philosopher's stone, believed by alchemists to turn base metals into gold or silver.

344. The reference may be to Bissari's praise of Tarabotti in the *Scorse olimpiche*. See n. 210.

110
TO SIGNOR N.

The conclusions made by Your Lordship are so false as to have no substance at all, when, because of the liveliness of my letters, you do not believe me to be as ill as I wrote you. I am very ill, afflicted, consumed, and I would almost say that whoever does not believe me, may God let him suffer the same for himself.

Yet I am the opposite of other people, because amid the greatest oppression of my ailments, my spirit revives the most. It seems that as much as my physicians open my corporeal veins in order to bleed me, so the vein of artistic inspiration opens within me, with such profusion that I suffer less from my affliction than from not being able to put my thoughts on paper. In this manner I composed *Paternal Tyranny*, when, during the nine months in which I languished in the hands of physicians, practically abandoned by them, my mind conceived the idea and formed that offspring in such a way that I most happily brought it forth, unlike other women who are accustomed to feel labor pains upon giving birth. Let this be said not out of arrogance but as an expression of the truth, to which I have always been partial. I offer you my respects.

111
TO THE MOST ILLUSTRIOUS AND EXCELLENT SIGNOR GIOVAN FRANCESCO LOREDANO[345]

In keeping with the commands of Your Excellency, which I will always worship as originating from the most benign heavens, I have sought Palavicino's *Joseph*[346] everywhere, but I have been unable to find him.

345. Tarabotti turns to her patron to tell him that she cannot find a book by Ferrante Pallavicino for which he asked her. As Zanette notes (*Suor Arcangela*, 350), it is impossible that that Loredano, such a powerful force in the Venetian publishing world, would look to a nun for a book penned by a writer as controversial as Pallavicino: instead, he made the request as a prank against the nun. Loredano's letter of response appears in his *Letters* (333). On this exchange with Loredano, see also letter 15, which postdates this one, in which Tarabotti scolds Loredano after he denies having asked her for the book.

346. *Joseph* (*Giuseppe* [Venice: C. Tomasini, 1637]) was one of four novels Pallavicino based on biblical stories.

I do not know if he is still in the cistern where his brothers left him or perhaps in Pharaoh's prison.[347] I would gladly search both places in order to serve Your Excellency, were I not myself imprisoned for eternity.

I asked news of him from the *Soul* of his father, whom you sent here,[348] but he could not tell me anything either. It cheers me, however, to think that the great patriarch should flee from and abhor being called the son of so impious a parent. Therefore I return the *Soul* to Your Excellency, who may know better than I how to implore him, given that your magic words are capable of turning every heart and every soul not only to serve you but also to worship you.[349]

He is accompanied by all the loftiest expressions of gratitude that my lowly pen knows how to compose. May your great and regal soul receive them and know that, although your kind visit with me may have been undertaken under another name, I glory in it immensely.

As to the rest, I beg you to present on my behalf my regards to the illustrious Signor Gio[vanni] D[andolo], your kinsman through the lineage of Adam.[350] I beg you also to believe that although I am a woman, I am not one of those who easily gives credence to what she is told by men. May that satisfy your divine intelligence, and I pledge myself eternally to Your Illustrious Excellency, etc.

347. In a series of allusions, the nun compares her search for Pallavicino's book to the story of Joseph in Gen. 37:21–28 and 39:1–20.

348. Tarabotti refers to *The Soul of Ferrante Pallavicino*, an anonymous work whose first part was probably written by Loredano, who had given a copy of the prohibited work to the nun. On the work and this exchange with Loredano, see also letter 15.

349. Condemning the scandalous content of the *Soul*, Tarabotti sends the work back to Loredano. It is likely that Tarabotti knew that the work was being attributed to Loredano but here, out of prudence, she pretends not to know this.

350. Tarabotti usually had a good rapport with Dandolo, but he let her down when he did not write a work in praise of women that she greatly desired. It is perhaps this disappointment that leads her to underscore that his relationship to Loredano is through Adam.

112
TO THE MOST EMINENT AND EXCELLENT
SIGNOR ENRICO CORNARO[351]

Your Eminent Lordship's usual kindness and my own devotion to you cause a certain hope to blossom in my heart that you might help me to obtain a favor I desire above all else. Your sweetest nature promises me your aid, since it concerns love. I say love because I have fallen in love with the most divine compositions of the illustrious Businello, and I would like you to have one composed to my liking. In return I offer to seek for you with my prayers some favors from Heaven, knowing well that men always want to be rewarded for their efforts with a prize of greater value: as the saying goes, *Omnis labor optat præmium.*[352]

But to conclude this matter, Your Eminent Lordship should know that five years have already passed since my beloved Regina departed this prison, taking with her the dearest part of myself.[353] At that time, to ease my pain I composed a funeral oration entitled *The Tears of Angela Tarabotti,*[354] and gave it to the sister of my dearly departed friend.[355] The illustrious lady in question decided that I should publish it along with certain other writings of mine that would be more at home in Vulcan's jaws than under the printing press. Nevertheless, I was born a subject and therefore I must obey, even though it might cause me to be ridiculed by people of letters.[356]

Thus in order to immortalize the gentlewoman in question, I come to request words from that golden pen that the greatest and most ancient poets would envy were they alive today. If you will agree

---

351. In this letter, written in 1650, Tarabotti turns to Cornaro to request that he send her a poem by Giovan Francesco Busenello for her *Tears*, the eulogy she wrote for Regina Donà. A composition of an "Incognito" appears at the beginning of the *Tears*. In letter 104, Tarabotti thanks Cornaro for sending the poem.

352. "Every effort desires reward."

353. Regina Donà died in 1645, and thus the letter dates to 1650.

354. The actual title of the work is *Le lagrime d'Arcangela Tarabotti*, but here the text reads "Angela."

355. Andriana Donà Malipiero.

356. Tarabotti several times in the *Letters* offers this explanation for the publication of the *Tears* and of the *Letters*.

to accept this honor, I will tell you that my most worthy Regina was of true Venetian blood. She wed herself to Christ at a very young age and she was a queen *non solum nomine sed etiam visu, verbo et opere.*[357]

With the support of Your Eminent Lordship, I will confidently await this grace from the person in question,[358] who I am sure will not refuse me, since I have discerned in his compositions that he is no less a friend to the Graces than to the Muses. Nor do I doubt that I will receive your pardon: since you are accustomed to performing the office of confessor and absolving innocent women of their sins, you will absolve me too, who innocently sins by bothering you with my request. I declare myself Your Noble Lordship's, etc.

113
TO THE MOST EXCELLENT
SIGNOR GIACOMO PIGHETTI[359]

The protestations of Your Eminent Lordship regarding your innocence in having neither suggested nor encouraged anyone to write against me would so thoroughly convince me that I would have no reason to doubt your sincerity, had I not the evidence in hand of your actions.

Dear Brother-in-Law, you in your prudence understand better than I that there is nothing that can remain hidden when it is on so many people's tongues, for in *ore duorum vel trium stat omne verum.*[360] Leaving aside the evidence which, having been entrusted to me under

357. "Not only in name but in appearance, word and works."

358. Giovan Francesco Busenello.

359. Tarabotti in this letter voices the profound disappointment she experienced when her brother-in-law Pighetti, who had encouraged her to publish her *Antisatire*, then urged Angelico Aprosio to write a biting response, *The Mask Lifted*, which brimmed with invective against the nun and her work. Beyond the concrete proof of his betrayal that she says she possesses, Tarabotti points out that Aprosio, a close friend of Pighetti's, would never have written a work against his sister-in-law without his consent. Tarabotti in any case succeeded in preventing the work's publication. Aprosio recycled some of the content for *Rinaldo's Shield* (*Lo scudo di Rinaldo* [Venice: Hertz, 1646]) which was published under one of Aprosio's many pseudonyms, Scipio Glareano; the personal attack against Tarabotti was almost entirely removed.

360. 2 Cor. 13:1, *In ore duorum vel trium testium stabit omne verbum* ("In the mouth of two or three witnesses shall every word stand"). Cf. also Deut. 19:15 and Matt. 18:16.

sacred seal, I cannot yet reveal, but will at the appropriate time be made public,[361] I offer clear proof: so dear a friend of yours would never have dared write against your sister-in-law without your assent and encouragement. I leave this to the judgment of those who know better than I, and I call Holy Truth as witness, even if I do not have your letters that instigated people to respond against me. I am not complaining that there were such responses, because she who writes always exposes herself to such trials. *Omnis scriptor habit contradictorem.*[362] But what truly pierces my soul is to hear that my sister's husband, loved and honored by me for his supreme virtues, was the one who encouraged this.

Our first impulses are not in our power, and therefore I cannot deny that I felt quite vexed when I first discovered this. It has been explained to me, however, that this is typical behavior nowadays. Nonetheless, thanks be to God, despite the fact that according to my enemies I have committed a great crime, I am not so friendless that I lack people who understand my motive.

If Your Eminent Lordship could recall the sentiments you expressed to me when first I showed you my *Antisatire*, you would not now behave in this way, for you never told me I should not publish it, but only suggested, I recall, that I take out a number of words that seemed to you too biased against Signor Buoninsegni, which I promptly did. Since I still have the manuscript, I can show you. So be it. God always protects innocence.

As to the apologies and other things that might follow, Your Eminent Lordship must believe me that no one in this fragile world is without some sinful stain, and I do not marvel that I am maligned, for wicked tongues dare even to slander God himself.

It was not ambition that persuaded me to publish this little work of mine, since it would be madness to build one's house on the praise of men who, if first they exalt, a moment later condemn and mistreat. Whence I care little whether or not they believe the *Paradise*

361. Aprosio subsequently wrote that Alvise Querini, secretary of the Riformatori dello Studio di Padova, had given a copy of Aprosio's manuscript to Girolamo Brusoni, who in turn sold it to Tarabotti (*Biblioteca aprosiana*, 167–70). Perhaps it was through Querini or Brusoni that Tarabotti gained her proof of Pighetti's involvement in the affair.

362. "Every writer has an opponent."

or any other writing is my own work, since I know well that virtue is disdained and despised in women.

> *Poiché qui spesso il vizio al Ciel s'inalza,*
> *E virtù 'l fianco trae povera e scalza.*[363]

Certainly these fellows must have little experience with writing, since they marvel that the style of the *Paradise* should be different from that of the *Antisatire*, whereby they show that they do not know that style must be varied according to the topic.

The fact is that all are free to do as they wish, and such clamor on Signor Buoninsegni's behalf is neither necessary or appropriate, for I know for certain that he declares himself not at all offended by me, and one should never expect unseemly remarks against a woman from a gentleman.

As for the rest, know that never did I strive to offend or jeopardize you; rather I have always esteemed your pen and loved you as a brother, although you did not return my affection, and I affectionately kiss your hands.

114
TO SIGNOR N.[364]

This excellent madame comes to honor you with her presence. She is ornamented with such sublime qualities that my pen admits it is unable to describe them as would befit her most lofty merit. It will suffice to say that she is the wife of that great Gildas who, like a new Mars, valorously defends the kingdom of Crete. May Your Lordship deign to offer her your servitude since she deserves to have the greatest potentates of the world bow to her, and I remain yours, etc.

---

363. "Since here vice is often raised to the heavens / and drags virtue by its side, poor and barefoot."

364. This letter of presentation is for Madame Gildas, to whom Tarabotti also addresses a letter; she was the wife of a French war hero in Crete (on his exploits, see for example Girolamo Brusoni, *Istoria dell'ultima guerra tra' veneziani e turchi* [Venice: Stefano Curti, 1673], bk. 7).

115
TO THE MOST ILLUSTRIOUS AND EXCELLENT
SIGNORA ELENA FOSCOLA[365]

It stands to reason that, if the heart on this occasion rushes to congratulate you on your excellent and most worthy husband's election to procurator, the pen also comes along to serve as the heart's voice. There would be so many things to say, and in particular, that any honor will always be inferior to his great merit, but it is not proper for me to express such thoughts since my most ardent servitude, which could besmirch me as partial, must prevent it. I will only say that here the glorious demonstrations of his excellence are extolled no less than your charity and courage. Like a new Esther you beseech victory for these people, yet not from Ahasuerus but from the Blessed Lord.[366] The glorious Judith will cede to you in the future, and Helen who was so renowned for her beauty will fall into oblivion.[367] An Elena who is beautiful in soul and body will provide new impetus to the pens of writers to fly to the heights of the eagle, who, always facing the sun, shares in its rays and its glory.[368] So fame circulates in this city. I ask that Your Excel-

---

365. Elena Molin married in 1624 Lunardo Foscolo (1588–1661), who became procurator of San Marco—the most prestigious office in the city after that of doge—on 20 April 1647 and who was celebrated in Venice for his military exploits (Cicogna cites a *Canzone al signor Leonardo Foscolo procuratore di San Marco, generale in Dalmazia ed Albania, per le sue gloriose imprese contro Turchi* [Venice: Andrea Baba, 1648]; see *Iscrizioni veneziane* [Venice: Giuseppe Orlandelli, 1824–53], 4:167). It is likely that Tarabotti made Elena's acquaintance through a fellow nun, Elena's aunt, of whom Tarabotti makes mention on several occasions. She may have been Laura Molin, who appears in convent documents as a chapter nun in 1650 (APV, Collezione Antica, Monalium, 1650, b. 4, 4v–5v).

366. That is, just as Esther intervened with her husband, king Ahasuerus of Persia, to save the Jews, so Elena may seek, with her prayers, a victory for the Christians in their struggle against the Turks.

367. Through her actions, Elena will prove herself more worthy than Judith, the biblical heroine often compared to Esther for her valorous defense of her people; she will also surpass Helen of Troy, who was beautiful in her person but not in her soul.

368. The eagle is associated in many cultures with the sun and with spirituality. The early Christians believed that every ten years an eagle flew near the sun to renew itself. It was said that the eagle looked directly at the sun, as the pure in soul contemplated God. Perhaps Tarabotti makes reference to the writer Aquila (the word means eagle) Barbara, of whom little is known, but with whom the nun exchanged several letters.

lency believe it, and in the meantime, implored by the lady your aunt to send her heartfelt congratulations, together we bow to you.

116

TO THE MOST ILLUSTRIOUS AND EXCELLENT SIGNOR FRANCESCO MARIA ZATI, RESIDENT OF TUSCANY AT THE MOST SERENE REPUBLIC OF VENICE[369]

If the Thracian musician[370] with his song convinced Pluto to free Eurydice from Hell, Your Illustrious Lordship with your saintly prayers beseeched His Divine Majesty to free Lady N. from convent Hell. Having learned that her departure is decreed for Saint Catherine's day,[371] a most happy turn of fate for her, she would like to thank you in person and she asks you no less for this favor than for your pardon, offering you her respects as I also do.

117

TO THE MOST ILLUSTRIOUS SIGNOR GIOVANNI POLANI[372]

I received both books, which are to my complete satisfaction because of the kindness and diligence of Your Illustrious Lordship.[373] I will not thank you, since my sisterly bond with you abhors such ceremony.[374]

369. This letter addresses the liberation of a certain Lady N. from the convent of Sant'Anna, thanks to the intervention of the Tuscan resident. Tarabotti makes reference to a similar situation in letter 41 to Enrico Cornaro.

370. Orpheus.

371. Likely the feast of Saint Catherine of Alexandria, observed on 25 November (Tarabotti's convent was founded in 1242 and dedicated to Saints Anne and Catherine), or else the feast of Saint Catherine of Siena, celebrated on 29 April (on Tarabotti's admiration for this saint, see Zanette, *Suor Arcangela*, 15–16).

372. In this letter Tarabotti addresses her friend Giovanni Polani, thanking him for books he sent her and asking him to give a copy of her *Convent Paradise* to an important literary figure whose name is not given in this letter.

373. It is unclear to which books Tarabotti refers: her own, or perhaps others procured by Polani at her request.

374. Tarabotti's warm relationship with Giovanni was established through her friendship with Betta Polani, his niece and the nun's dear friend.

I earnestly beseech you to honor me by passing along my *Paradise*, with the enclosed letter, to that heavenly swan who did not disdain to praise the glories of the most sterile and unhappy pen that writes today.[375] Please consider with your wisdom whether it is right to do this without a trace of temerity. Completely entrusting myself to your most prudent opinion, I will anxiously await your orders.

118
TO SIGNOR N.

If I have not advised your excellent Lordship before now of my efforts on your behalf with the illustrious Signor Vendramino,[376] please blame it on the continued indisposition that torments me and on the death of my most beloved sister.[377] The illustrious Signor Silvestro Valiero,[378] who has entered under your tutelage, must have told you about the quality of the exchanges I had and the efficacy of the requests I made to those excellent sirs. I have fulfilled and will fulfill the same duty with other persons whom I deem able to understand the admirable erudition of your excellent Lordship, whom I ask to remember me.

119
TO THE MOST ILLUSTRIOUS AND EXCELLENT MADAME DI AMÒ, AMBASSADRESS OF FRANCE[379]

Since we cannot come to you with our voice, the true expositor of affections, we come with pen and heart to express to Your Illustri-

---

375. It is not clear to whom Tarabotti refers here. Possibly she alludes to one of the authors whose verses are published in *Convent Paradise*, perhaps the famous poet Ciro di Pers.

376. Probably Andrea Vendramino, one of Tarabotti's correspondents, who was nephew of Tarabotti's dear friend and fellow nun in Sant'Anna, Regina Donà. Tarabotti evidently used this relationship to help the addressee of this letter.

377. Likely Camilla Tarabotti, who died 4 November 1644 (see Zanette, *Suor Arcangela*, 20).

378. Also a correspondent of Tarabotti's (see letter 52).

379. This letter to Anne des Hameaux is chronologically the last to be addressed to her in the collection. In addition to expressing Tarabotti's dismay at the departure of the ambassadress from Venice, it attests (through Tarabotti's use of the first-person plural throughout the letter) to the relationship the ambassadress had established with the nuns of Sant'Anna, who produced lacework for her.

ous Excellency the bitterness of the pain that pierces our soul at your departure.[380] It is a pain that despite the passage of time will never diminish, just as the effects of our most reverent servitude will be eternal in the eternity of your merit. We regret only that our frailty, just as it rendered us worthy of the most considerable favors from Your Excellencies,[381] will now cause us to live unhappily since we are not able to give you the greater signs of our servitude, as we wish and as befit your greatness. We have not lost hope, however, both for fulfillment and for approval where such kindness reigns.

It pains us not to be able to reduce the price as you requested, since these ladies swear that they would not work for anyone, no matter who it was, for less than two scudi for each piece of lace. We also received information from certain *maestre*[382] who say they wouldn't accept less than three ducats each for a *periolo*.[383]

I bring you this information from the mouth of Truth, and I remain your Excellency's, etc.

380. The French ambassador des Hameaux left Venice in 1645 (see ASV Collegio, *Cerimoniale*, 3.120–1; A. Baschet, *Les Archives de Venise: Histoire de la Chancellerie Secrète* [Paris: Henri Plon, 1870], 438).

381. In addition to Anne des Hameaux, Tarabotti here refers to other family members with whom she was in contact. She may intend Marguerite de Fiubet, Anne's niece with whom Tarabotti warmly corresponds (see letter 10) but who seems to have died before the des Hameaux's departure from Venice (see letter 121). She may also, or instead, refer to the ambassador himself.

382. In charitable institutions such as Venice's Casa delle Zitelle, whose female inhabitants produced lace, the *maestre* supervised the lacework.

383. Tarabotti uses the word *periolo*, which is perhaps *perolo* (Boerio), a kind of finishing or edging (here, of lace), worn on the head; Boerio calls it typical of "Paduan peasants," but Tarabotti is referring to an ornament for noblewomen.

120
TO THE MOST EXCELLENT SIGNOR
GIACOMO PIGHETTI[384]

Your Excellent Lordship's persistent opinion that I should publish these misshapen—or better mistaken—conceits throws me into great confusion, with different consequences. If I think about how kindly the divinity of your spirit looks upon them, I lose myself in obligation and I fear that perhaps your affection for me distorts that judgment which resides in you as in its true home. If I instead think that you applaud my writing based on the common opinion men have about my sex—that is, that because of our excessive ignorance everything is permissible—I become quite irritated. Among these thoughts I never, however, let myself believe that flattery leads Your Excellent Lordship to spur me to make public work that has nothing good in it, since this would do injury to your honesty, so alien to other men.

Be that as it may, I declare my writings not only unworthy of the presses but unfit to be looked upon by anyone other than my dear relatives. I know well that I have spoken out of innocence and truth, just as I confess for the rest to be ignorance itself. This limit so inborn in me must compel Your Excellent Lordship to keep under rigorous silence these expressions that certainly would encounter the fury of the arrogant sex. I pray that the Lord bestow every true blessing upon you.

121
TO THE MOST ILLUSTRIOUS AND EXCELLENT MADAME
D'AMÒ, AMBASSADRESS OF FRANCE[385]

The prudence of Your Illustrious Excellency will soothe within you the fierceness of that grief which has also struck us to the core at the death

384. The work of which Tarabotti speaks so modestly in this letter is the *Antisatire*, which she calls unworthy of being read by anyone but her brother-in-law (even if it is clear from other letters that the nun was actively involved in its publication). Despite her protests, Pighetti showed the manuscript to Aprosio, thereby sparking the subsequent conflict between Tarabotti and the Augustinian friar (see also letter 113).

385. Letter of consolation for the death of Marguerite de Fiubet, niece of Anne des Hameaux and a correspondent of Tarabotti's. The letter dates to after the pilgrimage of Anne and Marguerite to Rome (see letters 249 and 250), probably made in late 1644 or early 1645.

of Lady de Fiubet, our most beloved friend and exceptional patroness. From the most profound reaches of our heart we mourn with you, in keeping with those habits to which mortals are accustomed, while in truth it would be proper to rejoice that she has left these boundless miseries to enjoy and delight in the Elysian fields. May Your Excellency therefore take comfort and believe that the world was not fit for that precious Marguerite[386] whom the King of Glory desired to take unspoiled into his bosom. Swearing to you upon the candor of this leaf of paper that we will ceaselessly pray for the glory of that pious soul, we pray that the Lord accord you every consolation, remaining Your Excellency's, etc.

122

TO THE REVEREND FATHER N.[387]

The most courteous letter of Your Lordship spurs me to respond to you, whence once again you are the reason I speak, though religion greatly values silence.

Starting from the beginning, I say I thank you as profoundly as my frail state will allow for the anxiousness with which you sought to be apprised of my health and the sadness you felt over my sickness. However I will never agree that you need not account to God for making me break my silence. Remember that if Adam, asked by God why he ate the apple, blamed Eve, and she was punished for this reason, I will keep this example in mind, and if I am asked by our Lord at Judgment Day why I broke my silence, I will blame Father

386. As in other letters regarding Marguerite, Tarabotti plays on the many nuances of her name: in French and Italian, a *marguerite* or *margherita* is a daisy; in Latin, a pearl.

387. This biting letter is a response to Aprosio's efforts to dissuade Tarabotti from publishing the *Antisatire*. She expresses her intention to proceed despite the fact that such an action appears to conflict with the silence expected of nuns. She justifies her action in two ways: on the one hand, she reminds Aprosio that in other circumstances he himself encouraged her to break her silence; on the other, she insists on the importance of revealing the true nature of men. This letter is among the seven autograph letters in the Biblioteca Universitaria di Genova where it bears the date 14 April 1644 (BUG E VI 22, c. 133 [Francesca Medioli, "Alcune lettere autografe di Arcangela Tarabotti: Autocensura e immagine di sé," *Rivista di storia e letteratura religiosa* 32.1 (1996): 151–55]). Tarabotti made only slight changes to the letter for publication: the most important ones are noted below.

Ventimiglia.[388] Furthermore it is not wise for a good and upstanding preacher, as I hold you to be and as you are universally considered, to advise a woman religious to greet everyone, when the blessed Lord gave as a reminder or precept to his apostles: *Neminem per viam salutaveritis.*[389] I do not know why you think that, in coming to the parlor grille, I must account for my silence, given that my words are always aimed at exposing the truth of men's malice and therefore cannot but edify and yield more than I can do with silence. This is the perfection I am following to such an extent (praise be to my Bridegroom) that I hope to reach the Seraphim choir and also to be counted among those most holy virgins whom I joined when I wreathed my head with their sacred veils and also became one of the martyresses.

If my seclusion were greater than Domitian's, I would be determined to catch more flies than he did, yet I don't want to hunt down those who fly around stinging me.[390] In addition, I do not know why Your Lordship wishes to deprive me of those merits which are my due, and at the same time you desire my death, since yearning for me to pray in Paradise for your improvement is an infallible sign that you want me to go as a herald before you. This matter cannot be decided here, but you may nevertheless take comfort because even if I remain after your passing in convent Heaven, I promise to pray for the salvation of your soul.

Signor Buoninsegni may expect my *Antisatire* more than ever, since those things that are said against evil and in support of truth cannot be renounced by one who wishes to arrive at perfection. Quite the contrary, they must fervently be thrust into broad daylight in order that their spiritual benefits may be extracted, since it is much better (as you know) to preach with honesty than to keep silent out of negligence. The point is that, since Your Lordship is partial to Buoninsegni,

---

388. P[adre] V[enti] M[iglia].

389. Luke 10:4, "Greet no man by the way."

390. Domitian (51–96 CE), Roman emperor known for the cruelty with which he punished those who refused to honor him. Svetonius recounts that the emperor passed the time by capturing and killing flies with a pointed stylus (*Domitianus*, par. 3). A poem by Giovan Battista Lalli entitled *Domitian the Fly-Killer* (*La Moscheide, ovvero Domiziano il moschicida* [Venice: Giacomo Sarzina, 1624]), recounts the story of Domitian who, after being stung by a swarm of flies, declares war against them.

you would like me to refrain from speaking of him, and therefore you try to dissuade me by labeling this truth which is so pleasing to God as a satire and an improper battle for a woman religious. But be this as it may, I persevere in my righteous opinions, and therefore I will not yield from this one. Likewise, I will never yield my sense of obligation to you and to the reverend Father R.[391] for the acclamations and tributes your unparalleled kindnesses gave to my most imperfect works before those reverend mothers who had the good fortune to enjoy your fruitful sermons, of which we here were not worthy.[392] My obligations are even greater because, if we had enjoyed the blessing that you gave to the nuns of San Maffio in leaving Paradise open to them, I, as an Angel, would immediately have flown out of Paradise to have my *Paternal Tyranny* printed.[393]

To be initiated into an Italian Athenaeum[394] is such a great honor that, since I cannot offer adequate thanks, I will value it with my heart as greatly as I little merit it. Such excessive favors overwhelm me and show me that, if even you seem to desire my death, nonetheless you want to immortalize me.[395] Rest assured, Your Lordship, that I will always express my thanks to you from Paradise.

391. R[everendo] P[adre] R.

392. According to Zanette (*Suor Arcangela*, 255), Aprosio and this Father R., an unidentified preacher, visited the convent of San Matteo (Maffio) in Murano, where they spoke approvingly of Tarabotti's *Convent Paradise*. Tarabotti notes that the preachers did not deign to visit Sant'Anna.

393. Tarabotti plays on the word "paradise," alluding both to Aprosio's mention of her *Convent Paradise* during his visit to San Maffio, and to Aprosio's visit itself, which opened the door to Paradise. Therefore we can read: if Aprosio and his companion had opened the path to Paradise to the nuns of Sant'Anna as they did to those of San Maffio (through reading from *Convent Paradise* and by their presence), Tarabotti (as an "angel," for her name, "Arcangela") would have seized the occasion to flee the convent in order to publish her *Paternal Tyranny*, a work that represents the convent in a very different way than *Convent Paradise*.

394. In the autograph letter cited above (n. 387), Tarabotti writes that Aprosio not only apprised her of such a presentation but himself organized it ("That I am to be initiated *by you* into one of the Athenæa of Italy" [emphasis added]). Aprosio was a member of several academies and it is not clear to which one Tarabotti alludes. There is no record of such a presentation.

395. In the autograph letter (see above n. 387), Tarabotti offers praise for Aprosio that is absent from the published version. Translated, the original continues: "to immortalize me, with a mere stroke of your most glorious pen, which can rightly be called divine, since it

But perhaps I have dwelt too long on such chatter, and Your Reverend Lordship, who is to blame for this, will certainly feel pangs of conscience for having made me lose the favors of Heaven, since it is said of the one who is silent *elevabit se super se.*[396] I offer you my respects.

123

TO THE MOST ILLUSTRIOUS SIG[NOR] N.[397]

I am sending back to Your most Illustrious Lordship that *Ibraim* which, in order to be rightly called the *Illustrious Bassà*, has consacrated itself to your worth.[398]

To transcribe my works, you have found a man so old he seems like Time himself; but Time is winged, and this man so lazy that he could be compared to an ant; indeed he is like that old man who went searching for Maria in Ravenna.[399] He no longer knows how to hold a

---

enjoys not only its own immortality, but confers it upon others and upon me who has been dead and buried for many years."

396. "He will raise himself above himself." Cf. Lam. 3:27–28, where in the Vulgate we read *bonum est viro cum portaverit iugum ab adolescientia sua sedebit solitarius et tacebit quia levavit super se* ("It is good for a man, when he hath borne the yoke from his youth. He shall sit solitary, and hold his peace: because he hath taken it up upon himself"). This phrase was often cited as *quia levabit se super se,* as here (see, for example, Aelredus Rievallensi, *Speculum charitatis* [*PL* 195: 0543A]; Joannes Cassianus, *Collationes* [*PL* 49: 0967D]).

397. In this letter, Tarabotti criticizes her correspondent in a tone that is at once teasing and sharp. She also attempts to make arrangements for the marriage of a young girl. Because the heading of the printed letter abbreviates the title of the person to whom Tarabotti writes, it is unclear whether she addresses a man or a woman; the prickly tenor of the letter suggests a man, an assumption we follow in the letter's translation.

398. *Ibrahim, ou l'illustre Bassà* (Paris: A. de Sommaville, 1641–44) by Madeleine de Scudéry (1607–1701), a French poet and novelist. The book was translated into Italian in three parts. A translation of the second book (*Ibrahim, overo l'Illustre Bassa,* trans. P. Cerchiari) was published in Venice in 1646 by Valvasense, the favored publisher of the Accademia degli Incogniti and of Loredano. Loredano dedicated the third part of the book, an Italian translation probably issued in Venice, to Tarabotti (cf. Loredano, *Lettere,* 435). This third volume has not been found.

399. *Quel vecchio ch'andava cercando Maria per Ravenna.* "Cercare Maria per Ravenna" is a proverbial way of saying "to seek out something that turns out to be harmful," popularized by an anonymous fifteenth-century poem (reprinted in H. Varnhagen, *De verbis nonnullis*

pen, and it seems to me that he should follow the example of the Baron of N., who always prays to God that he be taken from this world when he is no longer able to serve women.[400]

I am waiting for the priest who in one trip will help in two ways. With his pen he will help to recopy, and with his aspergillum he may be able to chase away the spirits that surround me, since I am again suffering from a constriction in my chest.

The girl for whom we are seeking a husband under no circumstances wants Signor N. because (joking aside) her mother has learned that he has next to nothing, and she says that his forty years are excessive for her age. The one who is by trade a dyer[401] would be more to her taste in all ways. In short, a handsome, lively, and hard-working young man suits her better than a stern old fool like the widower who has been suggested. Your most Illustrious Lordship knows her needs: come up with something appropriate if you want approval. I bow to you.

124

TO THE MOST ILLUSTRIOUS SIGNORA
GUID'ASCANIA ORSI[402]

I leave it to the unparalleled prudence of Your Ladyship to consider how unbearable is the suffering that torments me more each day as a result of

---

linguae veteris francogallicae una cum fabella qual sermone italico composita et Maria per Ravenna inscripta [Erlangen: University of Erlangen, 1903]). In the poem, a beautiful young girl, Ginevra, is forced because of her father's avarice to marry an old man rather than the young Diomede with whom she has fallen in love. Deprived of Ginevra, Diomede leaves, but later comes back to town disguised as a female servant Maria. When the old man has to go away for several months on business, he wants someone to keep Ginevra company, so he searches for Maria throughout Ravenna, finally finding and convincing "her" to stay with his wife. This arrangement leads to the old man's cuckolding and death.

400. There may be some sexual innuendo in this reference, building on the allusion to the *Maria per Ravenna* tale; however, Tarabotti may simply refer to the gentlemanly help sometimes provided by noble men to women in need.

401. *Quel dai colori;* the suitor in question was probably a *vendecolori* (someone who made or sold dyes).

402. Tarabotti explains to her correspondent the origins of the *Tears*, which she composed in memory of Regina Donà.

the enormous loss of my Regina.[403] One must come to peace, however, with the will of our Lord and remember that we are all mortal.

As to the rest, you may be assured that the remainder of my life will be unhappy, since I must live separated in body from that beautiful soul which enjoys eternal delights in the Empyrean. I will assuage my heart's torment with the pleasure I experience in describing my continuing suffering and the admirable qualities of that queen[404] who has flown away to her eternal repose.

Your Illustrious Ladyship should know that on the very night in which my once beloved friend flew to the bosom of her Bridegroom and left me to suffer, deprived of the best part of myself, on that night, I say, my affection obliged me to compose some pages in her honor, but devoid of all good rhetorical order, confused in phrasing, poor in erudition, rich in error, and lacking in any decent qualities. I was aware of their imperfections, and although I was pierced through and beside myself with grief, I knew that they were unworthy of appearing in public and rather deserved to be buried for eternity. Therefore, having set them aside (since the illness that afflicts me daily did not allow me to revise and edit them to any kind of perfection), I threw them into the river Lethe.[405]

But lo and behold, the sister of my dearly departed companion came to visit me. Since a friend of mine had given her these scribblings, she begged me with great emotion to publish them.[406] I resisted, not wishing to oblige her at that time. Finally, won over by her entreaties, I gave them over to her.

If Your Illustrious Ladyship should happen to come upon them, be kind to them and believe me that although grief teaches the bereaved to render vivid their pain with words, my heart was unable

---

403. Until her death 31 March 1645, Regina Donà was Tarabotti's dearest convent friend. They entered the convent at the same time and took their vows together. The *Tears* center on Tarabotti's grief at Regina's death, but Tarabotti frequently uses the work also to justify her publication of the *Letters*, to which she appended the *Tears*.

404. In the original, Tarabotti makes a play on her friend's name Regina, which is also the Italian word for queen.

405. The mythological river of forgetfulness.

406. Regina's sister was Andriana Donà Malipiero, one of Tarabotti's correspondents and the dedicatee of the *Tears*.

to dictate well-chosen and lively conceits to my pen, since, being dead from grief and stunned by so great a loss, it knows not how to express anything of worth.

Adieu, my dear Lady.

125

TO THE MOST ILLUSTRIOUS SIGNOR COUNT COMMENDATOR PIETRO PAOLO BISSARI

The effects of Your Illustrious Lordship's favors reached me just as the Fates were about to cut the thread of my life, but, having seen me glorified so loftily by your celestial pen, they thought me immortal and spared me. My soul, too, was about to become immortal among the blessed chambers of Paradise but, blinded by the splendors of an Apollo, it returned to my breast and restored breath to my body, to Death's dismay. I don't know if I should say that such miracles were brought about by your divine compositions or by the thought of you. I well know that I was abandoned by my physicians and that your compositions seemed to be a magic capable of driving every ailment from my body.

On bended knee, therefore, I thank Your Illustrious Lordship with the humility mortals usually reserve for gods; and I will wait to express the depth of my debt to you until I have greater need. At present I am too agitated, a result not only of the constriction in my chest, but of the physicians who torment me incessantly with little mercy. I bow to you.

126

TO SIGNOR N.[407]

With all the hurry of N., Your Lordship[408] still discovered the anachronism I made in my other letter, and pointed it out to me, too. You

---

407. Tarabotti thanks her anonymous correspondent who noted an error she had made in a previous letter, confusing two Roman emperors. Tarabotti does not seem entirely pleased by her correspondent's correction and invites him not to complain too much about women.

408. V[ostra] S[ignoria].

must have sympathy for that illness which, in robbing me of my memory, brings discomfort and suffering to my unhappy self. Whence it came about that, since I was experiencing mortal pains in my heart, I recalled cruel Nero rather than lascivious Elagabalus.[409] I would like to thank you with the liveliest sentiments of my soul, but since they have all expired with my illness, I thank you with the weak state in which I find myself and which is indeed proportionate to the weakness of my pen. Your gracious displays bind me, your praise consoles me, and your kind letters cheer me. I cannot respond to you punctually because I can't think properly. I say you might, like Jove, make use of the eagle, but beyond that, you cannot employ the swan since you are its enemy.[410] Go ahead and exaggerate the cruelty of women, Your Lordship, but the numerous examples of men's wounds ought to impede your discussion of this subject. I regret that I cannot speak with you as I would about these matters, given my indisposition, but know that *sufficit bona voluntas*.[411] And do me the favor of apprising me precisely of N.'s conduct, about which, if it is not honorable, I'd rather not know. Adieu.

409. Tarabotti explains the anachronism thus: beset by illness when she was looking for a historical example for her previous letter, she thought first of the Roman emperor Nero (37–68 CE), known for extreme cruelty, rather than of Elagabalus, or Heliogabalus (c. 203–22 CE), an emperor famous for his licentiousness.

410. The eagle is often associated with Jove who, in love with the handsome son of Tros, Ganymede, transformed himself into an eagle and carried the youth away with him to Mount Olympus. Jove also took on the shape of a swan to seduce Leda. Tarabotti says that her correspondent would not be able to effect this second transformation because he is an enemy of swans, that is, of poets.

411. "Good will suffices." The expression is found in the *Regula Bullata* of Francis of Assisi (chap. 2), with reference to the conditions necessary for entering into the order of Friars Minor. One should rid oneself of all goods, but if that is not possible, good will is sufficient.

127
TO SIGNOR N.[412]

I delivered Your Lordship's letter directly into the hands of the illustrious Signor Vendramino,[413] and I will always consider it a singular
favor to have the honor of serving you. As to the composition, be assured that I have no need of encouragement in my ardent desire to
perfect it, but a constant constriction in my chest that consumes me,
may I say, to my very core and almost entirely takes my breath away,
assails me with such vehemence that it makes my body ache and causes me to throw my pen aside. I offer you my respects.

128
TO THE ILLUSTRIOUS SIGNORA N.[414]

Letters now arrive with such delay that the last time I sent off my post,
I received one from Your Illustrious Ladyship, from which I understand the matter to be just as I imagined it in my mind. I know the
sincerity of your heart, and I cannot without painful sentiment recall
having addressed those lines to Your Illustrious Ladyship, which, if
they have a certain shadow of diffidence, are nonetheless excusable.
Your kindness must excuse me, while I beg your pardon on bended
knee, since even God appreciates repentance and confession. I confess
to Your Illustrious Ladyship that I have erred and I await not just pardon, but a favor of your piety; nor can I believe that Signor N. would
refuse such a small thing to so great an intercessor as yourself. I know
well the vanities of youth, but if I ask for the compositions in their cur-

---

412. This letter, written during an episode of what Tarabotti termed the "constriction in
my chest," also highlights Tarabotti's role as an intermediary for others' letters, despite her
condition as a cloistered nun.

413. Perhaps Andrea Vendramino, the nephew of Regina Donà and the addressee of letter
85.

414. Once again Tarabotti's letters reveal the instability of epistolary communication. Here
we see how the slowness of the mail caused a misunderstanding. Excusing herself to her
correspondent, Tarabotti asks that she help her to retrieve some pages she had entrusted to
a certain Signor N. for transcription. Also notable in the letter is the mention of the war of
Candia (1645–69), about which the nun updates her correspondent, who is not presently
in Venice.

rent state (without him having to transcribe them as I had requested), he has no reason to refuse them to one who is his equal. Therefore make use of the authority of your patronage, for I am assured of a good outcome.

There are many things I would add in this regard, but I am in the hands of physicians who not only leave my veins exhausted of blood, but my eyesight weakened and myself practically devoid of spirit and energy. Your prayers, to which I heartily commend myself, would go a long way toward strengthening me.

As to the rest, the turmoil of war is quite great and there is fear that the kingdom of Crete may fall into the hands of the great lord,[415] to the detriment of all Christendom and particularly of the Crown of Spain.[416] Our armada, however, with the papal galleys and others, have left together to fight; in fact, it is said that we have had a great victory.[417] But there is no certainty. We must piously believe, as I truly pray, that the good Lord, after having so tried his beloved subjects, will recall that we are His people and forgive the many, many offenses of false Christians, if He so desires in His infinite mercy. I bow to your illustrious Ladyship.

---

415. The Ottoman sultan Ibrahim I, who defeated Venetian forces and conquered Candia in 1669.

416. It was suspected that Spain was attempting to exploit the tensions between Venice and the Turks to obtain more power in the Christian world (see S. Romanin, *Storia documentata di Venezia* [Venice: Pietro Naratovich, 1858], 7:416–47). A victory for the Turks would have blocked Spanish aspirations.

417. Venice had many victories, and many defeats, in the long war of Candia. It is possible that Tarabotti refers to the Venetian victory of May 1649 at Fochies, under the command of Jacopo Riva, for which "great rejoicing was had in Venice" (ibid., 415).

129

TO THE MOST ILLUSTRIOUS AND EXCELLENT MADAME ANNA DI GREMONVILLE, AMBASSADRESS OF FRANCE[418]

Your Excellency's kindness can delay favoring me with regard to the drapes and cradle,[419] since instead of reciting and singing epithalamia of love we must prepare the funeral rites for Death, which last night left its cadaver here in our convent when the Fates snipped the stem of life of a nun who was some one hundred years in age.

Let this suffice to ensure that your efforts are not in vain, and meanwhile I will not fail to entreat His Divine Goodness to grant you a male child, the image of you for the glory of posterity and our common consolation.

Mademoiselle di Ravan, having lately nursed in herself a certain, shall I say, jealousy, or rather envy, sowed in her heart by a great fear of falling from your grace, seems to be starting to hate her brother-to-be, if that is what he is, though still in the womb of Your Excellency. Together we bow to you.

130

TO THE MOST ILLUSTRIOUS AND EXCELLENT SIGNOR BERTUCCI VALIER

So that Your Excellency may see that not bold temerity but a just necessity brings me to the tribunal of your piety to ask new favors, I send you the enclosed. Since you are a new and always beneficent Jove, father of the Graces, I am certain that he who makes this request of me will, as a consequence, receive grace, and I favor although I do not merit it. If I trust too much, let Your Excellency attribute it to the experience of your unparalleled kindness that I have had on other oc-

---

418. Tarabotti updates her correspondent on recent affairs in the convent: preparations for a wedding, perhaps of a convent boarder, have been postponed because of the death of an elderly sister. She expresses hope that the ambassadress, who is pregnant, is carrying a boy. But she also informs her that one of her daughters, Mademoiselle (*Mamosella*) di Ravan, entrusted as a boarder to Tarabotti, is already jealous of her potential brother. Anne de Grémonville did in fact give birth to a son, baptized Marco in honor of the Republic that witnessed his birth.

419. It seems that the ambassadress was to help the bride to assemble her trousseau.

casions. Therefore, on bended knee, I wait for your divine kindness to honor him who seeks my aid and to console me as I desire.

In the meantime, I continue to pray unceasingly to our Lord for the return of your health and I wish you a lifetime as immortal as your name, most reverently kissing your robes.

131

TO SIGNOR N.[420]

If the illustrious baron of Copet[421] keeps his promise with regard to printing my book as he did to come with that lady, I believe that, if I awaited him in vain until the end of that day, I may wait for its publication until the end of my life without ever seeing it.

Yesterday I began to scheme for his permit[422] but given what has come of that personage's first promise to me I deem him to have been born in Normandy[423] and I will not proceed any further. I bow to you.

420. Tarabotti responds to her anonymous correspondent to express annoyance with a mutual acquaintance—a certain baron of Copet—who offered to publish one of her works, probably her *Paternal Tyranny*, likely in France.

421. Tarabotti does not elsewhere in the *Letters* mention this baron. Tarabotti speaks repeatedly in the *Letters* of her attempt to publish the work in France with the help of a young man named Colisson, who however let her down. It is not clear whether her efforts with the baron and with Colisson were related.

422. Tarabotti had evidently tried to help the baron in an affair in Venice, but she says she will no longer help him since he is not helping her.

423. Tarabotti repeatedly in the *Letters* refers to the supposed unreliability of the Normans.

132

TO THE MOST ILLUSTRIOUS SIGNOR LUIGI DE MATHEREL, RESIDENT OF FRANCE AT THE MOST SERENE REPUBLIC OF VENICE[424]

I delayed sending the rest of the book to Your Illustrious Lordship because of the promises of a certain person to transcribe it. But since he has not kept his word, I am more convinced than ever that it is truly a trait of men to promise much and deliver little. Therefore I resolve to send it to Your Illustrious Lordship in its current state, since it seems to me that the script is sufficiently clear. The division into paragraphs will be left to that person who must help me by following the marks of my pen.[425] I would write to him myself, but without knowing his name or title I hesitate to do so. Thus I entrust my child to Your Illustrious Lordship with all my love; and while I elect you as its godfather as it comes into the world, I beg you to gather it in the embrace of your authority, and I bow to you.

133

TO THE MOST ILLUSTRIOUS AND EXCELLENT SIGNORA RENATA DI CLARAMONTE, MARCHIONESS DI GALERANDA[426]

Those things that, long desired, torment the one who desires them, console the one who seeks them once obtained. After having anxiously awaited news of Your Excellency, I had the good fortune to receive a most kind letter of yours that filled my heart with consolation. I

424. Tarabotti persists in her efforts to have her *Paternal Tyranny* published in France with the help of the French diplomat Matharel (see also letter 58). A certain man did not fulfill his promise to the nun to transcribe the final part of work, so she has to send it to Matharel in rough copy.

425. It seems Tarabotti made notes on her manuscript indicating where she wished to have paragraph divisions.

426. It was through the Marchioness de Gallerande that Tarabotti met the marchioness's secretary, Colisson. This letter, full of admiration for the marchioness, is from the period in which Tarabotti's hope that the *Paternal Tyranny* would be published in France had not been displaced by bitter disappointment. The marchioness left Venice, together with other members of the French community, between 1647 and 1648 (Zanette, *Suor Arcangela*, 424).

feel new hope rise in me that I may yet enjoy the longed-for results of those promises which, by obliging you to favor me, bind me with enduring chains of eternal debt.

In the meantime, I pray to Heaven that these promises be fulfilled, for just as the star of the Lord showed itself to the holy Magi at the birth of Christ, so may the kindest star of Your Excellency show itself to be favorable to me with regard to the news I so desire and may it show me the road by which I may attain the precious treasure of your most precious favor. Wishing you a century of grace and prosperity in these holy holidays, and bowing to you, I give myself anew to Your Illustrious Excellency, etc.

134

TO THE MOST ILLUSTRIOUS SIGNOR LUIGI DI MATHEREL, RESIDENT OF FRANCE AT THE MOST SERENE REPUBLIC OF VENICE[427]

I wish Your Illustrious Lordship to favor me by personally sending the enclosed to the eminent cardinal Mazarin's librarian.[428] If the address is not appropriate in its titles or anything else, may your kindness deign to make a proper cover for it. In any case I beg you to make sure it reaches its destination safely for this matter is very important to me.

Please honor me, too, with a visit at your convenience, which will serve to bind me more greatly to your merit with chains of indissoluble obligation. I know I ask too much, but I also know that the goodness of Your Illustrious Lordship is immense, and I am yours, etc.

427. This letter belongs to a series of letters that tell the story of Tarabotti's attempt to print her *Paternal Tyranny* in France by entrusting it to Colisson. Tarabotti now turns not only to Matharel but, in letters that follow, to the powerful French prime minister Jules Mazarin and his librarian, Gabriel Naudé, to bring the affair to a conclusion.

428. The Italian-born Jules Mazarin (1602–61), cardinal and famous French statesman (see letter 136). Gabriel Naudé (1600–653; see below) was his librarian.

135

TO SIGNOR GABRIEL NAUDEO, LIBRARIAN OF THE MOST EMINENT CARDINAL MAZZARINO[429]

Just as I always considered the honor of those visits you once bestowed upon me, with the aid of that great Gremonville[430] who is so well known to the world, to be the result of my good fortune, so now I rely on the same to receive from your kindness a favor that will cause me to owe you my very life. Confident in your most courteous offers, I feel I have already received this favor. The declarations once made to me nourish my heart with these hopes and presage a most happy outcome to the affairs I am about to explain to you. If I did not take advantage of them before in practice, it was because I did not have occasion, and to bother important people unnecessarily is temerity.

Know, then, Your Lordship, that my soul is more agitated and confused than those of the damned. Sir Colisson,[431] son of sir Nicolo, doctor of law, citizen of Paris, a youth of about twenty-two years, visited me several times with the Marchioness di Galeranda, and displayed enormous delight in my compositions. Persuasively, with prayers and promises, he said and did enough that, with the added entreaties of that lady who is most kind, I finally gave him a work to be printed.[432] Now six months have passed in which I have had news neither of him

---

429. Gabriel Naudé, librarian to the cardinal Jules Mazarin. Sent to Italy in 1645 to gather books for the cardinal's library, Naudé arrived in December at Venice, the peninsula's printing capital. During his visit, he went repeatedly to converse with Tarabotti, and he asked her to contribute some of her works to the collection he was establishing. In this letter, addressed to Naudé after his return to France, Tarabotti asks for his help in resolving a problem that was causing her great anguish: the apparent loss of her *Paternal Tyranny*, which she had sent to France for publication. She desires that the librarian, and even the cardinal, help her to put the work to press, or at least that they send it back to her. Tarabotti sends this letter through the French resident in Venice Louis Matharel (see letter 134), together with another letter, addressed directly to the cardinal, which follows this one.

430. Nicolas Bretel de Grémonville, dear friend to Tarabotti, whom she met during his tenure as ambassador in Venice, probably hosted Naudé during his stay in the city. As we read in this letter, it was he who introduced Naudé to Tarabotti.

431. The secretary to the Marchioness de Gallerande, who is mentioned directly after.

432. *Paternal Tyranny*.

nor of the work,[433] which, since it is the offspring of my unrefined mind, it breaks my heart to have lost, and I fear I have been deceived by that fellow. Let your prudence consider, on the basis of the temerity that makes me turn to Your Most Eminent Lord with the enclosed,[434] whether having lost it pierces my soul. If, however, Your Lordship should deem it too improper, keep it and do not present it to that kindest prince.[435] Please do me the honor, too, of inquiring after the aforementioned youth and, if he cannot publish the work, may your goodness help me do so.

If the request is too great, make it more modest by simply returning the book to me safely. If I dare much without being worthy, may Your Lordship remember that prayers are offered to God even by infidels and He does not scorn them. Therefore do not disdain these prayers that I so fervently bring you with regard to the aforementioned matter, for I await your courteous response.

136

TO THE MOST EMINENT CARDINAL MAZZARINO[436]

The fame that brings its call to every angel of the universe reveals how, since Your Eminence is a true portrait of God on earth, whosoever appeals to your most high tribunal receives a righteous and per-

---

433. Tarabotti almost certainly composed this letter at the end of 1648, since she says that six months have passed since Colisson's departure along with the rest of the French community (see n. 426), and in the contemporaneous letter to Mazarin she refers to an event of November 1648 (see n. 438).

434. That is, the letter to Mazarin that follows this one in the printed collection.

435. We do not know if Naudé gave the letter to the cardinal (nor if Matharel sent the letter to Naudé). We have no evidence, either from Tarabotti's letter collection or from elsewhere, that the nun received a response to these letters.

436. Tarabotti now turns directly to the powerful cardinal to seek his help in recovering her *Paternal Tyranny* manuscript. Jules Mazarin (1602–61) was born near Rome and soon entered into diplomatic service for the Holy See. He spent some years in France in this capacity (1630–32) and returned there in 1640. Mazarin was not a consecrated priest, but he was named a cardinal in 1641. A figure of great authority, Mazarin became still more powerful following the death in 1643 of Louis XIII, thanks to the support of the queen regent, Anne of Austria. With this letter, therefore, Tarabotti turns to one of the highest authorities in France.

fect justice. That fame, I say, came to this prison and recounted how Your Eminence—who can be called a sun in the temple of the universe, spreading the rays of your splendor equally in every part of the world—appeared with the brightness of your light to honor the nobility of Venice as well. However, this Republic did not pretend, most Excellent Lord, to add honors to the purple which, dyed in the crimson that flowed from the veins of our God, consistently confers unrivaled honors and grandeur.[437] The nobility accepted you with universal applause into their *Consiglio Serenissimo*,[438] and the subjects, with devout fervor, worship the vastness of your merits with veneration.

Guided then by the universal acclamations and by my personal devotion, I would like to congratulate you on this and I dare not. But let my fears this time cede to my respect as I rejoice in this, reverently bowed at your sacred feet. Devotedly I kiss them as a sign of what all nations will have to do when you sit on Saint Peter's throne, which you merit by virtue of the perfection that shines within you, and bestow favors to the satisfaction of Christianity and the glory of the Vatican.[439]

May you, the image of kindness, receive these heartfelt wishes, and excusing such boldness, blame it on Signor Naudeo, who made wings for my boldness when he asked me for my works in order to house them in Your Eminence's most richly endowed library. And he must now seek your pardon. Also complicit in this crime (if it is a crime to worship a god) are the Signors Gremonville, who encouraged me to give my works to him.

Emboldened by such successes, I come before your supreme justice, and the reasons for my case will be explained to Your Eminence by your librarian. Meanwhile, since you are the Astraea[440] of this monarchy, I pray the depths of your mercy not to allow the city of Paris, which is called a Paradise for women,[441] to become an Inferno

---

437. "Purple" refers here to the purple robes worn by cardinals.

438. Tarabotti makes reference to the inscription of Mazarin into the Venetian nobility on 20 November 1648, upon a large payment to the Republic (see Zanette, *Suor Arcangela*, 425).

439. It was widely assumed that Mazarin had ambitions to the papacy, which were however never fulfilled.

440. The goddess of Justice.

441. Elsewhere, Tarabotti also describes France as a refuge for women: "In France, Germany and many northern provinces, women run households, handle money, and keep ac-

for me where I lose forever a work that I gave to be published to one who deceitfully denies it to me.

I know that you are adored by the French people and are the oracle of the universe, whence you will not permit that I alone fail to receive your kindness; and, as I wait for it, I wish an all-powerful scepter for Your Eminence's sacred hands, and I bow down to ask you for your holy blessing.

137
TO THE MOST ILLUSTRIOUS AND EXCELLENT
SIGNOR BERTUCCI VALIERO[442]

Even if I find myself in bed tormented by a fearsome constriction in my chest that often leads my soul into the jaws of death, my ears ring with the joyful news that in Your Lordship's most serene household a son has been born, at which I rejoice with all my soul. My heart, which was half dead in the languor of my illness, takes new life as it considers what glorious achievements the posterity of the great house of Valier promises for our native city. May Your Excellency and the excellent procurator not disdain to receive these strokes of my most reverent respect and appreciate the well wishes which issue forth from the candor of my most reverent servitude, while, glad for your joy, I will eternally sing:

> *Oh dèi del mar godete*
> *L'eroe che, nato a pena,*
> *Posto ha di gloria in seno al mar le mete.*
> *Teti*[443] *lieta è serena;*
> *Sempre in virtù di sì gran parto ondeggi.*

---

counts of merchandise; even noblewomen shop in the marketplace for their families' needs. They enjoy liberty and make use of that free will granted by the Giver of all good things…." (Tarabotti, *Paternal Tyranny*, ed. Panizza, 100).

442. Tarabotti congratulates her correspondent on the birth of his grandson (to Bertucci's son Silvestro). The child was born after Silvestro's nomination to *procuratore* in 1649 (see letter 93). Tarabotti encloses a composition praising the child's birth and comparing him to Achilles, born of a Nereid, to underscore the intrinsic link between the child and the sea.

443. Thetis, the most famous of the Nereides, or marine goddesses; mother of Achilles.

Dalla culla agitato,
Non dorme ei, no, ma per indurlo al sonno
Diano che dar gli ponno,
Le Nereidi vezzose:
In seno all'acque algose
Di margarite eoe letto gemmato;
Ché ben si deve a lui riposo tale,
Se da un nume dell'Adria ebbe il natale.[444]

138

TO THE MOST ILLUSTRIOUS SIGNOR COUNT COMMENDATOR PIETRO PAOLO BISSARI

In accordance with Your Illustrious Lordship's promise, I have been awaiting the Paradise of your compositions in order to cheer myself with such glory. My anticipation has been in vain, but never in vain is my most devoted respect. With such I wish Your Illustrious Lordship in these highest holidays an uninterrupted series of successes and honors, for you and for your house. I hope for you, with the new year, a century of life, and I most reverently kiss your hands, remaining Your Illustrious Lordship's, etc.

---

444. "O gods of the sea, delight / in the hero who, newly born/ has placed in his breast the goal of glory at sea. / Happy Thetis is serene; / May she always rock in the waves by virtue of so noble a birth. / Lulled by the cradle / He does not sleep, no, but to help him to slumber / Let the charming Nereides / give him what they can: / in the bosom of the marshy waters / a bed bejeweled with oriental pearls; / For well he deserves such a repose, / if he is born of an Adriatic deity."

139

TO THE MOST ILLUSTRIOUS AND EXCELLENT MADAME DI GREMONVILLE, AMBASSADRESS OF FRANCE[445]

Your Excellency, my absolute mistress, can embarrass me as you wish, but I pray you, on bended knee, not to do so in this way that torments me excessively.

Your illustrious daughters are provided adequate warmth and food, whence I swear to you, on the candor of this leaf of paper, that I treat them with as much love as I would if they had been born of my womb, and I serve them with the respect and diligence that their birth demands. You are not at all indebted to me for this, since when I chose to take them as charges, I also committed to serve them well.

Let Your Excellency rest assured of my devoted affection and of my unceasing servitude, as I, humbly offering you respects in their name, most devotedly kiss your hands, pleading that you cease to give me such excessively generous gifts.

140

TO THE MOST ILLUSTRIOUS SIGNOR N.[446]

Yesterday evening, amid the gloom of night and of my thoughts, the light of Your Illustrious Lordship's graceful conceits appeared to me and had the same effect on me that Saint Elmo's fire has on sailors,[447] illuminating me with its announcement of help for my dear vestal virgin. I realized then that such consolation came precisely from the palace whence royal favors are dispensed and where Your Illustrious

445. Tarabotti's affection for the Grémonville daughters, boarders in the convent of Sant'Anna, is evident in this letter, in which the nun declares that she loves the girls as if they were her own, and that they lack for nothing. The ambassadress's expressions of gratitude only embarrass the nun.

446. This letter addresses the affairs of certain women whom Tarabotti seeks to help. She thanks her correspondent for the help he has already offered his "dear vestal virgin" (*cara vestale*; another nun), and encourages him to persist in his efforts to aid other ladies of whom she writes in letters 22 and 104.

447. The electrical current observed around the mast of a ship, sometimes interpreted as a sign of hope. Saint Elmo is the patron saint of sailors.

Lordship, even if you fulfill the duties of Momus,[448] still holds straight the scales of Justice, who is also a lady.

It brought me no surprise to hear that iron is unyielding,[449] but I am amazed that you, with the magnet of your kindness, do not know how to draw it towards you, or rather that, by placing it in the fire of your authority and of your firmness, you are not able to soften it. It is certainly true that this is a quality of women, because it is said of one of us: *O mulier quae aemolisti durum, quae vicisti fortem.*[450] I do not want to believe, however, that you wish to be like wax, receiving so easily the imprint of the desires of Signor Ferro.[451] Rather I believe that your exceptional prudence will not give your irrevocable promise if the calculations mentioned by the most excellent Cornaro[452] have not been made first, calculations that could be quite advantageous to those ladies. I am alive with curiosity to know the arrangements, secure in the knowledge that this cloudy sky, supported on Your Illustrious Lordship's shoulders, could not hope for a brighter star.

To the maxim stating that the old are more apt to promise and the young to wait more patiently, I say that every rule bears an exception. Let this much suffice for those who can understand it, and I dedicate myself to Your Illustrious Lordship, etc.

141

TO SIGNOR N.[453]

I do not know what reasons move Your Lordship to speak with me in such a manner, since I have always respected you. It seems to me quite improper to hear myself told that writers might secretly censor my

---

448. That is, even if you always find something to criticize.

449. A reference to the Signor Ferro mentioned below (*ferro* = iron).

450. "O woman who mollified the hardened, who vanquished the strong."

451. Tarabotti also makes reference to this Signor Ferro in letter 22.

452. Probably the Enrico Cornaro to whom Tarabotti addresses several letters and who contributed a composition to her *Tears*.

453. This letter is addressed to Girolamo Brusoni and attests to the beginning of the deterioration of their friendship. Brusoni had evidently criticized the *Antisatire* and Tarabotti's efforts to suppress Aprosio's *Mask Lifted* that responded to it. Brusoni himself had warned her to expect other responses to her satire, including his own.

works. It is true that the infernal mouths of slanderers did not even spare God, but I am astonished that Your Lordship should express such ideas, for you profess all good intentions and have never been injured by me.

May God deprive me of life if I ever expected that senator to demand anything else of V[enti]M[iglia][454] except that he remove my name from his book, since it was not right for him to state it openly when I had disguised it.[455] These were my feelings. If Your Lordship and he know that you are making a mistake in responding against me and therefore decide not to do so, it is not necessary that you come after me with such chimeras. I am still that Angelica whom Your Lordship some time ago praised so highly,[456] and now my writings are so despicable? My *Paternal Tyranny* was a marvel then; now my utterances are heretical and unworthy? Anyone who can be silent in the face of such expressions is most prudent. I confess that I am unable to withstand them.

Go ahead and publish your sentiments freely to the whole world,[457] Signor, if your conscience does not prick you for speaking against the truth, and I give you my regards.

142

TO SIGNOR CAVALIER FRANCESCO PONA

I believe Heaven wanted to show Your Lordship that, even if I carry the name of Arcangela, I am not one of those who lives without sin in Paradise, as you say, and wanted to make you aware that in convent Paradise one can fall and sin. I truly regret that to prove this to you I had to fall, if not from Heaven to Hell, at least from a great height, with a mortal blow to the head. I then realized that your most kind conceits were paradoxes, since I did fall, since I did sin in impatience, and it

---

454. That is, Aprosio.

455. Tarabotti, who published the *Antisatire* with only the initials D.A.T. (D[onna] A[rcangela] T[arabotti]) sought to prevent Aprosio from revealing her as its author in his *Mask Lifted* (see letter 113). It is not clear from which senator Tarabotti sought support.

456. In his *Orestilla*, Brusoni alludes to Tarabotti through the character Laura, a forced nun and writer who is depicted positively and whose writing is praised.

457. Brusoni's response was entitled *Antisatire Satirized* (discussed in letter 99).

seemed to me that I was an angel, but of the shadows, since I was condemned to be quarantined in the dark with much other suffering. So be it. This pleases His Divine Majesty, and I too must most happily succumb to his salutary dispositions.

I regret that I was not able to respond to the courtesies of Your Lordship or to help your friend more than I regret not having been able to respond to the other miseries afflicting me. Please be so kind as to believe this, as I devotedly offer myself to Your most Excellent Lordship, etc.

143

TO SIGNORA BETTA POLANI

I cannot and do not wish to live any longer without hearing news of Your Illustrious Ladyship, for if I admire your virtues, I love your merit even more. The blows my most beloved Lady Betta's hammer inflicts on my heart are too great, and all the more so since I cannot fathom the reason behind your silence, which speaks to me in my heart and suggests a thousand reasons for uneasiness. I therefore await news of your good health to be able to rejoice a little amid so much suffering. Adieu my dear Lady.

144

TO THE MOST REVEREND SIGNOR N.[458]

If in the coming holy season, in which Earth and Heaven rejoice over the birth of our Lord, I were the only one neglecting to enliven my soul with spiritual joys, I would be the epitome of carelessness and would deserve the most severe punishment. In order not to risk such a failure and to be present for that miraculous night with the ox and the donkey, to warm the baby Jesus with the breath of my selfsame love, and to go no less with the shepherds than with the Magi to worship him and to offer him my heart in sacrifice, I pray Your Lordship to grant permission that Father N. may come comfort this soul which is

---

458. At the approach of the Christmas holidays, Tarabotti greets her correspondent, a man of the church, and asks him to grant permission to a certain Father N. to visit her in the convent.

oppressed and upset by many conflicts.[459] He promised me that when he obtained permission he would be ready to help me, and the displays of courtesy from Your Lordship allow me to hope that I will receive this favor.

In the meantime, just as it is from Heaven that angels announce peace to men of good will, I wish Your Lordship heartfelt peace and boundless joys in the coming year since, because you are a true servant of the Lord, you certainly deserve all spiritual and bodily graces. I bow to you.

145
TO THE MOST ILLUSTRIOUS SIGNORA ANDRIANA MALIPIERO

The most singular favors come from illustrious personages and the utmost trust develops where one professes the greatest servitude. I wish to suggest that I turn to Your Illustrious Ladyship, the dearest patroness to whom I have dedicated my devotion, for a favor that will result in my eternal debt.

I understand that the illustrious and excellent procurator Giustiniano[460] is the one whose task it is to choose military recruits; therefore I beseech your incomparable prudence to urge his excellency not to include the bearer of these letters in their number. This request is most just and proper, since he is married, with children, and neither he nor his wife has any male relatives to whom he could entrust his household. He suffers badly from dizziness and a weak heart, and if drafted he would be sent to die, not to fight. He will explain to you in greater detail the reasons that he cannot serve the people by means of arms, even though his heart is most disposed towards his prince and his country.

I know how much your kindness is swayed by dint of my intercessions, which have no basis other than the affection Your Illustrious Ladyship had for my most beloved Regina; and, on my knees, I beg

---

459. Following the reforms instituted at the Council of Trent, it became necessary, at least in theory, to obtain permission before visiting female convents.

460. The reference may be to Marco Giustiniano, nominated to the office of procurator in 1646.

you to treat this young man with the acts of compassion and charity that are innate to the royal grandeur of Your Illustrious Ladyship. Awaiting the favor, I remain Your Illustrious Ladyship's, etc.

146

TO THE MOST ILLUSTRIOUS SIGNORA AQUILA BARBARO

I am sending back to Your Illustrious Ladyship your composition which I found among some of my scribblings, and I confess to you that the relief I felt was beyond words when by happenstance I found in my hands that precious pearl which I had sought time and again.[461]

Believe me and be reassured that I will always be a devoted admirer of your worth, to which, with my heart in my pen, I offer myself always as Your Illustrious Ladyship's, etc.

147

TO THE MOST ILLUSTRIOUS AND EXCELLENT SIGNOR ANGELO EMO[462]

With undue excess of favors Your Excellency has delighted to adorn my most reverent servitude, while you deigned to honor me with your royal presence, in which one can admire much more than even your fame promised. I was therefore so bewildered and dazzled at the sight of the purple which gains splendor from your most divine qualities that my tongue at that moment could not produce anything but confusion. May your heroic compassion take pity upon me since you know that great lights always create darkness and that it was of little help to Semele to expect the appearance of Jove. Even if *in lumine tuo videbimus lumen*,[463] nevertheless amid the splendor of those lightening bolts I neglected to give to Your Excellency such thanks as are

461. The "precious pearl" (*margarita preziosa*) is an expression of praise for a lost work by Barbaro and perhaps a reference to its title.

462. Angelo Emo (1604–1681) belonged to the high aristocracy and held the office of State Inquisitor several times between the 1650s and 1670s. In this letter, Tarabotti begs the powerful Emo's pardon: overcome by the honor of his visit, she admits that she was unable to properly thank him for it or to speak to him about the affairs of a certain lady.

463. "In thy light we shall see light." See Ps. 35:10.

owed the supremacy of your merit and as my heart should have expressed. I also neglected to explain to you some details regarding the holdings of Lady N., which Signor N. can fill in. I beg the forgiveness of your kindness: to doubt it would be a sin against a most benign Jove. Before your most lofty throne I bow and kiss your garments and pledge myself to Your Excellency, etc.

148
TO THE MOST ILLUSTRIOUS AND
EXCELLENT SIGNOR N.[464]

The darkest ink of my pen presents itself before the splendor of Your Excellency to beg illumination, that it too might legitimately appear on the world's stage. It requests licenses from secretary Quirini[465] and from the reverend father inquisitor, and I do not believe Your Excellency will refuse a happy outcome to such a request when he sees delineated at the end of the work the praises of my most beloved friend. It is quite true that to sing the praise of so great a queen[466] one would need the quills of swans, eagles, and doves, but it is also true that they who give what they can, give what they should.

I confess to Your Excellency that this time my rosy blushes turn to pallor, for I ask favors for the roses that turned to eternal lilies in the lovely cheeks of my dear friend. Therefore, on bended knee, I beg Your Excellency to favor that blessed soul and obtain the licenses quickly for me (but let no one find out that I am seeking them).

I am constrained to ask humbly of you another, greater favor, for which I do not believe I shall be condemned by your kindness

464. In this letter to a powerful figure (Zanette suggests Bertucci Valier [see *Suor Arcangela*, 377], perhaps because of Valier's assistance in obtaining printing permission for the *Antisatire* [see letter 217]), Tarabotti asks for help in seeking printing permission from the government and from the church to publish her *Letters*, even if in another letter (157) she seems to indicate that she does not need such permission. As evidenced repeatedly in this letter collection, Tarabotti justifies the publication of the *Letters* by means of her *Tears* in honor of Regina Donà. To this request she adds another, from her friend Betta Polani: that her correspondent support the candidacy of an unidentified gentleman to the Pregadi.

465. Alvise Querini, secretary of the Riformatori dello Studio di Padova (see Aprosio, *Biblioteca aprosiana*, 169).

466. Tarabotti here plays on Regina's name, which means queen.

when I explain the motives that impel me to kneel before your kindest feet. Your Excellency must know that Lady N., my friend and foremost mistress, having resided in this convent for seventeen years,[467] understands the enduring and constantly renewed devotion I bear toward you, whence she entreated, or rather begged, me to ask a favor of Your Excellency which my heart does not dare transmit to my pen, nor my pen to write or my tongue to pronounce. Nonetheless your prudence well knows that *amicus est alter ego*,[468] so that, since I am another N. by virtue of friendship, I speak with her tongue and request the ballot for the Pregadi for the illustrious Signor N.[469] I know I could cry out, *Domine non sum digna*,[470] but I also know that the goodness and piety of Your Excellency exceed my unworthiness just as celestial deities surpass earthly creatures. I bow to you.

149

TO THE MOST ILLUSTRIOUS AND EXCELLENT MARCHIONESS DI GALERANDA[471]

Finally, after having written an infinity of letters to Your Excellency, I receive a few lines from you in which you inquire whether I am alive or dead. Thank God, I am quite alive and ready to oppose anyone who might swindle me, or rather to make sure that the swindler ends up swindled. I say this so that Signor Colisson knows that if my book,

467. That is, Betta Polani.

468. "A friend is another self." Cf. Aristotle, *Ethics*, 9.4.

469. The Consiglio dei Pregadi, or Venice's senate, voted on various issues including the appointment of political and administrative posts. Tarabotti asks her correspondent to use his influence to put Betta Polani's request to the senate itself.

470. "Lord, I am unworthy." See n. 174.

471. In this brusque letter, Tarabotti responds to the marchioness who had, after a long delay, sent news to Tarabotti about her *Paternal Tyranny*, the work Tarabotti had entrusted to her and to her secretary Colisson. Tarabotti, now quite skeptical of the marchioness, tells her of the rumors around Venice that Colisson is trying to trick Tarabotti and to publish the *Paternal Tyranny* under another name, probably his own. Tarabotti warns the marchioness that, if such a betrayal were enacted, there would be serious consequences. Tarabotti also updates the marchioness on the lacework she had requested before her departure: the work has been more difficult, and thus more costly, than expected, and Tarabotti therefore requests more money.

translated into the French language, or even in the Italian, were to be published under any name but my own, as is whispered here, instead of that fellow robbing glory from a poor little woman, he would earn disgrace and blame before the whole world. Your Excellency must believe me in this, and rest assured that he will soon see the proof for himself. I know, however, that a woman of such worth would never take part in such low dealings and therefore I will continue without any restraint against the aforesaid person.

As for the rest, the work was completed within the time stated in the document you left with me, in spite of unfavorable circumstances that conspired to prevent my serving you. Of the women who took on the job, some became ill and some left the convent. I had to look outside and the *maestre*[472] did not wish to respect the price established by your Excellency. At my own expense I had to purchase the rest at twenty lire an ounce from the Venice agent.[473] I had five other apple designs[474] made and Monsieur Martino can testify to all this. If your Excellency would like to have the collar you refer to, give the order to the Signors Lumaga[475] or others to count out the money, while I most reverently kiss your hands.

472. On the *maestre*, or mistresses, see n. 382.

473. *Quel della Venezia*: it is unclear whether Tarabotti refers here to a person or an entity.

474. Venetian lace was made with intricate designs of fruit, flowers, and animals (see E. Ricci, *Old Italian Lace* [London, W. Heinemann, 1913]).

475. On the Lumaga brothers, see n. 227. Given the time and expense Tarabotti alludes to, the collar the marchioness commissioned must have been an elaborate piece of lacework, very fashionable in the era, as can be observed in many contemporary paintings.

150
TO SIGNOR CAVALIER PONA[476]

I marveled greatly upon hearing from Signor N. himself that he expects venal reward for his virtuous efforts. I confess to Your Lordship that I am not accustomed to deal in this way with just anyone, let alone with persons like him, and it seems to me that praise which must be bought shows that the one who receives it does not deserve it. This is not the case for the excellent ambassador, enriched by nature with graces that would tire out the pen of Ovids and Homers in praising them. I communicate my opinion to you as to the person who introduced me to this gentleman; your kindness can therefore tell him that his words of praise will remain safe in my hands until, to fulfill his wish, he has found someone of greater authority and more sway with his excellency, because my mind loathes such self-interested dealings, and I cannot, I must not, and I do not want to do it.

If I can be of any other service, may Your Lordships employ me, for I will consider it an honor.

151
TO THE MOST ILLUSTRIOUS SIGNOR CESARE BALBI[477]

Your Illustrious Lordship's illness, of which your servant informed me, has caused great pain in my soul and in the hearts of these ladies. Your client in particular with fervent prayers to God implores

---

476. Tarabotti expresses to Pona her scorn for a certain Signor N., who had composed verse in praise of an ambassador, almost certainly Bretel de Grémonville, it seems at the nun's own request. The unnamed gentleman now wants a favor in exchange for the composition. Tarabotti insists that poems are composed for reward only when they are in honor of those who don't deserve them. Through Pona, Tarabotti encourages this poet to find use his verse to seek influence through someone else because the ambassador—her great friend—has no need of such bargains.

477. It is probable that this addressee is Cesare Balbi (1593–1660), a lawyer who held many prominent offices in the Republic. Podestà of Vicenza, he was hired in 1652 to become captain of ships in the war of Candia and in 1660 he was head of the Quarantia Criminale and vice counselor (Cappellari, *Campidoglio veneto*, ad vocem). Tarabotti writes this letter on behalf of a gentlewoman, client of Balbi and perhaps Tarabotti's convent sister, who was involved in a lawsuit and seeks an update on the matter.

that Heaven grant you health. She awaits from your most authoritative sponsorship and your prudent efforts an end to those torments she has suffered for many years in extreme poverty. Thus she often urges me to send for news of Your Illustrious Lordship's dealings with the Signors Aviani.[478] If you should not be able to help her, however, because you are ill, or perhaps caught up in household business, may you be so kind as to give me the honor of letting me know, so that she may see to her interests, which require rapid attention. This lady desires the landholdings to be seized so she may actually enjoy what she rightly expects. She reminds me of many details that will help her to get her due, but I do not intend to explain them to Your Illustrious Lordship because I do not wish to deviate from the right road of the jurists, since I never studied law. If this were to occur, however, you ought not marvel but pity a mole who, blind by nature, comes for proper guidance before an all-seeing Argus. Give me also some news of your condition, and command me for I ... , etc.

152
TO THE MOST NOBLE AND EXCELLENT SIGNOR
ENRICO CORNARO[479]

Because the greatest consolations cannot be fully enjoyed if they are not communicated to the dearest friends, I share with Your Eminent Lordship how the visit of the illustrious Businello to this place filled my soul with contentment. My desire was partly fulfilled, and, like that prophetic poet who held the Savior in his arms,[480] I will say in the future, *nunc dimittis*,[481] etc. I admired his regal bearing, I enjoyed his refined conversation, and I felt myself transformed from nun to muse when, in proximity to an Apollo who is a friend to each, I heard praise

478. The Aviani are named also in letter 80 to Giovanni Dandolo, there in regards to a lawsuit over land belonging to the Sant'Anna convent.

479. In this letter Tarabotti recounts to her addressee a visit from a common friend, the poet and musician Giovanni Francesco Busenello (1598–1659), who came masked, a practice which at the time was explicitly prohibited in convents (Zanette, *Suor Arcangela*, 337–38).

480. Simeon.

481. Cf. Luke 2:29: *Nunc dimittis servum tuum Domine* ("Now thou dost dismiss thy servant O Lord"). These are the first words from the Song of Simeon.

attributed to me that would have made Humility itself arrogant.[482] He was masked and therefore he could in the male fashion tell lies without blushing. Perhaps he kept his face from me out of compassion, mindful of the fate of Semele. Nonetheless the sun, although sometimes covered by clouds, always shines forth.

I pay my respects to the eminent lady[483] and I commend myself to you, etc.

153

TO THE MOST ILLUSTRIOUS SIGNORA BETTA POLANI

The constant renewal of my illness causes certain effects in me that one who did not know my nature might attribute to strangeness or poor manners. But, my beloved Lady, you know my mind, and matters are otherwise, because although I may contain all imperfections, I always feel such mortification when I fail in my debt to you that my pen cannot describe it. Believe me, therefore, Your Illustrious Ladyship, that there is no other reason that prevents me responding to the kind expressions of your affection than the oppression of this body, made wretched by illness and by the remedies of those who play Galen and Hippocrates.[484] My soul, however, is always engaged in loving you, just as now I pay you my respects with all my affections.

154

TO FATHER N.[485]

Wishing to provide satisfaction to Your Reverend Lordship, I send you a copy of the miraculous sonnets of B. May you, with your customary

---

482. Tarabotti refers both to the musical works of Busenello and to his visits to Sant'Anna.

483. Probably Cornaro's wife.

484. Tarabotti makes a sarcastic reference to contemporary physicians who make a mockery of the example provided by the greatest doctors of the ancient world (Hippocrates [c. 460–c. 370 BCE] and Galen [129–200 CE]).

485. Tarabotti sends Aprosio some poetry that a certain poet, here indicated only with the initial B. (see also letter 30 in which he is identified as Francesco), had written in her honor. On the matter see n. 110 and Aprosio, *Biblioteca aprosiana*, 172–75. Tarabotti indicates below that some may find the praise of her humorous, to their own detriment.

prudence, take care not to give them to everyone to read, for in reading such delightful writing, someone overly prone to laughter might encounter the disgrace of Philemon upon admiring his donkey eating figs.[486] And may your goodness excuse me if I bother you, and honor me with your commands which, since they are longed for by me, will be immediately carried out, and again I pledge and declare myself to Your Reverend Lordship.

155

TO THE MOST ILLUSTRIOUS SIGNORA ELENA FOSCOLO[487]

My spirit, which follows the soul of our dear Regina who has flown away to Heaven, has no words to express to Your Illustrious Ladyship the bitter news of so great a loss. You, who are all piety, must commiserate and sympathize with the bitterness of my grief, and receive the inauspicious news only as an expression of my most reverent obligation to you, since this is a time in which ink cedes to tears.

> *Né più giova amicizia o giova amore,*
> *Ahi lagrime, ahi dolore.*[488]

---

486. Valerius Maximus tells of Philemon, who, upon seeing a donkey eat figs from his tree, called a slave to chase the donkey away. By the time the slave arrived, the donkey had eaten all the figs. To reprimand the slave, Philemon suggested that at that point he might as well give the donkey some wine as well. Delighted with his joke, Philemon died from laughter (Valerius Maximus, *Memorable Doings and Sayings, Books 6–9*, trans. D. R. Shackleton Bailey [Cambridge: Harvard University Press, 2000], Loeb 493, 377).

487. Tarabotti tells her correspondent the news of Regina Donà's death.

488. Cf. Tasso, *Re Torrismondo*, act 5: *Che più giova amicizia o giova amore? / Ahi lagrime! ahi dolore!* ("What avails friendship? What avails love? / Oh tears, oh grief!" [*King Torrismondo*, ed. and trans. Maria Pastore Passaro [New York: Fordham University Press, 1997], 308–9).

156

TO THE MOST ILLUSTRIOUS COUNTESS OF S.[489]

It is the prerogative of singular beauty to earn respect and enslave desires. Enticed by the sight of Your Illustrious Ladyship, I live as your affectionate servant and I might almost say a worshiper of your virtues. I will exert every effort so that Your Illustrious Ladyship will be accommodated this week regarding the introduction of your illustrious daughter to the convent; and in case I should not currently be able (due to certain misfortunes) to be her servant as I desire, I will make sure that she is satisfactorily settled in a place perhaps better befitting her high station. May your kindness be assured of my servitude, my respect, and my love, if it is appropriate for me to say as much, while I in the meantime kiss you a thousand times.

157

TO SIGNOR N.[490]

I do not know what fate causes us to complain about one another constantly without reason. It is true that I did not immediately send the letters to Your Lordship, but the error, born of my incessant indisposition, merited understanding. From a letter of mine sent days ago to the apothecary, I thought you knew you would receive the letters of yours that I had in my possession, and in fact I awaited my own, as I asked of you. So be it. Everything moves backwards for those forced always to proceed through a third party. I will certainly send yours one of these days and you must do the same with my letters; if they have been printed or in what state they find themselves I do not know, and I will explain why.

---

489. The letter regards the acceptance of the countess's daughter as a boarder in the convent. If Tarabotti cannot be responsible for the girl herself, she assures the countess, she will find her an even more prestigious placement, befitting her station.

490. This letter, which gives important information about the publication of Tarabotti's *Letters*, is most probably directed to Girolamo Brusoni (see Zanette, *Suor Arcangela*, 376). In the letter's first part, Tarabotti speaks of a misunderstanding caused when their letters did not arrive: Tarabotti was supposed to return Brusoni's letters and Brusoni hers. It is clear that Tarabotti is deeply involved in planning her letter collection.

May Your Lordship know, therefore, that during the coldest rigors of this past winter, when I was abandoned by my physicians, I sent a little chest full of my rough scribblings to the illustrious Lady N.[491] She showed everything to the illustrious Signor N.,[492] who selected the best pieces; indeed, without regard to my own will in the matter, he planned to publish them. He gathered them from various people and especially from the illustrious and excellent Loredano, who is quite pleased and believes that my letters must not wait for the slowness of that Saturn you mention to me.[493] Indeed he knows that my pen vanquishes the vainglorious beneath all the signs of the zodiac, while my pages dare to appear so often before you, who is yet the prince of planets.[494] These are undeniable truths, and I laugh at fictions. Let them plot tricks, let them prepare deceits, let the liars exaggerate falsehoods, for in any case I will always be that unmasked Arcangela whom a certain reckless person wished to paint to the world as something different. I am she who created *Paternal Tyranny*, etc.: understand me who will, for I understand myself. Thus I reply that Saturn does not rule my hand and he does not record the strokes of my pen, which boldly presents itself before the greatest potentates, and anyone who wishes to insinuate otherwise to simple minds is lying.

Your Lordship will certainly not find my latest two books in the bookshops of Venice, for Signor Gremonville had only a few printed at my order and only for friends;[495] and because they are spiritual in nature they appeared under the sign of Virgo without passing before

---

491. Betta Polani (see letter 26).

492. Probably Giovanni Dandolo, who would subsequently write a letter of presentation for the letter collection.

493. Evidently Tarabotti had already encountered some difficulty in obtaining official permission to print her letter collection. She seems to say that she does not need such permission (even though she will continue to seek it; see letter 148). Zanette (*Suor Arcangela*, 376) explains that in contemporary astrology, the term "Saturn" could describe a slow, taciturn man, and he hypothesizes that Tarabotti might make reference to the patriarch Giovan Francecso Morosini, who had tried to prevent cloistered nuns from exchanging letters (ibid., 365–67).

494. The sun.

495. It is not clear to which books Tarabotti refers: not her *Convent Paradise* (1643) nor her *Antisatire* (1644), since Bretel de Grémonville was not yet in Venice and since the works had wide circulation. Since Tarabotti terms the works "spiritual", she may intend the devotional

the eyes of Saturn nor being flicked by the tail of the Scorpion.[496] I would offer to send them to you, but I would be mad to hand weapons over to one who harbors a perpetual disdain for me. I offer you my respects.

158

TO THE MOST ILLUSTRIOUS AND EXCELLENT MADAME ANNA DI GREMONVILLE, AMBASSADRESS OF FRANCE[497]

The humble compositions of my poor mind come before Your Illustrious Excellency only to obey your commands, for they recognize themselves unworthy of appearing before the eyes of the most eminent cardinal Giulio Mazzarino, the splendor of the Roman Church. Whatever their nature, beneath the sheltering shadow of so great a lady they dare to appear among the most celebrated writers in order to enter the most flourishing library of so virtuous a prince. They have hope that his unbending fairness will not allow the simple offspring of a consecrated virgin to be insulted. It remains for Your Excellency to beg his kind understanding for the imperfections of a *Paradise*, which, if rustic in style, is so because the religious state does not allow for refinement; and not to condemn the *Antisatire* as inappropriate to my state or as a vain and perhaps improper composition for one who professes religion in habit and heart. With this, perpetually admiring Your Excellency's merit, I now most reverently kiss the hands of the illustrious and excellent ambassador no less than your own, conveying to both of you the most humble respects of your illustrious daughters.[498]

---

works that Dandolo mentions in his presentation of the volume and that she mentions in letter 26.

496. Tarabotti continues her astrological metaphors: she presents herself as Virgo, or Virgin, and those who try to impede her as Saturn and Scorpio. From the metaphor, we gather that her books did not go through official channels, and they were not blocked by her detractors.

497. Evidently responding to a request, Tarabotti entrusts two of her works to the wife of the French ambassador for delivery to Cardinal Jules Mazarin's famous library.

498. Boarders at Sant'Anna.

159
TO SIGNOR N.

I would be most appreciative of the familiarity that Your Lordship uses with me were I not removed from all worldly affairs, or indeed dead to the world to live in God. Signor N., we must consider the fact that this life ends, and work to acquire an eternal one in glory. This soul, created in the image of Heaven, must there aspire as to its natural center; and we must at all costs not abandon the Creator in favor of his creatures.

I am sending the *bozzoladi*[499] with such complete affection as befits the immensity of your merit. I am sorry I do not have more, just as I am ashamed not to be able to procure for you *The Postman Robbed of His Mailbag*,[500] but such people, who usually arrive at night, do not frequent places like ours.

I continue to pray that the Lord fill Your Lordship with His holy grace, and I kiss your hands.

160
TO THE MOST ILLUSTRIOUS SIGNORA GUID'ASCANIA ORSI[501]

By guessing, at my failure to write, that my health is failing and not my affection, my respect, or my manners, Your Illustrious Ladyship thinks most prudently and makes it clear to me that the divinity of your spirit contains a prophetic element. My Illustrious Lady, your suspicions are well founded since most of the time I am besieged by a most fearsome constriction in my chest that, taking my breath away,

499. A type of sweet, probably produced in the convent (Boerio: *bozzolao*).

500. A controversial work by Ferrante Pallavicino (see also n. 56). Brusoni described it as the principal factor in Pallavicino's troubles with the Church (see L. Coci, introduction to *La retorica delle puttane* [Parma: Ugo Guanda, 1992], xxiv–xxv). Although Tarabotti says she cannot help her correspondent locate a copy, given the nature of the work, it is notable that he should have turned to her, a nun, to obtain a work whose circulation was prohibited in Venice (ibid., xxv).

501. Tarabotti turns to the Bolognese writer and nun Guid'Ascania Orsi for a report on what is being said about *Convent Paradise* in that city. Planning a reprinting, she wanted a sincere critique of the work in order to improve it. It does not appear, however, that the work was ever reprinted.

often tries to take my life as well. Thus sometimes I neglect to fulfill my debt with you, whom I so admire and value. Please look upon this circumstance with sympathy, as I do not doubt that your divine kindness will grant me pardon.

And since so many favors rain down upon me from your most liberal hand, I dare to hope for truth and sincerity from your candor with regards to what I am about to ask you. I beg your kindness to be so pleased as to tell me what opinion those lofty intellects have of my *Paradise*. Please be assured, however, that my goal is not to hear praise (all the more so because I know I do not deserve it), but only because, since I must reprint the book, I would follow the opinion of the majority of writers in revising it anew if I knew what they thought I should do, since I well know that Bologna is the mother of learning, the guardian of the virtuous, and the treasury of knowledge. For these reasons I will await from your kindness honest reports such as befit the illustrious nobility of your birth. Please do not feel any compunction in informing me of the work's weaknesses, because I would be blind if I did not view it as an index of imperfections.

I also pray that you excuse the lengthiness of this letter and that you honor me with your commands, and I respectfully kiss your hands.

161

TO THE MOST ILLUSTRIOUS DAUGHTERS OF MADAME DE GREMONVILLE[502]

My heartfelt affection (which I promise you is everlasting, even if it matters little to you) does not allow me to further postpone writing you even if I am in no condition to do so. I am revived by memory of you, I rejoice at your happy return to your homeland, and I pray that you share with me news of your health and of the progress you make in your virtues. Write to me and do not go back on your word, even if you are from Normandy. Love me even if I do not deserve it and

---

502. The Grémonville girls, now back in France, had been like daughters to Tarabotti during their time as boarders in Sant'Anna. It was common for young girls to live in the convent and be educated under the nuns' care and the bonds engendered were often strong, although here Tarabotti reprimands the girls for not reciprocating her affection.

command me since I desire your dear commands. And I kiss you and kiss you again a thousand times, as does Lady N. who invites you to her home, and all of these gentlewomen[503] send their warm regards.

162

TO SIGNOR N.[504]

I would not venture to guess the reason for which Your Lordship restrains his pen on a matter that is quite pressing for me. You know one of your letters will always effect in me such happiness as light creates for those who are in darkness, and if I gave to you my daughter, that is, my work, so you would make her a public woman in France, I intend to be her mother in any place or climate.

Please oblige me with some news, and if you were unable to do me the favor of publishing this composition, I will work to achieve such a goal with Signor Gremonville or with the most distinguished cardinal Mazzarino's librarian.[505]

Sometimes I lead myself astray with certain untrue sayings, but immediately that infallible truth comes back to me: that men must not be believed and that whoever trusts them deserves to be fooled. May Your Lordship please remove these thoughts from my heart by acting differently from the others, and then I will take back my words and substitute for them all those qualities that characterize your merit. In the meantime I offer you my respects and I await news of the lady marchioness whom I serve with reverent respect.[506]

---

503. The other nuns in Sant'Anna.

504. This letter is likely meant for the Frenchman Colisson, secretary to the Marchioness de Gallerande, to whom Tarabotti had entrusted a copy of her *Paternal Tyranny* in the hopes of publishing it in France. Not having heard anything more about it, the nun had begun to worry, and here—still hoping for a positive outcome—she asks for news of it.

505. That is, Gabriel Naudé.

506. The Marchioness de Gallerande, through whom Tarabotti made the acquaintance of Colisson.

163
TO THE MOST REVEREND SIGNOR N.[507]

I confess that I am unable to respond or correspond to the most accomplished letter, the kind displays, and the most courteous manner of Your Reverend Lordship as my debt and your merit would demand. Whence, restricting my affection within the limits of respect, I will say nothing else than this: every day I become more convinced of my long-held belief that men, like alchemists, know how to deceive and to make one thing appear as another. I have read a collection of kind and well-disguised lies written by one who should be the very ideal of truth: most kind, indeed, and dear lies from which, as from precious stones, I see my intellect—of itself quite dark—shining, adorned and glorified.

You say that I have reached the halfway point on the ladder Jacob saw in his dream,[508] and you do not realize that, if Jacob struggled all night with the angel of God (who in the end blessed him), I must always fight with certain devils who constantly speak ill of me. You poke fun at me by saying that shadows appear as substance to me, that I mistake fireflies for suns, and yet you are mistaken since I do not use spectacles which can greatly enlarge things. You call me a glorious martyress and you do not realize that my glories are destroyed by the tainted breath of a few snakes who know how to kill truth with a breath of lies. I would prefer, for the glory of God, to be a martyress of the Thracians[509] rather than to be martyred by these N.N. who, like lemons, have golden skin and bitter insides.[510] I cannot enjoy serene days in prison like Saint Paul[511] because my case is different. Mine is no prison, it is a hell where no hope of leaving can enter, and where

---

507. Tarabotti responds here to her correspondent's excessive (and, she says, unjustified) praise of her, lightly reprimanding him for these "kind untruths." In addition, she complains of the falseness of her fellow nuns.

508. That is, the ladder to Heaven; cf. Gen. 28:10–22.

509. The reference is to the many Christians martyred in Thrace at the order of emperor Marcus Aurelius Valerius Maximinianus.

510. Tarabotti refers here to the falseness of other nuns (the "certain devils", "a few snakes", and the "N.N." described above).

511. Imprisoned in Rome for two years.

my crying will continue until, with God's help, that prophetic saying can be realized within me: *Adimplebis me laetitia in vultu tuo.*[512]

But I must no longer bore the person I desire to serve. Moreover, since I feel I am vanquished by your favors, I cannot respond completely to your letters, since otherwise I would be foolishly attempting to do literary battle with the person I must humbly revere, as I now do. I pledge myself to Your Reverend Lordship, etc.

164

TO THE MOST ILLUSTRIOUS AND EXCELLENT SIGNORA RENATA DI CLARAMONTE, MARCHIONESS DI GALERANDA[513]

It surprises me greatly not to see the results of the most kind promises Your Excellency made since, even if the great do not care about obligation, ladies of your stature keep their word because of their gentility. I wrote two other letters in Italian, and now, since I received no response, I have resolved to have one written in French in order not to do a disservice to myself. Many things are disquieting my soul, and I confess to Your Excellency that with every mail delivery I see pass without your news, I feel my soul dying from pain. It is not that I doubt your goodwill, but I mistrust your secretary who, since he came into possession of the work to be printed, has allowed thirteen months to pass without sending any news. I know that the length of the journey, the distance of your land, and accidents of fate that might have occurred may have interfered with my wishes, and therefore my hopes still germinate in the favorable shade of Your Excellency. As for the rest, I know well exactly how much men should be believed. Your

512. Cf. Ps. 15:10. "Thou shalt fill me with joy with thy countenance" (Ps. 15:11, Douay-Rheims version).

513. The saga of *Paternal Tyranny* in France continues: in this letter, written just prior to letter 149 to the same correspondent, Tarabotti rebukes the marchioness for not having answered her letters and reminds her that thirteen months have passed without news of the manuscript from the marchioness's secretary Colisson. The nun still harbors hope, but eventually loses faith when Colisson insists that the work was never in his possession to begin with (see letter 174). Tarabotti affirms that she had this letter translated into French to be certain the marchioness would understand it: it is the only instance in the *Lettere* in which she speaks of a letter's translation.

lace collar will soon be sent,[514] and I have not seen letters on either of these matters that are tearing me apart. I beseech your kindness to act so that I receive news, which I will be awaiting as anxiously as expiating souls await prayers. In case your secretary encountered difficulty in having the work printed, I will write to Signor Gremonville or to the librarian of the most distinguished Mazzarino,[515] from whom I will receive every favor.

Please pardon, Your Excellency, the bother that I perhaps create with this letter, and please do not erase me so easily from your most worthy favor, which would effectively erase me from the book of life, for I am and will always be Your Illustrious Ladyship's, etc.

165

TO THE MOST ILLUSTRIOUS AND EXCELLENT MADAME ANNA DI GREMONVILLE, AMBASSADRESS OF FRANCE[516]

Only God knows how greatly it shamed me not to have kept my word with Your Excellency, since He sees into the innermost workings of the heart. Yesterday evening the messenger failed to come, and that is what caused my failure, which I hope will be condoned and pardoned by your clemency, since you know how to impart favors even to the most unworthy. I am returning to you your silverware but retain memory of great honors, for which I humbly thank you and I bow most deeply to you and to the illustrious and excellent ambassador.

I beseech Your Excellency to grace me with a visit from your illustrious daughters, as they promised, and to kiss them affectionately on my behalf. Tell the illustrious gentleman that we have now, with experience, come to learn how gentlemen of Normandy maintain their word.[517] Please excuse the bother, I beg you on bended knee, and again I bow to you.

---

514. Regarding this lace collar, see also letters 149 and 174.

515. Gabriel Naudé.

516. Tarabotti asks pardon for her delay in serving the ambassadress, due to a problem with the messenger. It seems Tarabotti had borrowed silver that she now returns. She also asks that the ambassadress send her daughters—former boarders at Sant'Anna—for a visit.

517. Tarabotti seems to be referring to Jacques Bretel de Grémonville (brother to the ambassador), who was supposed to help her publish *Paternal Tyranny* but disappointed her (see n.

166

TO THE MOST ILLUSTRIOUS SIGNOR LUIGI DI MATHAREL, RESIDENT OF FRANCE AT THE MOST SERENE REPUBLIC OF VENICE[518]

The most singular favor of a visit from Your Illustrious Lordship, which you most kindly bestowed upon me, summons an obligation that knows no limits. Whence to give you to understand how much I desire to repay such courtesy (and not seeing your messenger), I send you in response to your request these sacrilegious pages which have no other purpose than to defame and insult female divinity. May you receive them as a testament to my devotion and believe me that insults against women are avenged no less by earthly justice than by celestial. Let the printer[519] attest to this, since he already saw that, by pushing mens' insults out from the presses to expose them to the light of day, he has gained nothing but the quintessence of misery. To Your Illustrious Lordship however, who is the image of goodwill, I need not demonstrate the insanity of his line of reasoning, since I know that your most lofty intellect has no need of light to see clearly what is illuminated by itself.

I pray you well to return this to me when you have read it and to excuse me for the inconvenience, as I devote myself to Your Illustrious Lordship, etc.

167

TO THE MOST ILLUSTRIOUS SIGNORA ISABETTA PICCOLOMINI SCARPI[520]

Your Illustrious Ladyship will see from the enclosed note how much this awful woman has misled us with most false pretenses. If she

---

691). Other negative references to Normans can be found in letters 131 and 161.

518. Tarabotti thanks Matharel for a visit and lends him a scandalous treatise arguing women do not have souls. On this treatise and the controversy surrounding it, see n. 191.

519. Francesco Valvasense, punished in 1649 for printing this work (see n. 191).

520. Tarabotti asks her correspondent to intercede for her with regard to a commission for lacework. A third person, perhaps the marchioness de Gallerande (see letter 149), evidently did not wish to pay the established sum for work that had been completed.

would like to keep only half of the lace collar, I understand that I must return one hundred ducats. To Your Illustrious Ladyship, who in this affair has been a kind mediator and protector, I turn again for favors, which will further indebt me to you. What I would like to say is that I pray you for a visit, but shame and embarrassment do not permit me to express such a brazen request. I know however that a lady like you, graced with such lofty status and such fine judgment, knows how to understand even those who don't speak. Men in love would suffer terribly if their beloveds could not understand them by subtle hints. May Your Illustrious Ladyship know that you are my beloved and that I wait for a remedy from your merit and kindness without seeking it out. Please take pity on us, as I kiss you sincerely and remain Your Ladyship's, etc.

168

TO THE MOST ILLUSTRIOUS AND EXCELLENT SIGNOR BERTUCCI VALIERO[521]

The servitude that I profess out of obligation and desire upon Your Illustrious Excellency's great merit spurs me, with an excess of respectful boldness, to send you that work which—thanks only to your kindness and patronage—has gained splendors that have rendered it not unworthy to appear on the world's stage. That lovely and worthy sonnet, which makes my *Paradise* sparkle like a jewel, animated the book which, a stillbirth of my most sterile mind, is in itself of scant renown and even less merit. I confess that I would like to shield it from Your Excellency's greatness, but since I am not permitted to do so, I judge it better to come as if before a kind deity to reveal my failing myself. May you who are the patron of our century and the image of humanity and courtesy accept the devotion of my heart and read it with a kind eye, even if it is a labyrinth of mistakes. But a woman such

---

521. This letter was to accompany a copy of *Convent Paradise* offered by Tarabotti to her important correspondent. With the requisite declarations of modesty, the nun thanks Valiero for contributing a sonnet to the work, likely the sonnet ascribed to an "uncertain author" (*incerto*, 35) that follows the *Soliloquy to God*. In letter 218 we learn that due to an error Bertucci's sonnet was missing from the manuscript, but in this letter the problem seems to have been resolved.

as me, who doesn't have the knowledge required for perfect compositions, hopes she will be pitied by Your Excellency. I continue to pray
the supreme Lord to grant you the pinnacle of greatness which allows
nothing more for human desire to want, and I declare myself Your Illustrious Excellency's, etc.

169

TO THE MOST ILLUSTRIOUS SIGNOR LUIGI DE MATHAREL, RESIDENT OF FRANCE AT THE MOST SERENE REPUBLIC OF VENICE[522]

Even if I had already received news of the death of Signor Gremonville, who will live in eternal glory, I confess to Your Illustrious Lordship that my heart so abhorred such bitter news that my pen could
never form the letters to compose my words of condolence to madame. But now that you have assured me, I see with greater certainty
the obligations of my respect and I will write dolefully in a letter of the
loss that should be mourned by all pens.

May Your Illustrious Lordship with your usual kindness
please deliver it safely and not forget to favor me with regard to that
book that has brought extreme anguish to my mind. Signor Colisson
has wished to confirm with his actions my long–held opinion against
men. So be it. I am not saying, however, that some do not stray from
the usual path of other men, among whom you appear to me as a
miracle. May your kindness believe me, and I offer you my respects.

170

TO THE MOST ILLUSTRIOUS AND EXCELLENT MADAME ANNA DI GREMONVILLE, AMBASSADRESS OF FRANCE[523]

If the whole world laments the shocking event of poor Signor Gremonville's death, your Excellency can rest assured that it provoked in

---

522. Tarabotti received news of the death of Nicolas Bretel de Grémonville, which occurred
26 November 1648 (on Bretel de Grémonville, see n. 115). Here, she entrusts a letter of condolence for his widow to Matharel (see letter 170 below). She also asks for news regarding
her *Paternal Tyranny* manuscript given to Colisson.

523. The letter of condolence referred to in letter 169.

me above others the sort of extreme grief that can afflict one who idol-
ized his merit. My heart constantly rejected the bitter news, nor did it
want to believe what it so detested. In the end, after receiving many reports, so unexpectedly, I accepted the news from the resident himself,
who I admit revealed it more with the sorrow on his face and with his
tears than with words. Since then the fierceness of the pain afflicting
my heart, hesitant and bewildered at such a great loss, has not permitted such woeful words to be dictated to my pen. If at times it tried to
communicate to Your Excellency my most sorrowful condolences and
the whole convent's tears, it canceled those lines I dolefully wrote of
the death of one who must live eternally in posterity's memory. But
the attestations of that personage[524] increased my pain such that I resolve with a pounding heart, with eyes flooded with tears and with
trembling hand to send my most heartfelt condolences, and to pray
you to exhibit in this bitter circumstance the trait of prudence that
makes you known to the world as superior to other women, as kings
are superior in majesty to their subjects and vassals.

May you take consolation in your children who, as images of
their father, will have the power to comfort you. And rejoice that you
were paired in marriage with one of the greatest persons who has ever
glorified the world.

Death, my excellent Lady, is the only thing we can be sure of
in this voyage of ours. Your intelligence knows well that the body is a
tribute due to the earth and that the soul belongs to God, to whom it
flies in order to end the miseries of this life. Take comfort, and count
me once again among your most devoted, indeed ardent, servants.
With my heart tormented with grief, I bow to you and pledge myself
to Your Excellency, etc.

171

TO THE MOST ILLUSTRIOUS DAUGHTERS OF THE MOST EXCELLENT SIGNOR DI GREMONVILLE[525]

The deepest affection of my heart comes to lament with Your Illustrious Ladyships the death of your illustrious and excellent father. The

524. That is, of Matharel.

525. Another condolence letter for the death of Nicolas Bretel de Grémonville.

illustrious Ladies N. do the same, as do all these ladies who are most afflicted by so great a loss.[526] They feel pity in their souls for this misfortune, which could not be greater for you poor ladies, tested by so great a blow at so tender an age. However, since you possess in the youngest of years all the characteristics of true understanding, you will know how to regulate such vehement suffering with prudence. Praying you to do so, I kiss you a thousand times, begging for a line from you.

172

TO THE MOST ILLUSTRIOUS AND EXCELLENT SIGNOR GIOVAN FRANCESCO LOREDANO[527]

If with the sweet sound of his lyre Orpheus caused the beasts and plants to follow him, the gentle concert of Your Excellency's compositions attracts with its graceful style, in which all the graces blossom, the flowers of the holy Church's gardens, and causes the most stolid creatures of the world to marvel. With his song, Orpheus led his Eurydice from Pluto's kingdom, and the lines of Your Excellency have the power to calm the suffering of women condemned to a living hell. And because your *Clever Jests*, like a magnet to iron, have the ability to cause anyone who reads them to love and honor the fecundity of your genius and your most noble state, I therefore declare myself your sincere admirer and I bow to you.

---

526. Tarabotti most likely refers to the other nuns who knew the Grémonville daughters when they were boarders at the convent, and who became acquainted with the ambassador through his frequent visits to Sant'Anna.

527. Tarabotti constructs this letter upon a comparison between Loredano and Orpheus, the extraordinary musician of mythology. She praises in particular his *Clever Jests* (*Scherzi geniali*), whose first part was published for the first time in 1632 (Venice: Sarzina) and the second in 1634 (Venice: Sarzina). This work was almost as successful as Loredano's enormously popular letters. (On the editions of the *Scherzi*, see T. Menegatti, *"Ex ignoto notus": Bibliografia delle opere a stampa del Principe degli Incogniti: Giovan Francesco Loredano* [Padua: Il Poligrafo, 2000]).

173
TO THE MOST NOBLE AND EXCELLENT
SIGNOR NICOLO CRASSO[528]

The favors I receive from Your Eminent Lordship are so great in number and in quality that my pen, realizing that it does not know how to thank you properly, leaves this task to the devotion of my heart. I confess that when I turned to you, I did not dare, I feared, and was ashamed; but you, in whom all kindness is concentrated, encouraged my daring, caused me to take heart, and transformed my shame into ambition. Such things transcend the limits of humanity and generate marvel and wonder. The pen of Your Noble Lordship exudes gems so resplendent they are worthy of illuminating the funeral praises of a queen,[529] and my tongue does not dare praise her for fear of diminishing her glory. Therefore I admire, enjoy, and hold my tongue, begging that I may be permitted to place your precious name clearly on the work[530] in order to glorify her and defend her from the Aristarchs.[531]

As to the rest, begging Your Lordship's pardon, you do a great wrong to the Muses in supposing them to be enemies of the aged[532] for they, being virtuous young ladies, love virtue, not youth, in men, and even swans[533] sing as they die.

Your courteous declarations that you are obliged to serve me are kind misunderstandings, because as a nun I am bound by a vow of obedience and furthermore, being Your Lordship's inferior in all ways, you can be well assured that I do not boast of other glory in this world

---

528. Tarabotti thanks Crasso for the two introductory sonnets he wrote for the *Tears*, published along with the *Letters* (see also letters 75 and 76).

529. *Regina* (queen) = Regina Donà, for whom Tarabotti wrote the *Tears*.

530. The sonnets in fact appear under Crasso's name.

531. That is, from critics. Aristarch of Samothrace (c. 217–c. 145 BCE), was director of the library in Alexandria and a scholar of Homer. His name became synonymous with that of a severe critic.

532. Crasso evidently told Tarabotti this in the letter that accompanied the sonnets. Such a concept does not appear in the sonnets.

533. That is, poets.

than that of being kin[534] and servant to Your Eminent and Excellent Lordship.

174

TO THE MOST ILLUSTRIOUS AND EXCELLENT SIGNORA RENATA DI CLARAMONTE, MARCHIONESS DI GALERANDA[535]

Finally, after more than a year, I receive a printed leaf of my book, in which there are more errors than words, which shocks me since I know that Your Excellency's secretary was most well-versed in that typeface. It seems to have been produced in order to provoke laughter in the reader. The errors are so outrageous and numerous, of all kinds, that they change the meaning, distort the conceits, and I would be mad to wish it published in this form. Therefore I thank Your Excellency for your efforts on my behalf, and I entreat you to have the work consigned immediately into the hands of Monsieur Matarel's father,[536] for this will be the best gift I could receive from your greatness.

That Colisson has not seen my works—this is a story to tell to children, for I handed them over to him myself, and by his silence I can infer the enormity of his crime.[537] He will find this out, and soon, for

---

534. Zanette says that Crasso was a distant relative of Tarabotti's (*Suor Arcangela*, 378), perhaps basing himself on a manuscript of Apostolo Zeno, who writes that Crasso "was linked to her no less on the basis of friendship than on that of blood" (Medioli, "Reliability," 94, n. 15). It is possible that Zeno bases his assertion on Tarabotti's accounts here and in letter 191.

535. This rather curt letter discusses both the unfortunate results of Tarabotti's attempts to publish the *Paternal Tyranny* in France and the collar that the marchioness wanted Tarabotti to procure for her. At this time, the marchioness and her secretary had already returned to France; because of the distance, many misunderstandings arose between the nun and her correspondent. From the letter it appears that the first printed pages of the *Paternal Tyranny*, evidently sent by the marchioness to Tarabotti, are full of errors. Disappointed and outraged, Tarabotti asks the marchioness to return the manuscript.

536. The father of the French resident at Venice, Louis Matharel, evidently lived in France and would have been able to send the manuscript to his son, who had a good relationship with the nun.

537. Together with the *Paternal Tyranny*, Tarabotti had also given *Convent Hell* (see letter 232) to Colisson. In this letter it seems that Colisson denied ever receiving the works, perhaps trying to blame the problem on the marchioness.

although I should have to compromise my honor, my life, and I would almost say my soul, I am determined to show not only all France, but all the world, the deceitfulness of his dealings. I swear as much to Your Excellency on my word as a nun, and he will see whether a woman's pen can revenge itself of the insults it suffers in good faith. The very letters of Your Excellency, which contain so many contradictions on this subject, assure me of the truth of this fact.

I have delivered your collar to the lieutenant of the marquis, Monsieur Guisson.[538] Know that I needed no encouragement to serve you, and paid no attention to the fact that an extra thirty ducats was necessary in order to serve you in a timely fashion. All this was to my own detriment, however, with many other problems incurred by the delay in receiving the money. You forgot your promise that you would still honor the written agreement when the work was completed, but the women who did the work did not forget and wanted to be paid immediately.

Never mind, this is what usually happens to those who serve important people. In any case, I take pride in knowing that it was I who was disappointed, rather than I to disappoint. And although I have not studied the ways of the powerful, at least I have learned good manners, which, practiced by me in every instance, require that I humbly honor you, entreating you to have the book delivered immediately to the father of the resident here, who can always attest to the quantity of letters that I have sent you, although you complain that you have not received even one.

175

TO THE MOST ILLUSTRIOUS SIGNOR GIOVANNI DANDOLO[539]

This morning I had to listen to the complaints of those gentlemen whom I once commended to the piety, not the cruelty, of the excellent

538. On this collar, see letters 12, 149, and 164.

539. Tarabotti in this letter expresses frustration at the way in which someone, probably Loredano, received a petition from some people the nun had asked him to help. Dandolo served as an intermediary between the nun and Loredano also in other instances when she looked to Loredano for help for her friends (see letters 209, 229, and 230).

avogadore. If it seemed strange to me to hear that the prayers I made to his excellency had been tainted and that all the people I commended to him have always been unsuccessful, I leave Your Illustrious Lordship to consider. I do not know if I am the one who does not know how to make myself understood, or if he, feigning not to understand, enjoys making my very requests the punishment for my temerity. I well know that in the future my prayers and vows will not be brought before vipers nor thrown to the wind, because I will bring them before God, who listens righteously even to the weakest and does not scorn the unworthy. I inform Your Illustrious Lordship of this because, having elected you as my intercessor before his excellency, you too must therefore be part of this discussion. Come what may, these encounters will serve me *ad exemplum*.

In the meantime let Your Illustrious Lordship be assured that women, although perhaps without souls (as that madman said),[540] are well able to distinguish actions from idle chatter even if they do not have much education or learning. I offer my respects.

176
TO THE ILLUSTRIOUS AND EXCELLENT SIGNOR BERTUCCI VALIER[541]

No one can deny favors to the supreme authority of Your Excellency, and those who turn to your lofty protection cannot be refused what they seek. I received the book with the publishing privileges, thanks to your kindest support. And because I do not have thanks proportionate to your greatness, my heart struggles and confesses itself obliged forever to pray for your and your serene family's happiness. Nonetheless, because humble thanks are pleasing even to God, I thank Your

---

540. Tarabotti refers to the misogynous treatise circulating in Venice that asserted that women had no soul (see letter 59); Loredano was likely behind the Italian translation of the work.

541. In this letter Tarabotti thanks her powerful addressee for his help in obtaining permissions for one of her works, probably her *Antisatire* (see letter 217); another possibility is that the nun refers to the *Letters* themselves, for which Zanette hypothesizes that Bertucci intervened to secure the permissions (see n. 464). In this case, the nun would have inserted this letter into the collection after having received the permissions.

Excellency by confessing that I do not know how to thank you, and I reverently kiss your robes.

177

TO THE MOST ILLUSTRIOUS SIGNOR
GIOVANNI DANDOLO[542]

Finally Your Illustrious Lordship has honored me with that book, *On Woman*, which I so desired. But having seen for myself this lady in the hands of a man, I saw she had become a public woman and I was ashamed to house an excommunicated prostitute in this cloister. It is true that the noble air, the courteous manner, and the divine eloquence of the gentleman who brought her to me made me believe her a god. But what does it matter? The gods have always made mischief for women. Know, therefore, Your Illustrious Lordship, that if I have returned *On Woman*, I retain the obligation, and although you are greatly obliged regarding your promise to me, it is said that from debtors who don't pay one must collect what one can. I mean to say that, in exchange for the great debt you owe me, and among my most prized possessions, I will hold onto the two pages you sent me, for if they did not make jabs at women they would be most valuable.[543] At any rate, although they have a certain heretical flavor, I admire the words, and my mind wishes it could thank you in a manner proportionate to the immensity of your merit, but my pen cannot attempt the impossible. Therefore I will keep my silence, and I commend myself…, etc.

542. Tarabotti thanks Dandolo for a work on women titled *La Donna*, although it is clear that she is not pleased by what he has sent her. It is unclear to which work Tarabotti refers.

543. Tarabotti mentions here to another document that regards women. It is possible she refers to some preliminary pages of the work on women Dandolo was supposed to compose (see letter 7).

178
TO THE MOST ILLUSTRIOUS AND
EXCELLENT SIGNOR N.[544]

My heart predicts that, in a glorious metamorphosis, Your Illustrious Lordship will soon be transformed into an Excellency, and thus I anticipate the senate in acclaiming you as such. You always disdain women, but you borrow their purple vestments nonetheless.[545] Therefore, to make sure you receive them, I have found you a hat that will be absolutely yours alone to cover you from the shower of graces the Pregadi will rain down on you.[546] And why do I say graces, if your worthiest person contains all the best qualities and could rightly take the crown from Pluto and take possession both of his kingdom and of Proserpina?[547]

But joking aside, please meet tomorrow with the illustrious B., for we made a date with his wife. He has to leave Monday for his magistracy[548] and thus I thought it best not to put off the request. I shall behave warmly; if you are cold, all the worse for you.

544. Tarabotti sends this sarcastic letter to a man who is about to receive confirmation from the senate for a high position within the Republic. Rather than congratulate him, Tarabotti mocks him for his derision of women.

545. References to the debates on vanity: men criticized women for excessive vanity when they wore purple (an expensive color to produce, customarily worn by cardinals and those in high office), but it seems that men also sought the same luxuries. On the criticisms of women for their colorful clothing, see Tarabotti, *Antisatire*, 77–78.

546. It is unclear if this is a literal or a metaphorical hat.

547. Tarabotti continues to taunt her correspondent, comparing him to the god of the underworld. With the comparison, she insinuates that he will not receive his new post through his own merit, but yet he believes he can take whatever he wants.

548. Venetian nobles were stationed in various positions throughout the Republic's territories.

179
TO SIGNOR N.[549]

Your Lordship's meditations on the night of holy Christmas caused you to fall so deeply in love with silence that you cede nothing to the blessed Agathon, a great observer of this virtue.[550] And if I did not know that you are the most important teacher among philosophers, I would think you had become a disciple in the school of Socrates in order to learn how to keep your silence.[551] Truly was silence always praised by God's servants as well as by gentiles. Nonetheless, that mediocrity so commended by Aristotle is praiseworthy in our every action.[552] Be that as it may, if you wish to be the god Harpocrates,[553] I do not wish to be the goddess Angerona,[554] and therefore, caring little for the praise or glory of this world, breaking the silence with Your Lordship, I pray God to number me among those who *gloriam suam non in ore hominum ponunt sed intra conscientiam contegunt.*[555] And I beg you to see that if the recent solemnity had been Easter I would have believed you had gone with the disciples to Emmaus;[556] but since

---

549. In this letter which brims with resentment, Tarabotti reproaches her correspondent for his silence.

550. Saint Agathon of Egypt was a monk of the fourth century who went into the desert to live as a hermit.

551. Socrates used the dialogue to involve his interlocutor actively and to reveal to him his mistakes. Perhaps Tarabotti means that the interlocutor, at first sure in his opinion, would in the future more willingly remain silent knowing of his errors. Tarabotti may also confuse Socrates with Pythagoras, whose disciples had to observe silence for years.

552. Moderation was a fundamental virtue for Aristotle (see *Nichomachean Ethics*, 2.6–7).

553. In Greek iconography, coming originally from Egypt, he is a figure represented as a young boy who puts his finger on his mouth; because of this gesture, he became known as the god of silence.

554. Roman goddess, represented with her mouth bound and her index finger to her lips, in the act of imposing silence.

555. "Place their own glory not in the speech of men but conceal it in their own consciences." Cf. Gregorius I, *Homilae in Evangelia*, 12 (*PL* 76: 1119B).

556. The disciples who left Jerusalem after the crucifixion of Jesus went to the nearby village of Emmaus, where they saw Jesus risen.

it was Christmas, I find it harder to believe that you would have let yourself be slaughtered with the innocents.[557]

The mother prioress gave me, in your name, a blessed candle[558] and commissions me to thank you heartily in her name. This news occasioned great wonder in me because if candles are tongues of fire to beg God for the favors we ask, I do not understand their language, and because there was no accompanying note, I understood nothing more from its messages than that they reminded me of my obligations, which I ask Your Lordship to relieve me of with some command. In the meantime I offer myself to the lady your sister and to you I am ... , etc.

180
TO SIGNOR N.[559]

If I did not congratulate Your Lordship before now on your improvement, attribute the fault to my illness, whose sharpness so often steals my breath away and causes me each day to despise life more. This changeable and unseasonable weather is most harmful to my indisposition. I blush, however, always to complain, because even real and not imagined illnesses appear to be womanish caprices to some people.

Your Lordship must take care since you, too, are convalescing, and do not hurry with regard to the relics I sent you, while I entreat you to pray for me.

181
TO FATHER N.

My imperfect compositions have never merited the honors bestowed on me by Your Lordship's heavenly pen, but rather deserve to be anointed, with manners and words, as unseemly. Therefore I receive

557. Reference to the slaughter of the innocents at Herod's order, immediately after Christ's birth.

558. Perhaps on 2 February, the feast of Mary's purification, called also *festum candelarum* or Candelmas, when candles were blessed and sometimes given as presents.

559. Tarabotti rejoices with her unnamed addressee who has recovered from a period of bad health, but she complains of her own continuing physical suffering.

them as words meant to fill with hot air my ambition, which (thanks be to God) is not encouraged by the praise of men, who are for the most part flatterers, as Sanazaro said:

> *Tal ride del mio ben, che 'l viso simula,*
> *Tal piange del mio mal, che poi mi lacera,*
> *Dietro le spale con acuta limula.*[560]

Nonetheless, I thank Your Reverend Lordship, praying our Lord keep you, and I kiss your hands.

182

TO THE MOST ILLUSTRIOUS SIGNORA BETTA POLANI

In my continued poor health, my heart's afflictions, and my mind's agitation, my memory does not forget those debts which, owed to your great affection, will always live etched upon my heart. It is true that my pen, negligent perhaps, flees the opportunity to bring before Your Illustrious Ladyship's eyes conceits that are cold, full of suffering, and therefore also bothersome. I must, however, hope for your understanding, since you are kindness itself.

I write to you with the confusion caused by the confusion of my mind, which has produced the silence with which I have failed you. Therefore please excuse me for everything, while I, wishing you a happy and joyful feast of the Resurrection with many years full of contentment and prosperity, bow to you and kiss you, etc.

---

560. "This one smiles at my fortune, dissimulating her expression, / That one weeps at my misfortune, but then wounds me, / Behind my back, with sharpened blade." Jacopo Sannazaro ("Sanazaro," as Tarabotti writes in the Venetian way), *Arcadia*, ecloga 6. The quotation here, by either Tarabotti's or the press's error, substitutes *viso*, or "expression," in the first verse, for *riso*, or "laughter." Tarabotti quotes the same lines from Sannazaro (correctly) in her *Convent Hell* (bk. 3, 86).

183

TO THE MOST ILLUSTRIOUS AND EXCELLENT
SIGNOR MICHEL MINOTTO[561]

The happy news of the election of your most worthy person to the Pregadi reached me at a time when I was forbidden to use my pen to congratulate you as my devotion obliged me to do. My heart, however, which hoped for all the honors you deserve and for this boon to our native city, immediately had the messenger fly to execute the debt of my reverent obligation. But we must congratulate the Republic for having the good fortune of a senator worthy of governing a whole world. This much I tell you with my heart's voice. Jubilant about the happiness of Your Excellency I commend myself to you, etc.

184

TO SIGNOR CAVALIER FRANCESCO PONA[562]

I finally received from Lady Emilia della Pietade[563] that famous motet by Vittoria[564] that Your Excellent Lordship so desired, a gift you must appreciate as a sign of the respect that I eternally pledge to your most supreme merit. I send it without delay since, with Easter nigh, Christ's victories must be sung by a heavenly singer, as I judge the cloistered lady your daughter to be. In the meantime to both your Lord and Ladyship I wish bodily and spiritual victories and contentments in these most holy days, no less than in the coming holidays, offering you my respects, etc.

---

561. Michiel Minotto (1603–61), head of the Council of Ten (Barbaro, *Arbori*, ad vocem). Tarabotti congratulates him for his election to the senate.

562. Tarabotti composed this letter to accompany a religious motet to be sung by her correspondent's daughter, a nun.

563. La Pietà (or the Pio Ospedale della Pietà) was an orphanage whose female residents learned to play or sing in order to earn money for a dowry for marriage or convent. Lady Emilia was perhaps a teacher—or student—at this institution.

564. Tarabotti is likely referring to Tomás Luis de Victoria, or da Vittoria (c. 1548–1611), the famous Spanish composer and one of the most important composers of the Counter-Reformation. De Victoria wrote a series of motets linked to the commemoration of Holy Week (*Officium Hebdomadae Sanctae*, 1585).

185
TO THE MOST ILLUSTRIOUS SIGNOR N.[565]

Your Illustrious Lordship is the most mindless creature in the world, the most ungrateful beast on the face of the earth, and the most envious soul that God created! You forgot to help that lady, you don't reciprocate or indeed even recognize the favors I have done for you, and you envy my little learning, I can tell. Fearful that your absentmindedness may also cause you to forget about Baron N. who will soon submit a request to the Pregadi, I am reminding you, because to me it is a matter of great urgency. To Signor Loredano you can say that, even if I refused the share you allotted me, in any case I expect the letter promised to me and Thursday someone will go to fetch it. As for the rest, I write in pain, tormented by the constriction in my chest and closer to death than life.

For this I despise men, who are the most despicable things in the world. I don't fuel their ambition with fancy titles or honorifics, so that they know that even if many of them take pride in being noble, they too are nothing but three ounces of dirt, and even if they are wrapped in purple, they will end up like everyone else, and whoever has good sense

> *Conosce al fin tutti i mondani avanzi*
> *Sogni d'infermi, e folle de' romanzi.*[566]

---

565. The recipient of this angry letter was probably Aprosio or Brusoni.

566. "Knows in the end the world's remains are / sick men's dreams and storytellers' fables." Tarabotti bases the second of the two verses on Petrarch (*Triumph of Love*, 66), but may have added the first verse herself.

186
TO THE MOST ILLUSTRIOUS SIGNORA ELENA FOSCOLO[567]

The fierceness of the pain afflicting the anguished body of the illustrious Lady N.[568] has managed to keep her confined to bed with a fever, but has not had the power to erase those feelings of indebtedness and love that she eternally professes to Your Illustrious Ladyship and to your excellent consort.[569] Having seen that Your Illustrious Ladyship did not favor her as promised, she therefore requests, despite her truly unbearable anguish, news of Your Lord and Ladyships' health, worried that some ill has befallen you. She also requests that I relate to Your Excellency that Lady N.[570] has chosen as a remedy to go for a while to recover in the house of her illustrious uncle, a decision with which everyone is pleased. She was anguished by the suffering she endured during our most beloved Regina's illness and afflicted by the grief and pain of her blessed passing, in addition to the illness of the lady her aunt.[571] The lady awaited the visit of Your Illustrious Ladyship in order to have Your Excellency's advice and agreement, but because of the delay she has already taken her departure.

As for the rest, believe me, Your Illustrious Ladyship, that I have lost half of myself; my dear friend has flown to delight in the blessed gardens of Paradise and has left me so alone and anguished that I can barely express it because of the innermost pain in my heart. May Your Illustrious Ladyship take pity upon my endless suffering and excuse me if I do not express my condolences to you, since I do

---

567. This letter must have been composed shortly after the death of Regina Donà in 1645. The two Lady N.'s referred to in the letter are most likely relatives of Elena Foscolo, who had an aunt and, it seems, another relative in Sant'Anna. The first of these women, in ill health, awaits a visit from Elena and sends her news, through Tarabotti, of the second, who, grieving the death of Regina, has withdrawn from the convent to the home of an uncle.

568. From what we read in the remainder of the letter, it seems likely that this lady may be one of two nuns with the name of Foscolo who appear in the chapter lists of Sant'Anna in these years: Orsetta Foscolo or Maria Grazia Foscolo (APV, sez. Antica, licenze e decreti riguardanti le monache [1632–39], b. 4, 4v–5v).

569. Leonardo Foscolo (1588–1661; see n. 365).

570. That is, the second of the two ladies mentioned in this letter.

571. It appears that Elena and the second Lady N. mentioned here have this aunt (the first Lady N.) in common.

not know how to convey them in proportion to the loss. I offer you my respects in the name of the most illustrious Lady N. and together with her illustrious excellency to both of you I most humbly present my regards, and most respectfully I bow to all of your illustrious family. Please count me among your most humble servants and honor me with your most precious commands, since I am Your Illustrious Ladyship's, etc.

187

TO SIGNOR N.

Your Lordship has almost given more thought to and found greater mystery in that small and malformed *Gondola*[572] than the wisest and most intuitive thinkers have given to Saint Peter's bark.[573] But the fertility of your mind is able to extract from nothingness the most important ideas, worthy of other people besides a sick woman wracked by every grief. For this reason, recognizing that I am too incapable and ignorant to respond promptly to your courteous letter, I will abandon such a difficult undertaking so as not to gain a reputation for rashness with you whom I admire so greatly. I will only say simply that I sent you that trifling work[574] because Signor A.[575] told me that you were very fond of riding in a gondola. Nor was it my intention to suggest that you treat your most kind lady in that manner,[576] as you describe so charmingly, since your prudence does not need womanly advice in order to live well, much less regarding love, since all men are experts at it, even if usually false ones.

---

572. *The Gondola with Three Oars* (*La gondola a tre remi*) by Girolamo Brusoni (Venice: Storti, 1657), of which Tarabotti and her correspondent must have seen a manuscript copy.

573. In *That Women Are of the Same Species as Men*, Tarabotti uses the metaphor of Saint Peter's boat for the church (6); she may also refer to Giotto's mosaic in the portico of the Basilica of Saint Peter in Rome, the relocation of which was the object of debate in the Seicento.

574. That is, Brusoni's text.

575. A reconstruction from the original *S. A.* = S[ignor] A.

576. Tarabotti is likely referring to the sixth part of Brusoni's *Gondola*, in which the protagonist offers advice on marriage (*La gondola a tre remi*, ed. F. Lanza [Milan: Mazorati, 1971], 174).

I thank you for the *Fugitive*[577] you sent me, who traveled quite a distance if she was able to reach the vast sea of your Lordship's knowledge, and I must repeat to you how much satisfaction and consolation I derive from your judicious and graceful flights of fancy, and I respectfully bid you farewell.

188
TO THE EMINENT SIGNORE A. AND C. T[ARABOTTI][578]

A letter from Your Ladyships, come to comfort me when I least expected it, indebts me to your kindness. To comfort me, I say, because in it I found nothing but strokes of esteem and love without the barbs that you always tend to make. But let us forget those grievances and remember that we were all born of the same womb. Take heed, however, that this memory does not stir up for me thoughts like those of the first twins.[579] Take care of yourselves and ask of me whatever I am able to give and love me as much as you can, for I expect nothing more.

I do not respond to the gossip you report because you, too, know that it is men's usual rumor mongering. I cannot tell you anything about Lady L.[580] since she has moved house, and, to tell you the truth, it seems that we siblings love each other as much as cats and mice. At this time we know that whoever has good luck should enjoy it. We must learn this, since to tell the truth, everything seems good in the moment. And I embrace you affectionately.

---

577. Brusoni's *The Fugitive* (*La fuggitiva* [Venice, Sarzina, 1639]), a romantic roman à clef.

578. One of two letters addressed to Tarabotti's sisters (see also letter 106).

579. Cain and Abel.

580. Likely Tarabotti's sister Lorenzina, who remarried after the death in 1647 of her first husband, Pighetti (see Zanette, *Suor Arcangela*, 4).

189
TO SIGNOR N.[581]

My usual indisposition, which often leads me to the brink, was the reason that I did not respond immediately to Your Lordship's letter, which I do now with this letter in order to take revenge with the pen, since I have no other weapons. In terms of the response after which Your Lordship inquires, I say it is true that the gentlemen's first objection was not to your response, but I swear to God that it is quite true that a senator told me about it exactly as I wrote of it to you.[582] I must therefore complain that you charge me with using lies and tricks to get you to suspend publication, which is the farthest thing from the truth. Indeed I hope that soon you will be convinced whether it was to my liking that your work be printed. These are the last letters and syllables that I will write on this matter, because I am so vexed by the preponderance of gossip about my ill fortune that I cannot put it into words. May everyone expose his feelings against me openly to the world, and if this is not enough for Your Lordship, pile on a dozen more, for it matters not to me. In this circumstance I have undergone many trials. Saint Paul did not lightly say *Nulla fides hominibus*.[583] I repeat again, may you find contentment in your work and in every other thing that relates to me, since I in any case will always have satisfaction.

I gave the letter to the person for whom it was intended, and she thanks you for thinking of her, as I thank you for your good will in helping me, and I continue to pray our Lord that he grant you perfect health.

---

581. This letter dealing with the *Mask Lifted* is intended for Angelico Aprosio. Tarabotti again affirms that she never attempted to block the publication of this response to her *Antisatire*, even if, in effect, that was exactly what she did.

582. It is unclear to which senator Tarabotti refers. She seems here to refer to Aprosio's revelation of her name as the author of the *Antisatire*.

583. Cf. 2 Thess. 3:2: *non enum omnium est fides* ("for not all have faith"). Tarabotti alters the passage to indicate "there is no faith among men."

190

TO THE MOST ILLUSTRIOUS SIGNOR
FRANCESCO DA MULLA[584]

So that Your Illustrious Lordship may see that my statements are true, I am sending you a rough and unrefined copy of *Paternal Tyranny*, in exactly the state that I birthed it. You, on the basis of your great merit, have gained a privilege not conceded to others. Your divine kindness will pardon the complete imperfection of the work, since in your courtesy you are always inclined to understand others' shortcomings. Trusting your unequaled prudence, I will let you have the book for only three days, and I profess that Your Illustrious Lordship is always excluded from the masses of men whom I with reason condemn. I pray that the Giver of every good grant you the height of all honors and contentments, offering myself to Your Illustrious Lordship, etc.

191

TO THE MOST EMINENT AND EXCELLENT
SIGNOR NICOLÒ CRASSO

The universal pronouncements, which gloriously proclaim Your Excellent Lordship's reputation no less as the most courteous than as the most elevated intellect that lights our world, nourish a certain hope in me that I may obtain a favor whose exceptionality will always be considered by me as a singular example of my greatest debt. My request is just; you are the image of goodness, and thus I consider it to be superfluous to linger on excuses with your kindness, which it would be a great mistake to doubt. I consider that my temerity may be defended by that small affinity which we share,[585] in which, because of Your Lordship's rare qualities, I take more honor than in any other

---

584. The identity of this addressee is not completely certain. It is likely that Tarabotti writes to a certain Francesco son of Marino da Mulla whose name appears among the archives of Sant'Anna in a document dated 26 March 1634 (ASV, Cong. Rel. sopp., S. Anna, busta 5). According to Barbaro, Francesco son of Marino (1587–1653) was a civil judge (*Arbori*, ad vocem). Tarabotti entrusts him with a draft copy of *Paternal Tyranny* in the hopes that he will help quell the rumors that she was not the real author of the work.

585. Tarabotti and Crasso were distantly related (see letter 173).

stroke of luck. I offer you my heartfelt respects most affectionately and I worship you in spirit, waiting to be able to ask you the favor in person, and I bow to you.

192

TO THE MOST ILLUSTRIOUS SIGNORA
GUID'ASCANIA ORSI

I am obliged to come on bended knee to the feet of Your Illustrious Ladyship to beg pardon for the great mistake of having let three dispatches pass without honoring you with my letters. The fault for this lies in some great problems which do not make me unworthy of your forgiveness.

I have just received the package from the heavens of your kindness. Since it is full of marvels, it renders me as astounded by the beauty of the flowers as I am embarrassed by the exceptionality of the favor and the nobility of your generous heart. Your garden indeed produces flowers that exceed natural ones in quality, and it is quite fertile with fruit and every other worthy quality. With all the affection in my heart I thank you most humbly, begging you to honor me with your commands. I pray you not to mortify me by asking for the efforts of my weak pen, even if you are and will always be the absolute mistress of me and what is mine. I am more pleased that my book was appreciated by Your Illustrious Ladyship's intelligence than by all the applause that could come to me from anywhere else, and I will consider it to be my good luck and even greater honor to show you in time the responses that are being prepared against me.

In the meantime I lift my pen in order not to bore you further, remaining absolutely and eternally devoted to you with my heart.

193

TO THE MOST EXCELLENT SIGNOR GIACOMO PIGHETTI

The eminent Signor Paolo has just now attested again Your Excellent Lordship's innocence regarding the responses to my *Antisatire*. Having heard his reasonable responses and knowing the nobility of his mind, which is the true and proper center of the virtues, I would consider it to be a betrayal of myself if I did not drive out of my heart the impression that was planted there by much speculation. I do not mean however that I will set aside my opinion regarding Signor Robazza,[586] because I would do too much ill to what I know of your guileless-ness; I mean only that the affect, manner and way with which this sir explained Your Excellent Lordship's arguments convinced me of the sincerity of his candor. Nevertheless, in any case my mind is prepared to receive from everyone the replies to the *Antisatire*, since it is not my thought to impede the movement of those quills that dare to spread their wings even against God Himself.[587] Be assured, in the meantime, that despite the terrible tribulations we had between us because of my family's interests,[588] I have always retained the devotion I owe to you. It has risen to the ultimate degree because of the exceptional favor I received from the illustrious and excellent lady ambassadress,[589] lead-ing me to redouble more vigorously than ever a sisterly love toward you that renders me forever Your Excellent Lordship's, etc.

194
TO SIGNOR N.[590]

So that Your Reverend Lordship may know that it is not true that you do not intend to print your *Mask* with my name clearly visible and that I acted with just cause to have you erase it, I am sending you the frontispiece copied from the original in your own hand. If you can deny this, and insist that you didn't read it to many gentlemen with my name expressed and many times repeated, I will have to say that

---

586. No biographical information has been found regarding this Paolo Robazza.

587. In actuality Tarabotti attempted, successfully, to block the publication of Aprosio's *Mask Lifted*.

588. The precise nature of the tensions to which Tarabotti refers is unclear, but likely had to do with problems related to Pighetti's marriage to Tarabotti's sister Lorenzina.

589. It was likely Pighetti who suggested that the ambassador Bretel de Grémonville and his wife board their daughters with the nuns of Sant'Anna.

590. In this letter to Aprosio, Tarabotti scorns the friar's protestations of innocence with regard to his *Mask Lifted*, which he maintains was never intended to reveal her name as the author of the *Antisatire*. In response, Tarabotti confronts him with damning evidence: the original frontispiece of the *Mask Lifted*.

you have a more-than-divine intellect, since even God with all his omnipotence cannot make things that have happened not take place; and thus the Legislator said: *Quod factum est fieri non potest.*[591]

Let this be said to assure you that I did not expect anything from you except that you remove my name from that work so that the comedy of the *Mask Lifted* did not result in tragedy for anyone. As for your wanting to exaggerate your feelings against me, I don't recommend it. But exaggerate if you will, and know that the duty of a good preacher is to abhor evil but without ever naming the guilty. If I said that in this convent I am judged to be incapable of making a *Paradise* by myself, I was referring to what Your Reverend Lordship said to many people (insofar as it has been reported to me[592]), since in all things I always leave due room for the truth. Nevertheless let people believe what they will, since I give you infinite thanks for the praise you have attributed to me. Be cautious, in the meantime, that praising a woman who brims with every imperfection does not injure your notable intelligence and learning, and may our Lord keep you.

195

TO THE MOST EXCELLENT SIGNOR
GIACOMO PIGHETTI[593]

I received two most singular favors yesterday through the kindness of Your Excellent Lordship—whether to mark my debt to you for eternity, or to render me uncertain of what had been heartily assured me (no less by your authoritative attestations than by those of persons of

---

591. "What has been done cannot be redone." See Saint Thomas Aquinas, *Scriptum super sententiis*, 4, 13.2: *Sed quod factum est, fieri non potest; quia quod est, non fit* ("But what has been done cannot be redone, because what already exists cannot be made").

592. Allusion to the rumors, circulated by Aprosio, that Tarabotti was not the true author of *Convent Paradise*.

593. The tensions between Tarabotti and her brother-in-law regarding the responses to the *Antisatire* that Pighetti had solicited (see letters 86 and 113) seem in this letter to have dissipated. Pighetti had asked his sister-in-law for forgiveness, which she granted. The letter demonstrates, however, that the nun retains her resentment toward Angelico Aprosio, the author of one of these responses, *The Mask Lifted*. Tarabotti maintains that she would like Aprosio's response to be published and that open attack would be preferable to the lies that Aprosio was disseminating privately, behind her back.

esteem), I do not know. Whatever the case, if you offended me and now regret it, it is enough for me because *angelicum est emendare.*[594] It is true that I was aggrieved, revered Brother-in-law, that you supported those who responded with indecent sharpness to my *Antisatire,*[595] but I did not expect praise since I know that I possess no virtue worthy of being celebrated by your authoritative attestations. Have care, I beg you, not to harm yourself by exalting me, for I do not merit it. I feel myself so highly favored that in return I must be careful that your judgment does not lose anything in the estimation of others when you are heard to praise me, of whom others speak ill and with little respect.

Seek in this regard the counsel of Father V[enti] M[iglia],[596] who will certainly dissuade you from exposing yourself to such a danger. He himself is even now spreading the rumor (I do not know on what basis) that others had a hand in the *Convent Paradise*, adding that if the breviary could produce doctors, all the priests, friars and nuns would be such. Such things, however, move me to laughter more than anger, whence I declare that I can receive no greater favor than for him to respond to my *Antisatire* and make his opinions clear in writing to all the world, just as he spews them out with his voice. Stabs in the back come from a traitor, and words spoken in the absence of the person they insult cannot inflict harm; but *sermo vanus vanae conscientiae iudex est. Et absentem lacerans seipsum deturpat.*[597] Proof is necessary to make the truth clear, and for this reason I hope that the entire world hears his arguments against me, placing my hope in God that I will have pen enough to demonstrate the goal of his fabrications.

Your Excellent Lordship must excuse me if my long-windedness is an undue bother. I thank you for the honor conferred on me,

594. "It is angelic to make amends." Carolus Magnus, *Capitularia* (*PL* 97.241d).

595. As she believed Aprosio had done in his *Mask*.

596. Aprosio.

597. "Empty speech is the sign of an empty conscience, and insulting an absent person shames the speaker." Saint Gregory is repeatedly cited for the saying "Sermo vanus, vanae mentis index est," present also in Saint Thomas Aquinas, *Psalmos Davidis expositio a psalmo XI ad psalmum XX*. The word *Iudex* in Tarabotti's text may be an error for *index*. For the second part of the citation, cf. Walther, *Lateinishe Sprichtwoerter*, 2:7, 31: "Absentem rodere turpe."

through you, by the ambassadress of France,[598] a woman truly blessed with remarkable qualities, to whom Your Excellent Lordship is not at all inferior in grace or charming traits. I have always recognized, and now indeed have experienced this, requiring that I be Your Excellent Lordship's, etc.

196

TO THE MOST EXCELLENT SIGNOR GIACOMO PIGHETTI[599]

I receive Your most Excellent Lordship's kind praise as a gift from God, for it is presented to me by an angel.[600] Thus are celestial favors dispensed and they excite astonishment more than praise. My rough *Paradise* will boast of no other glory than to see itself enriched by your goodness and with the most precious treasures of the Latin language. It will acquire splendor from those erudite and original conceits that have no match in our time, while your words will make it shine luminously. Your compositions, which contain the most uplifting concepts, oblige every heart to devote excesses of affection and devotion to you; but this one, written for me who knows herself to be unworthy of so significant a favor, will earn my unending obligation for the rest of my life. I would like to thank you from the depths of my soul, but my mind, stunned by the brilliance of your pen, cannot and knows not how to form anything but confusion. I am certain, however, that with customary kindness Your Lordship will not only have compassion for the weakness of my skill, but that you will also distinguish, with your marvelous genius, the failings of my pen, and be pleased by the affection of my heart. Therefore blame yourself, or at least have

598. Pighetti had evidently recommended Tarabotti as the teacher for the daughters of the French ambassador Nicolas Bretel de Grémonville and his wife, Anne-Françoise. See also letter 193 and Zanette, *Suor Arcangela*, 263.

599. Tarabotti thanks her brother-in-law for the Latin composition he wrote for *Convent Paradise*. The composition praises Tarabotti and predicts her eternal fame.

600. This "angel" may refer either to Pighetti or to Angelico Aprosio, who was still, at the time of the *Paradise*'s publication, a friend of Tarabotti's. The etymologic play between *angelico/angelo* is present also in Pighetti's Latin composition for the *Paradise*, with obvious reference to the nun's name.

compassion for me, even though I do not deserve it, for I should be accustomed to the greatness of the virtue, grace, and favor I have admired in you and which you extend to me, without overwhelming me. Nonetheless, miracles are always miracles and will always astonish and confound those who most often know and are touched by them. I offer you the highest thanks I can for the honor conferred on me and I beg you to be assured that your suspicions are quite false and that I am sincerely Your Excellent Lordship's devoted sister-in-law and obliged servant, etc.

197

TO SIGNOR N.[601]

Yesterday I received a letter from Your Lordship that caused me to marvel more than a little upon hearing that I am poised to provoke the most celebrated pens in Italy. It would surely be great cowardice in my opinion if these fellows were to plot against a lone woman, for it is not appropriate for worthy gentlemen to engage in combat unless it is one-on-one, and it is often said that *nec Hercules contra duos*.[602] Let your Lordship's prudence consider if it is proper and chivalrous for an army of quills, educated in the greatest studies, to move against a woman who has not been able to fly except over the surface of scripture, guided by her simple nature. Let these gentlemen reply as much as they like, for I shall force myself to respond in my necessary defense with what my tenuous talent permits, just as now in order to serve others I have entered into the fray.[603] Thus I believe these learned men should treat only literary matters in their writing since my status and my vows do not allow for any other contest. And if they are gentle-

---

601. This letter is likely addressed to Aprosio or to Brusoni, given that it speaks of the continued literary battles that Tarabotti faced. Here, the nun refers to the hostile reaction elicited by her *Antisatire*. She sarcastically calls attention to her status as a woman and as a self-taught nun to demonstrate the absurdity of the fact that a group of men has lined up against her.

602. "Not even Hercules against two." Erasmus provides a version of this saying in his *Adagia* (1.5.39): *Ne Hercules quidem adversus duos.*

603. Tarabotti writes that she wrote the *Antisatire* at the prompting of noblewomen (see letters 33 and 207).

men, they will certainly not mind that I have defended my sex, and they will not make accusations regarding a work published not to offend but to defend.

I do not know how teasing jousts can be coupled with biting jabs. If it is a friendly clash to say that I write with a pen dipped in the ink of scorn, gossip, hatred, and desire for revenge, I cede to those who know better. Since I am female, I ought not to know the meaning of gossip, liar, audacious, temerarious, or similar words. These words are too improper and irregular to attack the depths of my ignorance; nonetheless, everyone is master of his own conceits and the reply is often even more biting. Adieu.

198
TO SIGNOR N.[604]

Only yesterday did I have the good fortune to meet with Signor Vendramino,[605] to whom I explained to the best of my weak ability Your Lordship's devout opinions. I found him not only full of gratitude and affection, but I might say worshipful of your merit. With weighty and respectful words he showed that he recognized you as the best pen in Europe. He made it clear to me how greatly he is obliged to prize and recognize the verses of Your Lordship and he left me in a state of confusion, since I know myself to be incapable of returning the praise that comes from so lofty an understanding. I report this to you in order to carry out your commands, and I attest to it on my word of honor. If that gentleman should speak differently, however, blame the inconstancy of his sex, or rather man's forked tongue. I say this to you in my defense, not to offend anyone, just as I assure you once again that I only failed in my debt to you regarding the favor you asked because I was still sick, which makes me worthy of forgiveness. I declare myself Your Illustrious and Excellent Lordship's, etc.

---

604. Tarabotti here refers to her addressee compliments from another gentleman, while also commenting upon the inescapable untrustworthiness of men.

605. Perhaps Andrea Vendramino, nephew of Regina Donà and addressee of the nun.

199

TO THE MOST ILLUSTRIOUS AND REVEREND SIGNOR FRANCESCO MARIA ZATI, RESIDENT OF TUSCANY AT THE MOST SERENE REPUBLIC OF VENICE

Your Illustrious Lordship's goodness, which like that of God receives the offerings of pure hearts with no other consideration, will certainly not scorn the happy wishes I bring you in these holy festivities, which I pray to God will be full of incomparable contentment and prosperity for Your Lordship. In this florid season I desire that graces may bloom in you, so that afterwards the best fruits may ripen in your most blessed person. You, who are a mine of all learning and versed in all the virtuous disciplines, thus know how to assess, I believe, people's hearts, minds, and desires, and therefore will know if these wishes are sincere.

As to the rest, my soul stood at my lips these last few days, and if Your Illustrious Lordship had come to visit me while marking the holy jubilee, you would have completed two works of mercy at once, visiting an invalid and a prisoner.

Please have compassion for my devoted respect, and do not blame me for being too forward. I bow to you.

200

TO THE MOST ILLUSTRIOUS SIGNORA ANDRIANA MALIPIERO[606]

Our convent's custom is this: as soon as the nuns have surrendered their souls to their Creator, their cells are closed and they are not reopened until the end of the month. Therefore Your Illustrious Ladyship may not receive the sleeves until the first of May. I tell you this much on behalf of your illustrious aunt, who is inconsolable in her

---

606. This letter to the sister of the deceased Regina Donà gives an idea of daily life within Sant'Anna: Tarabotti explains that, according to convent rules, Andriana must wait until the end of the month to enter into Regina's cell to take away her possessions. Andriana is particularly interested in taking back some sleeves, which were in contemporary clothing separable from dresses. It seems Regina had embellished these sleeves by hand.

grief.[607] Be assured, Your Illustrious Ladyship, that as soon as it is possible I will have them delivered to you.

This is all I have to say to you in this regard; as to the rest, I declare myself (although unworthy) to be in effect the sister you have lost, and in service and devotion the most humble and reverent servant your greatness has. If Your Illustrious Ladyship will honor me by kindly accepting so lowly an offer, I attest that this will be the appropriate way to diminish in some part the fierceness of my unbearable grief. May your kindness therefore accept the enjoyment of my reverent affection, while I, praying His Holy Goodness to grant all graces to Your Illustrious Ladyship, most respectfully bow to you.

201
TO THE MOST ILLUSTRIOUS SIGNOR GUID'ASCANIA ORSI

If I did not notify Your Illustrious Ladyship that I have begun breathing freely again after a constant illness of some duration, I would merit falling from grace again for this sin alone. It is very true that my improvement is a but a flash of lightning that is quickly followed by a horrible rumble of thunder and a lightning bolt which itself, if it did not incinerate me at once, consumes me over time with a constant burning. As a result I have no breath, I have lost my spirit, my limbs are limp, my heart half dead, but it belongs completely to Your Illustrious Ladyship. May your kindness not disdain it, while I always immensely enjoy your letters, which depict to me in vivid images your beautiful soul, which I worship. I will always be Your Illustrious Ladyship's, etc.

---

607. An aunt of Andriana's in Sant'Anna is mentioned also in letter 81.

202
TO THE MOST NOBLE AND EXCELLENT
SIGNOR ENRICO CORNARO[608]

I send Your Lordship two stillbirths of my mind, so different in content, style and conceits that they hardly seem to be siblings. Such thoughts are formed by those with little understanding of how one writes; but I esteem it superfluous to remind Your Lordship, who has perfect understanding of letters and of the most elegant Latin language, of the need to vary one's style in conformity with the content treated. I pray you to have compassion on the other imperfections that really do exist in the works, and not to judge with that malice used by men to censure the writings of women. Give no sinister meaning to any passage where I might speak too freely of myself, but attribute it all to excessive naiveté, while I, having become an admirer of your spirited and most lofty compositions, pray to our Lord an abundance of every grace for you. I beg you to consign the reports to this messenger, and I declare myself Your Lordship's, etc.

203
TO THE REVEREND MOTHER N.[609]

I received from Lady B. a corona of the glorious Virgin entitled *Contemplation of her Holiest Sorrows*[610] and I would like to thank Your

---

608. This letter accompanied two works that Tarabotti sent to her correspondent and literary champion. She tells him the two works are quite distinct in style and subject matter. It is not entirely clear which works Tarabotti discusses, but similar references in other letters (see, e.g., letter 113) might indicate her *Convent Paradise* and *Antisatire*, works so different that doubts were raised about whether they could be by the same author. The nun composed another missive, however, to Cornaro (letter 67), which accompanied the two works. Another possibility would be that Tarabotti here refers to *Convent Hell* and *Paternal Tyranny*, which are, however, closer in subject matter, or that she sent one of these latter works along with a devotional work, later lost, like the *The Paved Road to Heaven* (see Giovanni Dandolo's introductory letter).

609. Tarabotti in this letter writes of an exchange of works with a literary nun.

610. *Contemplazione de' suoi santissimi dolori*. This was a common theme for writers; it is unclear to whose work Tarabotti refers. By referring to the work as a *corona*, or rosary, Tarabotti emphasizes its meditative and spiritual qualities.

Ladyship, but because your favors are incomparable treasures, I have no words adequate to do so. With such a meditation, there is no doubt that a soul can lift its thoughts to such an understanding of God that it can even gain *Paradise*; whereas I, having received so efficient an instrument for lifting myself up, can send you nothing in grateful exchange but a Paradise. Look on it with a kind eye, for you will see the audacity of a sinner (as I am) in daring to create a *Convent Paradise*, in which blessed God keeps here on earth his dearest delights, which he perhaps meant to imply when he said *Delitiae meae esse cum filiis hominum*.[611] Also pray to the Lord that at the time of my death I may feel pain for offending Him equal to that suffered by the Virgin, so that by virtue of it I may then enjoy the true Paradise. I bow to you.

204

TO SIGNOR N.[612]

Yesterday Your Lordship sent me such beautiful roses that they made me believe it was the first of May rather than August. The choice and exquisite fruits appear to have been gathered in Earthly Paradise, for which I heartily thank you.

I was astonished to hear of the behavior of N., since many times he himself has praised with great excess your courtesy and kindness. Nonetheless I am accustomed to his stupidity, and I promise you that had he not served me for so many years I would let him go. His poor manners reveal him to be an ass dressed as a man, and therefore those with lofty sensibilities must not bother about being mistreated by one such as him. I would appreciate being informed if he has spent too much on certain things so that I can act accordingly. I declare myself Your Lordship's, etc.

---

611. Prov. 8:31: "My delights were to be with the children of men."

612. Thanking her addressee for a present, Tarabotti complains of another man long in her service whom she has begun to mistrust.

205
TO THE MOST ILLUSTRIOUS SIGNOR N.[613]

When Your Illustrious Lordship proposed that person to me, you did not hint at all that there was a hurry to resolve things, for if you had mentioned it, my desire to serve you well would have given wings to paper in order to seek the assent of the woman who will be the bride. I was waiting, however, to be able to earn in person that attention usually dedicated to cruelty in order to inform you with my weak words that the worthy qualities of the groom, sung by Your Illustrious Lordship, have been sufficiently authenticated. I was hoping (with the imperturbability so often demonstrated by yourself) to bring an end to this undertaking. I recalled that you sing,

> *La flemma è sicura*
> *La trotta non dura.*[614]

But I see that although Your Illustrious Lordship is all calm and patience when it comes to the affairs of others, you wish others to be all fire and fury, acting instantly. I will obey, and consider it my fortune to do so, offering you my respects.

---

613. In this letter Tarabotti is again the intermediary in a marriage negotiation. She scolds her addressee who is slow when working for others but expects others to act quickly for him.

614. "Slowness is certain / Hurry does not last." Tomaso Buoni provides the proverb *Trotto d'asino poco dura* ("The donkey's trot doesn't last") to mean that the donkey moves quickly only when food is near, and therefore only for his own interests (*Thesoro degli proverbi italiani*, part 2 [Venice: Gio. Battista Ciotti, 1606], 9).

206

TO THE MOST ILLUSTRIOUS SIGNOR N.[615]

The painter causes me to yearn for the strokes of his brush more than Alexander longed for those of Apelles.[616] I turn to Your Illustrious Lordship so that you may warn that good-for-nothing that he is defaulting on his debt. I realize, however, that you are inexperienced in matters of warfare, so I will turn to you instead in matters of love.

Do me the favor of letting your mother know that I adore her, and while I remain Your Illustrious Lordship's servant, I bow to that kindest lady.

207

TO SIGNOR N.[617]

With this brief response to Your Lordship's letter I will set forth the facts that I think are pertinent in defending my case. It is true that I composed the *Antisatire* at the urging of noblewomen, but on the assumption however that it would not be published.[618] These illustrious ladies chose to have it printed, and for this I am extremely mortified. I take consolation however that gentlewomen of that rank will be able to solicit others (besides me) to respond in my defense to the malicious men who attacked me, and that perhaps this will be to my benefit.[619]

---

615. This letter, in which the nun mentions a painter, might refer to a planned portrait of Tarabotti. Mention is made of this portrait in Loredano's biography by Antonio Lupis, *Vita di Giovan Francesco Loredan Senator Veneto* (Venice: Valvasense, 1663). From the letter it seems that the painter had put off the work; Tarabotti asks her addressee to encourage his speed.

616. See n. 239.

617. It is not certain to whom Tarabotti addresses this letter. It is one of the first to discuss the controversy surrounding the publication of the *Antisatire*, when the rumor spread that various responses to the work were being planned.

618. In several points Tarabotti assigns responsibility for the publication of the *Antisatire* to a group of noblewomen who urged her to respond to Buoninsegni's *Satire* (see also letter 33).

619. Although a handful of responses were in fact composed it does not seem that any were in favor of Tarabotti (in fact, quite the opposite: for example, Aprosio's *Mask Lifted*).

I marvel at the prudence of Your Lordship when you allow yourself to believe that Signor Buoninsegni, a much honored gentleman, fails to uphold standards of chivalry by taking up the pen against a woman.[620] Those who will speak against me will never be gentlemen and therefore I will disregard what they say.[621] To Your Lordship, who possesses all the qualities that befit a worthy gentleman, I say that I do not doubt your kindness, which, since it has benefited me at other times, requires that I confess my deep debt to you. Pay no mind, therefore, to the insinuations of malicious men, because such heaving waves against my innocence could not come from any other sea. Rest assured that I may have erred out of ignorance, but not malice. But it is superfluous to make such declarations to your kindness, which knows my modesty and my ways, which will always be respectful towards Your Lordship, to whom I am…, etc.

208
TO THE MOST ILLUSTRIOUS AND EXCELLENT SIGNOR ENRICO CORNER

The readiness with which Your Eminent Lordship promised me your kind assistance for the marriage of Lady N. already assured me of the favor, since I will receive it from such an eloquent Mercury.

I am writing to learn about the arrangement so as to be able truly to enjoy what my heart foresees. If I hope, if I trust in your ability, I am not unworthy of your favors—all the more so because I attest to you that the information I gave you regarding the bride is Gospel truth. May Your Eminent Lordship proceed willingly since you will receive a thousand blessings. A woman of her standing is capable of bringing happiness to a whole household. I offer you my respects.

620. Tarabotti's correspondent apparently reported that Buoninsegni was composing a response to the *Antisatire*.

621. Here the first part of the verb is missing in the original text due to a typesetter's error; however, Tarabotti's meaning is clear.

209
TO THE MOST ILLUSTRIOUS SIGNOR
GIOVANNI DANDOLO[622]

I am sending a commendation to the excellent *avogador* Loredano and I beg Your Illustrious Lordship to be the numen tutelare in this case. Please beseech his excellency for the honor that the case of Lauro Monte[623] be introduced by tomorrow, and I will not fail to beseech that both of you ascend that mount of perpetuity which all of the chosen have worked to reach with great effort.

210
TO SIGNOR N.[624]

If Your Lordship's supreme intelligence did not remove from my mind the reasons to disprove your opinions against women, I would like to have you recognize and admit again that suspicion is birthed of a male mind and should not be assigned to women with the bastardized name of suspiciousness.[625] Those who gave suspicion a masculine gender were most prudent, not dim-witted, since suspicion in men's imprudent decisions creates great damage. How many husbands have killed their faithful wives, driven only by an erroneous suspicion? How many princes have taken the lives of their truest friends, blinded by the shadow of such a perilous vice? Innocents are not condemned without trial before the female tribunal, but men are rightly judged since, having been found guilty, they have no other defense but that which they have begged from falsehood, so befitting of their mind. Because of the affection in which I hold the merits of Your Lordship,

622. Tarabotti turns to Dandolo as an intermediary with Loredano, whose help in a legal matter she seeks on behalf of an acquaintance. She asks Loredano's help directly with regard to the same matter in letter 40 and again, through another intermediary, in letter 215.

623. From letter 215 we learn only that Monte was from the area of Vicenza.

624. Irritated with her correspondent, but reluctant to abandon her high esteem of him, Tarabotti reminds him of the promise he made to help her obtain publishing privileges for one of her works, perhaps *Paternal Tyranny*, which she was never able to publish.

625. Tarabotti plays on the grammatical gender of the nouns *sospetto* (masculine) and *sospizione* (feminine).

I do not advise you to appeal to the tribunal of faith: since faith is an enemy of men, it cannot but proceed harshly against them, driven by the hatred it has conceived because of the unfaithfulness of your most inconstant sex.

I deem the difficulties of obtaining publishing privileges for that unpolished volume to be great, but I also expect that your skill, combined with your great desire to help me, cannot but bring me satisfaction. I do not wish to give up on the idea I have conceived of Your Lordship's sublime nature; indeed, I wish to continue in marvelous praise of your noble mind's gifts so as to further my desire to serve you, remaining your very illustrious Lordship's.

211

TO THE MOST ILLUSTRIOUS SIGNORA
GUID'ASCANIA ORSI

You will not criticize me for discourteousness in not responding to your gracious letter since the reasons that prevented me from doing so merit your understanding. The severe purge which I undertook at the beginning of the spring has hindered my pen, because the doctors have forbidden me to write in this period. My heart has been in constant distress, however, at the knowledge of my great failing, which Your Illustrious Ladyship, the image of benevolence, will kindly excuse.

As for the marriage you wrote about, you should know that the bride is the daughter of the excellent ambassador of his Caesarean majesty.[626]

The reports of the war are more positive, and I place my hope in divine goodness that the outcome will be different from the one everybody was whispering about.[627]

As for the rest, may it please you to return my affection and to enjoy the service I pledge to you eternally; and I commend myself to you, etc.

---

626. Likely the daughter of the ambassador of the Holy Roman Empire at Venice from 1648 to 1652, Johann Ferdinand von Portia (Bittner and Gross, *Repertorium*, 1:173).

627. The reference is to the war between Venice and the Turks over Crete.

212

TO THE MOST ILLUSTRIOUS SIGNORA N.

The marriage broker never came, and the young lady awaits him with bated breath.[628] She is pleased that the groom is young since, though she resembles Aurora, she doesn't want Tithonus as a husband.[629] She knows music, and therefore she could sing to him

> *Forsenato canuto,*
> *Lascia i vezzi e gli amori.*[630]

I think however that Your Illustrious Lordship would be better suited to any other profession but that of the marriage broker, since you are so averse to settling things, which is quite necessary for marriages.

Please forgive me if I joke with you, perhaps with excessive familiarity, and please accept as a jest that which I say in jest, since I am truly Your Illustrious Lordship's, etc.

213

TO SIGNOR N.[631]

I am not certain that I wrote anything to Your Lordship that deserves such offense and I have always respected your worth as I should. My ignorance may have been to blame, and a peevishness that, provoked by the continuous pain in which I live, throws me into a little fury that

---

628. Tarabotti puns here on *golla* (marriage broker) and the young lady (*novizza,* possibly a boarder in the convent) who awaits him with *gola aperta,* literally, with open throat.

629. That is, although she is young, as Aurora was, she doesn't want a husband who is old. Aurora asked the gods to grant her beloved Tithonus immortality, but neglected to ask that they grant him eternal youth.

630. "Crazed old man, / set aside your affectations and your amorous pursuits."

631. This letter, addressed to Girolamo Brusoni, may be dated to the early stages of the deterioration of their friendship, for it does not yet express the same degree of rancor that characterizes later letters. Tarabotti expresses pleasure at appearing as a lightly disguised character in certain of Brusoni's works: in his *Orestilla* (see also n. 456) and also other compositions from which she was subsequently erased. She also responds to Brusoni's insinuation that she is not capable of understanding the philosophical underpinnings of the *Orestilla.*

would at times send me crashing to the ground. In these moments my pen, guided more by passion than by reason, may perhaps have dictated some things that my heart would never allow. If this is true, and in fact it is most true, may Your Lordship, who embodies kindness, forgive me, and believe me that I was more surprised to hear that you had featured me in your compositions than to hear that you erased me. Be it as you wish, I will always enjoy the honor of appearing in those that have already been published.

I, too, would agree that my eyes were not worthy of admiring the many philosophic and political insights found in your *Orestilla* were it not for the fact that all printed books encounter the misfortune of falling beneath my gaze, which is as dim as a bat's. I have not spared the best books of the greatest thinkers, and the good politician Machiavelli did not disdain to be looked upon and leafed through by me, with permission of course of the *Superiori*.[632]

If Your Lordship has ripped up my letters, I feel obliged to respond in kind,[633] and your sister's letter—on my word I cannot find it because I spend more time confined to bed than on my feet, so everything ends up a mess. I will look for it right away in order to send it to you.

In the meantime, I declare I am quite familiar with the vanity of worldly glories when I consider the maxim of the wise man, *universa vanitas est omnis homo*.[634]

632. Tarabotti reports having read a striking variety of texts, including those of Machiavelli, all of whose works were on the *Index of Forbidden Books*. She insists, however, that she was granted permission to read all these books—perhaps a jab at Brusoni, who was perpetually in conflict with the church.

633. Zanette (*Suor Arcangela*, 372–73) maintains that both Brusoni and Tarabotti were lying about destroying one another's letters, perhaps because Brusoni writes in *Sogni di Parnaso* that he still has several of hers in his possession.

634. Cf. Ps. 38:6: "All things are vanity: every man is vanity."

214

TO THE MOST ILLUSTRIOUS AND REVEREND SIGNOR FRANCESCO MARIA ZATI, RESIDENT OF TUSCANY AT THE MOST SERENE REPUBLIC OF VENICE

Before Your Illustrious Lordship took leave of these prison bars, Signor N., as I expected, came to speak to me; but that beast disguised as a man told him that I was unavailable.[635] The gentleman therefore left, and when he came back yesterday evening he reassured me vehemently that the *Soul* of procurator Zeno cannot be found amongst the living and that it was an invention of certain people who said that they had heard that soul wandering around his palazzo.[636] God, who sees inside of people's hearts with no deception, knows how I regret not to being able to serve you, and you can deduce this no less from your infinite merit than from my enormous debt, which will always keep me in the service of Your Illustrious Lordship, etc.

215

TO THE MOST ILLUSTRIOUS SIGNORA N.

I don't know if either the merit of Your Illustrious Ladyship or your wisdom can transform, in a strange metamorphosis, a virgin sworn to silence into a loquacious Mercury.[637] Well do I know that I am obliged to serve you despite myself and against my nature, which is an inexorable enemy of secular matters.

Yesterday I wrote to Signor N. with the explanation that you gave me regarding the dog,[638] but my messenger found him in bed quite ill. I therefore beseech Your Illustrious Ladyship not to believe that his failure to receive your kind visit was voluntary, as I hinted to you, and I also pray you not to breathe a word of what I have told you

635. The identity of this Signor N. is unclear.

636. On this nonexistent work, see also n. 186.

637. Messenger of the gods.

638. *cagnina*: the Italian word, which is not clarified by the context, could refer to a female dog (*cagnolina*) or also to a type of wine produced in Cesena. In either case, Tarabotti appears to act on behalf of the convent. It is worth noting that although nuns were forbidden to keep dogs in the convent, they often did so (cf. Zanette, *Suor Arcangela*, 48).

about this. I would have many things to tell you regarding this and other details, but one must be cautious in speaking to one who dares to condemn even angels.

May it please you to present to the excellent *avogadore*[639] my humble explanations and my urgent prayers in support of the Vicentine Lauro Monte.[640] I remind you that, if the Lord transfigured atop a mountain revealed his glory to three of his apostles, he too should not disdain to transmit the graces and glories of his kindness onto this Monte in order to glorify a woman who is one of his most humble and devoted servants and who worships and admires his most worthy qualities.[641]

As for Lady N., despite the fact that some carped against her, it now augurs well that someone is setting people's minds straight. Thus if anyone wanted to take her in marriage, Your Illustrious Ladyship could attest to him that he will have in her that strong woman so sought after by Solomon.[642] She will be active in the governance of the house and contemplative in divining the desires of her spouse in order always to fulfill them. She will gladly undertake the management of his money, not to dissipate it but to increase it. In short that man will be able truly to say *mulieris bona beatus vir*,[643] in spite of those men who always grumble about their wives. Adieu.

216

TO THE MOST EMINENT SIGNOR N.

The honor of the command that Your Eminent Lordship issued to me will serve as an inscription in the book of my great debts to you. Please

---

639. Loredano.

640. See letters 40 and 209.

641. Cf. Matt. 17:1–9. Tarabotti compares Loredano to Christ by saying that the favors he distributes are like the graces bestowed by Christ upon his disciples Peter, Jacob, and John at the Transfiguration. She builds an elaborate metaphor around the surname of the man she is trying to help, *Monte*, which in Italian means "mount" or "mountain."

642. Probably a reference to Prov. 31:10–31, which describes the perfect wife, of whom it said that "strength and dignity are her clothing" (31:25).

643. Sirach 26:1: "Happy is the husband of a good wife."

continue to make use of me, as I will always work with every effort, and I offer you my respects.

217

TO THE MOST ILLUSTRIOUS AND EXCELLENT SIGNOR BERTUCCI VALIERO[644]

I send to Your Excellency my *Antisatire*, which will serve as true testimony that the inscription of A. and T. still resulted in a publishing privilege. Books have appeared and still appear that receive the approval of the *Superiori* even though they are printed without the authors' names, or with anagrams or just two or three initials, at the authors' whim.

Such an ordinary thing cannot be denied to the greatness of Your Excellency, whose mere gesture would suffice to make the impossible achievable; thus I, relying on your most powerful patronage, assuredly await favor, and I humbly kiss your garments.

218

TO THE MOST ILLUSTRIOUS AND EXCELLENT SIGNOR BERTUCCI VALIERO[645]

I heard with great embarrassment my brother's inquiry[646] regarding your contribution to my book, and I confess that I could not have committed so great an error. Nonetheless, I must quiet my soul and present my oversight to your greatness like a guilty woman worthy of punishment.

---

644. A triumphant Tarabotti sends Bertucci Valiero a copy of her newly printed *Antisatire*; she notes with satisfaction that the book has received—perhaps with his help—the necessary publishing privilege despite being published under her initials (D[onna] A.T.). Valiero also helped Tarabotti obtain publishing privileges for her *Letters* (see letter 148).

645. Tarabotti, mortified, confesses that the *Paradise* was sent off to the auditors for approval without Bertucci's composition. She blames the messenger to whom she entrusted the book. The composition seems finally to have made it into the book (see letter 168).

646. Tarabotti had two brothers, one older and one younger, but the reference is probably to her brother-in-law Pighetti, who facilitated and supported the nun's literary work.

Yet I remain perplexed, and it seems impossible to me that I could have sent the book to the censors for approval without your inscription. I fear that the messenger with whom I sent it must have left it out. Be that as it may, I ask Your Excellency's pardon, as I humbly thank you for your kind praise of my imperfections, and bowing deeply I pray that Heaven may bless you for generations to come and I most respectfully kiss your robes.

219

TO THE MOST ILLUSTRIOUS SIGNOR COUNT COMMENDATOR PIETRO PAOLO BISSARI[647]

The astonishments produced by the mind and pen of Your Illustrious Lordship have filled with marvelous delight whoever has had the good fortune to enjoy them. Your most charming *Bradamante* demonstrates to all that your divine intellect surpasses that of its first author just as Heaven reigns supreme over our lowly lives.[648] He was first to put it on paper, and Your Illustrious Lordship has resurrected it on the stage more beautiful and worthy than ever. One might say that he created a beautiful body, but Your Illustrious Lordship gave it a soul and showed the whole world the varied things that could previously be enjoyed only in imagination. The marvelous combat in air conducted by those two proud knights has earned everyone's applause.[649] These are not, however, the first glorious efforts of the illustrious count Pietro Paolo.[650] Commending the affair of the poor Mother Aviana to you,[651] I offer my respects together with hers.

---

647. Tarabotti celebrates a melodrama written by her correspondent, published as *La Brada-mante* (Venice: Valvasense, 1650).

648. Bissari greatly outdoes the author of the first work in which Bradamante appears. Tarabotti probably means Ariosto, whose "wise pen" Tarabotti celebrates in *Innocence Deceived* (6); although M. M. Boiardo first wrote of Bradamante.

649. The melodrama was performed in one of the Grimani theaters in Venice. It was published in the same year as Tarabotti's *Letters*, but this letter suggests that it was staged before the publication of the collection.

650. Among the works that Bissari had already published were his *Scorse Olimpiche*, which the nun perhaps admired particularly since they contained praise of her (see n. 210).

651. See n. 249.

220

TO THE MOST ILLUSTRIOUS AND EXCELLENT SIGNOR
GIOVAN FRANCESCO LOREDANO[652]

Your Illustrious Excellency would have shown favor to my most reverent devotion merely by deigning to receive the few alms for the souls of the departed[653] I sent you without confounding me by returning the favor with a greater one. I believe you have acted in such a way, however, so that I, seeing my error, might confess to meriting severe punishment, since as a subject I dared to show charity to my prince and with a vow of poverty I risked bringing the lowliest fruits of Puglia before your greatness and wealth.[654] I easily recognized the sweetness of your intellect and your courteous manner without you needing to reveal it to me with the sweet sugar you sent me, for which I give you the most humble thanks. I beg you to believe that I am and will always be Your Excellency's obliged servant, etc.

221

TO THE MOST ILLUSTRIOUS SIGNOR
GIOVANNI DANDOLO[655]

Although my heart, an oracle in matters relating to Your Illustrious Lordship, may have predicted that the purple robes to honor your glorious merits would be delayed, it cannot ever believe that spiteful envy was the cause of such harm, to your great detriment.[656] Nonetheless, who does not know that these are the fruits of blind Fortune? Un-

652. Tarabotti speaks in this letter about an exchange of gifts between her and her patron, literally an exchange of sweets, but it may also be an exchange of books. She describes her own gift as inadequate.

653. The *Soul of Ferrante Pallavicino* (see letter 15) or an offering for the soul of the departed, perhaps made at All Souls' Day (2 November).

654. If Tarabotti speaks literally, this reference to the fruits of Puglia is rather surprising, since, according to Boerio, Puglia signifies the land of plenty. If she speaks metaphorically she might be referring either to the author or the topic of a book that she sent to Loredano.

655. Tarabotti here consoles her correspondent who did not receive the honor she believes he deserved.

656. It is likely that Tarabotti here alludes, through the use of the color purple, to an honor or a position of prestige, as elsewhere in the *Letters*, and not to a specific post, even if offices

able to distinguish worthiness from unworthiness, she usually—with strange injustice—deprives the first of honors and rewards the second undeservingly. However, Your Illustrious Lordship, who is the epitome of prudence, must play a trick on this female, of whom it is said: mad, blind, and bestial is Fortune. Rest assured that with virtue's guidance you will find the contentment you deserve, arm in arm with happiness, who is also a female, and who welcomes only the truly virtuous, among whom Your Illustrious Lordship shines like the sun among the planets. The clouds have no power to obscure the sun for more than a moment, and gold cannot be stained. Therefore the cloudy thoughts of the malicious cannot obscure the glorious light which our city must concede to the greatness of your most resplendent merit, so that finally honor will in the end be the fitting reward for virtue. From the touchstone, these excellent senators will see spring forth the finest gold of the integrity, learning, valor, and goodness of Your Illustrious Lordship. Reminding you not speak with anyone about printing my book unless you first meet with me,[657] and sending you the letter of credit, I once again dedicate myself more than ever.

222

TO THE MOST ILLUSTRIOUS AND EXCELLENT SIGNOR BERTUCCI VALIERO[658]

Last Saturday the illustrious D. advised me in person of the very kind promises made to him by the goodness of Your Excellency with regard to his problem.[659] He praised the regal and courteous manner so well known to me, demonstrating clearly that Your Excellency must be the most admirable hero not just of this city but of all the world. He also mentioned the praise bestowed by your great self on my lowly per-

---

were often identified according to their corresponding dress (see P. Molmenti, *La storia di Venezia nella vita privata*, 2:408ff.).

657. Tarabotti refers to *Paternal Tyranny*, which she was trying to publish. Because of the book's controversial content, she here tries to control its publication herself; later she entrusts its publication to others, with negative results.

658. This is a letter of compliment in which Tarabotti expresses admiration for her highly stationed addressee, without neglecting to mention his praise of her.

659. The identity of this D. and the nature of his problem are unclear.

son, and confessed he was unable to relay it in the gracious manner in which Your Excellency was kind enough to present it. I went mute upon hearing about such graciousness and I understood that such important favors can be no better appreciated than with silence, since the gymnosophists venerated the sun with a finger to their mouths.[660] Nonetheless, my reverent devotion must pray unceasingly to Heaven that, just as on the miraculous night in which God was born honey and other marvelous things were seen to gush forth, so may we see flourish divine grace, sweetness, and astounding happiness in the persons of the excellent procurator,[661] his most noble wife, and their fortunate son, and in the new year new greatness abound for the great family of Your Excellency, whose robes I, bowing down, most humbly kiss.

223

TO THE MOST ILLUSTRIOUS AND EXCELLENT SIGNOR SEBASTIAN MICHIEL[662]

My ancient and always new devotion to the greatness of Your Excellency, who is the glory of this city, now requires that I heartily congratulate you on the happy occasion of the appointment of your excellent lord brother-in-law to procurator.[663] May Your Excellency receive this communication from the heart, and receive it as a prelude to those purple robes which will soon be honored by your noble person, to whom I most humbly bow.

660. A common literary image. See for example Pliny, *Naturalis historiae*, where we can read that the gymnosophists, philosophers and wise men of ancient India, used to stay in one position, with their eyes fixed on the sun, from morning till night (7.2).

661. Silvestro Valier, son of Bertucci.

662. Sebastiano q. Antonio Michiel (1597–1684) held various important offices in the Republic, among which counselor to Doge Francesco Erizzo. He was in contact with members of the Accademia degli Incogniti, through whom he perhaps knew Tarabotti (cf. Barbaro, *Arbori*, ad vocem; Cicogna, *Iscrizioni*, 6:658–59).

663. We do not know with certainty the identiy of this brother-in-law of Michiel's.

224
TO THE MOST ILLUSTRIOUS AND EXCELLENT SIGNOR N.

As I send *Convent Hell* to Your Excellency, I harbor a painful hell in my heart and am agitated by a certain fear that, in wandering the world, my work might engender such judgment against me as bad children often cause their parents. You will, in fact, see that it is an inferno of confusion, and it is true; but I believe you will have compassion for it, by virtue of my ready obedience. Always commending my entire will to you, I devote myself to you, etc.

225
TO SIGNOR N.[664]

The holy Christmas holiday requires me to interrupt Your Lordship's silence even if I know that our blessed Lord chose to be born at the hour in which all the world is quiet.[665] I cannot comprehend the cause of such silence; I well know that, examining my conscience these holy days, my memory has not brought before my eyes any fault committed against you, unless it be that of my natural flaws and weaknesses. If I did err out of ignorance, I beat my chest and beg your pardon. With a happy wish that you will have fame for your virtues, peace in your heart, and joyful events in the coming year, I commend myself to you, etc.

664. Tarabotti, confused by her correspondent's silence, sends him her Christmas greetings and excuses herself if she has offended him.

665. Christ is traditionally believed to have been born exactly at midnight. This belief is based on biblical verses that prophesied the birth of Christ in the middle of a silent night (Ws 18:14–16). Tarabotti says that she sends her correspondent Christmas wishes, breaking his silence, even though she knows that Christ was born at the most silent hour.

226
TO THE MOST ILLUSTRIOUS SIGNOR N.[666]

May this saying serve as an adequate response to the afflictions, sadness, and worry Your Illustrious Lordship describes to me: let he who is cause of his own misfortune blame himself. You found yourself in a florid city, far from the oppression of the Thracians,[667] and you willingly volunteered to go looking for war, hunger, and every adversity; in fact it seems that, having a wish to marry, you went out with your lantern seeking the plague as a wife. Nonetheless I have great compassion for you, despite being in a state worthy of compassion myself. But if Your Illustrious Lordship had reflected upon my affectionate counsel, you would have enjoyed better fortune here instead. Nonetheless, since there is usually no remedy for that which has already occurred, be prudent and believe me that in this world the happiness we imagine is but a shadow that vanishes just when we think we can embrace it. Let this be a consolation to you, and I most humbly bow to you.

227
TO THE MOST ILLUSTRIOUS AND EXCELLENT SIGNOR BERTUCCI VALIERO[668]

My frequent recourse to Your Excellency's kindness is worthy of your understanding, since it is with great reticence and only out of necessity that I dare respectfully to appeal to the sea of your most precious favor. Know, therefore, that my incessant indisposition has reduced me to a skeleton and in this state I can do nothing of any worth, let alone recopy my works without great damage to my health. I found someone else for this, but he is afraid to come here without official permission; whence, in order to avoid any unpleasantness with the

---

666. Tarabotti here demonstrates little compassion for her addressee, who, having left for a trip against the nun's advice, then encountered many problems.

667. She refers either to the reputation of ancient Thracians (see n. 509) or to the Islamic world, considered hostile. It might also be that her addressee traveled in the area of ancient Thrace, that is, in the central and southern Balkans.

668. Tarabotti asks her powerful addressee to obtain permission for a copyist to come to the convent. Afflicted by continuing bad health, she is not able to copy her manuscripts herself.

injudicious officials who care for appearances rather than substance, I humbly beg your greatness to grant him permission that he may sometimes present himself at the parlor grille. In the meantime, with my whole heart turned to God, I pray that Your Excellency will enjoy the greatest happiness and prosperity that His omnipotent hand can dispense, most humbly kissing your robes and also those of the excellent procurator.[669]

228
TO SIGNOR N.[670]

The respectful affection my heart has always held for the kind and noble Lady A. and the enormous obligation I have to Your Lordship prevent me from holding my tongue so easily now that I see a way to serve the two of you, whom I esteem and prize greatly. Your Lordship must be familiar with Lady N.'s thoughts on the matter, which in truth are worth considering, but because a solution must be found to so urgent an affair, I remind you of the illustrious Lady N., who will certainly take her in. If this agreement is acceptable to you and if you come to see me, you will hear every detail promptly.[671]

In the meantime, do not think me ineffective on such an occasion, and I send you this book in response to your request. If it has already been read by that lady, Your Lordship must return it to me and I will send another.

I beg you not to forget the quarter and eighth scudi since I will subtract the entire fifty you mentioned to me the other evening, and I will be eternally obliged to you.[672]

---

669. Bertucci's son, Silvestro Valier.

670. Tarabotti professes her devotion to her addressee and to a Lady A., perhaps his daughter, who is evidently unhappily married, and she puts herself at their service for some unspecified matters. She acts already as a literary intermediary, procuring books for a certain lady (perhaps Lady A.) at the correspondent's request.

671. It seems that Tarabotti was the go-between for the addressee, Lady A., and two women (both designated with an "N.") who were seeking a solution to Lady A's troubles. Tarabotti urges him to consider the offer of the second Lady N. because it seems more secure.

672. The reference may be to the matter that is hinted at above; in any case, Tarabotti has a clear economic stake.

I do not neglect to pray for the tranquility of that lady who merits the adoration of every heart, not the unjust treatment of a cruel husband, and I bow to you both.

229

TO THE MOST ILLUSTRIOUS AND EXCELLENT SIGNOR GIOVAN FRANCESCO LOREDANO[673]

It is my understanding that until now Your Excellency has kindly received the most humble requests presented to you in my name by the illustrious Signor Giovanni Dandolo in favor of the excellent Doctor Locatello, who is the bearer of this letter. He will explain his request to you, and I doubt that Your Excellency's sense of justness will deny him the favor he rightly seeks.

In the meantime, I will pray Heaven to shower you with all graces and grant you as many years as Nestor so that this part of the world may remained blessed under your felicitous command.[674] Most respectfully kissing your robes, I ask that you remember my devotion and obligation to your illustrious and excellent wife no less than to Your Illustrious Excellency.

230

TO SIGNOR N.[675]

I helped Signor Locatello with the letter, but even more with the effective commendation made through Signor Giovanni Dandolo to the excellent *avogadore.* I pray God to grant me a happy outcome, because

673. Tarabotti presented to Loredano, through Dandolo, a doctor by the name of Locatello, about whom little is known, but it is clear that he sought Loredano's help. It is possible that this is Ludovico Locatelli (d. 1657), a doctor and chemist from Bergamo who studied law and medicine in Padua and traveled in Italy, France, and Germany (cf. Joecher, *Allgemeines Gelehrten-Lexicon,* ad vocem).

674. Nestor, in Homer's poem, was the oldest and wisest of those who fought in the seige of Troy. He lived for three generations in recompense for all the years that were stolen from his uncles, killed by Apollo.

675. Tarabotti writes to a correspondent who seems to have employed the Locatello mentioned in the previous letter (letter 222). She informs him that she has introduced Locatello both by letter and in person through Giovanni Dandolo.

my greatest ambitions in this world are to serve Your Eminent Lordship and those who depend on you.[676] You may believe me because my pen does not know how to flatter or lie. As for the business with the scudi, I did not fail to write all this time, and each day I await the receipt, if what is promised to me is true.

In the meantime, I beg Your Lordship, if you are not able to go to the Vincentine territory, to return the presidents' letter to me or, better yet, send it to that person to be completed, because I am always upset by trying to do too much good there. So be it.

I honor your illustrious wife and all those in your house, remaining more than ever Your Noble and Excellent Lordship's, etc.

231
TO SIGNOR N.[677]

Were it an article of faith to believe that my nuns had disseminated the rumor Your Lordship mentions to me, I would certainly die a heretic, and I would sooner believe I had seen the devil make the sign of the cross than lend credence to such an impropriety.[678] Perhaps not all of them love me, it may be, but it would be no wonder, for it is impossible to unite so many wills and we can see in the infinity of men in the world that many do not even love God. Nevertheless, each of them knows and believes the truth with regard to my writing, for they all see me do it with their own eyes. I am not so dim that I would believe this if I did not have proof at hand. But let us move on, for these are things unworthy of reflection; indeed laughter and derision can be purchased for ready money.

---

676. She here intends Locatello.

677. In this letter to Girolamo Brusoni, Tarabotti reacts with annoyance to the rumors that she was not the true author of the works issued under her name, and specifically of the *Paradise*. Tarabotti vehemently denies this accusation throughout the *Letters*.

678. Tarabotti says she does not believe that her convent sisters spread the rumor that she did not author the works she published; if it were dogma to believe in such a betrayal, she says, she herself would be a heretic.

I will arrange to return your letters to you when I am assured that I will receive my own in return.[679]

As to the Ladies SS., I cannot, will not, and must not interfere with their resolutions, be they voluntary or coerced.[680]

I am stunned that Your Lordship declares to have spoken in your work on the topic of coerced nuns while, having seen my work, you were obliged not to speak of something so thoroughly discussed by me.[681] If *Paternal Tyranny* had not been read by worthy gentlemen before it came before your eyes, I confess that I would be greatly pained by such a metamorphosis.[682] But even among men, there are those who know and confess the truth and at the moment the editing of my lines is carried out only by a noble hand, a pure eye, and an innocent and sincere soul.

I would go on but the purge I am undergoing, rather than giving me relief, aggravates me in such a way that I am worse off than ever. Such are the miracles wrought by the skills of physicians today. So be it. Adieu.

---

679. Here Brusoni and Tarabotti were evidently supposed to give back letters they had exchanged, a practice that was not uncommon in the case of disagreement between two correspondents (as seems the case here) or when a writer wanted to have his or her own letters for their publication (see also n. 490).

680. Tarabotti might refer to two (or more) girls who have begun the process of becoming nuns.

681. Tarabotti refers to Brusoni's *Turbulence of the Vestals* (*Le turbolenze delle vestali*, subsequently published under the title of *Tragic Loves* [*Amori tragici*, without date, place, or publisher]), a work that dealt with convent life in the seventeenth century (on the change of title and the late publication of the work, see Zanette, *Suor Arcangela*, 176–77). Since Tarabotti already dealt with this topic in the *Paternal Tyranny*, which she showed to Brusoni, and in *Convent Hell*, Tarabotti felt betrayed that Brusoni discussed the same subject matter.

682. Tarabotti fears that the publication of Brusoni's work might raise doubts as to the authenticity of her *Paternal Tyranny*, which was still in manuscript form. Luckily, she writes, she had already had others read the work before Brusoni composed his, and she thus believes their testimony will disprove his charges of plagiarism against her.

232

TO THE MOST ILLUSTRIOUS AND EXCELLENT
SIGNORA RENATA DI CLARAMONTE,
MARCHIONESS DI GALERANDA[683]

Two offspring of my most sterile mind come to serve Your Excellency, but in exceptional circumstances. I would like the girl, who should remain withdrawn and far from worldly matters because in this city she would be looked at askance, to become a public woman in France.[684] The boy[685] must remain hidden even from the eyes of Heaven, as you guaranteed me with your irrevocable promise. Please do me the favor of telling your secretary that I have difficulty believing him because *multa fidem promissa levant*.[686] And as I declare myself your servant, I bitterly mourn Your Excellency's departure and I remain yours, etc.

233

TO SIGNOR N.[687]

Your Lordship has found the true way to gladden my heart, since the gentleness of your song stirred up a sweetness in me that, as it melts me completely, makes me forget whether I'm on Earth or in Heaven, where the blessed fully enjoy the music of the angels, whom Your Lordship certainly equals. I was not alone in my enjoyment, and all the sisters—full of delight—praise and extol you and worship the harmony of your divine singing and playing. Each of them would vie for the pleasure of being your syrinx. All of us, in short, more expectantly

683. Tarabotti writes to the marchioness shortly after her departure from Venice. According to other letters in the collection, Tarabotti had entrusted *Paternal Tyranny* to the marchioness and her secretary Colisson so that it could be published in France. In this letter, we learn that Tarabotti also gave them a second work, most certainly *Convent Hell*, which was too controversial in subject matter to be published at all.

684. That is, *Paternal Tyranny*; in the Italian the title is grammatically feminine (*La tirannia paterna*).

685. *Convent Hell*; in the Italian the title is grammatically masculine (*L'inferno monacale*). With "Heaven" Tarabotti may refer to Paris, which she elsewhere calls a "Heaven of women."

686. "Many promises undermine trust." Horace, *Epistularum*, 2.2.10.

687. Tarabotti writes to a singer who had entertained the nuns of Sant'Anna. On Tarabotti's passion for music and on convent recitals, see n. 101.

than ever await your return, when you will grace our ears with such a sweet concert, in which the refined musician so thoroughly masters theory and practice that we may say of you *vox tua dulcis est; favus distilans labia tua.*[688] I bow to you.

234

TO THE MOST ILLUSTRIOUS AND EXCELLENT SIGNOR NICOLO BRETEL DE GREMONVILLE, AMBASSADOR OF FRANCE TO THE MOST SERENE REPUBLIC OF VENICE[689]

The prolonged voyage of *Paternal Tyranny*[690] would lead even the calmest mind to worry that something had gone wrong. Whoever loves, fears. I am most apprehensive about the matter and I beseech Your Excellency not to disappoint my just desire to have it back. I will pay whatever cost necessary for its transport.

In truth I would merit reproach for being too naïve in giving it to a gentleman that I did not know were it not for the fact that he was the brother of Your Excellency, in whose service I remain.[691] Speaking in my defense is also the fact that at that time I had your illustrious daughters as such precious guarantee.[692]

Worldly things however often finish quite differently than we expect, and many times our assumptions are proved quite false. I turn

---

688. "Thy voice is sweet.... . Thy lips ... are as a dropping honeycomb"; cf. Song of Sol. 2:14 and 4:11. The second verse is used in the antiphony used for the birth and assumption of the Virgin Mary. See R.-J. Hesbert, *Corpus antiphonalium officii: Rerum ecclesiasticarum documenta*, ser. Maior, Fontes 9 (Rome: Herder, 1965), 3:225.

689. Tarabotti asks two favors of her friend: the first (and most urgent), that he help recover her *Paternal Tyranny* manuscript; the second favor regards a Cretan gentleman seeking a passport.

690. *T[irannia] P[aterna].*

691. Tarabotti faults herself for entrusting her precious manuscript to a gentleman she did not know, but the fact that he was her correspondent's brother, Jacques Bretel de Grémonville (1625–86), explains her mistake. Jacques was in the service of the Serenissima with the cavalry headed for Crete, but was later accused of spying (see Zanette, *Suor Arcangela*, 313–16). It is the first time that Tarabotti refers to this affair explicitly (see also n. 517), although she often affirms having given a copy of *Paternal Tyranny* to Colisson, the French secretary to the Marchioness di Galeranda.

692. The Grémonville daughters were boarders at Sant'Anna.

to Your Excellency's kindness for its recovery, and I ask for this favor with the humility that befits a request presented to your greatness.

I ask that you honor me by granting a passport to that Cretan gentleman whom I commended to you on other occasions for your support.

The excellent ambassadress will communicate in greater detail my desires, and in the meantime I humbly bow to Your Excellency, kissing most dearly your daughters and your son.

235
TO THE MOST ILLUSTRIOUS SIGNOR N.

I cannot without some grief consider the case of Signor N., even if I deem it to be a mistake that someone would have as their principal aim to fool the world. Nonetheless, everything is possible when things are done backwards most of the time and when judges look upon trials through self-serving lenses. I turn therefore to you, who were born to quiet any unease in my mind, so that you may get precise information about this matter and satisfy my curiosity to know when you come to see me. If I asked pardon for the trouble, it would intensify my repeated negligence at your repeated favors, which bind me to you with an eternal debt and make me ever Your Illustrious Lordship's, etc.

236
TO THE MOST ILLUSTRIOUS SIGNOR N.[693]

Yesterday I realized that Your Illustrious Lordship has readily passed from the role of defense attorney[694] to that of prosecutor,[695] but the tri-

693. In this letter, Tarabotti criticizes her correspondent for his involvement in accusations that she had written a letter that she denies having penned. Framing the case as a legal one, Tarabotti describes how her correspondent has gone from defending to attacking her. She declares that her innocence will only be reinforced by his efforts against her.

694. In the Italian, *contradittore*, a lawyer who represented defendants who had been indicted. We thank Ed Muir for his help translating this term.

695. In the Italian, *avogadore*. The powerful *avogadori di comun*, three in number, could arraign and arrest anyone, propose proceedings against them and suggest charges (cf. David Sanderson Chambers et al., *Venice: A Documentary History, 1450–1630* [Toronto: University of Toronto Press, 2001], 51–52).

als and the claims against my innocence will have that effect that the hammer usually has on the diamond, beautifying it with blows.

From simple words may you deduce great cunning, since in the end the plaintiff will be shown to be dishonest, the trial faulty, and the defense attorney a liar. It will never be established that I wrote that letter: the handwriting will make it clear to everyone, and if under your examination I confessed that it was mine, I did so as a joke and in an effort to satisfy you.

As for the proposal that was made to me, I have no adequate response since everyone knows that to figure out whether a woman is beautiful, you only need to look at her. I would like to hear from your great intellect what those three women from yesterday looked like. I believe you did not want to judge their beauty as Paris but to enjoy as Adonis.[696] You should therefore fear wild boars,[697] as I will always fear the judgment of those judges who are masters of love and tempt Susannas even when they are clothed.[698] They give the excuse that women set traps and capture men, saying

> *Ove n'andai rimasi preso al fin*
> *Ch'ella ha reti nel crin, e reti il crine.*[699]

Adieu.

696. That is, Tarabotti's correspondent has ulterior motives in his relationships with the women. Paris judged the beauty of Juno, Venus, and Athena; Adonis had relations with Venus and Proserpina.

697. That is, he should fear the fate of Adonis, killed by a wild boar.

698. Tarabotti, on the other hand, fears the fate reserved for women, who, like Susanna, are accused by men of crimes they did not commit. The Old Testament heroine Susanna was accused of adultery by elderly judges who attempted to besmirch her honor.

699. "Wherever I went I was eventually captured / Since she has snares in her locks, and her locks are snares."

237

TO SIGNOR N.[700]

Since lady N. is busy with other matters and cannot respond to Your Lordship's courteous letter, and since she heard that I am determined to write to you, she has asked me to thank you for your kindness in remembering us always, a favor for which these ladies send their kindest regards and remain in your debt, commending themselves quite earnestly to your prayers.

But as for me, if I want to speak with great sincerity, I am quite disgusted. If Your Lordship does not reveal to the world the truth of the matter regarding my *Paternal Tyranny*,[701] I will write as my weak talent prescribes, since, even if I do not have sufficient conceits or style to counter the strength of your pen, at least my innocence will serve as a shield. Truth, daughter of time, will expose the difference between one style and another, since yours is as marvelous and scientific as mine is foolish and artless. I confess to Your Lordship that when *Lost Occasions* came into my hands I knew that I had been thoroughly betrayed.[702] If you were only trying to make me the butt of a funny prank, aimed only at revealing your sincere opinion about my writings, you should have obeyed a certain decorum and not committed to paper something that in fact was not true and will never be so, for which your conscience will forever prick you. You and others may act as you wish, since I too at my whim will lift my mask and reveal my face, despite what liars say, and I offer you my respects.

---

700. Tarabotti addresses this letter to Brusoni. On the one hand, she sends the greetings of her sisters; on the other she upbraids him for disseminating the rumor that *Paternal Tyranny* was not entirely her own work and that he himself had had a hand in it.

701. *[T]irannia [P]aterna.*

702. The *Aborti dell'occasione* were published in 1641 (Venice: Sarzina) and reprinted a number of times. Brusoni would write in a later version of this work, published after Tarabotti's death in 1652, that *Paternal Tyranny* had been "reduced to ashes amidst the flames of [the nun's] funeral pyre; but from those ashes there rose again, almost like a phoenix, another work bearing the title *The Turmoil of the Vestal Virgins* [*Le turbolenze delle vestali*]" (see Zanette, *Suor Arcangela*, 176). Brusoni's *The Turmoil* was later published as *Tragic Loves* (*Amori Tragici*, without date, place, or publisher); like *Paternal Tyranny*, it addressed the problem of forced monachization. Tarabotti expresses elsewhere in the *Lettere* her irritation that Brusoni has plagiarized her (see letter 231).

238
TO THE MOST ILLUSTRIOUS SIGNOR N.[703]

If I with reckless presumption had dared to summon Your Illustrious Lordship to this place without anything to negotiate, I would deserve, beyond a refusal, a most severe punishment. But if I beseech you to come to hear my excuses for my unintentional failure, well may I and must I expect your pardon. If you grant me the opportunity to do so, I will explain sincerely the terrible circumstances that prevented you from receiving your due from the agreement and from my word which I always place ahead even of my life. In the meantime I swear to Your Illustrious Lordship on this unblemished page that a delay will be intolerable for me, since the enormity of the favor requires unrivaled urgency. So be it. These days whoever helps a friend hurts himself. Please take pity upon my pain and pardon the nuisance, and I bow to you most reverently.

239
TO SIGNOR CAVALIER FRANCESCO PONA

The perfection of Your Excellent Lordship's pen, combined with those of the blessed Elena,[704] arrived at a time when I was languishing in bed, despairing of my health, and hoping to finish my wanderings through this world. I was on the brink of death, tormented by a ceaseless constriction in my chest that at times makes me hate life and fear death. From your favors I regained my strength, because my mind, uplifted by seeing how worthily honored I had been, administered enough happiness to my heart that it was able to regain the senses that had taken leave of me as heralds of my soul. Let your prudence consider how deeply obliged I am for such an enormous favor, since I will save my thanks for when I feel better. For now, still weak from illness, I consecrate all of my frailty to you and I send you the attached panegyric in praise of a worthy doctor. Since Your Excellent Lordship

---

703. Here Tarabotti begs her correspondent's pardon for being unable to help him as she would have liked.

704. It seems that Pona had sent Tarabotti a work about the life of Saint Elena, perhaps a particular favorite of the nun based on their shared name (she was born Elena Cassandra).

is in no way inferior to him, I pray that you enjoy it, and I offer you my respects.

240
TO THE MOST ILLUSTRIOUS BETTA POLANI, MY DEAR AND ONLY LADY

Your most stubborn illness, which does not want to leave you, has made my heart leave my chest since I am not able to see you. I am agitated and ask everyone about medicines that might free you. Since this world is richly supplied with specialists in music, medicine and madness, I have received a lot of different opinions. Some recommend a moderate lifestyle while others suggest medicine; some suggest a live lizard; and everyone concurs that a good husband would be a cure. I who love you as myself will give you detailed accounts of everything I hear so that you may choose the course that seems best to you.

Look after yourself without so many Galens,[705] and do not become easily angered, because having your blood boil harms your health greatly. Do not expose yourself to the air, which is currently pestilent, so foggy and dark. The variation in the current weather can be fatal even for the healthy. The greatest help, however, will be your patience, your youth, and the good care you receive, which will certainly bring you back to full health.

In the meantime, I ask that you return my love, and I dearly kiss you, etc.

241
TO THE MOST ILLUSTRIOUS SIGNORA ALBA PORTI[706]

If my pen was slow to revere Your Illustrious Ladyship, and if my tongue was silent, my heart has always respected and indeed worshipped you as much as is possible.

---

705. That is, doctors (for Galen, the ancient physician and philosopher).

706. No information has been found regarding this Alba Porti. Tarabotti expresses admiration for her in this letter of introduction for an unidentified gentleman.

Please excuse my failing, and receive this most worthy gentleman who comes in my name to recognize your worth and to pledge my service to you again. I declare myself Your Ladyship's, etc.

242

TO THE MOST ILLUSTRIOUS SIGNORA
GUID'ASCANIA ORSI

Last week I suffered infernal torment to my heart because I had from Your Illustrious Ladyship no letters, which always seem like Paradise to me. I hope to God that this is not due to any ill cause, and if it was for a lack of fondness, I hope to return to full favor by reassuring you that I love you truly.

You must have received my letter recently in which I, as I am wont, beseech you for favors. If you are able to help me, I will ascribe it to my good luck, since my debts can be no greater, and I kiss you wholeheartedly.

243

TO THE SAME[707]

I received in its entirety everything that Your Illustrious Ladyship mentions. Even if I do not believe I have discharged my debts with unadorned graces, I gave to you all those thanks that my pen knew how to form. In the last dispatch I prayed you with great urgency to honor by means of your great authority the birth of the excellent French ambassador's son; I have the privilege of having his daughters as boarders in the convent and as my pupils.[708] I would be most grateful if one of the distinguished personages from there, through your mediation and authority, celebrated the birth of this boy who will be baptized by the Republic and will have the name Marco Bretel de Gremonville. I tell you this because perhaps this fact will present an opportunity to

---

707. Tarabotti asks Guid'Ascania Orsi of Bologna to solicit verses in honor of the birth of Marco Bretel de Grémonville, son of the French ambassador to Venice, from other Bolognese writers. These may be the poems included in letters 34 and 35, sent to the ambassador by Tarabotti to congratulate him on the baby's birth.

708. See letters 35 and 139.

writers to praise him, since writing about a birth is a boring topic, without much substance. It is a task for astrologers rather than poets. I will with bated breath await news as to whether I can be satisfied, and please do not refuse the burden of updating me. Dearly I kiss you and bow to you.

244

TO THE MOST ILLUSTRIOUS SIGNOR DI GREMONVILLE[709]

Your Illustrious Lordship's visit to this place, even though it was an exceptional honor for me, filled my soul with such sadness that it can never be removed from my heart until I hear the desired news that your health has returned. These ladies sympathized so greatly with you and felt so sorry for your mishap that all around the convent you could hear echoing "The poor gentleman! He was in such bad condition, I wish I had not seen him. What has happened to the looks, the grace, the vivaciousness and the spirit that made him shine bright amid other men?"

May you not lose courage, however, Your Illustrious Lordship, since a cure is imminent. Count Vasari[710] is quite able to treat you without pain and to bring you back to perfect health. This is proven by his experience, particularly with Countess Sacrati,[711] who can give you more information. She had been sent an explosive by some of her enemies, which almost killed her and leveled her house. Her whole body was riddled with bullets and nails, such that she was in infernal pain. The above-mentioned doctor cured her, and with gentle heat extracted all the bullets and nails and restored her to perfect health. Your Illustrious Lordship should not delay so that the pain you experience because of the musket shot that was lodged in you does not gain further foothold. Therefore heal yourself quickly, take care of yourself immediately, and enjoy the recognition that comes to you accompanied by my full affection, which is part of my eternal servitude to the great Gremonville family. I offer any help I can provide in any circum-

---

709. Grieved by the ill health of the ambassador, caused by ammunition lodged in his body, Tarabotti recommends a physician who has handled a similar case.

710. Unidentified.

711. Unidentified.

stance, I pay my respects to the French resident,[712] and I pledge myself to Your Illustrious Lordship, etc.

245
TO THE MOST ILLUSTRIOUS SIG[NOR] N.[713]

Your Illustrious Lordship's books are true proof no less of your kindness than of your admirable talent, which the world discovered when you were quite young. I will enjoy reading them and I will envy the accomplishments of their author, to whom I am eternally indebted, remaining Your Illustrious Lordship's, etc.

246
TO THE MOST ILLUSTRIOUS AQUILA BARBARO[714]

I received the graceful compositions of Your Illustrious Ladyship and I command you, as is my duty as a nun, to keep the treasures of your intellect hidden, since it seems to me that you wrong God, who endowed you so freely with qualities he does not share widely.

All of those attributes you deigned to assign to me are in fact yours, since you have the dignity of Parnassus, and only you truly possess all of the virtuous qualities that are by legend attributed to the chorus of the nine Muses. Your talent stuns all the literary men who have had the good fortune to enjoy perusing your florid poetry.

On the basis of your wonderful qualities, I pray you excuse me if I delayed in responding to you, a delay that was due to my tireless work to bring to press the present little volume, for which I had to be

---

712. Louis Matharel.

713. Tarabotti's abbreviation of the title creates ambiguity as to whether the correspondent is a man or a woman. For our translation we presume it is a man Tarabotti congratulates for an editorial success since, if it were a woman, Tarabotti would certainly have highlighted the exceptionality of her accomplishment.

714. Tarabotti expresses admiration here for her correspondent's compositions, but also apprehension that Aquila might run into trouble with the church on their account (see also letter 101 for a similar admonishment).

not only the author but the proof-reader.[715] You will also pardon (as I hope your inborn kindness allows) the imperfections of my pen and, even more, of my mind, which, uncultured and sterile, can produce nothing but the roughest thorns. If these thorns are regarded through the most courteous rays of your kindness, they may perhaps become fragrant roses of some worth because of you, whom I revere. I declare myself eternally Your Illustrious Ladyship's, etc.

247

TO THE MOST ILLUSTRIOUS AND EXCELLENT SIGNORA MADAMA GILDAS[716]

To defend myself before Your Illustrious Excellency for a failure of which I am completely innocent, I believe that the testimony of the illustrious count P[ietro] P[aolo] Bissaro[717] will be authoritative enough. Nonetheless, so as not to appear insufficiently respectful in the eyes of someone of your stature, whose greatness and commands must be honored and adored by everyone, I swear to you with most devout truth that I was not asked by anyone on the feast of Saint Anne to supply chairs for Your Excellency. The faintest suggestion of this in my ear (if not the entire request) would have caused me to fly straight up to Heaven to furnish you with chairs appropriate to your stature.

Know that I would consider it an honor, not to mention my good fortune, to be called your servant. I pray God to concede to Your Excellency, who is the phoenix of our age among women, an uninterrupted century of happiness. Most respectfully asking your pardon

---

715. Probably *Convent Paradise*, which, despite Tarabotti's efforts, was published with numerous errors. Or she may be referring to the *Antisatire*, which was reprinted due to the many errors in the first edition; but it seems she was no more content with the second (see Weaver, ed., *Satira e Antisatira*, 111–12).

716. Tarabotti excuses herself with her addressee (whose husband was a hero during the war of Candia) for a misunderstanding she attempts to clear up in the letter: she maintains that she did not previously understand that the lady was expecting her help in reserving spots during the feast of Saint Anne, the patron saint of Tarabotti's convent. Perhaps there was a concert or some other sort of performance, hosted inside the convent, that the addressee desired to attend.

717. The Vicentine writer was evidently of a friend of Gildas's as well as of Tarabotti's.

for the boldness with which I have undertaken to disturb you, I most humbly bow to you.

248

TO THE MOST ILLUSTRIOUS SIGNOR COUNT COMMENDATOR PIETRO PAOLO BISSARI[718]

If I did not send the dedication to Your Illustrious Lordship as quickly as I should have, it was because I planned to deliver it to you along with the *Antisatire*. I was not able to execute this desire born of my obligation, however, because it was impossible for me to retrieve it from the hands of the auditors. Now, in conformity with your honored command, I send it to you, and I reverently beg you to have compassion for the extreme imperfection of both works. Please forgive that devoted daring which, although I feel myself immersed in an ocean of infinite favors, does not allow me to fear shipwreck when I know I am navigating the sea of your kindness.

I had it transcribed in the manner you will see in the enclosed, and it seemed to me it was altered not just in meaning and spelling, but also in the method of promptly beginning clauses. Therefore I most respectfully pray Your Illustrious Lordship to excuse my tardiness, while I judge my rough thoughts unworthy of ever coming before the eyes of the most eloquent orator and celebrated poet of our time, for my heart reveres you as such. Therefore I am proud that good fortune has graced my *Antisatire* with your lines, which, to my greater glory, are certainly those of an Apollo if not an Apelles.[719]

I humbly ask to obtain from your divine voice the sonnet I desire, so that you may you excuse my temerity before his highness[720]; while I similarly beg you not to disdain that I am Your Illustrious Lordship's, etc.

---

718. Tarabotti sends Bissari the first version of the dedication to the *Antisatire*, addressed to Prince Leopoldo de' Medici (1617–75), brother to the Grand Duke of Tuscany, Ferdinando II (see letter 254); Tarabotti had asked Bissari for a sonnet in praise of Leopoldo, and she renews her request in this letter (on the exclusion of the sonnet from the final edition, see letter 254).

719. See n. 239.

720. Prince Leopoldo.

249

TO THE MOST ILLUSTRIOUS AND EXCELLENT MADAME D'AMÒ, AMBASSADRESS OF FRANCE[721]

I have carried out the commands of Your Illustrious Excellency with regard to the petition of indulgences offered me by your kindness. Perhaps you will think my requests excessive, because I am greedy for such favors, but you must excuse me for it is proper to wish for and desire an excess of spiritual favors. Many favors are requested with fervent prayers even of God, but he grants only those that he knows concern the good of our souls. Thus Your Illustrious Excellency may plead with His Holiness for that which your divine prudence deems most appropriate, for in any case I will always be bound to the greatness of your heart and your courtesy with chains of perpetual obligation. If I ask for great favors, I do so because they are somewhat proportionate to your greatness, which must seek them from the Vicar of God. I do so also in order not to wrong the magnanimous words with which your regal heart extravagantly honors me, who is both the lowest and the most devoted servant to adore your semidivine qualities.

May an easy journey follow your happy departure, in which you will have me together with N. to accompany you, serving you with our hearts and prayers. Nor we will fail to serve you with every proper diligence in the exquisiteness and speed of the work for which we have received the designs and the material together with such a sum of money from your unparalleled generosity that even a third would have sufficed to satisfy the demands of the workers, for Lady N. has no other goal than to serve you well. Your generous, even regal, hand nonetheless wished to confuse those who rightly trusted the simple and unbreakable word of so great lady as Your Excellency. Together with N., bowing most humbly, I beg you remember our service and

---

721. Tarabotti here turns to her addressee who is leaving for Rome on a pilgrimage. She asks her to obtain numerous indulgences from the new pope, Innocent X, proclaimed pope 4 October 1644. Brusoni recounts in his *Istoria d'Italia* (Venice: Antonio Tivanni, 1676, 409), that the ambassadress went to Rome "out of her religious devotion and in order to kiss the feet of the new pope." Despite tensions with France, the pope was charmed by the "graceful manner of speaking of that lady." Beyond the requests for the pilgrimage, Tarabotti thanks the ambassadress for generously paying for lacework the convent sisters had done for her.

devotion, not leaving it idle but favoring our respectfulness now and then with your commands.

250
TO THE MOST ILLUSTRIOUS SIGNORA MARGHERITA DI GIUBET[722]

Your Illustrious Ladyship's departure cannot take place without causing a painful feeling in my heart, as it will be deprived for some time of such a revered lady and mistress. During your absence, however, my respectful servitude and devoted affection for your immense merit will not be diminished by even the smallest part. I will live with the constant desire for your return, in order that my meager talents may glory in serving the most gracious, kind, and accomplished lady of France. May your mind welcome the offerings of my heart, utterly dedicated to your service.

At the holy house of Loreto[723] and in the holy places of Rome, I beg you for a sigh or a prayerful thought to God, since I know that a mere breath of devotion emitted from your wholly pure soul will certainly obtain for me every desired grace from His Divine Majesty. Similarly I beg you to excuse me to the excellent lady ambassadress if I have asked for too much in my petition, which is more an error of ignorance than of boldness and therefore worthy of pardon.[724] I leave aside the favor of bringing my book to print, because it seems to me this was not entirely pleasing to her excellency, according to whose wishes I must reverently rein in my own desires.[725] Under your most kind protection, however, I do not doubt your compassion and every

722. Tarabotti wishes a pleasant journey to the niece of the ambassadress, whom she accompanies in pilgrimage (see letter 249). Elsewhere in the letters this correspondent is called "de Fiubet" (see letters 10 and 121).

723. The holy house of Loreto is one of the most sacred pilgrimage sites in all of Christendom. By tradition it is the house of Nazareth where Mary was born and was visited by an angel and in which the word of God was incarnated.

724. See letter 249.

725. Tarabotti had evidently asked the ambassadress's help in publishing one of her books, probably *Paternal Tyranny*, in Rome.

favor. Wishing you a most prosperous journey and us your quick return, Lady N. and I respectfully kiss Your Illustrious Ladyship's hand.

251
TO THE MOST ILLUSTRIOUS AND EXCELLENT SIGNOR
GIOVAN FRANCESCO LOREDANO[726]

My heart's most reverent requests come before Your Illustrious Excellency's merit, which I have always admired in spirit, and they beg you to reveal the person who, speaking against that *Antisatire* I composed at the request of noble ladies, shows himself to be poorly versed in gentlemanly manners. My pen, however, is not intimidated by such an unforeseen encounter because, since it protects truth, it will receive conceits from truth itself where necessary. My little work seeks shelter and safe refuge with Your Excellency, who is the kind protector and valorous defender of the female sex. It implores you as a courteous gentleman to be the judge. If all lettered and virtuous people turn to you, and not in vain, as the refuge itself of virtue and letters, I more than anyone else, as a woman, although lacking in letters and virtue, must hope for aid. If I did not send it you sooner, know that I delayed only out of a reverent awe, as now the zeal of honor spurs me to use these inappropriate manners of bold trust. Humbly praying you for kind compassion, I most respectfully bow to you.

---

726. Tarabotti writes to the influential Loredano regarding the nascent controversy surrounding her *Antisatire*. She learned that someone had replied to the work in an ungentlemanly manner, and asks Loredano, always knowledgeable about happenings in the literary world, who this person was. It may be Aprosio, whose harsh response Tarabotti had still not, upon the writing of this letter, read. Aprosio's was one of many responses to the *Antisatire* (on these, see, for example, letters 99 and 113). It is surprising that Tarabotti, as we read in the letter, did not send her *Antisatire* immediately to Loredano.

252
TO THE MOST REVEREND FATHER N.[727]

I resolve to answer you more out good manners than because the letter of Your Reverend Lordship deserves it. Where there is no error, there is no need for amends. I don't admit to have erred since I published with the necessary permissions. If I did not clearly display my name in the *Antisatire*, it was out of a certain modesty, and not to correct that which I do not regret having done.

I do not think I am biased, and so I free Your Lordship from the chore of merely reading your response to others. I urge you not to keep this labor of your lofty intellect hidden from the world, since there is no need for you, for my sake and against your will, to be deprived of that praise and applause which have greeted you on other occasions and which are naturally due your famous compositions. If that senator honored me by forbidding you to publish it with my name, he did so because it was inappropriate to publish my name when I wanted it concealed; nor does this person expect anything else of you.

Speak freely, Your Lordship, and send your unfettered opinions to press, publishing them for all the world, for I will consider it my good fortune, especially since I do not intend to take any offense from you. I never presumed to keep you from publishing here or abroad, nor do I have any regard whatsoever for the injury with which you threaten me because it does not concern me.

I received the panegyric, but knowing that in this monastery of yours[728] no one believes the *Convent Paradise* to be my work, I deemed it a lapse of the pen intended to foment with wind my ambition which, thanks be to God, pays no heed to the flattery of men. I offer you my respects.

727. Tarabotti here returns to the controversy surrounding her *Antisatire*, explaining yet again how she was able to publish the work using only her initials. She refuses to ask the pardon of her addressee, the friar Angelico Aprosio, who criticized her for having blocked the publication of his *Mask Lifted*. The nun denies this accusation and coolly encourages the friar to circulate the work amongst his friends if he desires. She concludes by saying that she received from the friar's monastery a panegyric about *Convent Paradise*, towards which she demonstrates skepticism.

728. Aprosio resided at the Santo Stefano monastery in Venice (see *Biblioteca aprosiana*, 245).

253
TO THE MOST ILLUSTRIOUS AND EXCELLENT
SIGNOR PAOLO DONADO[729]

Your Excellency distributes favors in proportion to your great kindness and with disregard to the small worth of others. The sum of my debts had no need for increase, but rather of occasion in which I might demonstrate to you with my actions the desire I harbor within me to serve you. Thus could I free myself in some part from the burden of so many obligations, not because it is unpleasant to be beholden to you, but because it is unbearable for my good intentions not to be able to properly reciprocate.

Therefore, in order not to come up short in that little which does depend on my own power, with most devoted sentiment I give you infinite thanks for the lovely little book you sent me, and since my *Soliloquy* and *Paternal Tyranny* have reached me just now,[730] I send them both to you so as not to delay in your commands. I am certain that the divinity of your courteous spirit will not accuse me of excessive confidence for daring to bring such imperfect words before your eyes, since this is not the first time that I have made you aware of my shortcomings.

If it should seem to you that I delayed too long in showing these rough lines to you, be assured that nothing held me back but the respectful awareness I have always had of your intelligence, as superior in perspicacity to every other as every other light and planet is inferior to the vast rays of the sun. Therefore I beg the profundity of your wisdom not to disdain having compassion on the ignorance that is common to and characteristic of my sex and on the particular weakness of my own mind, naturally sterile and not at all cultivated by

729. There were many Paolo Donados (Donà) in Venice in the first half of the seventeenth century. One hypothesis is that this was a cousin of two of Tarabotti's friends, Regina Donà—Tarabotti's convent sister whose death she laments in the *Tears*—and Regina's sister Andriana Donà in Malipiero, with whom Tarabotti corresponded (see Barbaro, *Arbori*, ad vocem). This letter was intended to accompany two works that the nun was offering to Donado along with thanks for a book that he had lent her.

730. Tarabotti sends her addressee both *Paternal Tyranny* and her *Soliloquy to God* that opened the *Paradise*. She excuses herself for the errors in transcription in the *Paternal Tyranny*.

art and study. I know it is sensitive material that goes against political, if not Catholic, mores.[731] Because of the infinite mistakes of the pen, together with those of the intellect, it would be necessary to transcribe the entire work in order to present it you in the most befitting manner, but my serious indisposition will not permit it.

Thus I turn to the courtesy of Your Excellency who, transcending the confines of humanity, was able in your most glorious years to earn the crown of doctoral laurels around your temples, marvelously demonstrating that at an age when others are barely able to learn, you could have been the teacher of all. Therefore forgive all the shortcomings and overly free passages in this work as owing to the weakness of my talent and the naiveté of my understanding, while I pray to Heaven that you enjoy an abundance of all graces, and I remain your Excellency's, etc.

254

TO THE MOST ILLUSTRIOUS SIGNOR COUNT COMMENDATOR PIETRO PAOLO BISSARI[732]

I would merit severe punishment if, in publishing before the world the offspring of my sterile intelligence, I did not share it respectfully with the most worthy and virtuous gentleman to honor learning and arms in our century. I confess however to Your Illustrious Lordship that this is a self-interested gesture. If you deign to accept it, I will declare myself perpetually obliged to your kindness, for I will deem it my great glory that the enclosed little work should be looked upon with favor by so great a hero. Because it treats a subject favorable to ladies, I would have sent it to the illustrious ladies of your house, who are of such stature and position that all the honors of our sex are owed

---

731. In other words, she targets not religion but *raison d'état*. She expresses the same sentiment in an autograph letter to Aprosio, in which she writes of *Paternal Tyranny*, "I know the subject matter is awkward, but contrary to political, not Catholic, mores" (BUG, E VI 22, c. 122; Medioli, *La scrittura forzata*, 147). In fact much of this paragraph recycles, with changes in order and phrasing, the brief autograph letter to Aprosio.

732. Tarabotti sends her *Antisatire* to her friend Bissari, excusing herself for not having included a sonnet written for the work by Bissari.

to them.[733] But fearing that such an expression of my servitude and devotion might cause me to appear reckless to them, I resolved with greater confidence to turn to you for support.

Your Illustrious Lordship will see a chaos of errors, the greatest of which is, in my opinion, that of having changed the dedication, once meant for the serene Prince Leopold, now addressed to the serene great duchess. Since in this manner I was deprived of the honor of that most divine sonnet that would have been the soul of my otherwise imperfect writings.[734] I beg you to excuse this in particular and in general every other failing you will find in my book, and be assured of the most devoted reverence with which I bow deeply to Your Illustrious Lordship and to all your illustrious female kin.

255

TO THE MOST ILLUSTRIOUS SIGNORA ACQUILA BARBARA[735]

While my heart was already agitated and greatly troubled for fear that I could be accused by Your Illustrious Ladyship of ingratitude and that I might look with confusion upon the marvelous and beautiful conceits with which you honor me, now to render my obligation truly enormous I receive an idyll, the most gracious, refined, and worthy my ambition could have ever desired. Upon receiving such a composition, I was stunned by the greatness and singularity of the favor, but not so much so that I did not immediately recognize it as an eagle's flight of pen.[736] I received it with the reverence due so graceful a poem and so great a lady. I regret that it did not reach me in time to

---

733. Among other relatives, Tarabotti probably refers to Bissari's mother, Giulia, another of the nun's correspondents who had read her *Paradise*.

734. Tarabotti had initially intended to dedicate her *Antisatire* to Leopoldo de' Medici, who had been served by Francesco Buoninsegni, the author against whom the nun responded (see Weaver, *Satira e Antisatira*, 63, n. 107). Bissari had written a laudatory sonnet to include in the *Antisatire*, but when Tarabotti changed her mind and dedicated the work to Vittoria della Rovere, Grand Duchess of Tuscany, the sonnet was excluded.

735. Tarabotti here thanks Barbaro for an idyll that she had composed to accompany one of the nun's works (probably the *Paradise*). Tarabotti expresses her disappointment at the fact that the composition arrived too late to be included.

736. Tarabotti plays on her correspondent's name, which means eagle.

adorn my poor little book with such rich and precious gems, as it had already gone to press; I now most respectfully send this book to you. My mortification grew not only because I knew myself to be unworthy of such an honor, but because I saw taken from me the chance to enjoy the delicate fruits of the flourishing and fertile garden of Your Illustrious Ladyship's most lofty intellect. Whence I can call myself an unfortunate Tantalus who has been deprived, to his increasing distress, of tasting those flavorful apples that entice his lips from so close by. I will not for this reason fail to be Your Illustrious Ladyship's, etc.

256

TO THE MOST ILLUSTRIOUS SIGNORA BETTA POLANI[737]

The silence of Your Illustrious Ladyship speaks in my heart, causing me to worry that my negligence has resulted in your disfavor. My illustrious dear friend, my dear lady, I was negligent in responding to you, it is true, but I was hampered by serious causes. I ask pardon, I beg pardon, and I condemn my failing. Let Your Illustrious Ladyship's indignation condemn this failure and have pity, for the laws of necessity are harder than diamonds. In the meantime, I wish you incomparable happiness and contentment from Heaven for the coming holidays, and I pledge to you my innocence and my ardent affection, always remaining entirely Your Illustrious Ladyship's, etc.

THE END OF THE *LETTERS*

---

737. Tarabotti closes the collection on an intimate note with a letter to her closest correspondent.

THE TEARS
OF ARCANGELA TARABOTTI
UPON THE DEATH OF
THE MOST ILLUSTRIOUS
SIGNORA REGINA DONATI

DEDICATED TO THE MOST ILLUSTRIOUS
SIGNORA ANDRIANA MALIPIERO

GUERIGLI
VENICE
1650

MOST ILLUSTRIOUS SIGNORA[1]

In life, Suor Regina—Your Illustrious Ladyship's sister and my mistress—compelled all hearts to admire her, and in death she was accompanied by tears from every eye. I, who adored and admired her more than any other woman, and swore my devotion to her, suffered the anguish of a most painful death at her loss. I believe that God only permitted me to survive such pain so that I might memorialize her with perpetual tears.

I had already shed my tears on paper, and—persuaded to expose to the light through the black ink of print the offspring of my two loving eyes—I now resolve to protect them under cover of Your Illustrious Ladyship's heavenly virtue. I hope you will be pleased, because I know that God appreciates tears more than any other offering. If it should come to pass that you accept them with the kindness I yearn for, it will be my good fortune, since without your courtesy these poor dew drops have no hope of finding an oyster to transform them into pearls. I will not beg you to have mercy on them since, with the title Tears, I am convinced that they will find their way to the compassionate heart of Your Illustrious Ladyship, to whom I dedicate myself.

Your most humble and devoted servant,
D[onna] Arcangela Tarabotti

[...]

---

1. Tarabotti dedicated the *Tears* to Andriana Malipiero, sister of Regina Donà. On Malipiero, see letter 81. This encomiastic work was published along with the *Letters* and was in fact central to Tarabotti's justification of her epistolary project (see for example letters 112 and 148). The *Tears* constitute, however, a freestanding work which had its own title page, dedication and prefatory material. We present the work here in an excerpted form.

[…]

Born to the noble house of Donato was a queen, who, by her very name—Regina—and surname, presaged the qualities of prudence and virtue that would come to render her worthy of a scepter and destined to become, in the bloom of her youth, a gift worthy of being donated to God. […] It was clear that this was a queen destined by the omnipotent celestial Monarch to rule with righteously rigorous command all the most burning desires and ambitions that usually govern fragile humanity. Even at that most immature age, when youthful behaviour tends to be frivolous and vulgar, she (with the majesty truly befitting a queen) undertook no action which did not demonstrate her to be a true exemplar of faith, an ornament of her cloister, a perfect image of goodness. She showed herself to be a woman religious even before entering the convent. Reading the Holy Books, praying, and reciting the Office were familiar exercises to her; nor was there anything she enjoyed more than building small altars, at which (I believe) she offered her own heart in sacrifice to Jesus Christ, whom she had already chosen for her beloved Husband.

She entered adolescence, a time when it is customary for most people to give themselves over to silly love affairs. She, too, fell in love, but her love was directed at God, even though she did not lack temptations toward the usual vanities, since her beauty would have allowed her to conquer and command every heart. There never was a mirror fortunate enough to receive a vain gaze from her as she primped. She never tormented her locks with burning irons in order to create curls, nor were rouges or colors ever produced worthy enough of adding blush to that cheek upon which Nature planted crimson-colored blooms and cultivated lilies.

The time came to exchange palace for convent, opulence for poverty, finely appointed rooms for a bare cell, rich meals for austere fasts, soft silks for rough woolens, and domestic grandeur for enforced servitude. How readily she did so foretold, in my opinion, her spiritual virtues, which I shall try to sketch out in my rough style.

No man would have been worthy of possessing so precious a jewel; thus the King of Paradise, looking upon and admiring her, chose her for his heart's delight, for his dear bride, and kept her just as a gem in a treasure chest, within the blessed cloisters dedicated to the great mother of his virgin genetrix.[2] [...] She was the bride of Jesus Christ, for the beauty of a divine soul could not be conceded to an earthly groom. Her external beauty, the expression of her spiritual worth, took shape in a corporeal form of the loveliest sort that could be produced by the hands of the Omnipotent One, who created her Himself.

Her tall stature, regal presence, and noble bearing were beyond mortal ways, to the amazement of all. The fairness of her delicate complexion robbed the silvery Moon of its glory. Her eyes were two resplendent stars, beneath which the door to Paradise, adorned with pearls, could be seen to open. Lastly, this beautiful being was clearly the work of divine love, and could properly be called an angel who was flown to Heaven on the wings of her holy acts.

But let my pen cease to describe this outer beauty, which she always magnanimously disdained, except insofar as it was a shadow (so to speak) of the inner beauty of the pure and ornamented soul, a beauty that exists in divine affection and in the habit of virtue and faith. Here the eternal Lover chose to refine the affection of his Beloved through the fire of tribulation. He took away her parents, he stole a much-loved sister, and he deprived her of her closest relatives. She, resigned to divine good, calmed her will and overcame the impulses of nature which would have obliged her to grieve to excess, and willingly she submitted to the determinations of heavenly decrees. [...]

But more than any other virtue, the three religious vows of Obedience, Poverty, and Chastity could be seen to bear fruit in her. Therefore, since she knew that *meliore est obedientia, quam victima*,[3] she was always submissive and responsive to the commands of her superiors, so that it seemed that in obeying she anticipated their wishes. She loved poverty, since, born among riches, she deigned to live and die among the deprivations of a narrow and bare cell, to nourish her-

---

2. That is, Saint Anne, mother of Mary. Tarabotti and Donà served in the convent of Sant'Anna di Castello.

3. 1 Kings 15:22: "For obedience is better than sacrifice."

self on little food, and to dress herself in the most modest wools. I will not speak of her chastity: it would be an offense to her, since she was honesty itself.

Joined to these three rings of religious vows so perfectly observed by her were an infinite number (so to speak) of other various virtues, which comprised a precious chain that pulled her up to Heaven. [...] Never did this queen give herself over to accumulating treasures that were not spiritual in nature. Like a new Cleopatra, renowned for magnanimity and acting with virtuous liberality as a counterpoint to greed, she used the remainder of her income, granted her by the Mother Superior, for generous works of great charity. [...] I will leave off explaining the features of perfect charity in her, for in that immaculate soul one constantly saw shining the precious gem of charity, so that she could have been called the living and breathing image of so great a virtue. [...] It was no wonder that in adversity and tribulation, she—who was supported by divine virtue so that her actions might correspond to her name—imitated Saint Job.

This marvelous woman availed herself to such an extent of sobriety, and abstinence against gluttony, that not only did she never lose herself in gambling and drinking, but I can truthfully attest that even in the flower of her youth, she accustomed herself to never fully satiating herself at lunch or dinner, and she was so sparing in her drink that, despite an ardent thirst that bothered her daily, she merely wetted her lips, so to speak, with a tiny portion of wine, which she drank only to close the door to vice within her soul and open it to those virtues that lived inside and around her heart.

Never did that courageous soul find herself pricked by proud Envy; rather, in the face of this cruel monster, she took up the arms of neighborly love. Whence with great kindness she attracted the souls of all to serve her reverently, even (allow me to say) devoutly to adore her, and truly her heart was a treasure trove of kindness. She understood that the most noble hearts make greatness shine more luminously with rays of calmness and benevolence.

Finally, in order to compete with strong Alcides, in order to wholly sever the seven heads of mortal sin belonging to the Hydra of Hell, she was always the mortal and immortal enemy of idleness, never letting a minute go by without occupying herself either with the praise of her God, or in the tasks assigned to her or, finally, in the marvelous embroidery and ingenious stitching in which she easily surpassed the Paliadi, and stole the Araneae's glory.[4] Her beautiful hands were the most industrious ever made by God. Communicating to them the wonders of her intellect, and adding the exquisite layout of her stitches, the lovely decoration of the silk, the gracefully distributed beauty of the colors, and the well-placed riches of the golds and silvers, she created works so perfect that one might think them produced in the Empyrean Heaven, by the hands of angels, rather than here on earth, by a queen.

[...]

I will not discuss her religious observance, which was of such perfect excellence that not only did she respect and honor prelates, superiors, and her elders in years; but she even treated her inferiors with a certain respectful decorum that rendered her both lovable and laudable to all. She was generous, but not prodigal. She gave with no thought to receiving. She helped her friends, with no concern for herself, sharing with all of them, equally, her prudence, favors, and grace. She charitably remembered the needy with alms. In short, Astrea herself never had a more secure home here on earth than in this woman's heart.

Our heroine was as strong as she was just and prudent, for with great fortitude she always maintained a soul devoted to the service of God. She was immovable in her prudent decisions, from which she never swayed, except to fulfill Cicero's teaching that prudence consists in changing one's opinion if it means to change for the better. True strength consists just as much in restraint, neither boasting in prosperity nor lowering oneself to despair in adversity.

This rock of Christian fortitude conducted herself with strength in times of trial as well as prosperity. Never did she allow herself to be moved by the impetuous wind of ill fortune in a way that might mark her as cowardly, nor was she swayed by the benign aura

---

4. That is, Regina's skill surpassed that of the daughters of Pallas Athena and Arachne, both known for their weaving expertise; Ovid (*Metamorphoses*, bk. 6) recounts that the goodess was driven by jealousy to turn her mortal river into a spider (*aranea*).

of success that might cause some change in her toward imprudent happiness. She was a new, courageous Judith: after she, with valorous right arm, severed the head of Holofernes from the Devil, from his senses, and from their followers, she freed the city of her soul from the hands of that treacherous tyrant who watches over us always in order to harm us by stealing the precious treasure of divine grace. And who will not applaud the strength of so great a woman, close to whose valorous rays the shining light cast by the glories of the strongest Amazons, Deborahs, and Camillas would seem but sparks and shadows.

[…]

She always, however, dressed in clothes that befitted the modesty of her soul, never passing beyond the bounds of the appropriate. She had the most refined spirit that could be infused by God into a lovely soul inhabiting a beautiful body. Just as her facial features were like those of a most striking Sybil, so did she possess an analytical mind worthy of such a comparison. It seemed that she had a gift for prophesy, since she foresaw future events, and some time before she died, she foretold the end of her life with astute prediction. She could boast of such noble and remarkable abilities which, possessing heavenly graces, rendered her worthy of the governance of a whole world. Under her leadership, this monastery did indeed expect all the good fortune that awaits those subjects who are ruled by a prudent and righteous leader. And this was not without reason, since nothing more could be wished for in that soul, who in the bloom of youth gave such maturely ripened advice, and in old age would have acted in the most prudent fashion. She was prudent in responding, wise in conversing, shrewd in spotting a lie, clever in learning, fair in judging, patient in affairs, quick to settle matters, generous in giving, and most courteous with her favor. In giving advice she was more valuable than Cato, making her living proof of the German belief that women partake of some measure of Divinity. In the acumen of her advice she gained a reputation as the most lively and sublime intellect of our time.

Her retiring nature was awe-inspiring, her modesty unparalleled, and her goodness indescribable. She nourished in her mind, by natural inclination, various sayings of the Philosopher, which always held Christian-like traits at the center of moral virtue. In every action she preferred the middle path, as if, as Aristotle's disciple, she had learned that he says true virtue consists in avoiding extremes. To this end, she held on the scales of reason the impulses of the senses, which always flowed out of her, falling down to be trampled and crushed by her feet. On the contrary, her voluntary mortifications and her severe penitences rose supreme within her to dwell in her breast, where she embraced and caressed them. She said *medium semper est optimum*,[5] except in serving the King of Heaven. She had gotten to the point of acting virtuously by habit, an inclination she couldn't set aside in any circumstance.

[...]

Certain that her death was near, she never gave any sign of resentment or cowardliness; but she resigned herself fearlessly into the hands of her maker, and she girded herself to fight courageously against her bellicose fate, which even killed God himself in his human form.

I will leave aside discussion of her intense and arduous devotion, with which she tasted the manna of the sacrosanct Eucharist. And I will not recount how, with each of her sister nuns, she humbly discussed her sins. I will remain silent about the thousands of other external and internal indications of her perfect goodness. I will only say, that in breathing her last mortal breaths, while the enemy of souls was doing his utmost to trap and prey on this snow-white swan of purity, she—in order to relieve the torments and afflictions of the body and the soul—so close to leaving the beloved prison, said these words:

Exaudiat me Dominus in die tribulationis.[6]

Shortly after, she ended her life on earth in order to fly to eternal life in Heaven.

---

5. "Moderation is always the best path."

6. "May the Lord hear me on the day of tribulation." Cf. Ps. 19:2, "May the Lord hear thee in the day of tribulation" (*Exaudiat te Dominus in die tribulationis*).

Are not, are not these, marvels of nature and of grace? Are these accomplishments not more admirable than imitable? And wasn't she, in her birth, in her life, and in her death, a glory to her family and to her native city? An example of goodness and saintliness, the image of perfection and innocence?

But I am mad with grief, blinded by the rays of her merit. Blessed Soul, instead of bemoaning with inconsolable tears the loss of my heart which has fled along with you, why do I persist in praising you? The rites of your passage invite me to grieve your death sorrowfully. Yet the memory of a long, faithful, and trusted friendship causes me to lose my senses. I am more than half-dead, since I have lost my soul but remain alive, a most unhappy state. I am not alive, and yet I breathe? I live in Heaven in my mind, but I walk the earth, despising life. Ah, and yet many others are experiencing these same painful losses. If I wanted to delve into considering the universal suffering that occurred in this place for those who were her dear and close relatives, I would encounter an ocean of tears in which, a most unhappy shipwrecked soul, I would be submersed with no hope for my heart to find a serene harbor. But of my own, and not of others' suffering I must always so tortuously complain. In whose heart will I ever find again a true and loving faith? A paradigm of purest love? The expression of perfect friendship? We could certainly with truth say:

Amicus est alter ego.[7]

At present, no other emotions reign but adulation and falsity. Whoever praises you to your face, criticizes you behind your back. Whence one can with reason complain by saying: *Impia sub dulci mele, venena latent.*[8] You were never like this. Far from such iniquity, always sincere and faithful, you consecrated your heart to the virtue of friendship, showing yourself to be the Phoenix of affectionate and true friends.

I will ceaselessly carry a pain in my heart that will never disappear until it is reunited with your soul. Over the course of a quarter

7. "A friend is another self." Cf. Aristotle, *Ethics*, 9.4. Tarabotti uses the same saying in her *Letters* (letter 148).

8. "Deadly poisons are hidden in sweet honey." Cf. Ovid, *Amores* 1.8.104, *Impia sub dulci melle venena latent.*

century my heart became used to speaking with you on earth, and it yearns to come to enjoy your presence eternally in the Empyrean. Separated from you I cannot say that I live, if between tears and pain a mere sliver of a most unhappy life is conceded to me. You, having finished the most dangerous voyage through this world, fearlessly disembarked in a most serene harbor. But what remained for you to fear, when even among the gentiles the father of eloquence knew:

> *Che Mors timenda non est,*
> *Immortalitas animae sequitur.*[9]

In light of this knowledge that you so firmly grasped, you never feared death, and instead valorously met it head-on, and almost like an Amazon of Christ you fought against the enemies of our health, armed with no other weapons than Christian virtue and religious ornament; whence, crowned with other virtues, you flew to delight in eternal embraces, beatifying yourself in the infinite enjoyment of the highest good.

> *Virtude al Ciel ritorna,*
> *E dove in prima nacque al fin soggiorna.*[10]

Ah, and you no longer must say:

> *Satiabor cum aperverit Gloria tua.*[11]

You are already beyond this valley of tears; you are already enjoying your well-deserved glory, and you are already in the presence of that righteous Judge, who will pay you with an abundant reward for your past suffering.

[...]

---

9. "There is no need to fear death. / Immortality follows the soul."

10. "Virtue returns to Heaven, / And where first it was born, there it abides."

11. "I shall be satisfied when thy glory shall appear."

And if the passing of true friends begets tears, how will I be able to stop the grief dripping from my most tormented heart which, divided in half by the cruel Fates, was stolen from me? Indeed, how can I not weep inconsolably at my loss? But here I am raving: No, no—tears to such a great woman are small tribute; tears are ordinary and to be expected at the passing of anyone. New ways to mourn should be invented. Even if we could turn our hearts to tears at her funeral, there could be no sorrowful expression that rendered proper tribute to reach the height of such eminent worthiness. The pens of this world are not worthy to style her praise and her funeral orations, and instead we would need angelic ones in order to sketch the sublime qualities of such a deserving queen.

Take pity, O great soul, on this pain that afflicts me. Pardon the boldness of the pen that tries to praise you, and now that you have reached the throne of God, please don't disdain to present the prayers of your loved ones to His great Majesty. I would bewail, with ceaseless tears, your painful separation from me. But worthy of tears is only the death of those people whose life merited only laughter—those who, forgetful of living a good life, sink into a sleepy lethargy, reaching the end of their voyage almost like careless pilgrims, unprepared, whence they entrust a perpetual silence to posterity. But you, most beautiful Regina, crowned with grace, having risen to Heaven through the Milky Way, have left perpetual memory to the universe of your truly regal endeavors. Perhaps you laugh over the tears that I cry. You are enjoying that blessed and most loving union with God, which gives delight unsurpassed in joy and mirth. When you look down here, I believe, you disdain as useless our tears and the most bitter suffering that our hearts experience at your loss. It seems to you the madness of human ignorance to lament that goodness which, because it is infinite, cannot be understood by our inferior intellects.

You are (might we say) filled with satisfactions, because you are enjoying the immensity and infinity of every contentment. You are free, because where God is, there is true liberty. You possess the richness of all bliss, with eternal surety, with the highest joy. You enjoy true happiness, perfect knowledge, everlasting peace, a bond with divine love, boundless mercy, and infinite goodness. You live in gentle tranquility, you take part in a glorious friendship and you enjoy a most sweet harmony amid the ranks of angels. You are receiving the reward for your vigorous faith, and fulfilling your vision as you stand looking at God, you come to understand in his company the most arcane mysteries of the most Holy Trinity. You have gone to that great feast to which the supreme Lord invites all of his chosen people. O what most delectable foods you have tasted, blessed soul, at that sweet banquet, where God offered to serve the most fortunate guests, and to give them as their meal the clear knowledge of his divinity. You went with your lantern lit to wait for your Bridegroom, and have—along with other prudent virgins who performed saintly acts—received the reward for your religious deeds.

Beatify yourself, most pure soul, among those happy displays of crowns and banquets and the nuptial bed; but don't forget to tell your Bridegroom about our suffering. Understand our tears. Take pity on our distress. Set your eyes upon your monastery that you already, with your angelic qualities, transformed into an empyrean. Look again at your dear relatives who, now orphaned and abandoned by you, implore you. Remember, then, that love and that faithfulness which, with the bond of friendship, steadfastly held us together, for a quarter of a century without fail, almost as if we were most loving sisters. Accept these tears, which, even if they express the essence of my heart, are however only the weakest tribute to your great worth.

Bibliography

Archival and Manuscript Sources

Florence, Archivio di Stato (ASF)
    Mediceo del Principato, 6152, cc. 29r–v
    Mediceo del Principato, 6152, c. 31r–v
    Mediceo del Principato, 6152, c. 32r
Genoa, Biblioteca Universitaria (BUG)
    E VI 6, Int. I
    E VI 22, c. 122
    E VI 22, c. 129
    E VI 22, c. 133
Venice, Archivio Patriarcale (APV)
    Collezione Antica, *Licenze e decreti riguardanti le monache*
    [1632–1639], b. 4, 4v–5v
    Collezione Antica, *Monalium* 7
    Collezione Antica, *Monalium*, 1644; 1647; 1650
Venice, Archivio di Stato (ASV)
    Avogaria di Comun, *Indice di matrimoni patrizi per nome di donna*, 86, ter. 1 [reg. V., 87]
    Avogaria di Comun, *Libro d'oro*, Reg. IV, c. 164v
    Barbaro, M. *Alberi dei patrizi veneziani*
    Collegio, *Cerimoniali* III, pp. 120–21; p. 123r
    Collegio Esposizioni Principi, Registro 56, c. 154r
    Cong. Rel. sopp., Sant'Anna di Castello, busta 5
    Cong. Rel. sopp., Sant'Anna di Castello, busta 15, fasc. 4
    Cong. Rel. sopp. Sant'Anna di Castello, busta 17
    Sezione Notarile, *Testamenti*, b. 620.233
    Sezione Notarile, *Testamenti*, 83.35
Venice, Biblioteca del Museo Correr
    Barbaro, M. *Alberi dei patrizi veneziani*
Venice, Biblioteca Marciana (BMV)
    Cappellari, A. *Campidoglio veneto*, Marciana mss. Italiani, classe 7, n. 15–18, p. 577

Primary Sources

L'anima di Ferrante Pallavicino. Villafranca: Fallardi, 1643 [publishing information false].

L'anima di Ferrante Pallavicino ... Vigilia prima. Cologne: Lodovico Feiraldo, 1675.

Aprosio, Angelico. *La biblioteca aprosiana*. Bologna: Manolessi, 1673.

_____. *Lo scudo di Rinaldo*. Venice: Hertz, 1646.

Augustine, *Confessions*. Trans. Edward B. Pusey. New York: Modern Library, 1949.

Boethius. *Consolation of Philosophy*. Trans. Joel C. Relihan. Indianapolis: Hackett Publishing, 2001.

Brusoni, Girolamo. *Aborti dell'occasione*. Venice: Sarzina, 1641.

_____. *Amori tragici*. N.p., n.d.

_____. *La fuggitiva*. Venice, Sarzina, 1639.

_____. *La gondola a tre remi*. Venice: Storti, 1657. Reprint, *La gondola a tre remi*, ed. F. Lanza (Milan: Mazorati, 1971).

_____. *Istoria dell'ultima guerra tra' veneziani e turchi*. Venice: Stefano Curti, 1673.

_____. *Istoria d'Italia*. Venice: Antonio Tivanni, 1676.

_____. *Sogni di Parnaso*. N.p., 1660.

Buoninsegni, Francesco. "Satira." In *Satira e Antisatira*, ed. Elissa Weaver, 38–55. Rome: Salerno, 1998.

Bursati, Lucrezio. *La vittoria delle donne*. Venice: Evangelista Deuchino, 1621.

Cartari, Vincenzo. *Immagini degli dei de gl'antichi*. Venice: Tomasini, 1647.

Cereta, Laura. *Collected Letters of a Renaissance Feminist*. Ed. and trans. Diana Robin. The Other Voice in Early Modern Europe. Chicago: University of Chicago Press, 1997.

Che le donne non siano della specie degli uomini: Discorso piacevole. Lyon: Gasparo Ventura [Venice: Francesco Valvasense], 1647.

de Scudéry, Madeleine. *Ibrahim, ou l'illustre Bassà*. Paris: A. de Sommaville, 1641–44.

_____. *Ibrahim, overo l'illustre Bassà*. Trans. P. Cerchiari. Venice: Valvasense, 1646.

Fedele, Cassandra. *Letters and Orations.* Ed. and trans. Diana Robin. The Other Voice in Early Modern Europe. Chicago: University of Chicago Press, 2000.

Fonte, Moderata. *The Worth of Women.* Ed. and trans. Virginia Cox. The Other Voice in Early Modern Europe. Chicago: University of Chicago Press, 1997.

Fusconi, Giovan Battista. *Argiope.* Venice: Gio. Pietro Pinelli, 1649.

Le glorie degli Incogniti. Venice: Francesco Valvasense, 1647.

Grimani, Antonio [Bishop]. *Constitutioni, et decreti approvati nella sinoda diocesana, sopra la retta disciplina monacale sotto L'illustrissimo, & Reverendissimo Monsignor Antonio Grimani Vescovo di Torcello. L'anno della Natività del Nostro Signore. 1592. Il giorno 7. 8 & 9 d'aprile.* Venice: n.p., 1592.

Index librorum prohibitorum Alexandri XII pontificis maximi. Rome: Typographia Reverendae Camerae Apostolicae, 1664.

Lalli, Giovan Battista. *La Moscheide, ovvero Domiziano il moschicida.* Venice: Sarzina, 1624.

Loredano, Giovan Francesco. *Lettere.* Venice: Guerigli, 1655.

_____. *Lettere, prima parte.* Venice: Guerigli, 1665.

_____. *Novelle amorose.* Venice: Guerigli, 1656.

Lupis, Antonio. *Vita di Gio. Francesco Loredano Senator Veneto.* Venice: Valvasense, 1663.

Marinella, Lucrezia. *The Nobility and Excellence of Women, and the Defects and Vices of Men.* Ed. and trans. Anne Dunhill, intro. Letizia Panizza. The Other Voice in Early Modern Europe. Chicago: University of Chicago Press, 1999.

Morato, Fulvio Pellegrino. *Significato de' colori e de' mazzolli.* Pavia: Andrea Viani, 1593.

Nogarola, Isotta. *Complete Writings: Letterbook, Dialogue on Adam and Eve, Orations.* Ed. and trans. Margaret King and Diana Robin. The Other Voice in Early Modern Europe. Chicago: University of Chicago Press, 2004.

Ovid. *Ars amatoria.* Trans. Lewis May as *The Love Books of Ovid.* Whitefish, MT: Kessinger Publishing, 2005.

_____. *Metamorphoses.* Trans. Brookes More. Boston: Cornhill Publishing, 1922.

Pallavicino, Ferrante (Ginifacio Spironcini). *Corriero svaligiato.* Nuremberg [Venice]: Stoer, n.d. [but 1641]. Modern ed., ed. A. Marchi (Parma: Università di Parma, 1984).

———. *Giuseppe.* Venice: C. Tomasini, 1637.

Passi, Giuseppe. *I donneschi diffetti.* Venice: Iacobo Antonio Somasco, 1599.

Petrarch, Francesco. *Petrarch's Songbook.* Trans. James Wyatt Cook. New York: Medieval and Renaissance Texts and Studies, 1995.

———. *The Triumphs of Petrarch.* Trans. Ernest Hatch Wilkins. Chicago: University of Chicago Press, 1962.

Priuli, Lorenzo. *Ordini, & avvertimenti, che si devono osservare ne' Monasteri di Monache di Venetia: Sopra le visite, & clausura,* 10r. Venice, 1591.

Sansovino, F. *Venetia citta nobilissima et singolare.* Venice: Steffano Curti, 1663.

Tarabotti, Arcangela. "Antisatira" (1644). In *Satira e Antisatira,* ed. Elissa Weaver, 56–105. Rome: Salerno, 1998.

———. *Che le donne siano della spezie degli uomini: Difesa della donna* (1651). Ed. Letizia Panizza. London: Institute of Romance Studies, 1994.

———. *L'"Inferno monacale" di Arcangela Tarabotti.* Ed. Francesca Medioli. Turin: Rosenberg & Sellier, 1990.

———. *Lettere familiari e di complimento* (1650). Ed. Meredith Ray and Lynn Westwater. Turin: Rosenberg & Sellier, 2005.

———. *Paternal Tyranny* (1654). Ed. and trans. Letizia Panizza. The Other Voice in Early Modern Europe. Chicago: University of Chicago Press, 2004.

———. *Paradiso monacale.* Venice: Oddoni, 1643.

———. *La semplicità ingannata* (1654). Ed. Simona Bortot. Padua: Il Poligrafo, 2007.

———. "Women Are Not Human". In *"Women Are Not Human": An Anonymous Treatise and Its Responses.* Ed. and trans. Theresa Kenney. New York: Crossroad, 1998.

Tasso, Torquato. *Jersualem Delivered.* Trans. Ralph Nash. Detroit: Wayne State University Press, 1987.

———. *King Torrismondo.* Ed. and trans. Maria Pastore Passaro. New York: Fordham University Press, 1997.

Valiero, Andrea. *La storia della guerra di Candia.* Venice, 1679.

Secondary Sources

Barbierato, F. *Nella stanza dei circoli: Clavicula Salomonis e libri di magia a Venezia nei secoli XVII e XVIII.* Milan: Edizioni Sylvestre Bonnard, 2002.

Baschet, A. *Les archives de Venise, histoire de la Chancellerie Secrète.* Paris: Henri Plon, 1870.

Biga, Emilia. *Una polemica antifemminista del '600: La "Maschera scoperta" di Angelico Aprosio.* Ventimiglia: Civica Biblioteca Aprosiana, 1989.

Bittner, L., and L. Gross. *Repertorium der diplomatischen Vertreter aller Länder seit dem Westfälischen Frieden.* Oldenburg: G. Stalling, 1936–65.

Bousset, W. *The Antichrist Legend.* Trans. A. H. Keane. London: Hutchinson, 1896.

Bouwsma, William J. *Venice and the Defence of Republican Liberty.* Berkeley: University of California Press, 1968.

Buoni, Tomaso. *Thesoro degli proverbi italiani,* part 2. Venice: Gio. Battista Ciotti, 1606.

Camillocci, Daniela Soffaroli. "La monaca esemplare: Lettere spirituali di madre Battistina Vernazza [1497–1587]." In *Per lettera: La scrittura epistolare femminile tra archivio e tipografia secoli XV–XVII,* ed. G. Zarri, 235–61. Rome: Viella, 1999.

Cannizzaro, Nina. "Studies on Guido Casono, 1561–1642, and Venetian Academies." Ph.D. dissertation, Harvard University, 2001.

Cicogna. E. *Iscrizioni veneziane.* Venice: Giuseppe Orlandelli, 1824–53.

––––––. *Storia dei Dogi di Venezia.* Venice: Giuseppe Grimaldo, 1864.

Chabod, Federico. *La politica di Paolo Sarpi.* Venice: Istituto per la Collaborazione Culturale, 1962.

Chojnacki, Stanley. *Women and Men in Renaissance Venice: Twelve Essays on Patrician Society.* Baltimore: John Hopkins University Press, 2000.

Clough, Cecil H. "The Cult of Antiquity: Letters and Letter Collections." In *Cultural Aspects of the Italian Renaissance: Essays in*

Honor of Paul Oskar Kristeller, ed. Cecil H. Clough, 33–67. Manchester: Manchester University Press, 1976.

Coci, Laura. Introduction to Ferrante Pallavicino, *La retorica delle puttane*. Ed. Laura Coci. Parma: Ugo Guanda, 1992.

Constable, Giles. *Letters and Letter-collections*. Turnhout, Belgium: Éditions Brepols, 1976.

Costa-Zalessow, N. "Tarabotti's 'La semplicità ingannata' and Its Twentieth-Century Interpreters, with Unpublished Documents Regarding Its Condemnation to the Index." *Italica* 78 (2001): 314–25.

Cox, Virginia. *Women's Writing in Italy, 1400–1650*. Baltimore: Johns Hopkins University Press, 2008.

Cozzi, Gaetano. *Paolo Sarpi tra Venezia e l'Europa*. Turin: Einaudi, 1979.

———. "I rapporti tra stato e chiesa." In *La chiesa veneta tra Riforma protestante e cattolica*, ed. Giuseppe Gullino. Venice: Edizioni Studium, 1990.

Cozzi, Gaetano, and Luisa Cozzi. "Paolo Sarpi." In *Storia della cultura veneta: Il Seicento*, vol. 4, part 2, ed. Girolamo Arnaldi and Manlio Pastore Stocchi, 1–36. Vicenza: Neri Pozza, 1983.

Creytens, Raimondo. "La giurisprudenza della Sacra Congregazione del Concilio nella questione della clausura delle monache (1564–1576)." In *La Sacra Congregazione del Concilio, quarto centenario dalla fondazione (1564–1964): Studi e ricerche*. Vatican City: n. p., 1964.

———. "La riforma dei monasteri femminili dopo i Decreti Tridentini." In *Il Concilio di Trento e la riforma tridentina: Atti del convegno storico internazionale*. Rome: Herder, 1965.

De Rubeis, Flavia. "La scrittura forzata: Le lettere autografe di Arcangela Tarabotti." *Rivista di Storia e Letteratura Religiosa* 32.1 (1996): 142–45.

Fumaroli, Marc. "Genèse de l'épistolographie classique: Rhetorique humaniste de la lettre, de Petrarche à Juste Lipse." *Revue d'Histoire Litteraire de la France* 78 (1978): 886–905.

Giustiniani, Vito. "La communication érudite: Les lettres humanistes et l'article moderne de revue." In *La correspondance de Erasme et l'epistolographie humaniste*, 109–33. Brussels: Éditions de l'Université de Bruxelles, 1985.

Graziosi, Elisabetta. "Arcipelago sommerso: Le rime delle monache tra obbedienza e trasgressione." In *I monasteri femminili come centri di cultura fra Rinascimento e Barocco: Atti del convegno storico internazionale, Bologna, 8–10 dicembre 2000*, ed. Gabriella Zarri and Gianna Pomata, 146–81. Rome: Edizioni di Storia e Letteratura, 2005.

_____. "Scrivere in convento: Devozione, encomio, persuasione nelle rime delle monache fra Cinque e Seicento." In *Donne, disciplina, creanza cristiana dal XV al XVII secolo*, ed. Gabriella Zarri, 303–31. Rome: Edizioni di Storia della Letteratura, 1996.

Henderson, Judith Rice. "On Reading the Rhetoric of the Renaissance Letter." In *Renaissance Rhetoric*, ed. Heinrich F. Plett, 143–62. Berlin: Walter de Gruyter, 1993.

Hesbert, R.-J. *Corpus antiphonalium officii: Rerum ecclesiasticarum documenta*. Ser. Maior, Fontes ix. Rome: Herder, 1965.

Infelise, Mario. "Books and Politics in Arcangela Tarabotti's Venice." In *Arcangela Tarabotti: A Literary Nun in Baroque Venice*, ed. Elissa Weaver, 57–72. Ravenna: Longo, 2006.

_____. "La crise de la librairie venetienne, 1620–1650." In *Le livre et l'historien: Études offertes à Henri-Jean Martin*, ed. Frédéric Barbier et al., 343–52. Geneva: Droz, 1997.

_____. "Ex ignotus notus? Note sul tipografo Sarzina e l'Accademia degli Incogniti." In *Libri tipografi biblioteche: Ricerche storiche offerte a Luigi Balsamo*, 207–23. Florence: Olschki, 1997.

_____. "Libri e politica nella Venezia di Arcangela Tarabotti." *Annali di Storia Moderna e Contemporanea* 8 [2002]: 31–45.

Jed, Stephanie. "Arcangela Tarabotti and Gabriel Naudé: Libraries, Taxonomies and *Ragion di Stato*." In *Arcangela Tarabotti: A Literary Nun in Baroque Venice*, ed. Elissa Weaver, 129–40. Ravenna: Longo, 2006.

Jöcher, C. G. *Allgemeines Gelehrten-Lexikon*. Leipzig: Johann Friedrich Gleditsch, 1750–51.

Kendrick, Robert. *Celestial Sirens: Nuns and Their Music in Early Modern Milan*. Oxford: Clarendon Press, 1996.

Kenney, Theresa, ed. *"Women Are Not Human"*: *An Anonymous Treatise and Its Responses.* New York: Crossroad, 1998.

King, Margaret, and Albert Rabil Jr. *Her Immaculate Hand: Selected Works by and about the Women Humanists of Quattrocento Italy.* Binghamton, NY: Medieval and Renaissance Texts and Studies, 1983; 2nd rev. paperback ed., 1991.

Laven, Mary. "Cast Out and Shut In: The Experience of Nuns in Counter-Reformation Venice." In *At the Margins: Minority Groups in Premodern Italy*, ed. Stephen J. Milner, 72–93. Mineapolis: University of Minnesota Press, 2005.

_____. *Virgins of Venice: Broken Vows and Cloistered Lives in the Renaissance Convent.* New York: Penguin, 2002.

Legrenzi, D., ed. *Piccola galleria poetica di donne veneziane. Strennetta per l'anno nuovo, compilata da D.L..* Mestre: Strennetta per l'anno nuovo, 1852.

Lowe, Kate. *Nuns' Chronicles and Convent Culture in Renaissance and Counter-Reformation Italy.* Cambridge: Cambridge University Press, 2003.

Maylender, Michele. *Storia delle accademie d'Italia.* Bologna: Licinio Cappelli, 1930.

Medioli, Francesca. "Alcune lettere autografe di Arcangela Tarabotti: Autocensura e immagine di sé." *Rivista di storia e letteratura religiosa* 32.1 (1996): 133–41 and 146–55.

_____. "Arcangela Tarabotti's Reliability about Herself: Publication and Self-Representation (Together with a Small Collection of Previously Unpublished Letters)." *The Italianist* 23 (2003): 54–101.

_____. "La clausura delle monache nell'amministrazione della congregazione romana sopra i regolari." In *Il monachesimo femminile in Italia dall'alto medioevo al secolo XVII a confronto con l'oggi: Atti del VI convegno del Centro Studi Farfensi, Santa Vittoria in Matenano, 21–24 settembre, 1995*, ed. Gabriella Zarri, 249–82. Nagrine [Verona]: Il Segno dei Gabrielli Editori, 1997.

_____. "The Dimensions of the Cloister: Enclosure, Constraint, and Protection in Seventeenth Century Italy." In *Time, Space, and Women's Lives in Early Modern Italy*, ed. Anne Jacobson Schutte, Thomas Kuehn, and Silvana Seidel Menchi, 165–80. Kirksville, MO: Truman State University Press, 2001.

_____. "Monacazioni forzate: Donne ribelle al proprio destino." *Clio: Trimestrale di Studi Storici* 30 (1994): 431–54.

_____. "Monache e monacazioni nel Seicento." In "De monialibus [secoli 16–18]," by Gabriella Zarri, Francesca Medioli, and Paola Vismara Chiappa. *Rivista di Storia e Letteratura Religiosa* 33.3 (1997): 676–78.

Melzi, G. *Dizionario di opere anonime e pseudonime di scrittori italiani…* . Milan: Pirola, 1848.

Menegatti, T. *"Ex ignoto notus": Bibliografia delle opere a stampa del Principe degli Incogniti: Giovan Francesco Loredano*. Padua: Il Poligrafo, 2000.

Miato, Monica. *L'Accademia degli Incogniti di Giovan Francesco Loredan, Venezia (1630–1661)*. Florence: Leo Olschki, 1998.

Molmenti, P. *La storia di Venezia nella vita privata dale origini alla caduta della Repubblica*, vol. 5. Bergamo: Istituto italiano d'arti grafiche, 1910–12.

Monson, Craig. *Disembodied Voices: Music and Culture in an Early Modern Italian Convent*. Berkeley: University of California Press, 1995.

Muir, Edward. *Civic Ritual in Renaissance Venice*. Princeton: Princeton University Press, 1981.

Odorisio, Ginevra Conti. *Donna e società nel Seicento*. Rome: Bulzoni, 1979.

Paolin, Giovanna. *Lo spazio del silenzio: Monacazioni forzate, clausura e proposte di vita religiosa femminile nell'eta moderna*. Pordenone: Biblioteca dell'Immagine, 1996.

Parodi, S. *IV Centenario dell'Accademia della Crusca: Catalogo degli accademici dalla fondazione*. Florence: Accademia della Crusca, 1983.

Portigliotti, Giuseppe. *Penombre claustrali*. Milan: Fratelli Treves, 1930.

Prevost, M., and R. d'Amat, eds. *Dictionnaire de biographie française*. Vol. 7. Paris: Librairie Letouzez et Ané, 1956.

Priuli, Lorenzo. *Ordini, & avvertimenti, che si devono osservare ne' Monasteri di Monache di Venetia: Sopra le visite, & clausura*, 10r. Venice, 1591.

Prodi, Paolo. "Chiesa e società." In *Storia di Venezia*, vol. 6, *Dal Rinascimento al Barocco*, ed. Gaetano Cozzi and Paolo Prodi, 305–39. Rome: Istituto della Enciclopedia Italiana "Giovanni Treccani," 1994.

Quondam, Amedeo. *Le carte messaggere: Retorica e modelli di comunicazione epistolare. Per un indice di libri di lettere del Cinquecento*. Rome: Bulzoni, 1981.

Ray, Meredith K. "Letters and Lace: Arcangela Tarabotti and Convent Culture in Seicento Venice." In *Early Modern Women and Transnational Communities of Letters*, ed. Julie Campbell and Ann Larsen. Farnham, U.K.: Ashgate, 2009.

_____. "Letters from the Cloister: Defending the Literary Self in Arcangela Tarabotti's *Lettere familiari e di complimento*." *Italica* 81.1 (2004): 24–43.

_____. "Making the Private Public: Arcangela Tarabotti's *Lettere familiari*." In *Arcangela Tarabotti: A Literary Nun in Baroque Venice*, ed. Elissa Weaver, 173–89. Ravenna: Longo, 2006.

_____. *Writing Gender in Women's Letter Collections of the Italian Renaissance*. Toronto: University of Toronto Press, 2009.

Ricci, E. *Old Italian Lace*. London: Heinemann, 1913.

Robin, Diana. "Cassandra Fedele's *Epistolae* (1488–1521): Biography as Ef-facement." In *The Rhetorics of Life-Writing in Early Modern Europe: Forms of Biography from Cassandra Fedele to Louis XIV*, ed. Thomas F. Mayer and D. R. Woolf, 187–98. Ann Arbor: University of Michigan Press, 1995.

_____. *Filelfo in Milan: Writings 1451–1477*. Princeton: Princeton University Press, 1991.

Romanin, S. *Storia documentata di Venezia*. Venice: Pietro Naratovich, 1858.

Rosa, Mario. "La religiosa." In *L'uomo barocco*, ed. Rosario Villeri, 219–67. Rome: La Terza, 1991.

Schutte, Anne Jacobson. "The Permeable Cloister?" In *Arcangela Tarabotti: A Literary Nun in Baroque Venice*, ed. Elissa Weaver, 19–36. Ravenna: Longo, 2006.

Sperling, Jutta Gisela. *Convents and the Body Politic in Late Renaissance Venice*. Chicago: University of Chicago Press, 1999.

Spini, Giorgio. *Ricerca dei libertini: La teoria dell'impostura delle religioni nel Seicento veneziano*. Florence: La Nuova Italia, 1983.

Strocchia, Sharon. "Taken into Custody: Girls and Convent Guardianship in Renaissance Florence." *Renaissance Studies* 17 (2003): 177–200.

Ulvioni, Paolo. "Accademie e cultura in Italia dalla Controriforma all'Arcadia: Il caso veneziano." *Libri e Documenti* 5 (1970): 21–75.

_____. "Stampa e censura a Venezia nel Seicento." *Archivio Veneto* 104.139 (1975): 45–93.

Varnhagen, H. *De verbis nonnullis linguae veteris francogallicae una cum fabella qual sermone italico composita et Maria per Ravenna inscripta*. Erlangen: University of Erlangen, 1903.

Walther, H. *Lateinische Sprichwoerter und Sentenzen des Mittelalters und der fruehen Neuzeit in alphabetischer Anordnung*. Vol. 2, part 7. Carmina medii aevi posterioris Latina. Göttingen: Vandenhoeck & Ruprecht, 1982.

Weaver, Elissa, ed. *Arcangela Tarabotti: A Literary Nun in Baroque Venice*. Ravenna: Longo, 2006.

_____. *Convent Theater in Early Modern Italy: Spiritual Fun and Learning for Women*. Cambridge: Cambridge University Press, 2002.

_____, ed. *Satira e Antisatira*. Rome: Salerno, 1998.

Westwater, Lynn Lara. "The Disquieting Voice: Women's Writing and Antifeminism in Seventeenth-Century Venice." Ph.D. dissertation, University of Chicago, 2003.

_____. "A Cloistered Nun Abroad: Arcangela Tarabotti's International Literary Career." *Intersections: Yearbook for Early Modern Studies. Volume 14: Women Writing Back, Writing Women Back: Transnational Perspectives from the Late Middle Ages to the Dawn of the Modern Era*. Leiden: Brill, 2010.

_____. "A Rediscovered Friendship in the Republic of Letters: The Unpublished Correspondence of Arcangela Tarabotti and Ismaël Bouillau." *Renaissance Quarterly* 65, no. 1 (forthcoming, 2012).

_____. "The Trenchant Pen: Humor in the *Lettere* of Arcangela Tarabotti." In *Arcangela Tarabotti: A Literary Nun in Baroque Venice*, ed. Elissa Weaver, 158–72. Ravenna: Longo, 2006.

Zanette, Emilio. *Suor Arcangela monaca del Seicento veneziano.* Rome and Venice: Istituto per la Collaborazione Culturale, 1960.

Zarri, Gabriella. "Monasteri femminili e città (secoli XV–XVIII)." In *Storia d'Italia*, vol. 9, *La chiesa e il potere politico*, ed. Giorgio Chittolini and Giovanni Miccoli, 359–429. Turin: Einaudi, 1986.

_____. *Per lettera: La scrittura epistolare femminile tra archivio e tipografia, secoli XV–XVII.* Rome: Viella, 1999.

_____. *Recinti: Donne, claustra e matrimonio nella prima età moderna.* Bologna: Il Mulino, 2000.

_____. *Sante vive: Profezie di corte e devozione femminile tra '400 e '500.* Turin: Rosenberg & Sellier, 1990.

_____. "Venetian Convents and Civic Ritual." In *Arcangela Tarabotti: A Literary Nun in Baroque Venice*, ed. Elissa Weaver, 37–56. Ravenna: Longo, 2006.

Zarri, Gabriella, and Gianna Pomata, eds. *I monasteri femminili come centri di cultura fra Rinascimento e Barocco: Atti del convegno storico internazionale, Bologna, 8–10 dicembre 2000.* Rome: Edizioni di Storia e Letteratura, 2005.

Zupko, Ronald E. *Italian Weights and Measures from the Middle Ages to the Nineteenth Century.* Philadelphia: American Philosophical Society, 1981.

Accademia degli Incogniti, 8

Accademia della Crusca, 71n63

Amò, Madame d' (Madame des Hameaux) (Tarabotti's letters to), 101–102, 169–170, 171–172, 277–278

Anima del Zeno (*Soul of Zeno*), 32, 113n186, 118, 154

Anima di Ferrante Pallavicino (Soul of Ferrante Pallavicino), 32, 118, 162nn348–349, 256n653

anonymous correspondents, 26

Antisatira (*Antisatire*) (Tarabotti), 13, 14, 19, 36, 60n34, 125n232

   Andrea Valiero and, 126

   Bertucci Valiero and, 254

   criticism of, 72n66

   Giacomo Pighetti and, 164n359, 236n593, 237

   question of authorship, 73n72

   strategy for publication of, 89n114

   Tarabotti on, 10n24, 80, 151–152, 165–166, 171n384, 172–175, 246–247, 279, 280, 282–283

   Tarabotti's identity, 193n455, 235n590

   vanity and, 223n545

Antisatira satirizzata (*Antisatire Satirized*) (Brusoni), 151, 152

Aprosio, Angelico, 19, 25–26, 36, 66n46, 93n125, 99nn141–142, 140n274, 152n313, 164n359, 172–175, 236n593, 280n728

Aretino, Pietro, 15–16, 17, 61n37

Argiope (Fusconi), 111n179

Aviani, Signors, 131n249, 201

Balbi, Cesare (Tarabotti's letters to), 200–201

Baratotti, Galerana (Tarabotti), 11

Barbara, Aquila, 27

   Tarabotti's letters to, 154–155, 274–275, 283–284

Biblioteca aprosiana (*Aprosian Library*) (Aprosio), 88n110

Bissari, Giulia, 56–57

Bissari, Pietro Paolo, 24, 25n58, 53n13, 275

   on Tarabotti, 119n210

   Tarabotti's letters to, 53, 55–56, 67–68, 118–119, 159, 160, 178, 190, 255, 282–283

Bradamante (Bissari), 255

Brusoni, Girolamo, 20, 72n66, 80n86, 107n166, 108nn168–169, 140n274, 141n278, 165n361, 192n453,

193nn456–457, 204n490,
264n679, 264n681, 269n700,
269n702
Buoninsegni, Francesco, 80, 81,
247
Busenello, Giovanni Francesco,
128, 156n331, 201n479

Cassandra, Elena (Arcangela
Tarabotti), 1
Catherine of Siena, 21
Cereta, Laura, 16–17
*Che le donne siano della spezie
degli uomini (That Women
Are of the Same Species as
Men)* (Tarabotti), 15, 37,
78n82, 114n191
Claramonte, Renata di (Cler-
mont-Gallerande, Renée de),
28–29, 124n226, 209n506
(Tarabotti's letters to),
184–185, 198–199,
211–212, 219–220, 265
coerced monachization, 1, 2,
5–6, 12
Colisson, 29, 183n421, 186,
198n471, 209n504, 211n513,
215, 219
*Contemplazioni dell'anima
amante (Contemplations of
the Loving Soul* (Tarabotti),
40, 50n7, 82
*Contemplazioni de' suoi
santissimi dolori (Contemplation of her Holiest Sorrows)*,
243

*Contro 'l lusso donnesco satira
menippea (A Menippean
Satire against Female Vanity)*
(Buoninsegni), 13
Convent Hell (Tarabotti), see
Inferno monacale
Convent Light (Tarabotti), see
Luce monacale
Convent Paradise (Tarabotti),
see *Paradiso monacale*
Copet, Baron of, 183
Cornaro, Enrico, 25
Tarabotti's letters to, 97,
120–121, 129–130,
156–157, 163–164,
201–202, 243, 247
*Corriero svaligiato (The Post-
man Robbed of His Mailbag)*
(Pallavicino), 69n55, 207
Council of Trent, 5
Crasso, Nicolò, 25, 25n62, 39,
127n236
Tarabotti's letters to, 127–128,
218–219, 233–234
Cremonini, Cesare, 127n236
Crocebianca, Giovanni, 60
cultural and economic ex-
change in the *Letters*, 31–33

Dandolo, Enrico, 58
Dandolo, Giovanni
number of letters to, 24
pseudonym of, 59n27
on Tarabotti, 49–50
Tarabotti's letters to, 57–59,
63–65, 94, 95–96, 110–
111, 118, 127, 131–132,

143–145, 220–221, 222, 248, 256–257

Dandolo, Matteo (Tarabotti's letters to), 94–95, 120

Decree on Regulars and Nuns, Chapter 17 (1563), 5–6

De Divinitate Feminae (On Women's Divinity) (Dandolo), 57n21, 60

Del secretario (Sansovino), 17

Disputatio nova contra mulieres, qua probatur eas homines non esse (New Disputation Against Women in Which It Is Proved That They Are Not Human), 14

Donà, Regina, 38, 84n100, 128n238, 203n487

Donado, Paolo (Tarabotti's letters to), 281–282

Emo, Angelo (Tarabotti's letters to), 196–197

epistolary network of Tarabotti, 22–31

  Accademia degli Incogniti, 23–24

  Angelico Aprosio, 25–26

  Anne-Françoise de Loménie, 28

  anonymous correspondents, 26

  Aquila Barbara, 27

  Bertucci Valier, 22

  Betta Polani, 27

  correspondence with women, 26–28

  Enrico Cornaro, 25

  Francesco Erizzo, 22

  Francesco Molino, 22

  Francesco Pona, 25

  Francesco Zati, 22

  Giacomo Pighetti, 25

  Giovan Francesco Loredano, 24

  Giovanni Dandolo, 24

  Guid'Ascania Orsi, 27

  important figures in, 22

  Jean des Hameaux, 28

  Jules Mazarin, 22

  literary figures in, 23

  "Mother N.," 28

  Nicolas Bretel de Grémonville, 28

  Nicolò Crasso, 25

  number of published letters, 22

  Odoardo Farnese, 22

  Pietro Paolo Bissari, 24

  Renée de Clermont-Galerande, 28–29

  Silvestro Valier, 22

  Vittoria della Rovere, 22

epistolary tradition and Tarabotti, 15–19

  See also nuns and letter writing

Ercole geromicida (Hercules Slayer of Geryon), 152

Erizzo, Francesco, 22

  Tarabotti's letters to, 51–52, 76–77, 109–110

Farnese, Ferdinando (Tarabot-
ti's letters to), 71–75
Farnese, Odoardo, 22, 71n65
Fedele, Cassandra, 16
Ferro, Signor, 79
Fiubet, Marguerite de
(Tarabotti's letters to), 62–63,
172, 278-279
Foscola, Elena (Tarabotti's
letters to), 167–168, 203,
229–230
Foscolo, Nicolò (Tarabotti's
letters to), 77–78
Fuggitiva (The Fugitive) (Bru-
soni), 231n577
*Funerali delle pompe femi-
nili (Funeral for Feminine
Luxury)* (Foccacci), 151
Fusconi, Giovan Battista,
111n179

Galeranda, Marchioness di, see
Claramonte, Renata di
Gildas, Signora (Tarabotti's
letters to), 166n364, 275–276
Giubet, Margherita di, ee
Fiubet, Marguerite de
Giuseppe (Joseph) (Pallavicino),
161, 162n347
*Gondola a tre remi (Gondola
with Three Oars)* (Brusoni),
230n572
Grémonville, Anna di (Anne
de Grémonville) (Tarabotti's
letters to), 182, 191, 206, 212,
215–216

Grémonville, de (daughters)
(Tarabotti's letters to),
208–209, 216–217
Grémonville, Jacques Bretel de,
212n517
Grémonville, Nicolas Bretel de,
22, 28, 30, 186n430
Tarabotti's letters to, 90–91,
92–93, 97–98, 137–140,
151–154, 266–267,
273–274
Grimani, Antonio, 20

Hameaux, Anne des, 62n38
Hameaux, Jean des, 28, 62n38
Hameaux, Madame des, see
Amò, Madame d' (Tarabotti's
letters to)

*Ibrahim, ou l'illustre Bassà
(Ibraim, or the Illustrious
Bassà)* (de Scudéry), 175
Index of Forbidden Books
(Clement VIII's), 8, 53n14,
251n632
Infelise, Mario, 9
Inferno monacale (Convent Hell)
(Tarabotti), 4, 6, 9, 12, 36,
219n537, 259, 264n681
Innocence Deceived (Tarabotti),
see *Semplicità ingannata*
Inquisition, the, 114n191

Julius II (Pope), 7

lacework, 32, 101nn146–148,
199

Lagrime di Arcangela Tarabotti per la morte della illustrissima signora Regina Donati (Tears of Arcangela Tarabotti upon the Death of the Most Illustrious Signora Regina Donati) (Tarabotti), 15, 36, 38–40, 163
    dedication, 286
    text of, 287–296
lettera familiare, 16
letterbooks, 17–18
Lettere familiari e di complimento (Letters Familiar and Formal) (Tarabotti)
    afterlife of, 35–38
    arrangement of, 29–30
    cultural and economic exchange in, 31–33
    dedication of, 48
    defense of women, 30
    importance of, 15
    publication of, 29
    purpose of, 30–31
    reaction to, 35–37
    reprinting of, 38
    strategic purposes in, 29
    style and rhetoric in, 33–35
    the *Letters* by recipients
        A. and C. Tarabotti, 158, 231
        Alba Porti, 271–272
        Andrea Valiero, 125–126
        Andrea Vendramino, 134
        Andriana Malipiero, 132–133, 195–196, 241–242
        Angelo Emo, 196–197

Anna di Grémonville, 182, 206, 212, 215–216
Aquila Barbara, 154–155, 274–275, 283–284
Bertucci Valiero, 145–146, 182–183, 189–190, 214–215, 221–222, 254–255, 257–258, 260–261
Betta Polani, 82–83, 88–89, 103–104, 114–115, 129, 147–148, 149–150, 194, 202, 226, 271, 284
Cardinal Mazzarino, 186–189
Cavalier Pona, 200
Cesare Balbi, 200–201
Countess S., 85–86, 141–142
d'Amò, Madame (Madame des Hameaux), 101–102, 169–170, 171–172, 277–278
Elena Foscola, 167–168, 203, 229–230
Enrico Cornaro, 97, 120–121, 129–130, 156–157, 163–164, 201–202, 243, 247
Ferdinando Farnese, 71–75
Francesco da Mulla, 233
Francesco Erizzo, 51–52, 76–77, 109–110
Francesco Maria Zati, 70–71, 133, 168, 241, 252
Francesco Molino, 115–116
Francesco Pona, 104–105, 193–194, 227, 270–271

Galeranda, Marchioness
di, 198–199, 211–212,
219–220, 265
Giacomo Pighetti, 116,
135–136, 164–166, 171,
236–239
Gildas, Signora, 275–276
Giovan Francesco Loredano,
61–62, 68–70, 75, 96,
112–114, 154, 159–160,
161–162, 217, 256, 262,
279
Giovanni Dandolo, 57–59,
63–65, 94, 95–96, 110–
111, 118, 127, 131–132,
143–145, 220–221, 222,
248, 256–257
Giovanni Polani, 60–61,
86–88, 168–169
Giulia Bissari, 56–57
Grémonville, de (daughters),
208–209, 216–217
Grémonville, Madame di,
191
Guid'Ascania Orsi,
81–82, 102, 125, 176–178,
207–208, 234, 242, 249,
272–273
Isabetta Piccolomini Scarpi,
65–66, 156, 213–214
Lorenzo Pisani, 126–127
Louis Matharel, 112
Luigi de Matherel, 184, 185,
213, 215
Marguerite de Fiubet
(Margherita di Giubet),
62–63, 278–279

Marin Polani, 148–149
Matteo Dandolo, 94–95, 120
Michiel Minotto, 227
N., Countess, 55
N., Father, 66–67, 93–94,
105–106, 111, 172–175,
202–203, 225–226, 280
N., Mother, 243–244
N. Negri, 54–55
N., Signor, 78–80, 83–84,
98, 99–101, 103, 107–109,
130, 133, 136, 140–143,
151, 155, 157–158,
161, 166, 169, 175–176,
178–180, 183, 191–193,
194–195, 197–198,
204–206, 209, 210–211,
223–225, 228, 230–231,
235–236, 239–240,
244–247, 248–249,
250–251, 253–254,
259–260, 261–262,
262–264, 265–266,
267–270, 274
N., Signora, 84, 88, 121–123,
124, 180–181, 250,
252–253
Nicolas Bretel de Gré-
monville, 90–91, 92–93,
97–98, 137–140, 151–154,
266–267
Nicolò Crasso, 127–128,
218–219, 233–234
Nicolò Foscolos, 77–78
Paolo Donado, 281–282
Pietro Ottoboni, 117

Pietro Paolo Bissari, 53,
55–56, 67–68, 118–119,
159, 160, 178, 190, 255,
282–283
Renata di Claramonte,
184–185
S., Countess, 204
Sebastian Michiel, 258
Silvestro Valier, 106–107
Vittoria della Rovere, 89–90,
134, 146–147
Lettere volgari di diversi nobilis-
simi uomini (Vernacular
Letters of Various Noble Men)
(Manuzio), 18
Letters to Atticus, Quintus and
Brutus (Cicero), 15
life and works of Tarabotti, 1–2,
10–15
Locatello, Signor, 262–263
Loménie, Anne-Françoise de,
28
Loredano, Giovan Francesco
as ally of Tarabotti, 24,
112n184
Tarabotti's letters to, 61–62,
68–70, 75, 96, 112–114,
154, 159–160, 161–162,
217, 256, 262, 279
Luca, Giovan Battista de, 5
Luce monacale (Convent Light)
(Tarabotti), 40, 50n7, 83

Malipiero, Andriana, 39,
132n250
Lagrime di Arcangela
Tarabotti per la morte
della illustrissima signora
Regina Donati (The Tears
of Arcangela Tarabotti
upon the Death of the Most
Illustrious Signora Regina
Donati), 286n1
Tarabotti's letters to, 132–
133, 195–196, 241–242
Mantova, Osanna da, 21
Marinella, Lucrezia, 85n103
Maschera scoperta (The Mask
Lifted) (Aprosio), 36, 73,
93n125, 151, 164n359,
193n455, 232, 235, 235n590,
236
Matharel, Luigi de (Louis Math-
arel), 112n181, 219n536
Tarabotti's letters to, 112,
184, 185, 213, 215
Mazarin, Jules (Cardinal Maz-
zarino), 20, 22, 187n436
Tarabotti's letters to, 187–189
Medioli, Francesca, 37
Michiel, Sebastian (Tarabotti's
letters to), 258
Minotto, Michiel (Tarabotti's
letters to), 227
Molin, Domenico, 116n198
Molin, Elena, 167n365
Molino, Francesco, 22, 116n199
Tarabotti's letters to, 115–116
Morosin, Giovan Francecso,
205n493
Mulla, Francesco da (Tarabotti's
letters to), 233
music, 85n101

N., Countess (Tarabotti's letters
  to), 55
N., Father (Tarabotti's letters
  to), 66–67, 93–94, 105–106,
  111, 172–175, 202–203,
  225–226, 280
N., Lady, 84, 140
N., Mother, 28
Tarabotti's letters to, 243–244
N., Signor, 200, 252
N., Signor (Tarabotti's letters to)
  of anger, 224–225, 228, 246,
    269
  of anxiety about her work,
    209
  of apology, etc., 250–251,
    259, 270
  asking for help, 78–80,
    99–101, 130, 194–195,
    197–198, 267
  on the Baron of Copet, 183
  on being ill, 133
  on a benefice, etc., 83–84
  on *Inferno monacale (Con-
    vent Hell)*, 259
  on *Paradiso monacale
    (Convent Paradise)*,
    136n262, 151
  criticism of, 80, 108–109,
    155, 175–176, 192–193,
    245, 248–249, 267–268
  on criticism of her work,
    103, 263–264
  defense of the *Antisatira
    (Antisatire)*, 246–247
  on errors in the *Paradise*,
    136, 140–141, 142-143
of friendship, 207, 260
on gift giving, 98
on her handicap, 107–108
on his praise of her, etc.,
  210–211
on the *Maschera scoperta
  (The Mask Lifted)*, 232,
  235–236
matchmaking, etc., 261–262
on paternal tyranny, 151
on *Tirannia paterna (Paternal Tyranny)*, 161, 269
of praise, 169, 274
of presentation, 166
on printing of her work,
  204–206, 124
of sarcasm, 223, 239–240
on Signor Locatello, 262–263
of thanks, 157–158, 178–180,
  191–192, 230–231, 244,
  253–254, 265–266
on the untrustworthiness of
  men, etc., 240
N., Signora (Tarabotti's letters to), 84, 88, 121–123,
  180–181, 250, 252–253
Naudé, Gabriel, 186n429
Negri, N. (Tarabotti's letters to),
  54–55
Nogarola, Isotta, 16
nuns and letter writing, 19–22
  See also epistolary tradition
    and Tarabotti

Odorisio, Ginevra Conti, 37
*Olivo geroglifico (Hieroglyphic
  Olive Branch)*, 76, 77n80

Orsi, Guid'Ascania, 11n28, 27, 77n80
Olivo geroglifico (Hieroglyphic Olive Branch), 76, 77n80, 125
    Tarabotti's letters to, 81–82, 102, 125, 176–178, 207–208, 234, 242, 249, 272–273
Ottoboni, Pietro (Tarabotti's letters to), 117

Pallavicino, Ferrante, 9
Paradiso monacale (Convent Paradise) (Tarabotti), 13–14, 37, 39, 60, 126
    encomiastic poem for, 85n103
    errors in, 136, 140–141
    Giovanni Polani and, 87
    letter of presentation, 86n106
    question of authorship, 73n72, 105n161, 153n320, 236n592, 280
    Tarabotti on, 151, 153, 207–208, 214–215
Paternal Tyranny (Tarabotti), see *Tirannia paterna*
Paved Road to Heaven (Tarabotti), see *Via lastricata per andare al cielo*
Penombre claustrali (Portigliotti), 37
Pighetti, Giacomo, 14, 25, 70, 139, 164n359

Tarabotti's letters to, 116, 135–136, 164–166, 171, 236–239
Pisani, Lorenzo (Tarabotti's letters to), 126–127
Polani, Betta, 27, 136n263, 205n491
    Tarabotti's letters to, 82–83, 88–89, 103–104, 114–115, 129, 147–148, 149–150, 194, 202, 226, 271, 284
Polani, Giovanni, 168n374
    Tarabotti's letters to, 60–61, 86–88, 168–169
Polani, Marin (Tarabotti's letters to), 148–149
Pona, Francesco, 25, 104n159
    Tarabotti's letters to, 104–105, 193–194, 200, 227, 270–271
Porti, Alba (Tarabotti's letters to), 271–272
Portigliotti, Giuseppe, 37
Priuli, Lorenzo, 20

querelle on the merits of women, 14n38
Querini, Alvise, 197n465

Rovere, Vittoria della, 19, 22, 72n67
Antisatira (Antisatire) (Tarabotti) and, 89n114
    Tarabotti's letters to, 89–90, 134, 146–147

S., Countess (Tarabotti's letters
to), 85–86, 141–142, 204
Saint Elmo's fire, 191
Sansovino, Francesco, 17
Sarpi, Paolo, 8
Satira (Satire) (Buoninsegni), 90
Scarpi, Isabetta Piccolomini, 28
Tarabotti's letters to, 65–66,
156, 213–214
*Semplicità ingannata (Innocence
Deceived)* (Tarabotti), 11–12,
36n76, 112n182
Index of Forbidden Books,
53n14
serbanza, 31–32
Sperling, Jutta, 3
style and rhetoric of the *Letters*,
33–35

Tarabotti, A. and C. (Tarabotti's
letters to), 158, 231
Tarabotti, Arcangela
Accademia degli Incogniti
and, 9
Angelico Aprosio and,
93n125
answering a misogynous
treatise, 14–15
on the *Antisatira (Antisatire)*,
74n76, 151–152, 165–166,
171n384, 172–175,
246–247, 279, 280,
282–283
autograph letters, 19n48
birth name of, 1
on *Paradiso monacale
(Convent Paradise)*,

73n72, 151, 153, 207–208,
214–215, 280
criticism of, 13–14
education of, 10
epistolary communication,
importance of, 19–20
family of, 3
handicap of, 3
on *Tirannia paterna (Paternal Tyranny)*, 161, 193,
211–212, 257n657, 264,
266–267, 269
pseudonym of, 11
publication of her cor-
respondence, 21
published work of, 10–11
serbanza and, 31–32
style and rhetoric of, 33–35
*Tears of Arcangela Tarabotti
upon the Death of the
Most Illustrious Signora
Regina Donati* (Tarabotti),
see *Lagrime di Arcangela
Tarabotti per la morte della
illustrissima signora Regina
Donati*
*That Women Are of the Same
Species as Men* (Tarabotti),
see *Che le donne siano della
spezie degli uomini*
Tiepolo, Giovanni, 4
*Tirannia paterna (Paternal
Tyranny)* (Tarabotti), 4, 9, 11,
19, 28, 29, 36, 101n145
Colisson and, 29, 183n421,
186, 198n471, 209n504,
211n513, 215, 219n537

Francesco da Mulla and, 233
letters to Cardinal Mazzarino
concerning, 186–189
Marchioness di Galeranda
and, 198–199
publication of, 124n224, 147,
184n424, 185n427
Renée Clermont de Gal-
lerande and, 124n226
Tarabotti on, 161, 193,
211–212, 219–220,
257n657, 264, 266–267,
269
Vittoria della Rovere and,
146n291, 147
Tolentini, Maria Cadena dei,
89n112
translation note, 41–43
Turbolenze delle vestali
(Turbulence of the Vestals)
(Brusoni), 264n681

Valier, Silvestro, 22, 106n162,
145, 258n661
Tarabotti's letters to, 106–107
Valiero, Andrea (Tarabotti's
letters to), 125–126
Valiero, Bertucci, 22, 106n163
Tarabotti's letters to, 145–
146, 182–183, 189–190,
214–215, 221–222,
254–255, 257–258,
260–261
Valvasense, Francesco,
114n191, 213n519
Vendramino, Andrea, 134n257
Tarabotti's letters to, 134

Venice, 2–3, 6–9
Accademia degli Incogniti, 8
civic mythology of, 6
convents, importance of, 6–7
freedom of the press, 8–9
Index of Forbidden Books
(Clement VIII's), 8
interdiction and excom-
munication, 8
reaction to the Council of
Trent, 7
relationships with the Holy
See, 7–9
See also women, convents,
and society in seven-
teenth-century Venice
Vernazza, Battistina, 21
Via lastricata per andare al
cielo (Paved Road to Heaven)
(Tarabotti), 40, 49, 50n7, 83,
83n92
Victoria, Tomás Luis de (da
Vittoria), 227n564

women, convents, and society in seventeenth-century
Venice, 2–6
women, querelle on the merits
of, 14n38

Zanette, Emilio, 37
Zarri, Gabriella, 6, 7
Zati, Maria Francesco, 22, 32
Tarabotti's letters to, 70–71,
133, 168, 241, 252